PAUL TILLICH AND THE POSSIBILITY OF
REVELATION THROUGH FILM

OXFORD THEOLOGICAL MONOGRAPHS

Editorial Committee

J. BARTON   N. J. BIGGAR
M. J. EDWARDS   P. S. FIDDES
G. D. FLOOD   D. N. J. MACCULLOCH
          C. C. ROWLAND

OXFORD THEOLOGICAL MONOGRAPHS

THE THEOLOGICAL EPISTEMOLOGY OF AUGUSTINE'S *DE TRINITATE*
Luigi Gioia (2008)

THE SONG OF SONGS AND THE EROS OF GOD
A Study in Biblical Intertextuality
Edmée Kingsmill (2009)

ROBERT SPAEMANN'S PHILOSOPHY OF THE HUMAN PERSON
Nature, Freedom, and the Critique of Modernity
Holger Zaborowski (2010)

OUT-OF-BODY AND NEAR-DEATH EXPERIENCES
Brain-State Phenomena or Glimpses of Immortality?
Michael N. Marsh (2010)

WHAT IS A LOLLARD?
Dissent and Belief in Late Medieval England
J. Patrick Hornbeck II (2010)

EVANGELICAL FREE WILL
Phillip Melanchthon's Doctrinal Journey on the Origins of Free Will
Gregory Graybill (2010)

ISAIAH AFTER EXILE
The Author of Third Isaiah as Reader and Redactor of the Book
Jacob Stromberg (2010)

CONTRASTING IMAGES OF THE BOOK OF REVELATION
IN LATE MEDIEVAL AND EARLY MODERN ART
A Case Study in Visual Exegesis
Natasha F. H. O'Hear (2010)

KIERKEGAARD'S CRITIQUE OF CHRISTIAN NATIONALISM
Stephen Backhouse (2011)

GENDER ISSUES IN ANCIENT AND REFORMATION
TRANSLATIONS OF GENESIS 1–4
Helen Kraus (2011)

BLAKE'S JERUSALEM AS VISIONARY THEATRE
Entering the Divine Body
Suzanne Sklar (2011)

Paul Tillich and the Possibility of Revelation through Film

A Theoretical Account Grounded by Empirical Research into the Experiences of Filmgoers

JONATHAN BRANT

OXFORD
UNIVERSITY PRESS

Great Clarendon Street, Oxford OX2 6DP

Oxford University Press is a department of the University of Oxford.
It furthers the University's objective of excellence in research, scholarship,
and education by publishing worldwide in

Oxford New York

Auckland Cape Town Dar es Salaam Hong Kong Karachi
Kuala Lumpur Madrid Melbourne Mexico City Nairobi
New Delhi Shanghai Taipei Toronto

With offices in

Argentina Austria Brazil Chile Czech Republic France Greece
Guatemala Hungary Italy Japan Poland Portugal Singapore
South Korea Switzerland Thailand Turkey Ukraine Vietnam

Oxford is a registered trade mark of Oxford University Press
in the UK and in certain other countries

Published in the United States
by Oxford University Press Inc., New York

© Jonathan Brant 2012

The moral rights of the author have been asserted
Database right Oxford University Press (maker)

First published 2012

All rights reserved. No part of this publication may be reproduced,
stored in a retrieval system, or transmitted, in any form or by any means,
without the prior permission in writing of Oxford University Press,
or as expressly permitted by law, or under terms agreed with the appropriate
reprographics rights organization. Enquiries concerning reproduction
outside the scope of the above should be sent to the Rights Department,
Oxford University Press, at the address above

You must not circulate this book in any other binding or cover
and you must impose the same condition on any acquirer

British Library Cataloguing in Publication Data

Data available

Library of Congress Cataloging in Publication Data
Library of Congress Control Number: 2011944150

Typeset by SPI Publisher Services, Pondicherry, India
Printed in Great Britain
on acid-free paper by
MPG Books Group, Bodmin and King's Lynn

ISBN 978–0–19–963934–2

1 3 5 7 9 10 8 6 4 2

Dedicated to Tricia and Isaac, naturally

Acknowledgements

I would like to thank my D.Phil. supervisor, Professor George Pattison, for unstinting support throughout my time at Oxford University. There are other academics whose input has been vital: Dr Pete Ward of King's College, London was influential in the genesis of the research, discussed many of its ideas and read a draft of the manuscript; also Dr Gabriella Elgenius, Dr Heather Hamill, and the support staff at the Department of Sociology, University of Oxford aided me in the preparation and the enactment of the empirical research that forms part of this book. Fellow students have also contributed more than they might imagine and, more importantly, have enlivened the journey. Professor Paul Fiddes and Dr Jolyon Mitchell examined the thesis that forms the basis of this monograph. In their engagement with my work they managed to balance generous-spirited reading with searching critical evaluation. Their comments and suggestions have, I hope, been incorporated into and improved this published version.

The empirical research would, of course, have been impossible without the cooperation of the Latin American filmgoers who gave of their time and shared their lives and their love of film with me. The staff of the *Cinemateca Uruguaya* provided me with credentials, an excellent location to conduct the interviews and access to their remarkable archives and libraries.

For the provision of financial resources, I would like to thank the Arts and Humanities Research Council for the doctoral research award that made study with the Theology Faculty of the University of Oxford a possibility. Trinity College, Oxford also provided me with a Graduate Research Award which helped with the expenses of the two research trips.

Most importantly, I would like to thank my family—especially my wife, my son, and my parents—for their unwavering love and generosity, expressed in so many different ways.

Contents

List of Tables	ix
List of Abbreviations	x
Part I Imagining a Research Project	1
Cabra marcado para morrer	1
Introduction	5
I.1 The purpose and genesis of the project	5
I.2 An overview of the book	9
1. Religion and Film	15
1.1 Description: Religion and film through the twentieth century	15
1.2 Evaluation: From 'film *qua* film' to 'multiple perspectives'	21
1.3 Imagination: How to research the possibility of revelation through film	44
Part II The Theology of Paul Tillich	47
Walk the Line	47
2. A Theology of Revelation through Culture	49
2.1 Reasons for the turn to Paul Tillich	49
2.2 A theoretical account of the possibility of revelation through culture	50
3. From High Culture to Popular Culture and Film	82
3.1 Paul Tillich: Theologian of popular culture?	83
3.2 Paul Tillich: Theologian of film?	95
Part III The Empirical Research	113
Blow-Up	113
4. Researching Filmgoers' Experiences	117
4.1 Selecting a research paradigm and developing a methodology	118
4.2 The methods and instruments of the qualitative research	135
5. Contextualizing the Research Data	156
5.1 On experiences resembling Tillich's theoretical account	156
5.2 On the setting for the research project: Montevideo, Uruguay	157
5.3 On engagement with Latin American cinema	159
5.4 On the importance of the *Cinemateca* film club	167

	5.5 On respondents' use of religious language	171
	5.6 On the respondents and the films: Focus on dictatorship	179
6.	Grounding the Theoretical Account	182
	6.1 Theory-driven analysis: On the six aspects of the revelatory experience	183
	6.2 Data-driven analysis: From individual moment to communal life-practice	205

Part IV Illuminations — 215
Nueve reinas — 215

7. The Theory in Light of the Empirical Research — 219
   7.1 The film-viewer encounter in light of the empirical research — 221
   7.2 The 'Spiritual Community' in light of the empirical research — 223
   7.3 The event of revelation in light of the empirical research — 227
   7.4 The content of revelation in light of the empirical research — 230

Appendices — 236
Index of Films Referenced — 248
Bibliography — 250
Index — 265

List of Tables

Table 5.1. Films by subject matter	168
Table 5.2. Film characteristic by its importance	171
Table 5.3. Experience by location, companions, and time	171
Table 6.1. The interview respondents selected for congruity	182
Table 6.2. The interview respondents selected for difference	183

List of Abbreviations

The following works by Paul Tillich which are frequently cited in the book are referred to throughout the text by the following abbreviations.

AA   *On Art and Architecture,* ed. John Dillenberger and Jane Dillenberger (New York: Crossroad, 1987).

ST1   *Systematic Theology, Volume 1* (London: Nisbet, 1953).

ST2   *Systematic Theology, Volume 2* (Chicago, IL: University of Chicago, 1957).

ST3   *Systematic Theology, Volume 3* (Chicago, IL: University of Chicago, 1963).

TC   *Theology of Culture* (New York: Oxford University Press, 1959).

> **LWLies:**
> What do you love about movies?
>
> **Iñárritu:**
> About movies?
>
> **LWLies:**
> About movies.
>
> **Iñárritu:**
> Wow. There are so many angles. What do I love about the movies? I think a way to put it is that, besides the fact that I can eat popcorn without guilt, I think that it reminds me of and reveals to me things about the human condition that I'm not aware of until that moment. It brings me closer to the things that I should be close to, but I have forgotten. When a film touches me on that level, it reminds me of my own life, and it gives me a justification for this complex life that we are living. It puts me in touch with the source and the reason and the meaning of life.[1]

---

[1] Alejandro Gonzalez Iñárritu, 'Interview', *Little White Lies: Truth and Movies* film magazine, Issue 9, December 2006 – January 2007, p. 19.

Part I

Imagining a Research Project

CABRA MARCADO PARA MORRER, DIR. BY EDUARDO COUTINHO (1985)

I have made it my practice to introduce some of the key themes of each part of this monograph by means of a short passage focusing on a particular film which has been an aid to my reflection upon these themes. The first of these films, *Cabra marcado para morrer*, is a unique piece of cinema, the result of the serendipitous interplay of historical circumstance and directorial persistence. The project had its genesis in 1962 when the Brazilian director Eduardo Coutinho, disgusted by the brutal assassination of yet another trade unionist, decided to write and film the biography of one such leader. His chosen subject was João Pedro Teixera, an illiterate peasant whose organization of the disenfranchised farmers of north-east Brazil led to his being murdered by thugs in the pay of the military and of the local landowning elite. Coutinho named his film *Cabra marcado para morrer*, which can be translated as *Guy Marked for Death*, to highlight the inevitable fate of such leaders.

Teixera left behind a wife and nine children and a leaderless movement, many of whom fled to a region named Galileia where the peasants had already won their fight for ownership and control of the land. In 1964 Coutinho brought a crew and equipment to Galileia and, using Texeira's real-life wife, Elisabete, family, and supporters as his principal actors, he began filming. However, on 1 April, 35 days into filming and with 40 per cent of the story shot, Brazil suffered a *coup d'état* and the military seized power. As army units swept across Brazil to retake peasant-controlled regions like Galileia, film production was halted and cast and crew were forced to separate, flee, and hide. While most of those involved escaped capture and imprisonment, locals were tortured until they revealed where the film equipment and film stock had been hidden. These were confiscated and used to make propaganda in which the military claimed that Coutinho had been directing a communist instructional film, supposedly teaching murderous, rebellious peasants how to use machine guns.[1]

That would have been the end of *Cabra marcado para morrer* were it not for the fact that the film negatives had been sent to be developed in laboratories in Rio de Janeiro in the days immediately preceding the coup. The director was eventually able to reclaim this material, and in 1981 he returned to work on a radically revised version of the project. Abandoning the idea of a biopic, Coutinho instead decided to investigate what had become of Teixera's family and friends through the hard years of the dictatorship. Coutinho combed Galileia and the surrounding regions to locate and interview those who remained and those, like Teixera's wife and children, who had been scattered.

In its final form, the film is a poignant and compelling mixture of the black-and-white recreated scenes from Teixera's life, which are interspersed with newsreel footage, plus the interviews and documentary-style investigative journalism that were filmed in colour twenty years later. *Cabra marcado para morrer* is a variegated, audio-visual collage that offers a moving impression of the harsh life-experiences of an oppressed but resilient minority; it is 'a synthesis, at once political, social, anthropological, and filmic'.[2]

A Uruguayan filmgoer, interviewed in the course of the empirical research that forms part of this book, identified the viewing of *Cabra marcado para morrer* as an experience that had marked him deeply. In his memory one scene stood out. Having recovered the film stock and resurrected the project, Coutinho has returned to a village in Galileia and gathered together all those who had participated in the original filming. The camera pans across an impoverished, dusty village, lingering on incongruous piles of expensive, modern film equipment, and then settles on the golden orb of the sun as it sets behind distant, purple mountains. As darkness falls, a crowd forms in front of a canvas sheet that has been hung up between two rough, wooden poles in the central space of the village.

Coutinho's cameraman is placed to one side, at the midpoint between screen and audience, and initially he focuses on the stooped bodies and deeply lined faces of the elderly peasants. Suddenly the village and the audience disappear, replaced by a blinding flare of light as a projector is switched on. Slowly the camera swings away from the light and around towards the screen, where the recovered footage of the original biopic plays and scenes of life in a village almost identical to the one where the crowd has gathered flicker in black and white across the makeshift canvas screen.

---

[1] For an introduction to the film, see Timothy Barnard and Peter Rist, eds, *South American Cinema: A Critical Filmography 1915–1994* (Austin, TX: University of Texas Press, 1998), pp. 199–201.
[2] Robert Stam and Ismail Xavier, 'Transformation of National Allegory: Brazilian Cinema from Dictatorship to Redemocratization', in Michael T. Martin, ed., *New Latin American Cinema, Volume II: Studies of National Cinemas* (Detroit, MI: Wayne State University Press, 1997), pp. 295–322, especially 318.

When the camera turns back towards the audience, their faces are lit up not only by the reflected light from the screen but by the emotion that is generated by seeing their younger, un-bent and un-lined selves. As the footage plays, the audience laugh and cry and call to one another, totally transfixed by this glimpse of their shared past. The camera keeps up this back-and-forth movement for some time and the shot-reverse-shot sequence uncovers something strange. The audience gathered in the village are shot in life-like colour, yet the rapturous attention of these peasants, directed towards the simple canvas screen, invests the old black-and-white images with a remarkable power.

This scene has a strange beauty, but beyond the aesthetic it also offers a pre-textual, filmic commentary on the complex and multi-layered interplay between pro-filmic reality, film text, and audience. In fact, if reflected upon, the scene prefigures many of the questions and concepts that will be discussed throughout this book. First, the scene highlights the way in which the impact of a film upon its viewers can be, and perhaps always is, affected by the unique relations that exist between each particular viewer and each particular film; in this case the connection is as immediate as seeing a younger self on screen. Second, the panning back and forth between screen and audience, and the view this affords of the audience's reactions and interactions, highlights the rarely considered communal dimension of the film-watching experience. Third, the context given to this scene by the whole film, and the whole underlying historical narrative in which it is set, highlights the political dimension of film-making and film-viewing. Fourth, the obvious impact of the film images playing on the makeshift screen, which move the viewers to laughter and to tears, highlights the potential alchemy of the film-making and film-projecting process, which presents its audience with a remarkably potent species of hyper-reality.

Cecilia Gomez, co-chair of the City of Angels Film Festival, has spoken of her experience of another Latin American open-air projection. By talking of a moment when she 'encountered God under the stars in Havana', she creates a link to the central focus of this monograph:

> It was black and white on the screen under a black sky full of white stars [. . .] My heart strained at its moorings as the film came alive on a large sheet strung between two pillars. This is indeed a strange tribute, for I don't remember the name of the film, and in my nine-year-old memory only fragments survived, yet I know that the God alive in the film, whose holy presence stopped the soldiers from desecrating his church, was the same God who danced with us children in that history-paved patio, the God who made me weep.[3]

In this monograph I consider the possibility of revelation through film.

---

[3] Cecilia Gomez, quoted in Robert K. Johnston, *Reel Spirituality: Theology and Film in Dialogue* (Grand Rapids, MI: Baker Academic, 2000), p. 157.

Introduction

I.1 THE PURPOSE AND GENESIS OF THE PROJECT

A startling proliferation of texts, conferences, and courses bear witness to burgeoning academic interest in the relation between religion and film. This monograph considers the possibility of religious revelation through film. It begins with a reading of Paul Tillich's theology of revelation through culture and then designs and enacts an original project of empirical research in order to ground this account in the experiences of a group of filmgoers. The research provides fresh insights into the way in which film functions and impacts on its viewers and also offers an unusual perspective on the strengths and weaknesses of Tillich's theology of revelation.

The decision to open with commentary on a Brazilian film and the story of a Cuban experience is more than incidental. My work has a particular interest in Latin American cinema because it was in Latin America that the intellectual puzzle and central research questions that drive the project arose and developed.[1] It is thus for autobiographical rather than theoretical reasons that the empirical research focuses on Latin American filmgoers and takes place in Argentina and Uruguay.[2]

My interest in the possibility of revelation occurring in the experience of film-watching arose out of Christian pastoral work in the Anglican Diocese of Uruguay. The authors of *The Practice of Cultural Studies* write: 'Projects start with an idea—a question, concept, hunch, feeling of anger or identification, half-grasped experience, or a difference or strangeness evoking curiosity or

---

[1] 'Intellectual puzzle' is a phrase used frequently in qualitative research literature to describe the primitive questions, still conceived in 'layman's terms', that lie at the root of many academic research projects. See, for example, Jennifer Mason, *Qualitative Researching* (London: Sage, 1996), p. 14.

[2] I am also sympathetic to the view that those engaged in studying religion and film might adapt a concept drawn from Liberation Theology and 'exercise an option for world cinema': Gaye Williams Ortiz, 'World Cinema: Opportunities for Dialogue with Religion and Theology', in Robert K. Johnston, ed., *Reframing Theology and Film: New Focus for an Emerging Discipline* (Grand Rapids, MI: Baker Academic, 2007), pp. 73–87, especially 84–5.

wonder.'³ In this case, a troubling question arose as to whether urban young people, many of whom were almost completely alienated from the natural environment, were left without access to the *general revelation* that Christians normally associate with the beauty of the created order.⁴ More positively, this puzzle led to the consideration of whether such revelation could be mediated instead through the global popular-entertainment culture in which all, from richest to poorest, were immersed.⁵ More specifically, was it possible that Uruguayan films had greater potential to be the media of such revelation because of their resonance with the young peoples' daily lives?⁶

The questions that emerged from the intellectual puzzle were first considered in dialogue with books of what might be labelled 'evangelical popular theology'. These books—authored, published, and read by evangelical Christians—not only allow for but increasingly advocate and celebrate the possibility of divine revelation beyond the direct influence of Bible reading or gospel proclamation, through the creations of contemporary culture, including art, fashion, TV, film, music, and even transvestite cabaret!⁷ The very titles of the publications are remarkable in the context of evangelicalism.⁸ See, for example: *A Matrix of Meanings: Finding God in Popular Culture*;⁹ *How Movies Helped Save My Soul: Finding Spiritual Fingerprints in Culturally Significant Films*;¹⁰ *Reflections on the Movies: Hearing God in the Unlikeliest of Places*;¹¹ *Eyes Wide Open: Looking for God in Popular Culture*, for example.¹²

---

³ Richard Johnson, Deborah Chambers, Parvati Raghuram, and Estella Tincknell, *The Practice of Cultural Studies* (London: Sage, 2004), pp. 63–4.

⁴ Psalm 19, verse 1: 'The heavens declare the glory of God; the skies proclaim the work of his hands.'

⁵ Tom Beaudoin memorably described this global popular culture as the 'amniotic fluid' within which recent generations have grown up: *Virtual Faith: The Irreverent Spiritual Quest of Generation X* (San Francisco, CA: Jossey-Bass, 2000), p. 21.

⁶ At the time, *25 Watts* (Juan Pablo Rebella and Pablo Stoll, 2001) portrayed a day in the life of a group of young friends from the middle-class milieu, while *Aparte* (Mario Handler, 2002) was a docudrama about the violent and socially dislocated lives of slum-dwellers which featured cousins and friends of young people I worked with.

⁷ For this last, see Michael Riddell, *Threshold of the Future: Reforming the Church in the Post-Christian West* (London: SPCK, 1998), p. 121.

⁸ Throughout history, two of the pejoratives most frequently directed at evangelicals label them as 'cultural philistines' and 'revelational bibliolaters'. See, for example, Matthew Arnold, *Culture and Anarchy*, ed. Samuel Lipman (London: Yale University Press, 1994), pp. 100–103 and 105. While Arnold addresses non-conformism generally, later studies have laid the blame at the door of the evangelical party; see Donald Davie, *A Gathered Church: The Literature of the English Dissenting Interest, 1700–1930* (London: Routledge and Kegan Paul, 1978), pp. 3 and 56–9.

⁹ Craig Detweiler and Barry Taylor, *A Matrix of Meanings: Finding God in Popular Culture* (Grand Rapids, MI: Baker Academic, 2003).

¹⁰ Gareth Higgins, *How Movies Helped Save My Soul: Finding Spiritual Fingerprints in Culturally Significant Films* (Lake Mary, FL: Relevant Books, 2003).

¹¹ Ken Gire, *Reflections on the Movies: Hearing God in the Unlikeliest of Places* (Colorado Springs, CO: Cook Communications Ministries, 2000).

¹² W. D. Romanowski, *Eyes Wide Open: Looking for God in Popular Culture* (Grand Rapids, MI: Brazos Press, 2001).

The most radical of these books argue that culture is not just a helpful conversation partner for the theologically pre-informed but a possible medium of God's presence—'God might be lurking in the songs, shows and films kids continually return to for solace and meaning';[13] of divine encounter—'art forms help us not only to know about God, but to actually experience God';[14] of divine disclosure or revelation—'a means of grace whereby God speaks to us';[15] and, possibly, of healing and salvation—'an encounter with God to heal us'.[16] While interesting, these books were clearly not substantial enough to form the basis of an academic study of the possibility of revelation through film. Therefore, once returned to Oxford to study for a postgraduate degree, I began to expand my reading both within the religion and film discourse and within modern academic theology.[17]

Although the reasons for my focus on this topic are personal, even the briefest consideration of the history of writing on religion and film shows that my interest in the (possibly) religious potency of film is far from unique. One pervasive characteristic of the discourse is interest in film not merely as self-contained text but as functional—having an extra-textual effect (whether morally debasing or religiously potent) on its audience. To date, the various strategies utilized by religion–film writers to interpret and explicate the impact of films have remained essentially bi-polar: acting as if the religious meaning and power were suspended somewhere between the scholar and the film

---

[13] Detweiler and Taylor, *Matrix*, p. 9; also Gire, *Reflections*, p. 44; Johnston, *Beauty*, p. 11.
[14] Johnston, *Spirituality*, p. 17, also *Beauty*, p. 176; and Riddell, *Threshold*, p. 121; Higgins, *Movies*, p. xvii; Gire, *Reflections*, pp. 43–4.
[15] Gire, *Reflections*, pp. 11, also 38, 43, and 50; and Detweiler and Taylor, *Matrix*, pp. 16–17; Johnston, *Spirituality*, pp. 14, 93, 97, and 161; Mark Stibbe and J. John, *Passion for the Movies: Spiritual Insights from Contemporary Films* (Milton Keynes: Authentic Media, 2005), p. viii.
[16] Higgins, *Movies*, pp. xvii, also 255; and Johnston, *Beauty*, pp. 33 and 178.
[17] I began with my own tradition, developing a reading of the twentieth-century evangelical theology of revelation. Although the evangelical theology of revelation does not play a large part in my final account, it is important to recognize this stage in the development of my thought as it inevitably influences my engagement with Paul Tillich; and this, in turn, impacts upon the empirical research and, therefore, the grounded account. I focused on three key moments in the development of evangelical doctrine: at the turn of the century, Benjamin Breckenridge Warfield, for example, *Calvin and Augustine* (Philadelphia, PA: The Presbyterian and Reformed Publishing Company, 1956) and *Revelation and Inspiration* (New York: Oxford University Press, 1927); in mid century, Carl F. H. Henry, for example, *God, Revelation and Authority—The God Who Speaks and Shows, 1: Preliminary Considerations* (Waco, TX: Word, 1976); *God, Revelation and Authority—The God Who Speaks and Shows, 2: Fifteen Theses, Part One* (Waco, TX: Word, 1976); *God, Revelation and Authority—The God Who Speaks and Shows, 3: Fifteen Theses, Part Two* (Waco, TX: Word, 1979); *God, Revelation and Authority—The God Who Speaks and Shows, 4: Fifteen Theses, Part Three* (Waco, TX: Word, 1979); and at the close of the century a range of more positive treatments, including Gabriel J. Fackre, *The Doctrine of Revelation: A Narrative Interpretation* (Edinburgh: Edinburgh University Press, 1997); Stanley Grenz, *Revisioning Evangelical Theology: A Fresh Agenda for the 21st Century* (Downers Grove, IL: Inter-Varsity Press, 1993); Kern R. Trembath, *Divine Revelation: Our Moral Relation with God* (Oxford: Oxford University Press, 1991).

text.[18] In contrast, I am convinced that the best account of the possibility of revelation through film may be produced by first presenting a strong and particular theory and then refining the theory through careful and respectful attention to empirically generated data. This method avoids the problems inherent in beginning with a generalized, non-specific approach to religion and addresses the glaring lack of audience data that undermines the religion–film discourse's efforts to speak meaningfully of the potential religious impact of films upon their viewers.

However, previous attempts to integrate empirical research into theology have not always proved successful, and it is clear that the appropriate articulation of the two halves of the research project is essential. I reached the conclusion that in order to achieve the desired ends of this project, the theological, theoretical half of the research needed to be *prioritized* but should not be *privileged*. In practice, Tillich's theory was used as a heuristic lens to investigate and analyze particular experiences of particular filmgoers. In other words, although this monograph considers the possibility of revelation through film and incorporates empirical research, it does not set out to prove that revelation occurs, still less to try to predict the prevalence of revelatory occurrences across any given population. Rather, the goal is to develop a grounded account of the possibility of revelation through film in full knowledge of the fact that all theological accounts are contestable, human constructions, what Paul Tillich would refer to as creative acts of *theoria* (ST3, 62).

In spite of the specificity of this particular project, I hope that the methodology developed and employed here should be flexible enough to be utilized to investigate the same theological concept (the possibility of revelation through film) but with reference to other cinematic contexts (for example, Scandinavian cinema or screenings at the local multiplex); or other cultural media (for example, the possibility of revelation through music or literature); or, indeed, to develop grounded accounts of other theological loci at the point at which they intersect with lived experience (for example, the possibility that new birth in Christ through adult baptism affects self-image).[19]

---

[18] In some cases the experience of encountering God in the film-watching experience predates both faith commitment and academic interest in religion and film. See, for example, Greg Garrett's account of the importance of the film *Pulp Fiction* in his coming to Christian faith: *The Gospel According to Hollywood* (London: Westminster John Knox Press, 2007), pp. xiii–xv.

[19] This interest in developing methodology was shared by Paul Tillich. In the Preface to the first volume of his *magnum opus*, *Systematic Theology*, he declares that the methodology he has developed, correlation, should be considered the 'subject' of his entire project, while the discussion of the traditional theological problems is merely an 'illustration' of correlation in action (*ST1*, x).

I.2 AN OVERVIEW OF THE BOOK

A project that develops over a number of years, spans two continents, utilizes two languages, and shows little respect for the (sometimes contested) boundaries between the academic disciplines of systematic theology, film studies, and social science is necessarily complex. Therefore, this Introduction will offer a brief account of the final form of the monograph in order to orient the reader.[20]

This project is primarily an exercise in theology and film and may be located within the burgeoning academic discourse that marries theology or religious studies with film studies and film theory.[21] Chapter 1, Religion and Film, sets aside the question of revelation and presents a survey of writing on religion and film. The purpose of the chapter is threefold: first, to describe the religion and film discourse; second, to evaluate best practice in the discourse in light of the most common criticisms; third, to extrapolate from the description and evaluation in order to imagine what kind of research project would be best suited to the development of an account of the possibility of revelation through film. It emerges that such a project is best served by beginning with a strong theoretical account which can then be grounded by engaging directly with actual filmgoers.

In response to the findings of the survey of the religion–film discourse, Part II of this book, The Theology of Paul Tillich, develops a theoretical account of the possibility of revelation through film that will form the basis of the grounded account. Although Tillich is frequently referenced by academics concerned with religion and film, many of these citations are dependent upon secondary sources or are limited to engagement with a few popular tropes. In order to avoid a shallow misconstrual of Tillich's complex theory, Chapter 2, Revelation through Culture, presents in-depth analysis in four stages, seeking to understand his theology of revelation in the context of his wider *oeuvre*.

---

[20] The various disciplines that are united in this monograph each have their own culture and conventions, and differences may be noted with respect to the style or register of writing. Compare, for example, Paul Tillich's detached, analytical style (*ST1*, 3–8) with the first-person perspective of classics of qualitative research such as William Foote Whyte, *Street Corner Society: The Social Structure of an Italian Slum* (London: University of Chicago Press, 1981); or, more recently, Elliot Liebow, *Tell Them Who I Am: The Lives of Homeless Women* (London: Penguin, 1995). Also, religion–film writing sits at the boundary between the academic and the popular registers. Compare, for example, the similar intent but very different tone and style of Larry J. Kretizer's academic and theoretical approach in *Pauline Images in Fiction and Film: On Reversing the Hermeneutical Flow* (Sheffield: Sheffield Academic Press, 1999); and Robert Jewett's more popular style in *Saint Paul at the Movies: The Apostle's Dialogue with American Culture* (Louisville, KY: Westminster John Knox, 1993). The varying requirements of the different disciplines cause some slippage in writing style through this book. A more autobiographical tone may be noted in this Introduction and in the chapters relating to the empirical research.

[21] Melanie J. Wright comments on the coming to maturity of this discourse in her *Religion and Film: An Introduction* (London: I. B. Tauris, 2007), p. 11. Another sign of maturity is the recent publication of a reader and a companion by an established academic press: Jolyon Mitchell and S. Brent Plate, eds, *The Religion and Film Reader* (London: Routledge, 2007); and John Lyden, ed., *The Routledge Companion to Religion and Film* (London: Routledge, 2009).

First, Paul Tillich's autobiographical statements are considered.[22] Second, Tillich's pre-exilic German writings provide a general exposition of his understanding of the relation between culture and revelation.[23] The third stage develops the reading in conversation with the most complete statement of Tillich's theory which is found in *Systematic Theology* (*ST*, 1–3).[24] At this point an important biographical experience of Tillich's, an encounter with Alessandro Botticelli's painting *Madonna with Singing Angels*, is used to organize and structure the account of the possibility of revelation through culture.[25] In the fourth and final stage, the debate engendered by Tillich's theology is briefly surveyed. It is noted that questions cluster around the appropriateness of the interplay of philosophy and doctrine in Tillich's theology, and around his careful circumscription of the knowledge-content of revelation. Overall, the analysis uncovers a complex but compelling account of revelation through culture that emphasizes the salvific and healing power of revelatory experiences rather than their communicative potential.

The task of Chapter 3, From High Culture to Popular Culture and Film, is to provide a theoretical justification for the application of Tillich's theology to the medium of film. This work is necessary because Tillich was very much a theologian of high culture and of high culture art forms like modernist painting; he had very little interest in (or respect for) popular culture, within which category he placed all, or certainly most, film.[26] The first section considers the different ways in which contemporary theologians writing about popular culture appropriate Tillich's thought. I argue that one common approach fails to distinguish between two senses of the word 'religion' in Tillich's writings and, therefore, wrongly assumes that his method of correlation is too positivist with respect to revelation, doctrine, and religious

---

[22] Paul Tillich, 'Autobiographical Reflections', pp. 3–21, in C. W. Kegley and R. W. Bretall, eds, *The Theology of Paul Tillich* (New York: Macmillan, 1961); and 'On the Boundary', pp. 297–352, in id., *The Boundaries of Our Being* (London: Collins, 1973).

[23] Paul Tillich, 'On the Idea of a Theology of Culture', in Mark Kline Taylor, *Paul Tillich: Theologian of the Boundaries* (London: Collins Liturgical Publications, 1987), pp. 35–54; *The Religious Situation*, tr. H. Richard Niebuhr (London: Thames and Hudson, 1956); *The Socialist Decision*, tr. Franklin Sherman (London: Harper & Row, 1977); *The Protestant Era*, tr. James Luther Adams (London: Nisbet, 1951).

[24] Other, later, works are also considered, for example, collections of his sermons:Paul Tillich, *The Shaking of the Foundations* (London: SCM Press, 1949); and *The Boundaries of Our Being* (London: Collins, 1973); and other works such as the best-selling *The Courage to Be* (London: Yale University Press, 1952) and *Theology of Culture* (New York: Oxford University Press, 1959).

[25] For Tillich's own accounts of this experience, see Paul Tillich, 'One Moment of Beauty', pp. 234–5, and 'Art and Society', p. 12, in id., *On Art and Architecture*, ed. John Dillenberger and Jane Dillenberger (New York: Crossroad, 1987), hereon known as *AA*.

[26] In all of Tillich's writings there appears to be only one direct, positive reference to film: he comments on Ingmar Bergman's *The Seventh Seal* and Alain Resnais' *Marienbad* (sic) in 'Religion and Art in Contemporary Development', in *AA*, pp. 165–87, especially 169. There is a less generous, offhand comment referring to the falsely happy endings in 'perverted and perverting cinemas' in the sermon 'Born in the Grave', in *Shaking*, pp. 166–73.

Introduction

institutions.[27] A more nuanced reading of Tillich suggests that his approach to culture actually mediates between the traditional academic predilection for high culture and contemporary interest in popular or mass culture.[28]

The second section of the chapter considers the appropriateness of the application of Tillich's theology of revelation to film in particular. It begins with a survey of religion–film scholars' approaches to Tillich's thought.[29] Then it offers an extended thought experiment which suggests that the unique characteristics of film give it precisely the kind of breakthrough potential that Tillich associated with his most favoured art form, expressionist painting.[30]

Part III, The Empirical Research, concerns the research project that was enacted in 2007 in Argentina and Uruguay. I was fortunate to receive support and training in empirical research methods from the Sociology Department of Oxford University.[31] This training emphasized the iterative nature of qualitative research, and accordingly the final research project involved a pilot study in the UK; a first stage of questionnaire research investigating a large group of filmgoers attending South American film festivals; and, following collation and analysis of the questionnaire data, a series of in-depth, semi-structured interviews with a carefully sampled selection of these respondents. It was analysis of these interviews that gave rise to the most important body of data used to ground the theoretical account of the possibility of revelation through film.

The key decisions that underly this research are discussed in Chapter 4, Researching Filmgoers' Experiences. The chapter progresses from the general to the specific through what might be thought of as four concentric circles,

---

[27] For example, Gordon Lynch, *Understanding Theology and Popular Culture* (Oxford: Blackwell, 2005), especially pp. 101–5.

[28] For example, the way in which Tillich addresses and analyzes the whole of the cultural situation in science, economy, art, politics, and religion in *The Religious Situation*. For this approach I am indebted to Kelton Cobb, *The Blackwell Guide to Theology and Popular Culture* (Oxford: Blackwell, 2005).

[29] As practised, for example, by Carl Skrade, 'Theology and Films', in John C. Cooper and Carl Skrade, eds, *Celluloid and Symbols* (Philadelphia, PA: Fortress Press, 1970), pp. 1–24; Michael Bird, 'Film as Hierophany', in John R. May and Michael Bird, eds, *Religion in Film* (Knoxville, TN: University of Tennessee Press, 1982), pp. 3–22; and Clive Marsh, 'Film and Theologies of Culture', in Clive Marsh and Gaye Ortiz, eds, *Explorations in Theology and Film: Movies and Meaning* (Oxford: Blackwell, 1997), pp. 21–34.

[30] This thought experiment builds upon the work of realist theorists of film such as Siegfried Kracauer, *From Caligari to Hitler: A Psychological History of the German Film*, revised and expanded edn (Oxford: Princeton University Press, 2004) and *Theory of Film: The Redemption of Physical Reality* (Chichester: Princeton University Press, 1997); and André Bazin, *What is Cinema? Volume I*, ed. and tr. Hugh Gray (London: University of California Press, 1967); and *What is Cinema? Volume II*, ed. and tr. Hugh Gray (London: University of California Press, 1972).

[31] Dr Gabriella Elgenius taught the *Qualitative Research Methods Seminar*, Oxford University Department of Sociology, Hilary Term 2007.

with the largest being the research paradigm and the smallest being the research instruments. A survey of the historical development of research into the relationship that exists between film and viewer identifies the research paradigm best suited to the generation of the kind of data required to ground the theoretical account.[32] The chosen paradigm, qualitative research, is then introduced.[33] A discussion of appropriate methodology addresses the relationship between the two components of the research project (the theoretical account and the empirical research) in light of previous attempts to integrate empirical research into theology. The conclusion is reached that for the purposes of this project the theoretical, theological account is to be *prioritized* but should not be *privileged*. One way in which this decision to prioritize without privileging is practised is by speaking of the *possibility* of revelation through film. This acknowledges that many of the participants who contribute their stories to the empirical research would not believe in divine revelation. Speaking of possibility is a way of attending to their position and recognizing that any final decision over whether or not revelation occurs, and indeed over whether or not revelation is even a sensible concept, is a decision taken on the basis of commitments that precede the work undertaken in writing, contributing to, or reading this monograph.

The second section of Chapter 4 examines the design and enactment of the empirical research, focusing on the methods of qualitative research and the particular instruments which are used for data generation in this project.[34] It is in this section that the phrase 'grounded account' is discussed in detail. Specifically, I address the difference between the grounded account that is the goal of this project and the grounded theory approach to research that is prominent in qualitative studies.[35]

---

[32] This survey draws upon key texts, including Theodor W. Adorno and Max Horkheimer, *Dialectic of Enlightenment* (London: Verso, 1997); Laura Mulvey, 'Visual Pleasure and Narrative Cinema', in Leo Braudy and Marshall Cohen, eds, *Film Theory and Criticism: Introductory Readings*, 5th edn (Oxford: Oxford University Press, 1999), pp. 833–44; and David Morley and Charlotte Brunsdon, *The Nationwide Television Studies* (London: Routledge, 1999).

[33] Two qualitative studies which address the relation between film and viewer are considered as examples of good practice: Mark Jancovich and Lucy Faire with Sarah Stubbings, *The Place of the Audience: Cultural Geographies of Film Consumption* (London: British Film Institute, 2003); and Annette Hill, *Shocking Entertainment: Viewer Response to Violent Movies* (Luton: University of Luton Press, 1997).

[34] In addition to those books already mentioned above, these studies in ethnographic and qualitative methodology were particularly helpful: Martin Hammersley and Paul Atkinson, *Ethnography: Principles in Practice*, 2nd edn (London: Routledge, 1995); Paula Saukko, *Doing Research in Cultural Studies: An Introduction to Classical and New Methodological Approaches* (London: Sage, 2003); Dorothy Pawluch, William Shaffir, and Charlene Miall, *Doing Ethnography: Studying Everyday Life* (Toronto: Canadian Scholars' Press, 2005).

[35] What is meant by 'grounded account' will be discussed in detail in section 4.2.1, with reference to the work on 'grounded theory' by Barney Glaser and Anselm Strauss; see, for example, Barney Glaser and Anselm Strauss, *Discovering Grounded Theory* (London: Weidenfeld

Introduction 13

Chapter 5, Contextualizing the Research Data, considers the results of the questionnaire surveys and attempts to map out the general features of filmgoers' experiences, and to draw attention to key questions that are raised and will be revisited in the qualitative interviews. The chapter also offers extended introductions to three important features of the research context. First, the nation of Uruguay is introduced; the recent political history and the unusual religious culture of the country are later considered in more detail.[36] Second, there is an overview of the development and contemporary reality of Latin American cinema.[37] Thirdly, there is a section about the *Cinemateca Uruguaya*. The *Cinemateca* is the cinema club of which all the interview respondents were members. As the project develops it becomes clear that this institution is more central to this grounded account of revelation through film than might have been expected.[38] Clearly, the goal of these sections cannot be an exhaustive cultural history. Rather, the purpose is to contextualize the empirical research, providing a background against which the data generated by the respondent interviews may more clearly be seen.

Chapter 6, Grounding the Theoretical Account, presents the results of analysis of the data generated by the ten long, qualitative interviews. In the first section of the chapter, the approach to the data is governed by the conceptual categories derived from Tillich's theoretical account of revelation. In the second section, the conceptual categories taken from the theoretical account are set aside and analysis concentrates on identifying unexpected themes and developing fresh categories out of the data. A new way of looking at the possibility of revelation through film emerges. Now the emphasis is on the community rather than the individual, and on sustained life-practice

---

and Nicolson, 1967); and Anselm Strauss and Juliet Corbin, *Basics of Qualitative Research: Grounded Theory Procedures and Techniques* (London: Sage, 1990).

[36] This section drew upon works including Roger Geymonat, ed., *Las religiones en el Uruguay: algunas aproximaciones* (Montevideo: Ediciones La Gotera, 2004); Virginia Martínez, *Tiempos de dictadura 1973–1985: hechos, voces, documentos: la represión y la resistencia día a día*, 3rd edn (Montevideo, Uruguay: Ediciones de la Banda Oriental, 2005); Gerardo Caetano and José Rilla, *Breve historia de la dictadura: 1973–1985*, 2nd edn (Montevideo, Uruguay: Ediciones de la Banda Oriental, 1998).

[37] Both English language introductions to the cinema of Latin American and primary texts by Latin American film-makers (in English and Spanish) are utilized: for example, Deborah Shaw, *Contemporary Cinema of Latin America: 10 Key Films* (London: Continuum, 2003); and John King, *Magical Reels: A History of Cinema in Latin America*, new edn (London: Verso, 2000); Julio García Espinosa, 'For an Imperfect Cinema', in Michael T. Martin, ed., *New Latin American Cinema, Volume I: Theory, Practices and Transcontinental Articulations* (Detroit, MI: Wayne State University Press, 1997), pp. 71–82; and Fernando Solanas, *La mirada: reflexiones sobre cine y cultura* (Buenos Aires, Argentina: Puntosur Editores, 1989).

[38] Online articles were most useful for this research, for example, *Cinemateca Uruguaya*, 'Documentos institucionales' <http://www.*Cinemateca*.org.uy/institucional.html> (accessed 13 June 2008).

rather than momentary experience. This move results in the reinstatement of certain of the social and political aspects of Tillich's thought.

A grounded account is never final or closed; rather than an end result it is an ongoing process. Chapter 7, The Theory in Light of the Empirical Research, is one moment in this ongoing process. Consideration of the results of the empirical research present a challenge to the contemporary religion and film discourse and suggest engagement with parts of Tillich's theology as yet unconsidered, for example, his presentation of the 'spiritual community' (ST3, 149-61). In light of questions raised by the empirical research, Tillich's approach is contrasted with essays on revelation by Paul Ricoeur and Rowan Williams.[39] The chapter closes with the suggestion that Tillich's account is sensitive and compelling precisely because of its phenomenological attentiveness to real-life experience, notably his own experience, of the power of art. However, it also suggests that it might be helpful to identify a stronger link than Tillich allows between the subject matter of the artwork, the content of revelation, and the effect of revelation.

---

[39] Rowan Williams, 'Trinity and Revelation', in id., *On Christian Theology* (Oxford: Blackwell, 2000), pp. 131-47; Paul Ricoeur, 'Toward a Hermeneutic of the Idea of Revelation', in *Harvard Theological Review*, 70.1-2 (1977), pp. 1-37.

1

Religion and Film

In this chapter I shall undertake three tasks. The first is descriptive: a survey of the religion and film discourse as it has developed in the United States and the United Kingdom; in later chapters the monograph will be less parochial and Anglophone as it draws non-religious theorists and world cinema into the conversation.[1] The second task is evaluative: considering the discourse in light of the criticisms most commonly directed at religion–film writings. The third task is imaginative: building upon the description and evaluation of the discourse, I will explain how my thinking developed and led to the general structure of this research project, an approach which I believe is capable of producing a good account of the possibility of revelation through film. The questions that arise as a consequence are noted and will be addressed as they become pertinent in the development of this study.

1.1 DESCRIPTION: RELIGION AND FILM THROUGH THE TWENTIETH CENTURY

According to legend, the birth of the cinema can be located and dated with great precision: on the evening of 28 December 1895 in the Grand Café of Paris, the Lumière brothers entertained a paying audience with projections of short films they had photographed on their *Cinématographe* machine. No genesis is as clear-cut as such creation myths would have us believe, and behind this event lay advances in the photographic depiction of movement, notably by Thomas Edison, and a pre-history of motion picture entertainments like the Magic

---

[1] Film theorist Robert Stam notes the importance of world cinema from the very beginnings of the new art, in *Film Theory: An Introduction* (Oxford: Blackwell, 2000), pp. 18–22. The religion and film discourse has also become more attentive to world cinema in recent years. I have already referenced Gaye Williams Ortiz's essay in Johnston, *Reframing*, and other publications evidence this attention, for example Brent S. Plate, ed., *Representing Religion in World Cinema: Filmmaking, Mythmaking, Culture Making* (New York: Palgrave Macmillan, 2003); and John Lyden, ed., *The Routledge Companion to Religion and Film* (London: Routledge, 2009).

Lantern and the Zoetrope.² Nonetheless it was an important breakthrough, and after 1895 the new art/entertainment developed rapidly.³

Cinema turned to religion almost immediately. In 1896 *The Horitz Passion Play* was shot and screened in Paris.⁴ Five more 'Jesus films' followed before the turn of the century but, as the Roman Catholic theologian Lloyd Baugh points out, 'If the representation of Jesus Christ was a constant theme in the six traditional arts, one might well expect it to be a theme of the seventh art, the cinema.'⁵ Early cinematic appropriation of the Jesus story soon led to the use of other religious source material, particularly melodramatic and sexually-charged narratives like those of Samson and Delilah, or Salome dancing to claim John the Baptist's head. This immediately begged questions about the film-makers' motivations and about the films' impact: were these sacred or profane productions? Did they promote piety or prurience?⁶

Such ambivalence with regard to the explicitly or implicitly religious intent, content, and effects of film pervades the history of religion's relation to the medium. The struggle to resolve this tension is a characteristic preoccupation of the writings on religion and film, and, as a result, it is possible to offer a brief, narrative overview highlighting the dominant interests that set the tone of the discourse at different periods.

The first period was characterized by enthusiasm and the desire to harness the potential of the new medium. The early move to religious subject matter, noted above, may be seen as both partially constituting and simultaneously reflecting a general sense of optimism within the Christian church at the birth of cinema. Articles written in religious and general-interest publications extol film's virtues with regard to mission, where its presentational and affective power was seen as a boon to gospel proclamation;⁷ in Christian education, where it was compared to Jesus' parables in its use of contemporary settings and narrative excitement; and as a source of wholesome recreation for the working population.⁸

---

² There is an interesting grace note here in the involvement of clerics in this primordial development; see Terry Lindvall, 'Silent Cinema and Religion: An Overview (1895–1930), in John Lyden, ed., *The Routledge Companion to Religion and Film* (Routledge: London, 2009), pp. 13–31, especially 13.

³ Robert Sklar, *Film: An International History of the Medium*, 2nd edn (New York: Prentice Hall, 2002), pp. 16–22; and Jack C. Ellis, *A History of Film*, 4th edn (Needham, MS: Allyn & Bacon, 1995), p. 3.

⁴ Johnston, *Spirituality*, p. 32.

⁵ Lloyd Baugh, S. J., *Imaging the Divine: Jesus and Christ Figures in Film* (Kansas City, MO: Sheed & Ward, 1997), p. viii.

⁶ Ivan Butler, *Religion in the Cinema* (London: Zwemmer, 1969), pp. 9–12.

⁷ Johnston notes that early in the twentieth century Herbert Booth, son of the Salvation Army founders William and Catherine, produced short films for evangelistic campaigns in Australia: *Spirituality*, p. 32.

⁸ Herbert Jump, 'The Religious Possibilities of the Motion Picture', pp. 14–24; and Percy Stickney Grant, 'If Christ Went to the Movies', in Mitchell and Plate, eds, *The Religion and Film Reader*, pp. 27–31.

In the 1920s Cecil B. DeMille's epics highlighted the complexity of film's relation to religion. *The Ten Commandments* (1923) and *King of Kings* (1927) utilized biblical subject matter, but have been described by film historian Jack Ellis as 'religiosity cum sex and spectacle'[9] and by theologian Robert Johnston as 'religious gloss over salacious scenes'.[10] In response to such quasi-religious spectaculars (and to the burgeoning genre of amoral gangster films), the predominant approach of organized religion towards the cinema began to shift from celebration towards opprobrium. The second period of the engagement of religion and film is characterized by the attempt to influence the output of the film industry.

Religious institutions played an important role in the development of instruments for the censorship and classification of film. In the US, the long-standing Hays Production Code (in force approximately 1930–66) was an attempt at self-regulation by the Motion Picture Producers and Distributors of America, but it clearly resulted from the mobilization of grass-roots religious movements like 'The National Board of Censorship' (founded 1909). In the UK, the clergy and organizations like the Mothers' Union were among the most vociferous campaigners for the setting up of the British Board of Film Censors (BBFC) in 1912.[11]

Perhaps the single most important piece of writing of this period is that of Pope Pius XI in '*Vigilanti Cura*: On the Motion Pictures', written to the US Episcopate in 1936. In this encyclical, the Pope commended with 'gratitude' the formation of the immensely powerful pressure group the 'Legion of Decency'. He also encouraged the US church to 'serve the needs of the entire catholic world' by seeing to it that bad films which 'occasion sin and create prejudice' and damage the 'nation's moral fibre' be replaced with films 'directed toward the noble end of promoting the highest ideals and the truest standard of life'.[12]

Another predominant interest and approach seems to have gained ground from the late 1960s as a result of separate developments in film and theology. On the side of film, the 1950s and 1960s saw the rise of the European *auteurs*, serious film-makers who frequently engaged with religious and spiritual themes: Robert Bresson's *Diary of a Country Priest* (1951), Ingmar Bergman's *The Seventh Seal* (1957), Federico Fellini's *La Dolce Vita* (1960), and Pier

---

[9] Ellis, *A History of Film*, p. 110.
[10] Johnston, *Spirituality*, p. 33; Butler notes that the orgy scenes were actually toned down for the 1956 re-make: *Religion*, p. 15.
[11] Jeffrey Richards, 'British Film Censorship', in Robert Murphy, ed., *The British Cinema Book*, 2nd edn (London: British Film Institute, 2001), pp. 155–62, especially 155–6.
[12] Pope Pius XI, '*Vigilanti Cura*: On the Motion Pictures', <http://www.vatican.va/holy_father/pius_xi/encyclicals/documents/hf_p-xi_enc_29061936_vigilanti-cura_en.html> (accessed 28 August 2008).

Paolo Pasolini's *The Gospel According to St Matthew* (1964) all provide good examples.

Meanwhile, within the religious academy there was a turn to radical or secular theology which afforded the contemporary arts an expanded role in the development of theological thought. Two of the authors most associated with this theology, William Hamilton (who co-authored *Radical Theology and the Death of God* (1968) with Thomas Altizer) and Harvey Cox (author of *The Secular City* (1965)), wrote essays in the 1970 religion–film publication *Celluloid and Symbols*.[13] The philosopher John Cooper and the theologian Carl Skrade edited this volume and expressed their desire to speak across the chasm that had arisen between religious and secular people. Their simple thesis that cinema, 'the most vital and significant of the contemporary arts', 'can serve as the basis for a fruitful dialogue between the church and the world' led to theological readings that focused on the existential questions and potential symbols of renewal found in 'serious' cinema.[14]

Theology Through Film, by Neil Hurley, was also published in 1970. Hurley believed that 'movies are for the masses what theology is for an elite'. He argued that because 'religious transcendence [. . .] the dynamic piston in man's movement toward truth' is active in both spheres, film as much as theology can lead to 'transcredal' affirmations of religious truth. These are 'universal points of consensus' compatible with, but not prescribed by, the author's Roman Catholic Christianity.[15]

Through the 1970s and 1980s this style of theological engagement with film continued. The Roman Catholic author John May co-edited *Film Odyssey* and *Religion in Film*, championing a method that went beyond moral judgements and moved towards understanding the religious nature of film in relation to humanity's quest for ultimate meaning.[16] A Protestant writer of great influence through the 1970s and 1980s was the editor of *The Christian Advocate* and *The Christian Century* magazines, James Wall. From his article in *Celluloid and Symbol* onwards, Wall's contribution was to argue that the religious capacity of film was located not in its narrative (the discursive) but in the 'evocative power' of the overall artistic vision of its director (the presentational) which 'calls us all to receive the gift of life'.[17]

---

[13] William Hamilton, 'Bergman and Polanski on the Death of God', pp. 61–74; and Harvey Cox, 'The Purpose of the Grotesque in Fellini's Films', pp. 89–106, in Cooper and Skrade, *Celluloid*.

[14] Cooper and Skrade, *Celluloid*, p. viii; Skrade, 'Theology', pp. 3 and 17–20.

[15] Neil Hurley, *Theology Through Film* (London: Harper & Row, 1970), pp. ix, 8, and 13.

[16] Ernest Ferlita and John R. May, *Film Odyssey: The Art of Film as Search for Meaning* (New York: Paulist Press, 1976), pp. 1–15; and May and Bird, *Religion*, pp. vii–xi.

[17] James M. Wall, 'Biblical Spectaculars and Secular Man', in John C. Cooper and Carl Skrade, eds, *Celluloid and Symbols* (Philadelphia, PA: Fortress Press, 1970), pp. 51–60, especially 53 and 60.

As much of this body of writing engages with Paul Tillich and with the theology of revelation, it will be considered in more detail in Chapter 3. For the purposes of this brief narrative, what is important is the way this body of work moves beyond the pedagogical potential or moral failings of film and towards theological dialogue and the possibility of the religious (or religion-like) functioning of film.

The 1990s saw an exponential growth in writing on religion and film. As the twentieth century gave way to the twenty-first, the most serious discussions in the field began to exhibit a more self-referential character. The religion–film discourse had taken on many of the characteristic 'markers'—specific courses, publications, and conferences—of an independent academic discipline and the predominant interest turned toward methodology; the appropriate theoretical apparatus for religion–film dialogue; and the discourse's relation to other disciplines.[18]

As recently as 2007, Robert Johnston edited *Reframing Theology and Film: New Focus for an Emerging Discipline*. This book was the product 'of a three year consultation on theology and film [involving ...] fifteen scholars, church leaders, and filmmakers from Europe and the United States to come together to share ideas and to strategise on the discipline of theology and film'.[19] In 2008, Christopher Deacy and Gaye Williams Ortiz published *Theology and Film: Challenging the Sacred/Secular Divide*, which opens with an extended essay on 'Methodology'.[20] *The Routledge Companion to Religion and Film*, edited by John Lyden and published in 2009, is acutely sensitive to the way in which 'the field of Religion and Film [... makes] use of the methodological approaches of its parent disciplines'. One whole section of the *Companion* is devoted to consideration of the contribution of different academic approaches to the study of religion and film.[21]

There are three main subsets of contemporary religion–film writing. First, there are those who approach film from a background in biblical studies. In 1993, books were published by Larry Kreitzer in the UK, *The New Testament in Fiction and Film: On Reversing the Hermeneutical Flow*,[22] and by Robert Jewett in the US, *St Paul at the Movies: The Apostle's Dialogue with American Culture*.[23] While there are notable differences in approach (Kreitzer's work is closely argued and academic while Jewett's style and choice of films are more

---

[18] Melanie J. Wright, *Religion and Film: An Introduction* (London: I. B. Tauris, 2007), p. 11.
[19] Robert K. Johnston, *Reframing Theology and Film: New Focus for an Emerging Discipline* (Grand Rapids, MI: Baker Academic, 2007), p. 9.
[20] Christopher Deacy and Gaye Williams Ortiz, *Theology and Film: Challenging the Sacred/Secular Divide* (Oxford: Blackwell, 2008), pp. 3–75.
[21] John Lyden, 'Introduction', in id., *Companion*, pp. 1–10, especially 1 and 6–7.
[22] Larry J. Kreitzer, *The New Testament in Fiction and Film: On Reversing the Hermeneutical Flow* (Sheffield: Sheffield Academic Press, 1993).
[23] As referenced in the Introduction.

populist), both aim to generate new insights into biblical texts by examining them in light of similar tropes in classic or popular films.

A separate stream of writing, also arising out of biblical studies, has an ideological rather than hermeneutical intent. In fact, some of the most academically demanding writing on religion–film can be found where biblical studies scholars enter the discourse, drawing on literary and film theory to fund their engagement with the visual and narrative aspects of film presentation. In her introduction to a special issue of *Semeia: An Experimental Journal in Biblical Criticism*, Alice Bach writes: 'Like most cultural critics, we are engaged with cataloguing the power relations and the macropolitics that shape cultural representations of biblical tropes and narratives.'[24]

Second, there are those who continue more or less in the tradition of the early 1970s, engaging film using the tools of contemporary theology. The essays brought together in the UK's most influential religion–film publication, *Explorations in Theology and Film*, would fit this category.[25] In the US, Robert Johnston and Roy Anker write from explicitly theological perspectives, seeing film as a locus for 'divine encounter' (Johnston) and for the catching of divine 'Light' (Anker).[26]

Finally, there are those who approach the religion–film nexus from the disciplines of religious studies, social studies, and cultural studies. Margaret Miles was one of the first to argue for the 'fruitfulness of the cultural studies approach', in her book *Seeing and Believing*.[27] More recently Melanie Wright has written *Religion and Film*, and this is likely to prove to be an influential blueprint for this kind of engagement. Bergeson and Greeley have written as social scientists on the ongoing influence of the religious imagination in *God in the Movies*.[28] Cultural studies approaches are increasingly interested in film as a locus for religious or religion-like activity, often with a particular emphasis on the myth-like character of film.[29] A characteristic that separates these

---

[24] Alice Bach, '"Throw Them to the Lions, Sire": Transforming Biblical Narratives into Hollywood Spectaculars', in *Semeia: An Experimental Journal in Biblical Criticism*, 74.1 (1996), pp. 1–13, especially 3–4. More recently, Erin Runions, *How Hysterical: Identification and Resistance in Bible and Film* (London: Palgrave Macmillan, 2003), especially p. 2 for a summary of her purpose.

[25] Marsh and Ortiz, *Explorations*.

[26] For example, Johnston, *Spirituality*, pp. 57–8; and Roy M. Anker, *Catching Light: Looking for God in the Movies* (Cambridge: Eerdmans, 2004), pp. 1–18.

[27] Margaret R. Miles, *Seeing and Believing: Religion and Values in the Movies* (Boston, MA: Beacon Press, 1996), p. 27.

[28] Albert J. Bergeson and Andrew M. Greeley, *God in the Movies* (London: Transaction Press, 2000).

[29] See, for example, Joel W. Martin and Conrad E. Ostwalt, eds, *Screening the Sacred: Religion, Myth and Ideology in Popular American Film* (Oxford: Westview Press, 1995); Paul V. M. Flesher and Robert Torry, *Film and Religion: An Introduction* (Nashville, TX: Abingdon Press, 2007); and Bernard Brandon Scott, *Hollywood Dreams and Biblical Stories* (Minneapolis, MN: Fortress Press, 1994).

works from most of those that preceded them in the 1960s and 1970s is a willingness to engage not just with 'serious' films made by respected *auteurs* but also with popular film.

This brief overview demonstrates that one pervasive characteristic of the religion–film discourse is interest in film not merely as a self-contained text but as functional: having an extra-textual, extra-diegetic effect (whether morally debasing or religiously potent) on its audience. However, the various strategies utilized for the interpretation and explication of films have remained essentially bi-polar, acting as if the religious meaning and power were suspended somewhere between the scholar and the film text. A central tenet of this monograph is that more attention must be paid to the actual viewer in any interpretation of the meaning or power of a film.[30]

1.2 EVALUATION: FROM 'FILM *QUA* FILM' TO 'MULTIPLE PERSPECTIVES'

1.2.1 Criticizing the critics

In the brief narrative of development offered above, it was noted that in recent times the discourse has become more self-referential. Since the late 1990s, a number of pieces of robust criticism have been written by scholars working within religion–film. At the close of *Explorations in Theology and Film*, David Jasper sounded a cautionary note: 'We must [...] be perpetually watchful that the illusions of the screen do not also include the illusion of theology in a mere celluloid simulacrum of redemption and salvation.'[31] A year later, Brent S. Plate (who went on to co-edit *Imag(in)ing Otherness: Filmic Visions of Living Together* (1999)[32] with Jasper) looked to develop a 'religious visuality of film'. He first criticized previous work for its overly literary and narrative focus, lack of true 'interdisciplinarity', and for 'following Hollywood's slick and

---

[30] This is not to disparage scholars' opinions or disregard the fact that scholars also experience films as 'viewers'. However, it is important to recognize that the very fact of being a scholar influences this experience. For example, see Douglas E. Cowan's 'Preface' to his *Sacred Terror: Religion and Horror on the Silver Screen* (Waco, TX: Baylor University Press, 2008), where he notes that his experience of viewing horror as a sociologist of religion is completely different to his earlier experience as a layperson, pp. 12–13. See also the same author's *Sacred Space: The Quest for Transcendence in Science Fiction Film and Television* (Waco, TX: Baylor University Press, 2010).
[31] David Jasper, 'On Systematizing the Unsystematic: A Response', in Marsh and Ortiz, *Explorations*, pp. 235–44.
[32] S. Brent Plate and David Jasper, eds, *Imag(in)ing Otherness: Filmic Visions of Living Together* (Atlanta, GA: Scholars Press, 1999).

subversive path'.³³ More recently, Melanie Wright has accused her peers of theologically driven instrumentalism, theoretical naïveté, solipsistic interpretation, and inconsistent film selection. 'Could it be that—despite the growing bibliography and plethora of courses—*film is not really being studied at all?*'³⁴

The most prolific (and occasionally 'vitriolic'³⁵) critic is Steve Nolan, a Baptist minister who wrote his PhD thesis on the relation between film theory and Christian liturgy. He has published a series of articles in *Literature and Theology* (1998), *Reviews in Religion and Theology* (2002), *Mediating Religion: Conversations in Media, Religion and Culture* (2003), and *Flickering Images: Theology and Film in Dialogue* (2005).³⁶ He invariably begins with plangent regret for the errors of his predecessors. Tracing the roots of contemporary religion–film engagement to the US, Nolan focuses on three authors mentioned above: James Wall, John May, and Neil Hurley. He considers their work to be impoverished by their reliance on the *auteur* theory of film studies, and their ignorance of 'film theory's encounter with "Marxism and psychoanalysis on the terrain of semiotics"', which had recently taken place in Europe.³⁷ These authors are also too literary in their readings. May 'fails in his attempt to treat film in terms of the language of film, and his conception of film as "visual story" entirely misses the specific operations of film as experience'.³⁸ Nolan's third concern is most clearly spelled out in relation to Hurley, who is guilty of 'theological sleight of hand' in the way he 'masks the already committed nature of his method'.³⁹ Here he prefigures a criticism later made by Wright, who believes that many writers fail to recognize that their religious commitments 'are not the starting points of theory but are themselves data that must not be neglected'.⁴⁰

Those who approach film from a biblical studies perspective fare little better in Nolan's account. Kreitzer's work is disappointing as a result of its 'redaction critical preoccupation' and its being 'uncritically innocent' of theory.⁴¹ Although he is less dismissive of Martin and Ostwalt, they are included in the concluding summary of the failings of the past. Nolan would doubtless agree with Plate that their project 'originally so hopefully interdisciplinary turns out

---

³³ S. Brent Plate, 'Religion/Literature/Film: Toward a Religious Visuality of Film', in *Literature and Theology*, 12.1 (1998), pp. 16–38, especially 34.
³⁴ Wright, *Religion*, pp. 11–22, especially 22.
³⁵ Deacy and Ortiz, *Challenging*, p. 8.
³⁶ Steve Nolan, 'Understanding Films: Reading in the Gaps', in Anthony J. Clarke and Paul S. Fiddes, eds, *Flickering Images: Theology and Film in Dialogue*, Regent's Study Guides 12 (Oxford: Regent's Park College, 2005), pp. 25–48; 'Towards a New Religious Film Criticism: Using Film to Understand Religious Identity Rather than Locate Cinematic Analogue', in Jolyon Mitchell and Sophia Marriage, eds, *Mediating Religion: Conversations in Media, Religion and Culture* (London: T&T Clark, 2003), pp. 169–78; 'The Books of the Films: Trends in Religious Film-Analysis', in *Literature and Theology*, 12.1 (1998), pp. 1–14.
³⁷ Nolan, 'Trends', p. 1.   ³⁸ Ibid., p. 4.   ³⁹ Ibid., p. 6.
⁴⁰ Wright, *Religion*, p. 12.   ⁴¹ Nolan, 'Trends', pp. 7–8.

to be wholly subsumed by religious studies methodologies'.[42] In his more recent articles, Nolan judges the result of these failings to be the reduction of religious film criticism to an inappropriate and 'futile pursuit of cinematic analogue' to religious questions and doctrines.[43] He concludes:

> Problems have largely been due to the over reliance of religious film-analysts on (out-dated) literary categories of interpretation, combined with their failure to engage seriously with the categories of contemporary film theory. Future religious film-analysis must learn to treat film *qua* film, and to engage with its large and highly theorised body of literature.[44]

The concerns of critics like Jasper, Plate, Wright, and Nolan may be summarized as identifying four failings: first, engagement is too literary and narrative-focused, not really dealing with 'film *qua* film'; second, theological baggage is smuggled in and then, intentionally or unintentionally, read *onto* the film text; third, there is a lack of rigour in film selection; fourth, the cumulative result is the unexpected absence of true interdisciplinarity and dialogue. These are severe criticisms that, if correct, undermine the whole discourse. But are they *necessarily* correct?

Actually, these critics with their rallying cry of 'film *qua* film' produce more heat than light because they are just as situated, just as guilty of ideologically freighted rhetoric, as the authors they denounce. In what follows, I will argue that while these critics are not ignorant of developments in film theory and studies, they fail to take account of the fact that film theory is not monolithic but utilizes a number of theoretical rubrics. In the words of Robert Stam, film theory should be seen as 'an evolving body of concepts designed to account for the cinema in all its dimensions (aesthetic, social, psychological) for an interpretive community of scholars, critics, and interested spectators'.[45] Stam advocates 'theoretical cubism', which he construes as 'the deployment of multiple perspectives and grids. Each grid has its blind spots and insights; each needs the "excess seeing" of the other grids.'[46]

Nolan's papers, published over a long period, best illustrate my contention. Writing in 1998, he appears innocently to believe that 'ideological–semiotic–psychoanalytic' film theory is definitive, and it is on this basis that he critiques Wall, May, Hurley, et al.[47] Rewriting his article in 2003, he has the good grace to recognize that his chosen theoretical apparatus has its detractors and to list some of the most pertinent treatments in his footnotes.[48] In 2005, the title of his unpublished PhD describes his thesis as drawing on '1970s Lacanian film theory'.[49] This careful circumscription of his work is admirable, but it is

---

[42] Plate, 'Religion/Literature/Film', p. 17.   [43] Nolan, 'Criticism', pp. 169 and 177.
[44] Nolan, 'Trends', p. 11.   [45] Stam, *Theory*, p. 6.   [46] Ibid., p. 1.
[47] Nolan, 'Trends', p. 1.   [48] Nolan, 'Criticism', p. 177.
[49] Steve Nolan, unpublished PhD thesis, *Faithful Representations: an application of 1970s Lacanian film theory to the subject of liturgical subjectivity* (Manchester University, 2005).

notable that throughout this time he has not given the same benefit to the writers he criticizes. Here he proceeds as though his theoretical position were the universally valid norm of 'correct' film analysis.

In point of fact, David Bordwell considers this approach to be guilty of precisely the error Nolan sees in writers like Hurley; it does little more than use films to illustrate its own preconceived ideas.[50] Melanie Wright also rejects the kind of theory utilized by Nolan as 'totalizing' and implying 'that the normal viewer is "duped" by what he or she sees'.[51] Wright is making a move to locate the religion–film discourse within 'the territory of cultural studies, into which much of film studies has been shifting'[52] and her criticisms of previous writers must be seen in the light of her need to justify this move. Similar observations could be made with regard to the ideologically motivated film engagements of Jasper and Plate. They believe that only 'two-edged, ironic, difficult and ambiguous' films can be religiously relevant, because only these films problematize our viewing and help us to uncover buried ideologies.[53]

If these critics can be questioned because they mistook their particular theoretical apparatus for a universally valid norm, what might provide a more appropriate critical approach?

1.2.2 A particular and comparative approach to evaluation

The evaluation offered in this chapter is more attuned to the concrete. It will be structured around particular films that have been the subject of multiple treatments. The focus will be on scholars' analysis of these particular films and will only shift to their theoretical accounts as a means of understanding the method, purpose, and successfulness of their engagement. Finally, it will be comparative, assessing the work of those writing on religion–film against their peers and against authors from the wider sphere of film studies and theory.

A few practical notes are required with regard to this approach. First, an important datum is immediately generated: the near impossibility of finding a film that is treated by more than one or two religion–film authors implies that the critics are probably correct in suggesting that there is no consensus as to what constitutes a religiously-meaningful or religiously-functioning film. Four films will be considered: *The Passion of the Christ* (Gibson, 2004); *La Passion de Jeanne d'Arc* (Dreyer, 1928); *The Godfather* and its sequels (Coppola, 1972, 1974, 1990); and *Mean Streets* (Scorsese, 1973). These films have been chosen

---

[50] David Bordwell, *Making Meaning: Inference and Rhetoric in the Interpretation of Cinema* (Cambridge, MA: Harvard University Press, 1989); see, for example, his chapter 'Rhetoric in Action' on various interpretations of the film *Psycho*, pp. 224–48.
[51] Wright, *Religion*, pp. 27 and 49.
[52] Ibid., p. 27.
[53] Jasper, 'Systematising', p. 244; Plate, 'Religion/Literature/Film', p. 23.

not because of their intrinsic merit or a common theme, rather because they bring together a sufficient number of influential scholars.[54] The implications of this focus on particular treatments of particular films cut both ways: on the one hand it means that it cannot be proven that the typical criticisms are not true of other writings in the discourse; on the other hand it does allow for the presentation of particular examples of where the criticisms are founded and unfounded. This concrete and particular approach will not create a 'neat' survey, but I believe it allows for a fairer assessment of the potential strengths and weaknesses of the discourse and points towards the type of project that would be appropriate for investigation of the possibility of revelation through film.

Treatments of <u>The Passion of the Christ</u> Across the spectrum of religion–film writings there is a widespread belief that confessional, explicitly religious and Bible-based films are less interesting and less religiously powerful than those that treat similar subjects ambiguously, implicitly, and tangentially.[55] Nonetheless, it is hard to ignore such films completely, especially if, like Gibson's *The Passion*, they generate a cultural storm. Here I will begin with books by Flesher and Torry and Richard Walsh before widening the engagement to include other writers.[56]

One question recurs: why was this ultra-violent film so readily accepted by certain religious audiences who might have been expected to reject an 18-certificate Jesus film? With regard to the central task of this chapter, the evaluation of the discourse, consideration of which treatments offer the most illuminating answers to this question will cast doubt upon the assumption that there is a single *correct* approach to films. It will show that many different styles of engagement can contribute to understanding of the nature and impact of a film.

Flesher and Torry are US cultural studies scholars who, together, have taught a class on film's use of religion for the past ten years. With regard to *The Passion of the Christ* they focus on the way Gibson expands a brief gospel reference to Pilate's wife (known to tradition as 'Claudia') and uses this character to guide the audience's reception of the narrative. Most importantly, they note that Gibson inserts into his film a lengthy argument between Pilate and Claudia on the nature of truth. While Pilate's conception of *truth* extends

---

[54] The religion–film discourse tends to generate a large number of occasional essays, many by scholars whose primary expertise is in other fields. For the purposes of my evaluation I have focused on scholars for whom religion–film is their primary expertise, or who have produced at least one book-length work on the subject, or have been active in the field for an extended period.

[55] For one discussion of this see Ann Hardy, *Film, Spirituality and Hierophany* (Lampeter, University of Wales: Religious Experience Research Centre, 2002), pp. 16–20; also Wall, 'Spectaculars', especially p. 52.

[56] Flesher and Torry, *Film*; and Richard Walsh, *Finding St. Paul in Film* (London: T&T Clark, 2005).

no further than orders from his superiors, Claudia is interested in a more existential, self-validating *Truth* centred on the person of Jesus. As a result of this conversation, Gibson is able to contrast Pilate, who on this account knows full well who Jesus is but condemns him anyway on the basis of his self-interested earthbound *truth*, with Claudia, who is portrayed positively as an example of a convert to the *Truth*.[57]

Flesher and Torry look closely at the techniques employed by Gibson to encourage the audience to identify with Claudia. They note that Claudia is repeatedly portrayed as a spectator looking down upon Christ's suffering from a window. This corresponds with the audience's role as spectators and onlookers and their distanced point of view. Claudia's response to the suffering she views is to show compassion, which is considered by Flesher and Torry to be a type of conversion motif.

> The film's converts—such as Claudia and Simon—function as models for what Gibson hopes will be the response of his audience [...] On and off screen the viewers are sharing the same experience [...] It is not *imitatio Christi* but *imitatio conversorum*.[58]

This analysis is best assessed in light of Flesher and Torry's stated methodology and purpose. It is no accident that Flesher and Torry choose to focus on Gibson's deviation from the gospel accounts. Their analytical method is derived not from film studies or theory but from targumic criticism, which is a technique used to uncover the purpose of new phrases and meanings inserted by scribes translating biblical texts from Hebrew to Aramaic in the early centuries of the Christian Era.[59]

In the case of *The Passion*, this approach enables Flesher and Torry to put forward one hypothesis as to why evangelical Christians were so positive about a graphically violent film structured around Roman Catholic ritual and mysticism. Their analysis of Gibson's use of Claudia highlights 'a "traditional," in essence anti-modernist, depiction of religious "truth" and an evangelistic intent, both of which are highly attractive to the evangelical constituency in early twenty-first century America'.[60]

Another scholar, Richard Walsh, considers *The Passion* in his book, *Finding St. Paul in Film*. In a chapter entitled 'Gospels of Death' he focuses on the unrelenting violence of the film, 'Everything is sweat and blood, flayed body, and grim anguish'.[61] He is particularly interested in how Gibson's Jesus chooses and intentionally increases his own suffering.

---

[57] Flesher and Torry, *Film*, p. 165.
[58] Ibid., p. 166.
[59] Flesher and Torry describe their method, giving ancient and modern examples, in the Introduction to *Film*, pp. 1–24.
[60] Ibid., p. 159.
[61] Walsh, *St. Paul*, p. 85.

After a whipping that would have killed a 'normal man,' Gibson's Christ catches Mary's eye and rises slowly from the ground to endure more suffering. This suffering is not the apocalyptic prelude to glory. This Christ is already triumphant in his suffering, in this slow rise [...] Gibson's Christ is 'a tough dude who can take a licking and keep on ticking.'[62]

Walsh is surely correct to assume that a particular theological position underpins this ultra-violent passion. But it is the way he *deploys* film against this theological position that makes his approach unusual.

Walsh writes about Pauline thought in the movies and acknowledges that something approximating Gibson's concept of the passion can be found in the Pauline corpus. However, Walsh argues that this is something that Paul struggles with and holds in tension with other viewpoints.

[Gibson] is far more certain about justice than Paul because he is the heir of a long-standing, legalistic reflection that begins with Tertullian and proceeds through the development of medieval penance and Anselm's feudalistic reflections on the atonement [...] With such at its imaginative centre, it is no wonder that Western Christianity has also sponsored Crusades, Inquisitions, Colonizing Missions, Empires, Hell, and, at the movies, religious horror like *The Passion of the Christ*.[63]

Walsh's dislike of this position is clear and coheres with the overall purpose of his book, for this is not primarily a work of religious film criticism but a work of theology. The filmic portrayals of Pauline thought are a means to the end, which is the uncovering and undermining of certain *theological* ideologies. In his introduction Walsh states:

By pursuing the issue of multiple Pauls in Christian discourse and at the movies, I wish to make it difficult to render Paul our ideological ally [...] If our construct is 'St. Paul' we arrogate divine authority to ourselves and to our plans. When I speak of watching Paul, then, I am really talking about watching those of us who construct Paul for our own agendas.[64]

Walsh is even more explicit in his conclusion, where he links *The Passion* to cruciform Western Christianity and evangelical and pre-Vatican II Christology. His ultimate goal is to move away from such 'Gospels of Death' towards a more liberal and healthy-minded way of believing.[65]

Before returning to Walsh it is worth briefly considering other engagements with *The Passion*. One of the most theologically dogmatic of the analyses of the violence in the film is offered by Robert Johnston. His essay *The Passion as Dynamic Icon* summarizes three major theological interpretations of the cross before concluding:

---

[62] Ibid., p. 85.　　[63] Ibid., p. 88.　　[64] Ibid., p. 10.　　[65] Ibid., pp. 180-1.

> The root of the controversy surrounding *The Passion of the Christ* is Gibson's desire to (re)turn the church's interpretation of the cross to more 'classical' and 'objective' viewpoints, in contradistinction to much of the overly 'subjective' emphasis typical of current scholarship in mainline and progressive Catholic and Protestant churches.[66]

In marked contrast to Walsh, Johnston makes no secret of either his approval of this move, nor of his affirmation of the artistic and religious merits of the film.[67]

Mark Goodacre also offers an *apologia* for the violence. However, in contrast to Johnston he does not focus on theology or the relation of the film text to the gospel text, but on the film-making apparatus and the visual effects produced:

> Those who talk about the relentless, gratuitous or pornographic nature of this section of the film [the flogging] tend to ignore several important elements. The extent of the violence depicted is mitigated by the fact that the camera itself cannot bear to look on and repeatedly draws away sometimes so far that you can only hear it in the distance [...] In short, the camera chooses not to gaze. The viewer is encouraged not to look and is often not allowed to look.[68]

This would appear to be precisely the kind of treatment of 'film *qua* film' that the critics considered above demand. Yet the question must be asked: which account, Johnston's or Goodacre's, actually tells us most about this film, its production values and its reception?

The value of Goodacre's move is undermined by the fact that the supposedly mitigating effect of Gibson's camerawork seems to pass unnoticed even by sophisticated film critics. For example, in a review in *Sight and Sound*, Mark Kermode uses pornographically-tinged terminology to describe Gibson's film as 'a fetishised adulation of supermasochistic screen violence'.[69] In spite of Goodacre's visually focused technique, I think Johnston adds more to our understanding of why so many devout viewers were prepared to overlook the extreme screen violence. Whatever we think of his theological or critical opinions, he is probably correct when he says, 'Evangelical viewers and millions of lay Catholics have responded to the movie

---

[66] Robert K. Johnston, '*The Passion* as Dynamic Icon: A Theological Reflection', in S. Brent Plate, ed., *Mel Gibson's Film and Its Critics: Re-Viewing the Passion* (New York: Palgrave Macmillan, 2004), pp. 55–70, especially 65.

[67] Johnston, 'Passion', pp. 66–8.

[68] Mark Goodacre, 'The Power of *The Passion*: Reacting and Over-reacting to Gibson's Artistic Vision', in Kathleen Corley and Robert Webb, eds, *Jesus and Mel Gibson's The Passion of the Christ: The Film, the Gospels and the Claims of History* (London: Continuum, 2004), pp. 28–44, especially 35.

[69] Mark Kermode, 'Review—*The Passion of the Christ*', pp. 62–3 in *Sight and Sound* (London: BFI, April 2004).

so powerfully because Gibson's emphases resonate with their churches' own understanding.'[70]

The Passion is unique; nonetheless I believe consideration of treatments of this film have further undermined the typical criticisms of the religion–film discourse. Flesher and Torry use a, supposedly discredited, literary-theory-based technique and in the process develop an interesting proposal about the mechanism by which the film works to draw its audience into a particular position of identification. Walsh and Johnston wrote from (very different) explicit theological positions, but the comparison of the work of Goodacre and Johnston suggests, against the critics, that there are times when a theological reading is entirely appropriate and can offer the best route to understanding a film and its impact upon its viewers.

Before turning to the next film, it is important to notice that, with the exception of Walsh, all of these writers have been concerned to move from merely intra- or inter-textual readings to consideration of extra-textual effects of the film upon the viewer or audience. In the case of Goodacre, I used Kermode's review to question the likelihood that the elements of the film he described would have the implied effect upon viewers. In the absence of empirical evidence, the proposals of the other writers must also be considered unproved theses.

An empirical investigation into viewer experience of *The Passion* has been published. Although the study was not designed to address the specific questions considered above, some of the results that emerged from the 5,000-person survey confirm the theoretically derived hypotheses. For example, 'the pattern was remarkably consistent; namely, religious conservatives were the most moved by the film'.[71] However, it is important to note that this kind of empirical investigation also generates results that could never have been predicted on the basis of theoretically driven interpretations of the film and its impact. For example, it was found that women were far less concerned by the violence than men, and that, in general, there was a complete inversion of the usual demographic patterns relating to viewer response to screen violence.[72] The reasons for this inversion are currently unknown and could only be uncovered through a second round of research using more focused questions and qualitative interviews with the relevant sample of respondents.

Having raised the potential importance of empirical research, I will continue to note ways in which other religion–film scholars considered in this survey are beginning to try to ground their assumptions about film's impact upon

---

[70] Johnston, '*Passion*', p. 65.
[71] Robert H. Woods, Michael C. Jindra, and Jason D. Barker, 'The Audience Responds to *The Passion of the Christ*', in Plate, *Re-viewing*, pp. 163–80, especially 174.
[72] Woods et al., 'Audience', pp. 175–6.

30 Part I Imagining a Research Project

audiences in theoretical accounts of the religion-like nature of film and in attention to the voice of actual viewers.

<u>Treatments of *La Passion de Jeanne d'Arc*</u> Censored on release, lost to fire, and then resurrected from the bowels of a Danish mental hospital, the history of *La Passion de Jeanne d'Arc* is almost as dramatic as the events it portrays. Carl Theodor Dreyer was a Danish film-maker whose work covered six decades (from *The President* (1918) to *Gertrud* (1964)). David Bordwell has written of Dreyer's 'holy seriousness'. 'Dreyer's seriousness was "holy" in a double sense: not only did he treat his work almost as a sacred calling, but his art itself sought the spiritual.'[73] I will focus on treatments of *Jeanne* by Melanie Wright and Paul Schrader but, again, I will draw some voices from outside the religion–film discourse into the conversation. The key question in this instance is what makes a religious film: subject matter, style, or context? For the purposes of the general evaluation of the discourse, this discussion relates to the issue of film selection.

Having briefly discussed Melanie Wright's critique of the current state of the religion and film discourse above, I now turn to her constructive project. She discusses Dreyer's film with reference to: narrative; style; cultural and religious context; and reception. Wright is attracted to this film because as a silent film, and a highly stylized and affectively powerful one, it confounds the over-emphasis on narrative that she believes is typical of religious engagement with film. For Wright, 'the challenge of working with *Jeanne* may serve as a test for methodologies in religion and film'.[74]

In her discussion of narrative, Wright identifies the sources which Dreyer drew upon but emphasizes that he was not aiming for historical accuracy: 'for Dreyer, an authentic narrative is not necessarily a factually reliable one'.[75] He incorporated and discarded tropes from the historical sources in order to fund his wider project, most notably his careful construction of the Christ-figure typology.[76] Wright locates Dreyer's decision for a claustrophobic setting and compressed time period in 'classical conceptions of drama, especially those originating with Aristotle's *poetics*'.[77]

As one of those critics who have demanded engagement with 'film *qua* film', Wright necessarily takes her time over discussion of the film's style. She contends that subject matter alone cannot make a film religious. It is necessary to 'probe more deeply' to the 'qualities' that make the film religious.[78] Wright negotiates 'a moderating path between the extremes of thematic and formalist criticism', attempting to avoid the tendency to solipsistic over-interpretation of the thematic critic, and the inability of the formalist to allow for the 'emotional and cognitive dimensions of the viewer experience'.[79]

---

[73] David Bordwell, *Filmguide to La Passion de Jeanne d'Arc* (London: Indiana University Press, 1973), p. 9.
[74] Wright, *Religion*, p. 35.   [75] Ibid., p. 37.   [76] Ibid., p. 40.
[77] Ibid., p. 47.   [78] Ibid., p. 40.   [79] Ibid., pp. 41–2.

The use of close-ups, the repeated and challenging cuts, the negation of depth and so on, may function partly to emphasise that meaning is enacted [a formalist reading]. But in combination they divert attention *away* from externals in a way that encourages viewers to experience the encounter between Jeanne and her judges as a timeless and present conflict, rather than a distant historical event. From a religion and film perspective, this emphasis on interiority is particularly interesting, since it resonates with the ideological subtext of the film, and suggests that religiosity, or spirituality, stands in opposition to institutions and outward forms.[80]

I believe that it is in the study of the context in which the film was made and into which it was released that Wright's wide-ranging method makes its greatest contribution. For Wright, the film's release in 1928 must be seen against the background of Jeanne's veneration in 1903, beatification in 1909, canonization in 1920, and the quincentenary of her victories in 1929. Any treatment of the reception of this film that fails to take this chronology into account must be considered defective; such a potent religious presence in the public imagination was bound to influence the way audiences experienced the film and the meanings they took from it.

Unfortunately, when Wright moves to consider this, she notes that evidence of non-professional, non-elite reception is hard to come by. This means that, having passed through the four stages of analysis, Wright's essay seems to fade gradually to grey; there is little meat to take off the bones of the analysis. It is hard to say much about the impact of the film in the absence of more 'empirical, evidence-based data', and the religious studies insight seems to be limited to Wright's contention that the film tells us something about a view of the religious or the spiritual as 'interiority'.[81]

In fact, Wright's treatment adds little to the interpretation of the film offered by the 'secular' theorist David Bordwell in his 1973 *Filmguide*. After an overview of the plot and creation of the film, he offers an extensive analysis of its visual style, to which I will return below, before concluding:

> The film is, in the first place, a great work of religious art—not in any narrowly doctrinal sense but in the sense that it depicts, as a vital possibility, man's transcendence of material limitations in search of spiritual order [...] the film's very style and form embody religious experience [...] transforming the diffuse, elusive shimmer of religious ecstasy into the purified intense luminescence of aesthetic experience.[82]

If Wright's analysis does not offer many fresh insights into the film, it is only fair to note that understanding *Jeanne* is secondary to understanding *how* to understand *Jeanne*; Wright's stated purpose is to model a new methodological

---

[80] Ibid., p. 46.   [81] Ibid., p. 51.   [82] Bordwell, *Filmguide*, p. 67.

approach.[83] Cultural studies methodology 'offers a discursive space in which the oft-touted dialogue between religious (or theological) studies and film studies is perhaps newly possible'.[84]

This cultural studies approach involves a 'widening' of interest, from film texts and authors to the complex interrelations that exist between texts, authors, institutions, audiences, and contexts or cultures. Moving away from the polarity that privileges either author (*auteur* theory) or reader (reader response theory), the 'multidimensional' cultural studies approach 'traces the ways in which films acquire meanings by triangulating between film "texts", contexts and audiences'.[85] This 'multidimensional' approach, which assumes that the religious content or value of a film cannot be reduced to a particular characteristic but is constructed in, always particular, interactions between film, viewer, and context, is important in the development of the shape of this monograph.

The second religion–film scholar to be considered in relation to *Jeanne* is Paul Schrader. At the time of writing his main theoretical work, *Transcendental Style in Film*, he was a young Californian academic with strong ideas about what makes a religious film; now he is known as a screenwriter and director with writing credits including *Taxi Driver* and *The Last Temptation of Christ*.[86] In his work Schrader draws on film theory and studies, backed up by extensive readings in philosophical and theological aesthetics, and it is impossible to understand his treatment of a particular film without some knowledge of his complex wider project.

Schrader believed that directors such as Yasujiro Ozu (1903–63), Robert Bresson (1901–99), and Carl Dreyer (1889–1968) were exemplars of a universal cinematic style that was uniquely capable of representing the holy, the invisible, the ineffable—the transcendent.

> This common form was not determined by the film-makers' personalities, culture, politics, economics, or morality. It is instead the result of two universal contingencies: the desire to express the Transcendent in art and the nature of the film medium. In the final result no other factors can give this style its universality.[87]

The role of the critic or theorist is to describe the material, immanent, and precise temporal means—*mise en scène*, camerawork, editing, dialogue, narrative—that the film-maker uses in order to express transcendence. Schrader's thesis is that the expression of transcendence is achieved through the gradual replacement of what he calls 'abundant' cinematic means, which maintain the

---

[83] Wright, *Religion*, pp. 5–6.   [84] Ibid., p. 27.   [85] Ibid., pp. 26 and 30.
[86] For an up-to-date filmography, see International Movie Database, 'Paul Schrader', <http://www.imdb.com/name/nm0001707/> (accessed 12 December 2008).
[87] Paul Schrader, *Transcendental Style in Film: Ozu, Bresson, Dreyer* (London: University of California Press, 1972), p. 3.

viewer's interest, with 'sparse' means, which elevate the viewer's soul. When all the abundant means have been stripped away, a moment of stasis is achieved and the transcendent may be encountered.

Schrader argues that Dreyer never achieved the pure transcendent moment and that his work is an amalgam of three different styles. *Kammerspiel*, which provides the raw material for Dreyer's work, is based upon Strindberg's 'Intimate Theatre' of small social groups, located in reduced spatial situations, with an emphasis on psychological drama. Schrader argues persuasively that in Dreyer's *oeuvre* this raw material is transformed by the action upon it of two other styles, the expressionist and the transcendental.[88]

Schrader identifies expressionistic tendencies in *Jeanne* in the camera angles, extreme close-ups, and settings (designed by Hermann Warm, who also performed this function in *The Cabinet of Dr Caligari* (1920), a celebrated expressionist film).

> The architecture of Joan's world literally conspires against her; like the faces of her inquisitors, the halls, doorways, furniture are on the offensive, striking, swooping at her with oblique angles, attacking her with hard-edged chunks of black and white [...] craggy ridges, puffy cheeks, bulbous eyebrows, sclerotic warts, globes of sweat [...] The faces of Joan's oppressors are genuinely oppressive. [This is typical of] the Expressionist tradition: an innocent female victim trapped and terrorized by ghastly demonic distorted faces.[89]

Kammerspiel and expressionism do not exhaust the stylistic elements: '*The Passion of Joan of Arc* is much more than a chamber-play with an overlay of expressionism [...] it also has that "other" quality [it] contains some of the elements of transcendental style.'[90]

But, for Schrader, Dreyer's failure can be seen if his *Jeanne* is compared with Robert Bresson's film on the same subject.[91] In particular, he contrasts the ends of the two works. In the final sequence of Dreyer's film the camera pulls away from *Jeanne*'s martyrdom at the stake to show rioting crowds being attacked by soldiers, before finally panning up towards heaven.

> Any attempts Dreyer may have made at stasis collapse in the final moments of *Passion*. Joan's martyrdom is thrown into a simmering social context [...] the last scene sequence takes the viewer off the transcendental hook. He may interpret Joan's death psychologically, sociologically or spiritually, and given such a choice the viewer's natural preference is for either of the first two.[92]

In contrast, Bresson's camera remains fixed upon the martyr at the stake.

---

[88] Ibid., pp. 114–16.   [89] Ibid., p. 122.   [90] Ibid., p. 124.
[91] Robert Bresson's *The Trial of Joan of Arc* was released in 1962.
[92] Schrader, *Transcendental*, pp. 122–6.

> When the image stops, the viewer keeps going, moving deeper and deeper, one might say *into* the image. This is the 'miracle' of sacred art. If it occurs, the viewer has moved past the point where any 'temporal means' (abundant or sparse) are of any avail. He has moved beyond the province of art.[93]

There are many points at which Schrader's thesis might be contested. His desire for a 'universal' style, untouched by ideological or cultural particularity, seems dated, as does a theology that places the transcendent in such complete opposition to the material and carnal. It is also possible that his thesis is less unique that it might seem; his discussion of sparse and abundant means is similar to Bordwell's use of the concrete and the abstract with regard to the style and spiritual power of *Jeanne*.[94] Later work, for example *Images of the Passion* by Peter Fraser, has married a similar focus on formal style with a more grounded theological discussion of the 'divine intrusion' into film.[95] However, no other work is as completely immersed in, or shows such complete mastery of, the history of the technical and theoretical development of the film medium as Schrader's.

Once again, it should be noted that Schrader is not content with textual analysis; he is another of those writers who believe that film is not merely a text to be interpreted, but a medium of religious experience:

> Transcendental style can take a viewer through the trials of experience to the expression of the Transcendent; it can return him to experience from a calm region untouched by the vagaries of emotion or personality. Transcendental style can bring us nearer to that silence, that invisible image, in which the parallel lines of religion and art meet and interpenetrate.[96]

This is a powerful statement (of faith?) but, as Wright has pointed out, developments in film studies and theory since the early 1970s problematize such statements. It can no longer be assumed that the spectator is 'sutured in' to the film-watching experience in such a way that an expert can extrapolate from the text to the viewer.

With regard to the question as to whether content, style, or context make a film religiously interesting, meaningful, or powerful, it seems certain that Schrader would point to the style; whereas, in this case at least, Wright might point to the context and the religious fervour surrounding the figure of *Jeanne* at the time of its first release. This discussion shows why film selection within the religion–film discourse can appear idiosyncratic. While it can be argued that this particular example is religiously relevant based on

---

[93] Ibid., p. 161.
[94] Bordwell, *Filmguide*, pp. 22–9.
[95] Peter Fraser, *Images of the Passion: The Sacramental Mode in Film* (London: Flicks Books, 1998), especially p. 3.
[96] Schrader, *Transcendental*, p. 169.

Religion and Film 35

content, style, *and* context, many films might legitimately be considered religiously relevant based on one of these characteristics: content, style, *or* context. I would suggest that it is not universal rules that are required, but rather the discipline of clearly and explicitly explaining on what basis a film is considered.

Treatments of the *Godfather* trilogy In this section I will look at two treatments of the *Godfather* trilogy of films. Roy Anker and John Lyden both consider the explicit violence of the *Godfather* films, but offer conflicting accounts of its effect upon the audience. With regard to the evaluation of the discourse as a whole, this discussion engenders questions which are related to the dangers of reading *onto* film texts and the need for a fully articulated account of film's religious impact upon audiences.

The overall 'architecture' of Roy Anker's book, *Catching Light: Looking for God in the Movies*, is that of a classic redemptive arc: from the discussion of the presence of 'divine Light' in film in the Introduction; to 'Darkness Visible'; then 'Light Shines in the Darkness'; and finishing with 'Fables of Light' and 'Found'.[97] Within the 'Darkness Visible' section is a chapter entitled 'Utterly Lost: Michael Corleone's Descent in *The Godfather* Saga'. It is an extended exegesis of the 'moral–spiritual fate', that is to say 'the fall' of Michael Corleone.[98]

Anker deals at length with the subject of violence. He claims that the director of the *Godfather* films, Francis Ford Coppola, neatly subverted the studio chiefs' desire for a violence of 'lurid titillation' by presenting them with violence that 'not only looks but feels horrific'. Remarkably, Anker can argue: 'Coppola's most effective assertion of the intrinsic goodness of life emerges most clearly and forcefully—and unexpectedly—in his treatment of the abundant and graphic violence in the films.'[99]

Specifically, Anker identifies a three-stage 'signature construction of violence', involving a set-up of 'tranquil moments of goodness and beauty', followed by 'vivid use of sudden and extreme violence', and concluding with 'a kind of parting meditation [. . .] that broods on the carnage to emphasise the real human toll of the violence'.[100] Anker moves swiftly to theological commentary:

> The tripartite structure of Coppola's stylization of violence makes clear that all violence invariably and essentially opposes the goodness of life. To make his point still more pointed and emphatic, he regularly situates that violence within the context of Christian imagery and ritual. Not only does the violence disrupt the

---

[97] Anker, *Light*, p. 18.
[98] Ibid., for example pp. 42 and 65.
[99] Ibid., p. 57.
[100] Ibid., pp. 59–60.

natural goodness of life, but it specifically transgresses the core theological and moral values of the Western world's major religious tradition.[101]

As I have made clear, my goal is to judge works of religion and film against their own purposes and methodological decisions. Therefore, it is necessary to move at this point to Anker's description of his *modus operandi*. In the Introduction, Anker is at pains to distinguish his own method from one which works by 'preemptively bringing to bear external categories with which to analyze the story, whether those categories be sociological, political, or religious'.[102] Instead, he wants 'to understand the "text" of the film experience itself as fully as possible, and then, after the fact, to discover with what religious categories that "lived experience" might fit'.[103]

In the particular case of the violence of the *Godfather* films, he appears, initially, to have followed his methodological process to the letter. His theological observation seems to be built upon careful consideration of the film text and to be legitimated by the fact that the director juxtaposes the violence with religious ritual (most notably the inter-cutting between baptismal sacrament and 'murderous evil' at the end of the first film). However, a brief consideration of other religion and film treatments of *The Godfather* calls Anker's reading into question.

John May has written about these films on a number of occasions, also drawing attention to the richness of contrast that Coppola achieves by juxtaposing violence and crime with family celebration and religious ritual, but scrutinizing far more closely than Anker the extent to which the films 'romanticize' organized crime and violence.[104] Another frequent contributor to the religion–film discourse, Eric Christianson, also interprets the violence very differently from Anker. In 'An Ethic You Can't Refuse? Assessing the Godfather Trilogy', Christianson studies the film against the background of the Hays Production Code that was 'put to rest' just four years before *The Godfather* began production.[105] He sees Coppola's signature 'cinematic rhetoric' of violence as meaning that 'we are not so much appalled as entertained, even amused'.[106] These conflicting interpretations raise the possibility that the position of the *Godfather* chapter within Anker's overall, theologically motivated, structure might be driving his reading at this point.

This by no means erases the merits of Anker's book. I have already noted Walsh's use of film to critique theology; there is no reason why film should not be used to illustrate theology. In fact it might be argued that this is precisely

---

[101] Ibid., p. 60.   [102] Ibid., p. 12.   [103] Ibid., p. 12.
[104] Ferlita and May, *Odyssey*, pp. 86–90, especially 88; and May and Bird, *Religion*, pp. 163–9.
[105] Eric S. Christianson, 'An Ethic You Can't Refuse? Assessing the Godfather Trilogy', in Eric S. Christianson, Peter Francis, and William R. Telford, eds, *Cinema Divinité: Religion, Theology and the Bible in Film* (London: SCM Press, 2005), pp. 110–23.
[106] Christianson, 'Ethic', p. 118.

what Gerard Loughlin does in his book, *Alien Sex: The Body and Desire in Cinema and Theology*.[107] Here Loughlin uses films like the *Alien* trilogy, Christopher Nolan's *Memento*, and Kubrick's *A Clockwork Orange* to explore the relationship between sexual desire for the other, even the *alien* other, and the stream of Christian theology that links sexual desire to the divine eros that draws us towards God. The difference between Anker and Loughlin is that the latter is open about the priority of his theological project and admits that his choice of film is unsystematic: 'They are films I have seen and enjoyed, and deemed appropriate for the ideas I wanted to explore but most are not overly "religious" or overly concerned with the body and desire.'[108]

It is also important to note that the critics of religion and film are wrong when they contend that theology and philosophy are unique in *using* film in this way. One of the most widely referenced books about the *Godfather* films is Chris Messenger's *The Godfather and American Culture*, which uses literary theory to interpret the way these stories have impacted on American culture.[109]

As with so many of the authors considered, Anker also writes about the affective power of films. Indeed, his book opens with an anecdote about the way a viewing of *Superman* completely changed the demeanour of a harassed single mother.[110] Anker relates this impact to the revelation of divine Light through film. However, there is little theology offered to underwrite this, nor is there consideration of the mechanism by which this might occur (beyond allusion to the possibility that audiences might catch the Light as characters come to see or sense this Light in their on-screen experiences).[111]

The second scholar whose interpretation of the *Godfather* films will be considered in detail is John Lyden. Lyden's book *Film as Religion: Myths, Morals and Rituals* is one of the most widely referenced recent works in religion–film. Its influence seems to lie in the fact that it offers a fresh theoretical account of the mechanism by which films create their religious impact upon audiences.[112]

Lyden's discussion of *The Godfather I* and *II* draws on film studies research in the gangster genre, noting that early moral concerns (that resulted in the

---

[107] Gerard Loughlin, *Alien Sex: The Body and Desire in Cinema and Theology* (Oxford: Blackwell, 2004).

[108] Loughlin, *Alien*, pp. ix–x. Indeed, my own use of films to introduce some of the themes of each part of this thesis is another example of using films illustratively and as aids to theological reflection. Stephen Mulhall argues for the appropriateness of this practice with respect to philosophy in his book *On Film* (London: Routledge, 2002).

[109] Chris Messenger, *The Godfather and American Culture: How the Corleones Became "Our Gang"* (New York: New York State University Publishing, 2002).

[110] Anker, *Light*, pp. ix and 1.

[111] Ibid., p. 13.

[112] John Lyden, *Film as Religion: Myths, Morals, and Rituals* (London: New York University Press, 2003).

Hays Code) have been replaced by ideological critiques that draw attention to the relation of these films to the aspirations of disenfranchised minorities.[113] However, Lyden questions the simplistic assumptions of both approaches: the conservative right who think such films are dangerously revolutionary; and the liberal left who believe that these liminal fantasies of revenge and escape are cathartic and dissipate any pressure for change. Lyden argues that the *Godfather* films are complex on both the moral and the ideological registers: inviting us to identify with criminal violence but also challenging us to condemn our own complicity; subverting the American Dream by featuring 'the gangster who gains wealth and American identity, but at the cost of his ethnic and family identity'.[114] Showing sensitivity to the role of the particular audience member, Lyden contends that the impact of such a film 'depends on what one brings to it'.[115] Unfortunately, he concludes with what sounds like little more than a commendation of film's ability to encourage us to think for ourselves:

> There is not an obvious 'moral' to the story, and to moralize its point is to simplify a complex text to which audiences will return precisely because it is both evocative and provocative of a range of values and concerns. This is the role of all great myths: to provide a resource for an ongoing wrestling with our own cultural questions.[116]

This recourse to the language of myth must be seen in light of Lyden's overall theory. He utilizes the anthropological and functional approach to religion of Mircea Eliade and, more immediately, Clifford Geertz in his essay 'Religion as a Cultural System' (1996).[117] On this account, religion is a human enterprise that creates 'models of' and 'models for' reality. Through telling and re-telling in myth, and repeated enactment in ritual, these models have a moral impact on society. Therefore, Lyden can argue that films function as religion because they are myths recounted within their own ritual space and generating an impact. He is particularly interested in the cathartic effect of cinematic sacrifice and violence: 'film offers a separation from the everyday as viewers temporarily accept it as an alternate reality'; this 'can affect one's behaviour in the postliminal reintegration into society'.[118]

Due to this emphasis on the religious function of film, Lyden argues not for an interdisciplinary dialogue between religion and film but an 'inter-religious' dialogue.[119] He also expresses preference for simple readings of films, 'what the average film goer might discover in a film', not the 'hidden meanings in the films that can be detected only by the scholar who is trained in abstruse methods of analysis'.[120] Lyden claims to use published audience studies as well as personal observation to ground his analysis, but, in the Conclusion, he

---

[113] Ibid., pp. 153–6. [114] Ibid., p. 162. [115] Ibid., p. 156.
[116] Ibid., p. 163. [117] As discussed by ibid., pp. 41–8.
[118] Ibid., p. 102. [119] Ibid., pp. 108–9. [120] Ibid., p. 108.

admits that the audience studies were not much use as the public tends not to be eloquent about the ways in which films have affected them.[121]

It seems clear that Lyden's theoretical work is attractive because it offers a new way of imagining the film–religion interaction and, in myth and ritual, suggests a mechanism for understanding the effects of films on audiences. However, focusing on treatments of particular films uncovers the limitations of Lyden's approach. While an emphasis on simple readings protects him from the charge of solipsism, it leads, as with the *Godfather* films, to rather banal and uninteresting film analysis. Similarly an overly generalized definition of religion can offer an account for the way the general category of film may be considered religion-like, but is silent with respect to the way *particular* films might have *particular* religious effects on *particular* viewers.

The potential weakness of the conceptual apparatus deployed by Lyden is highlighted by a debate carried out in the *Journal of Religion and Film* between Lyden and Clive Marsh. In an article in 1997, Lyden compared and contrasted two approaches to religion–film: the ideological approach, that tended to critique film too harshly; and the religious approach, that tended to commend film too naively. His desire was for a third way that held the two approaches together in an aporetic and non-rational fusion.[122] Writing in 1998, Marsh commends Lyden but argues that he fails to pay enough attention to the fact that there is no pristine, neutral position from which to conduct an engagement with film. It is Marsh's next move that is interesting. Rather than assuming that religious studies offer at least the nearest approximation to this objectivity, he argues that engagement should be more explicitly theological. 'Religious interpreters of film need to be more aware of, and consciously working from, the particular hermeneutical (including theological) traditions within which they stand.'[123] The final section of this survey will consider a project that in many ways resembles Marsh's proposal.

Christopher Deacy on *Mean Streets* Christopher Deacy discusses Martin Scorsese's *Mean Streets* in his book *Screen Christologies: Redemption and the Medium of Film*. I believe that Christopher Deacy's work, in this book and beyond, brings together many of the different strands of discussion that have been raised in this survey.

First, Deacy's is an explicitly theological project, and consideration of treatments of *The Passion* and the debate between Lyden and Marsh suggest that this can be a positive trait. Second, he is quite intentional and explicit

---

[121] Ibid., p. 246.
[122] See, John Lyden, 'To Commend or Critique? The Question of Religion and Film Studies', in *Journal of Religion and Film*, 1.2 (1997), <http://www.unomaha.edu/jrf/tocommend.htm> (accessed 28 August 2008).
[123] See, Clive Marsh, 'Religion, Theology and Film in a Postmodern Age: A Response to John Lyden', in *Journal of Religion and Film*, 2.1 (1998), <http://www.unomaha.edu/jrf/marshrel.htm> (accessed 28 August 2008).

about the criteria of his film selection. Third, he makes excellent use of film studies. Fourth, his tight focus, with regard to both theology and film, allows him to address a particular issue in detail; he avoids the bland readings offered by, for example, Wright and Lyden. Finally, Deacy does not simply assume an impact upon the audience but is concerned throughout to address the fundamental questions about how this might occur and how it might be shown to have occurred.

Mean Streets (1973) is another gangster film by another Italian–American director that was released right between *The Godfather* (1972) and *The Godfather Part II* (1974). However, as one of Martin Scorsese's earliest films, this is a low-budget production from a director who was just beginning to discover his trademark style.

Deacy's reading of *Mean Streets* is concentrated on the search for redemption of one of its central characters, Charlie, played by Harvey Keitel. Religious and guilt-ridden, Charlie feels that the penance required by the church is insufficient to redeem a sinner of his magnitude.[124] According to Deacy, Charlie takes on a penance of his own by attempting to save the life of his 'irresponsible, reckless, and untrustworthy cousin, Johnny Boy (Robert De-Niro)'.[125] 'Johnny Boy, in effect, is the cross that Charlie must bear.'[126] The sacrifice must be one of 'pain and blood', but Deacy believes there is a hint of redemptive hope in the way Scorsese presents the aftermath of the shooting and car wreck that represent this sacrifice.

> The theme of redemption through suffering is [...] symbolised in the fact that the car hits a fire hydrant which then erupts in a fountain of cleansing water, which could be said to *bathe* Charlie as he stands before the palpable carnage of what he has done, and for which he must take responsibility.[127]

Deacy's analysis of this gangster film is underwritten by extensive work in four separate fields: the wider *noir* genre; other films of Martin Scorsese; a theological account of redemption; and the complex interplay between film text and audience. On the basis of this work Deacy argues that:

> Scorsese's films may be seen to bear witness to the Christian model of redemption through protagonists who may be read as functional equivalents of Christ, in the respect that—in line with an Antiochene Christology—any redemption that is attained has an intrinsically human dimension, and is achieved at the cost of immense physical and psychological suffering.[128]

In the viewer, this can result in an 'introspective, wholly personal and, at times, painful and protracted experience [of redemption], facilitated by a complex

---

[124] Christopher Deacy, *Screen Christologies: Redemption and the Medium of Film* (Cardiff: University of Wales, 2001), p. 108.
[125] Ibid., p. 109. [126] Ibid., pp. 109–10.
[127] Ibid., p. 110. [128] Ibid., p. 104.

interaction and exchange between the film "text" and its audience'.[129] Deacy is making large claims here and it is not surprising that his thesis has been criticized, notably by Steve Nolan. In what follows I will consider Nolan's critique and give my opinion as to where it is justified and where Deacy has been misrepresented or misunderstood. At times this will involve looking outside the religion–film discourse to other writing about Scorsese.

Nolan is just as dogmatic here as in the more general critical essays that were considered above. His assessment of *Screen Christologies* is sometimes brutal: 'theologically and methodologically confused' and 'an example of what currently passes as religious film analysis'.[130] He does identify three important issues. First, Nolan believes that in order to see cinema as a site of religious activity Deacy resorts to an argument based on the concept of 'implicit religion'. Nolan rightly points out that this broad interpretation of religion is almost meaningless; if it can encompass cultural activities such as flag waving and communal singing it is unsurprising that Deacy is able to argue for film's inclusion. Second, Nolan accuses Deacy of hermeneutical dishonesty: viewing film through the spectacles of religion means that Deacy is 'sure to find what he is looking for'.[131] Third, Nolan believes that Deacy is unable to offer any convincing link between the cinematic text and its effect on audiences: 'he seems to confuse films whose diegesis is redemptive of characters with films as redemptive of their audience'.[132]

I think that Nolan's first criticism correctly identifies a weakness in the way that Deacy structures his book. Deacy mistakenly chooses to begin with a generalized description of religion as a universal human activity that, in our time, has moved outside the narrow institutional channels that were characteristic of its past. He certainly sounds vague when he states that 'it is at least apparent that there are certain underlying themes intrinsic to some pictures into which discordant and heterogeneous audiences can at least potentially tap, and which thereby open such films to a possible religious interpretation'.[133] Deacy's work would have been far more convincing if his project had resembled Marsh's proposal still more closely and had foregrounded the strong and particular account of Christian redemption that he deals with in detail in later chapters. He might then explicitly have based his overall approach to the religious and redemptive potential of film upon the universal dimension of Christian soteriology, avoiding the vagueness of the generalized religious approach.[134]

---

[129] Ibid., p. 92.
[130] Steve Nolan, 'Review: *Screen Christologies* by Christopher Deacy', in *Reviews in Religion and Theology*, 9.5 (2002), pp. 460–65, especially 460 and 464.
[131] Nolan, 'Review', p. 460.   [132] Ibid., p. 462.   [133] Deacy, *Screen*, p. 13.
[134] Mikkel Fugl Heskjaer has written a fascinating essay that touches upon the importance of how we understand religious content in 'Religion in New Danish Cinema', in Geert Hallback and Annika Hvithamar, eds, *Recent Releases: The Bible in Contemporary Cinema* (Sheffied: Sheffield

Nolan's second criticism implies that Deacy is guilty of projecting his theological reading onto the films—'he is sure to find what he is looking for'. However, this charge is unsubstantiated. In the first instance, Deacy has the advantage of being able to demonstrate the substantial similarity between his Antiochene Christology and Scorsese's portrayal of Jesus in *The Last Temptation of Christ* (1988).[135] Second, his readings of theological themes and redemptive significance in Scorsese's *noir* films are confirmed by similar readings in 'secular' film criticism and studies. For example, Casillo's book *Gangster Priest*, which is written with the intent of shedding light on Italian–American culture and therefore has no religious axe to grind, mirrors both Deacy's general understanding of Scorsese's work and his specific reading of *Mean Streets*.

> What Scorsese has attempted in these Italian American films, with the mob as his chief example, is a general statement on the psychology and sociology of violence, and specifically its relationship to the sacred. A non-practicing Catholic but a Catholic nonetheless, he has always been concerned with the central religious problem of violence, sometimes extolling bloody redemptive sacrifice and sometimes absolute religious pacifism.[136]

And with regard to the close of *Mean Streets*:

> Charlie extricates himself from the demolished car and falls to his knees with hands outstretched, as if in supplication. His hand wound recalls the stigmata of St Francis of Assisi, his model of the Christian life. The combination of water and shed blood evokes the Gospel passage in which blood and water flow from Christ's side as the sign of divine sacrifice, and with it the cleansing of sin through the release of the Spirit into the world.[137]

Deacy's reading of *Mean Streets* is also reinforced by Scorsese's own account of the making of the film. In fact, the relevant chapter in *Scorsese on Scorsese* opens with a header taken from the first lines of the film when Charlie observes: 'You don't make up for your sins in church—you do it in the

---

Phoenix Press, 2008), pp. 30–49, especially 31 and 33. He writes: 'One way of analyzing the variety of religious filmmaking is to differentiate religious films along an axis, or continuum, ranging from overtly explicit religious content, to implicit, sometimes even hardly discernible, religious elements. At one end of the continuum are films that deal with theological questions and issues, often associated with official religion [. . .] The other end of the continuum consists of films portraying religious matters that belong either to non-official religions or what have been termed 'banal' religions [e.g. some forms of nationalism].' From this he creates a figure upon which he plots a number of recent religious films.

[135] For Deacy's own commentary on this film, see *Screen*, pp. 85–9.
[136] Robert Casillo, *Gangster Priest: The Italian American Cinema of Martin Scorsese* (London: University of Toronto Press, 2006), p. xviii.
[137] Casillo, *Gangster*, p. 219.

streets.'[138] Deacy should be exonerated from the charge of reading his theology onto the film text.

Nolan's third criticism, that there is no convincing link between the film and its effect on the audience, echoes a concern that I have raised throughout this survey. Within *Screen Christologies* itself, Deacy concludes his analysis of each film with a section on 'The Role of the Audience'.[139] Here Deacy is dependent on published reviews and essays which can lead, as we have seen in the cases of both Wright and Lyden, to rather bland conclusions. It is only with regard to Scorsese's later and critically acclaimed film *Taxi Driver* (1976), which charts the inexorable journey of lonely Vietnam veteran and taxi driver Travis Bickle towards an explosion of vigilante violence, that Deacy finds accounts which go some way to substantiating his theory of the redemptive impact upon the audience. In his analysis of a review by Westerbeck, Deacy writes:

> Not only does he [Westerbeck] posit *Taxi Driver* as a site of potential religious experience, but he construes it as a religious experience of 'the most binding and fanatical kind', amounting indeed to 'a conversion'. Consequently, therefore, having gone to the cinema 'to see an expose of someone else's life, we come away having got something even better: an apology for our own lives'.[140]

In fact, Deacy fully recognizes the weight of Nolan's criticism at this point, and in his subsequent work in articles and books he has attempted to fill the vacuum of audience data by recourse to the chatrooms and messageboards of internet film sites. Nonetheless, to date Deacy has been able to do little more than prove the truth of Lyden's contention that much of what is written in these contexts by 'ordinary' audience members is remarkable only for its banality.[141]

Screen Christologies is by no means a perfect book but Deacy is working hard to address its chief failing, the absence of the audience member's voice, in his later works. Nolan's other criticism of the implicit approach to religion hits home, but the resources to respond are present within the book itself. In line with Marsh's proposal, it can be argued that earlier use of the particular theological account which is at the core of the book might have provided a firmer basis for Deacy's contention that film can be a site of redemptive activity.

---

[138] Ian Christie and David Thompson, eds, *Scorsese on Scorsese* (London: Faber & Faber, 1996), p. 38.
[139] Deacy, *Screen*, pp. 111–13, for *Mean Streets*.
[140] Ibid., p. 120.
[141] See Christopher Deacy, 'Paradise Lost or Paradise Learned? Sin and Salvation in *Pleasantville*', in Mitchell and Marriage, eds, *Mediating Religion*, pp. 201–10; and 'Redemption Revisited: Doing Theology at *Shawshank*', in *Journal of Contemporary Religion*, 21.2 (2006), pp. 149–62; and *Faith in Film* (Aldershot: Ashgate, 2005).

1.3 IMAGINATION: HOW TO RESEARCH THE POSSIBILITY OF REVELATION THROUGH FILM

The evaluation carried out in the previous section focused on the concrete and the particular, instead of trying to capture the religion–film discourse within one conceptual account. This allows for fresh reflection on the veracity of the four major criticisms usually levelled against writing about religion and film.

First, it was noted that the lack of consensus over what constituted a religiously interesting film adds weight to the original critics' contention that there is a lack of rigour in film selection. However, the process of evaluation has also shown that to some degree this is inevitable. There are multiple ways of understanding what makes a film 'religious' (for example, content, style, or context), but when films are selected wisely the interpretations of those writing within the religion–film discourse tend to be corroborated by 'secular' treatments.

Second, the evaluation suggests that it is wrong to accuse the religion–film discourse of a literary bias. It has been shown that there are many treatments that focus on the visual or stylistic aspects of film. In any case, it may be argued that 'film *qua* film' is an illusion. Film is an irreducibly complex amalgam, and 'literary style' criticism should take its place alongside other analytical tools to be taken up when it suits the purpose of the writer.

Third, it may be argued that what is sometimes pejoratively labelled 'theological baggage' may, in fact, be of great importance. There is some justification for arguing that engagement with a film on the basis of a strong and specific theological account is to be preferred over a generalized religious studies account, as it allows for greater specificity in the religion–film dialogue. However, all engagements should be open about their method and theoretical frameworks, and self-reflexive in regard to their readings, if they are to avoid being charged with simply projecting their viewpoints onto films.

Finally, the charge that dialogue and interdisciplinarity are absent from the discourse is frequently related to the critic's desire to justify one particular mode of engagement. It has been shown that religion–film writing is eclectic, but then so are film studies and film theory. It is increasingly acknowledged in this field that the best engagement with film, whether religious or secular, is multidimensional,[142] multi-perspectival,[143] and hybrid.[144]

In light of the descriptive and evaluative tasks undertaken in this chapter, it is possible to imagine the kind of project that might produce a good account of the possibility of revelation through film and contribute to the development of

---

[142] Wright, *Religion*, p. 26.
[143] Stam, *Theory*, p. 8.
[144] Brian Baker, 'Key Concepts in Film Studies', in Christianson et al., *Cinema Divinité*, pp. 44–60, especially 57.

the religion–film discourse. Drawing the voice of the actual viewer into the account is of first importance. The project should address the glaring lack of audience data that undermines the religion–film discourse's efforts to speak meaningfully of the potential religious impact of films upon their audiences.[145] Second, the project should not be restricted to one mode of engagement with film. Instead, it should draw upon a range of tools and methods in order to describe films and the film-viewing experience in as much detail, and from as many perspectives, as possible. Finally, the project should not shy away from serious theology or be content to proceed upon the basis of lowest-common-denominator definitions of religion and revelation.

Such a proposal generates many important questions. On what basis would the particular theological account of the possibility of revelation be chosen? What style of empirical research is best suited to provide the kind of audience data required? How will two bodies of research, theoretical and empirical, be related? These questions will be addressed as they arise in the development of this study and especially in the focal methodological discussion which takes place in Chapter 4.

---

[145] Even the most recent books on method considered above lack direct engagement with the audience (or even the theoretically constructed spectator), for example, Deacy and Ortiz, *Challenging*. Johnston, *Reframing* contains a group of essays entitled 'Engaging the Experience of the Viewer', but these draw upon theoretical accounts rather than empirical research, for example, Gordon Lynch, 'Film and the Subjective Turn: How the Sociology of Religion Can Contribute to Theological Readings of Film', pp. 109–25; and Rebecca Ver Straten-McSparran, 'Polanyi's Personal Knowledge and Watching Movies', pp. 162–78. (The exception is Catherine M. Barsotti, 'Películas: ¿A Gaze from Reel to Real?', pp. 179–201, but here the films are used as discussion starters rather than being considered in their own right.) The same is true of John Lyden's *Companion*, where Clive Marsh's chapter, 'Audience reception', pp. 255–74, despite being an excellent, mature essay by a scholar long active in the field, remains at the level of theory and theoreticians, and doesn't offer a single quote from an audience member even when it engages with reception studies of a particular film.

Part II

The Theology of Paul Tillich

WALK THE LINE, DIR. BY JAMES MANGOLD (2005)

In *Walk the Line* (2005), the Oscar-winning biopic of Johnny Cash, writer and director James Mangold creates a scene that illustrates two aspects of the relation between religion and culture.

Cash's self-taught musical trio contrive a career-making opportunity to play for the producer Sam Phillips at his Nashville studio. Nervous to the point of musical incapacity, they play safe and cover a well-known gospel song. But their lack of conviction bores the world-weary Phillips. He tells the band: 'I'm sorry. I can't market gospel no more [. . .] I don't record material that doesn't sell, Mr Cash. And gospel, like that, doesn't sell.'

The vacant grin of the gospel balladeer slides off Cash's face and we glimpse the passion beneath. This is a man who believes it is his destiny to sing. As the verbal interchanges between Phillips and Cash develop, the director ratchets up the tension with a series of reverse shots (back and forth between Cash and Phillips) that gradually close in until each face fills the screen. Finally Phillips cuts loose:

> If you was hit by a truck—and you was lying out in that gutter dying—and you had time to sing *one* song. Huh? One song, people would remember before you're dirt. One song that would let God know what you felt about your time here on earth [. . .] You're telling me that's the song that you'd sing [. . .] Or would you sing something different, something real, something you felt, because I'm telling you right now that's the kind of song that people really want to hear. That's the kind of song that truly saves people.

Cash is stung. Over the objections of his band he launches into a song of his own making, and immediately there's a harsh, raw authenticity. The camera is still in tight. But while Phillips looks straight into the lens, giving the impression his eyes are riveted on Cash, Cash is shown with face contorted, eyes unsettlingly skewed away from the camera. The viewer is confronted with the dislocated stare of the sightless, the *petit mal* of the epileptic, or, perhaps, the ecstasy of the saint.

The scene illustrates two important aspects of the interplay between religion and culture. First, there is Phillips' professed reason for rejecting the gospel cover. He can't sell it. Economics rather than theology, or even taste, is seen to determine which religious products prosper. Neither theology nor culture is purely about texts and their interpretation; they are also about the conditions of the production of those texts, the networks of distribution that make them available (or not), and the complex ways in which they are received and interpreted.[1]

The second aspect of the interplay is seen in the interchange between Phillips and Cash. As passions rose Phillips taunted Cash, challenging him to produce something with real relevance, with real bite. Phillips wanted existential, human truth. He was not interested in religious dogma domesticated by the church and rendered toothless by a thousand 'plays' on commercial radio stations. But are these two 'truths' parallel lines or might they intersect? Can the finite break through to the infinite? Can human cultural creation be revelatory, not just because it incidentally mirrors narratives or 'truth' already given in Scripture and tradition, but because its very human authenticity, coupled with its aesthetic power, enable the hearer or the viewer to encounter something of the Truth of the divine? Phillips seemed to think so. 'That's the kind of song that truly saves people.'

A German immigrant, a philosopher–theologian, who was perhaps sitting at his desk at Union Theological Seminary in New York when Johnny Cash first sang for Sam Phillips in Nashville in 1953, thought so too. Paul Tillich took the revelatory potential of human artistic creation most seriously. Although an immensely complex thinker, sometimes referred to as 'the theologian's theologian', the huge volume of sales of collections of his sermons and philosophical works, such as *The Courage to Be*, and his popularity on college campuses and with other young people, show that concealed within his complex theorizing was a message that spoke powerfully to his time and society.[2] This part of the monograph explores Paul Tillich's theory of the possibility of revelation through culture in sufficient depth and detail to delve beneath the often repeated (and occasionally inaccurate) popular accounts of his theology of culture. A second task undertaken is that of considering the appropriateness of applying Tillich's theory to the contemporary popular culture medium of film.

---

[1] With respect to religious music, see, for example, Peter Ward, *Selling Worship: How What We Sing Has Changed the Church* (Bletchley, UK: Paternoster, 2005).

[2] 'A theologian's theologian' is applied to Tillich by Gustave A. Weigel, SJ, 'Contemporaneous Protestantism and Paul Tillich, in *Theological Studies*, 11.2 (1950), pp. 177–202, especially 177.

2

A Theology of Revelation through Culture

At the close of the last chapter I declared my intention, which developed out of description and evaluation of the strengths and weaknesses of the religion–film discourse, to base this account of the possibility of revelation through film upon a particular Christian theology of revelation, rather than on a broad definition of religion and a generalized notion of revelation. For this particular theological account I now turn to Paul Tillich, and whilst it is only in extended engagement with his thought that the true grounds for this decision may be seen, it will be appropriate to offer some initial justification for this choice.

2.1 REASONS FOR THE TURN TO PAUL TILLICH

Tillich may be considered the twentieth century's foremost Protestant theologian of culture.[1] Moreover, he was very interested in the visual arts and acknowledged a close connection between this interest and his theology of revelation.[2] In the Foreword to a book of essays and lectures published towards the close of his life in 1959, Tillich wrote: 'The purpose of this book is indicated in its title: *Theology of Culture*. The title is an abbreviation of the title of my first published speech ["On the Idea of a Theology of Culture"]. It is a source of great satisfaction to me that after the passing of forty years I can take the title for this volume from my first important public speech' (*TC*, v–vi).

Second, he was an important influence on the most attractive of the works of popular theology in which I first encountered the possibility of revelation through film. Of particular importance was Robert Johnston's *Reel Spirituality*, which seemed to move towards the kind of theory of revelation I was interested in (i.e. one that did not depend upon prior theological and religious knowledge in the

---

[1] Various understandings of 'culture' and, in particular, the appropriateness of applying Tillich's high culture-focused thought to a medium like film will be discussed below.
[2] See, for example, Paul Tillich, 'On the Boundary', in id., *The Boundaries of Our Being*, pp. 297–352, especially 306–7, and discussed later in this chapter.

recipients). In order to underwrite his understanding of the possibility of 'divine encounter' in the film-watching experience, Johnston uses Tillich's autobiographical experience of 'revelation' in the contemplation of a painting by Alessandro Botticelli as illustrative of the way in which God can speak through human cultural creations.[3] He also draws upon Tillich's theoretical analysis of the power of various styles of modern art to explain how images can 'become mediators of ultimate reality [...] to transport the viewer to some more central place'.[4]

Third, Tillich is the most frequently referenced theologian in the wider religion–film discourse. Specifically, he is the theologian to whom many religion–film writers turn when they wish to develop a theological account to fund their engagement.[5] His theology has been central to programmatic essays in the most important volumes of the last forty years. Essays such as Carl Skrade's 'Theology and Film' in *Celluloid and Symbols* (1970), Michael Bird's 'Film as Hierophany' in *Religion in Film* (1982), and Clive Marsh's 'Film and Theologies of Culture' in *Explorations in Theology and Film* (1997) are all heavily reliant on Tillich and will be considered in Chapter 3. Some of these appropriations of Tillich's theology use his theory to describe something analogous to revelation through film.

2.2 A THEORETICAL ACCOUNT OF THE POSSIBILITY OF REVELATION THROUGH CULTURE

Understanding what Tillich means by revelation demands a plan of engagement.[6] In an effort to do justice to Tillich's thought, this reading of his theology of revelation will proceed through four stages, generally moving from broad overview to close analysis. The goal is an account that highlights continuity without either homogenizing a body of work that developed over many decades, or succumbing to the risk of eisegesis, reading later developments back into earlier work.[7]

---

[3] Johnston, *Spirituality*, p. 68.
[4] Ibid., pp. 77–8.
[5] Marsh, 'Film', p. 30.
[6] Tillich drew upon a remarkable breadth of influences, and this is reflected in the complexity of his thought (Avery Dulles, *Revelation Theology: A History* (New York: Herder and Herder, 1969), pp. 104–8) and, sometimes, the opacity of his language. (There is a helpful discussion of this problem, complete with Tillich's brief response to the criticisms, in Charles W. Kegley and Robert W. Bretall, eds, *The Theology of Paul Tillich* (New York: Macmillan, 1961), pp. 132–6 and 329–31; also Heinz Ratschow, 'Preface', in Michael Palmer, ed., *Paul Tillich: Writings in the Philosophy of Culture: Main Works II* (New York: De Gruyter—Evangelisches Verlagswerk GmbH, 1990), p. x.).
[7] Tillich himself used a similar method in his analysis of Karl Marx's thought; see *The Socialist Decision*, p. 163, n4.

Initially, two autobiographical statements will be considered and two key dispositions that infuse Tillich's life and thought will be noted. Second, his early, German writings will be addressed: in particular, the lecture *On the Idea of a Theology of Culture* (1919), the books *The Religious Situation* (1926) and *The Socialist Decision* (1933), and the essays that were collected in the volume *The Protestant Era* (the original essays date from 1922 to 1946). These writings will be used to provide a first general exposition of the relation between culture and revelation. The third stage will focus on the most complete statement of Tillich's theory which is found in *Systematic Theology* (*ST*, 1-3) but will be supplemented by reference to other writings of the later, American period, including *The Courage to Be* (1952) and *Theology of Culture* (1959).

At this point my reading of Tillich will be organized by focusing on a particular experience in Tillich's life: his encounter with Botticelli's painting *Madonna and Singing Angels* in the Kaiser Friedrich Museum at the end of World War I. The appropriateness of this methodological move and its theoretical implications will be discussed with particular reference to the way it emphasizes the mystic and individualistic aspects of the revelatory encounter.

Finally, the debate engendered by Tillich's work will be briefly surveyed. As the primary intent of this project is to ground Tillich's account by correlation with an empirically generated body of data (rather than through engagement with other textual sources), the issues that arise from this discussion will be held in parentheses while the empirical research project is constructed and enacted, but will be revisited in the concluding chapter.

2.2.1 The autobiographical sources

Two autobiographical essays, 'Autobiographical Reflections'[8] and 'On the Boundary',[9] provide an insight into the genesis of two trends in Tillich's thought which have direct consequences for the relation between culture and revelation: first, a romanticism that assumes the infinite can be accessed through the finite; and, second, the impact of these experiences upon his doctrine of revelation.[10]

---

[8] Paul Tillich, 'Autobiographical Reflections', in C. W. Kegley and R. W. Bretall, eds, *The Theology of Paul Tillich* (New York: Macmillan, 1961), pp. 3-21, especially 3 for inferred time of writing.

[9] Paul Tillich, 'On the Boundary', in id., *The Boundaries of Our Being* (London: Collins, 1973), pp. 297-352.

[10] For a brief biography, see David H. Kelsey, 'Paul Tillich', in David Ford, *The Modern Theologians: An Introduction to Christian Theology Since 1918*, 3rd edn (Oxford: Blackwell, 2005), pp. 62-75, especially 62-3.

Tillich identifies a romantic disposition in his feeling and thinking from his earliest years.[11] He recognizes three contributing factors: mystical experiences of nature; German romantic literature; and finally, his lifelong Lutheranism.[12] Tillich rejected Calvin's insistence that the finite is not capable of the infinite—'*non capax infiniti*'.

> This difference means that on the Lutheran ground the vision of the presence of the infinite in everything finite was theologically affirmed, whereas on Calvinistic ground such an attitude is suspect of pantheism and the divine transcendence is understood in a way which for a Lutheran is suspect of deism.[13]

Tillich links this romantic imagination to the creative endeavours of culture and then to the development of his theory.[14] He cites a wartime experience of the Botticelli painting, *Madonna with Singing Angels*, as particularly profound and revelatory. As this experience is used to structure the engagement with Tillich's thought later in this chapter, and is also an important part of the interviews that provide the data within the empirical section of this project, I will present here the full text of Tillich's own description of the experience, as written for a popular magazine:

> Strangely, I first found the existence of beauty in the trenches of World War I. To take my mind off the mud, blood and death of the Western front, I thumbed through the picture magazines at the field bookstores. In some of them I found reproductions of the great and moving paintings of the ages. At rest camps and in the lulls in the bitter battles, I huddled in dugouts studying this "new world" by candle and lantern light. But at the end of the war I still had never seen the original paintings in all their glory.
>
> Going to Berlin, I hurried to the Kaiser Friederich Museum. There on the wall was a picture that had comforted me in battle: *Madonna with Singing Angels*, painted by Sandro Botticelli in the fifteenth century. Gazing up at it, I felt a state approaching ecstasy. In the beauty of the painting there was Beauty itself. It shone through the colours of the paint as the light of day shines through the stained-glass windows of a medieval church. As I stood there, bathed in the beauty its painter had envisioned so long ago, something of the divine source of all things came through to me. I turned away shaken.
>
> That moment has affected my whole life, given me the keys for the interpretation of human existence, brought vital joy and spiritual truth. I compare it with what is usually called revelation in the language of religion.[15]

---

[11] Tillich, 'Reflections', pp. 3-5, and 'Boundary', pp. 304-5.
[12] Tillich, 'Boundary', p. 335.
[13] Tillich, 'Reflections', p. 5.
[14] Tillich, 'Boundary', p. 305.
[15] Paul Tillich, 'One Moment of Beauty' in *AA*, 234-5. Further accounts of this experience can be found in Tillich's own words in 'Boundary', pp. 306-7; 'Art and Society', p. 12; and as described by his biographers, Wilhelm and Marion Pauck, *Life*, p. 76.

A Theology of Revelation through Culture 53

With respect to the importance of this and other experiences, Tillich stated, 'Out of the philosophical and theological reflection that followed these experiences, I developed some fundamental categories of philosophy of religion and culture, viz., form and substance.'[16]

> If a person who had been deeply moved by the mosaics of Ravenna, the ceiling paintings of the Sistine Chapel, or the portraits of the older Rembrandt, were asked whether his experience had been religious or cultural, he would find the question difficult to answer. It might be correct to say that the experience is cultural in form and religious in substance. It is cultural because it is not attached to a specific ritual act; but it is religious because it touches on the question of the Absolute and the limits of human existence.[17]

This leads Tillich to pronounce that, 'As religion is the substance of culture, so culture is the form of religion.'[18] Most importantly for this monograph, Tillich links such experiences and his reflection upon them with his theory of revelation. 'The concept of the "breakthrough", which dominates my theory of revelation, is an example of the use of this insight.'[19]

2.2.2 The early works pre-exile

Consideration of Tillich's lecture, 'On the Idea of a Theology of Culture', will highlight the radical character of Tillich's understanding of revelation; proceed to a first discussion of the underlying dynamics of cultural creation; and finish with a fuller exposition of the double relation of religion to culture in form and substance.[20]

In the first section of his essay, Tillich aims to differentiate between theology and religious philosophy (or the science of religion). He argues that 'religion' is basic while theology is a secondary discourse, located within a particular confessional tradition—in this case the Christian tradition. This entails a complete negation of conservative models of theology. First, Tillich rejects the inductive method: 'theology is not a scientific presentation of a special complex of revelation'.[21] Second, he discounts and discards the conservative view of Scripture because it 'presupposes a concept of supernaturally authoritative revelation; but this concept has been overcome by the wave of religious–historical insights'.[22]

From his discussion of the philosophy of religion and theology, Tillich moves to the relationship between culture and religion. In discussing the nature of religion, he summarizes the theories of three great thinkers. Hegel

---

[16] Tillich, 'Boundary', p. 306. [17] Ibid., p. 331. [18] Ibid., p. 332.
[19] Ibid., pp. 306-7. [20] Tillich, 'Idea', p. 35-54.
[21] Ibid., p. 37. [22] Ibid., p. 37.

assigned religion to 'the theoretical sphere of the mind'; Kant to 'the practical sphere'; and Schleiermacher to 'the realm of feeling'; Tillich says that religion 'is an attitude of the spirit in which practical, theoretical and emotional elements are united to form a complex whole'.[23] This 'attitude of the spirit' constitutes a 'religious consciousness' or 'religious potency' but, importantly, it can only be actualized through cultural functions.

> In forms like these, religion is actualized; the religious principle only exists in connection with cultural functions outside the sphere of religion. The religious function does not form a principle in the life of the spirit beside others; the absolute value of the religious consciousness would break down barriers of that kind. But the religious principle is actualized in all spheres of spiritual and cultural life.[24]

This is the first moment in the relationship between culture and religion; the substance of religion, its potency, is actualized in the forms of culture.

Tillich then goes further. It is not only the case that all religious actualization must be through culture; it is also true that all cultural creation is inherently religious. In other words, returning to Tillich's own formulation, not only is culture the form of religion but religion is the substance of culture. Such a statement demands a particular conceptualization of religion, and Tillich offers 'directedness towards the Unconditional' (Niebuhr's translation) or 'the experience of the unconditioned' (Nuovo's translation).[25] Religion is clearly not 'a new reality, alongside or above other things'.[26] It is possible, therefore, for a theology of culture to produce:

> A general religious analysis of all cultural creations; it provides a historical-philosophical and typological classification of the great cultural creations according to the religious substance realized in them; and it produces from its own concrete religious standpoint the ideal outline of a culture penetrated by religion.[27]

The Religious Situation might be construed as Tillich undertaking just such a task. It provides an extensive worked example of the theoretical concepts already outlined, addressed, by Tillich himself, to a concrete historical situation. From the author's preface through to the final page, Tillich emphasizes the importance of the readers' participation. The book was not an exercise in academic scholarship but an attempt to foment change in the volatile German situation.[28]

---

[23] Ibid., p. 39.   [24] Ibid., p. 40.
[25] Ibid., pp. 40–41.   [26] Ibid., p. 41.
[27] Ibid., p. 43. Note: for Tillich the term 'ideal' is always ambiguous and intrinsically tensioned; the role of the theologian of culture is never as 'a religious cultural system-builder'.
[28] Tillich, *Situation*, pp. 27 and 219.

A Theology of Revelation through Culture

In this book the figures of temporality and eternity are central, they are the principal metaphors that represent the relation between cultural form (temporality) and religious substance (eternity).[29] Tillich believes that Germany stands at a key (*kairos*) moment in its history where the temporal may be invaded by the eternal. Tillich's argument is that to understand, and therefore be in a position to seize, the present moment, attention must be paid to the 'whole contemporary world'.[30]

> [Human religion] is not the only phenomenon which bears witness to the ultimate and in some periods it is not even the most important [...] one of the most important characteristics of a time has been defined when we have discovered which of the various aspects of culture is the most expressive of its real meaning.[31]

The third decade of the twentieth century, he suggests, may only be understood when seen against the background of 'the capitalist society in the nineteenth century'. He characterized this society as 'an extreme example of a self-assertive, self-sufficient type of existence'[32] but believed that certain cultural movements had begun to shake this self-sufficient status quo. Witness to the ultimate could be perceived in each of the spheres of human life that Tillich analyzed in the three major sections of the book: 'the spheres of science and art',[33] 'politics and ethics',[34] and finally 'religion'.[35] Tillich ascribed exceptional powers of expression, apprehension, meaning, and revelation to art.[36] For Tillich, 'The revolt against the spirit of capitalist society has been least ambiguously expressed in painting since the beginning of the century.'[37]

The typical painting of the nineteenth century was 'bourgeois'. The forms of impressionism and naturalism are 'the perfect forms of self-sufficient finitude'.[38] There is creative genius, 'But nowhere does one break through to the eternal, to the unconditioned content of reality which lies beyond the antithesis of subject and object.'[39] Nonetheless, great figures like Paul Cézanne, Vincent van Gogh, and Edvard Munch provided the basis for 'new forces' to develop and 'restored things to their real metaphysical meaning [...] the abyss of Being was evoked in lines, colours and plastic forms'.[40] However, in the contemporary Expressionist painters, 'the transcendental reference in things to that which lies beyond them' was most perfectly expressed.[41]

As expressionism is very important to Tillich's theory, not least to his Christology and to the central interests of this monograph, it will be considered in greater detail in the next chapter. At this point, it is only necessary to note that for Tillich the term 'expressionism' transcended the particular

---

[29] Ibid., pp. 36–7. [30] Ibid., p. 25. [31] Ibid., pp. 36–7.
[32] Ibid., pp. 42–7. [33] Ibid., p. 55. [34] Ibid., p. 103.
[35] Ibid., p. 155. [36] Ibid., pp. 85–6 and 91. [37] Ibid., p. 86.
[38] Ibid., p. 86. [39] Ibid., pp. 86–7. [40] Ibid., p. 88. [41] Ibid., p. 88.

movements so named by art historians, and incorporated any artistic style that was particularly well-suited to facilitating the breakthrough from surface form to substantial depth. In *The Religious Situation*, this close association of revelation with the breakthrough means that the ostensible subject matter of the artwork, its content, is relatively unimportant, and that therefore there is nothing particularly revelatory about overtly religious subject matter.

> The religious art of capitalist society reduces the traditional religious symbols to the level of middle-class morality and robs them of their transcendence and their sacramental character [...] It is not an exaggeration to ascribe more of the quality of sacredness to a still-life by Cezanne or a tree by van Gogh than to a picture of Jesus by Uhde.[42]

Tillich concluded the book by suggesting a possible route towards a culture more appropriately infused by the eternal. Again, a development in the visual arts was influential: Tillich's turn to 'belief-ful realism' was inspired by the 'New Realism' paintings of George Grosz and Otto Dix.[43] Belief-ful realism united a reference to the transcendent eternal source of meaning and being with the sober-eyed depiction of the scientist or realist artist of things as they are.[44] Practically and politically, Tillich saw 'religious socialism' as the best exemplar of this attitude and the most likely route beyond the self-sufficient 'autonomy' of capitalist culture, not to a new 'heteronomy' where the religious institutions dictate the forms of culture, but to a 'theonomy' where all cultural creation is infused with the eternal.[45] This development will be considered more carefully in relation to Tillich's work *The Socialist Decision*.

The Socialist Decision, as its title implies, is a yet more practical book, 'a summons' to a decision for socialism on the part of the German people.[46] Tillich believed that there were only two possible alternatives to socialism. The conservative romantic approach preferred a nation led by a monarch, but such a 'movement that no longer questions the rightness of its own assumptions has become ossified'.[47] The more radical revolutionary romantic approach demanded a charismatic leader (*Führer*), but here the danger was even greater: 'The hegemony of the myth of origin means the domination of violence and

---

[42] Ibid., pp. 88–9.

[43] Ibid., pp. 90 and 218–19. Note: the coherency and accuracy of Tillich's interpretation of the history of art in general and various movements in modern art in particular are contested. (See, for example, John Dillenberger, 'Introduction', in *AA*, pp. ix–xxviii, especially xiv and xviii–xxii; and Wilhelm and Marion Pauck, *Paul Tillich: His Life and Thought, Volume I: Life* (London: Collins, 1977), pp. 75–9.) It should at least be noted that he often used artistic terms with both a narrower (art historical) sense and a broader sense in his theorizing.

[44] H. Richard Niebuhr, 'Translator's Preface', in Paul Tillich, *The Religious Situation*, tr. H. Richard Niebuhr (London: Thames and Hudson, 1956), pp. 9–24.

[45] Tillich, *Situation*, pp. 116 and 176–7. Again, such a goal must be read with due regard to Tillich's sensitivity to the impossibility of actually creating such an ideal culture.

[46] Tillich, *Decision*, pp. xxxi–xxxiii.

[47] Ibid., p. xxxiii.

death.'[48] Tillich believed that religious socialism offered a way forward because it was, in essence, a prophetic movement capable of puncturing the hegemony of assumptions and myths that characterized the other social movements.[49]

In the theoretical and theological writings collected in *The Protestant Era*, Tillich suggests that such prophetic criticism is most clearly instantiated in the history of Protestantism. Tillich defines the Protestant Principle as 'the power of criticising and transforming each of its historical manifestations'.[50] Once again, he connects this to the interrelation between time and eternity, form and substance. A cluster of essays address this theme and make it possible to tease out the way in which the critical principle challenges the hegemony of one particular myth of origin and, at the right *kairos* instant, allows for the inbreaking of the eternal and the revelation of a more authentically theonomous culture.

For Tillich, this critical principle is connected with the historical character of Christianity in contrast to, for example, the cyclical view of time which reached its zenith in Greek culture. He writes:

> In Christianity time triumphs over space. The irreversible, unrepeatable character of time, its meaningful directedness, replaces the cyclic, ever recurrent becoming and passing away. A 'gracious' destiny that brings salvation in time and history subdues a demonic fate which denies the new in history.[51]

Grace and salvation enter into history in the *kairos* moment. 'Kairos in its *unique* and universal sense is, for Christian faith, the appearing of Jesus as the Christ.'[52] The 'God of time is the God of history': 'Tragedy and injustice belong to the gods of space; historical fulfilment and justice belong to the God who acts in time and through time, uniting the separated space of his universe in love' (*TC*, 38).

> History comes from and moves toward periods of theonomy, i.e., periods in which the conditioned is opened to the unconditional without claiming to be unconditioned itself. Theonomy unites the absolute and the relative element in the interpretation of history, the demand that everything relative become the vehicle of the absolute and the insight that nothing relative can ever be absolute itself.[53]

What has been learned through consideration of the writings of Tillich's early German period? First, the foundation of all of Tillich's thought is the complete interpenetration of culture and religion. 'Religion is the life-blood, the inner power, the ultimate meaning of all life. The "sacred" or the "holy" inflames, imbues, inspires, all reality and all aspects of existence. There is no profane nature or history, no profane ego, and no profane world.'[54] Religious depth is,

---

[48] Ibid., p. 162. [49] Ibid., p. 160. [50] Tillich, *Protestant*, p. xxxvii.
[51] Ibid., p. 8. [52] Ibid., p. 53. [53] Ibid., p. 53. [54] Ibid., p. 49.

therefore, the substance which inheres in all cultural forms, from the particular painting or poem to the general style or orientation of a national culture. At certain times, the cultural form becomes transparent to its religious substance; the surface is broken and the depth encountered; the conditioned is opened up to the unconditional; and the temporal is infused by the eternal. Such periods may be considered as events of revelation. However, they are not revelatory of information or knowledge. Instead, Tillich states that what is revealed is grace and salvation.

Three further points may be noted. First, in these early writings the focus is rarely on the individual and almost always on society. Second, the *kairos* time of breakthrough from surface to depth, form to substance, culture to religion, is frequently related to a span measured in years not seconds. Third, the analysis that is developed is not primarily concerned with individual artworks but with the whole *style* of art of a society. The emphasis of these writings on the communal, on extended periods of time, and on culture as a whole provides a counterbalance to the focus on the individual, the momentary, and the particular artwork in the reading of *Systematic Theology* that follows.

2.2.3 *Systematic Theology*

Commentators note two changes in Tillich's American-period approach, particularly after World War II. First, a change from concrete political involvement to existentialism—from 'the political expectation that infused his earlier Religious Socialism [...] to humankind suspended in an inner void, a vacuum, laden with angst that theologians of culture must address'.[55] Tillich himself writes in the Preface to *The Protestant Era*:

> It was the 'ecstatic' experience of the belief in a kairos which, after the first World War, created or at least initiated, most of the ideas presented in this book. There is no such ecstatic experience after the second World War, but a general feeling that more darkness than light is lying ahead of us. An element of cynical realism is prevailing today, as an element of utopian hope was prevailing at that earlier time.[56]

Second, a change from the priority of 'meaning' to the category of 'being'. This can be seen, for example, in his conceptualization of God as 'basis of meaning and abyss of meaning' in 1924, but 'being-itself' and 'ground and abyss of being' in 1951.[57] Taken together, these two changes can be seen as a move to 'ontological existentialism'.

---

[55] Taylor, *Boundaries*, pp. 119 and also 21–2.
[56] Tillich, *Protestant*, p. xlv.
[57] Palmer, *Writings*, p. 2.

> [Ontological existentialism] tries to identify and describe existential states which, although described in personal, even autobiographical concreteness, in virtue of their ontological character point to a common dimension of depth underlying different cultural–linguistic frameworks of interpretation.[58]

Tillich developed a unique method in the three volumes of his *Systematic Theology*, in the Preface of which he defines his aim as 'a theological system written from an apologetic point of view and carried through in a continuous correlation with philosophy' (*ST1*, x).

Correlation is important enough to be considered the 'subject' of the entire project, while the discussion of the traditional theological problems acts as an 'illustration' of correlation in action (*ST1*, x). Correlation replaces three inadequate methodologies: first, the 'supranaturalistic' that assumes 'revealed truths which have fallen into the human situation like strange bodies from a strange world'; second, the 'naturalistic' or 'humanistic' that assumes all truth is the creation of humanity; and finally the 'dualistic', or Thomist, where a supernatural edifice is built upon natural foundations.

> The method of correlation solves this historical and systematic riddle by resolving natural theology into the analysis of existence and by resolving supranatural theology into the answers given to the questions implied in existence. (*ST1*, 73)

The method of correlation will be considered in far more detail in the next chapter, where recent attempts to apply Tillich's theory to theological engagement with popular culture will be considered. There I will argue that many recent appropriations of correlation fail to pay sufficient attention to one of Tillich's construals of 'religion' as something which stands behind, but is not reducible to, the revealed truths of particular religious traditions. Even in the paragraphs immediately preceding this, it should be noted that correlation cannot simply be reduced to culture's questions and the answers of Christian doctrine. Supranatural theology is explicitly distinguished from 'revealed truths' and therefore is not the source of the answers but rather is 'resolved into the answers'. More importantly, correlation is the 'subject' of the project while the traditional theological loci are the 'illustrations'. The possibility

---

[58] Christoph Schwöbel, 'Paul Tillich', pp. 638–42, especially 640 in Alister McGrath, ed., *The Blackwell Encyclopedia of Modern Christian Thought* (Oxford: Blackwell, 1993). Two comments: first, this definition's similarity to the insights of 'belief-ful realism' should serve to warn against the assumption of a complete break, as there is also much continuity; second, the emphasis on ontology might seem 'old-fashioned' in today's discourse. Some commentators have described Tillich's thought as Platonic or Plotinian; see J. Heywood Thomas, 'Foreword', in T. A. O'Meara and C. D. Weisser, eds, *Paul Tillich in Catholic Thought* (London: Darton, Longman and Todd, 1965), p. vii; and simply 'out of place in the vigorously language-centred and deconstructive landscapes of the present day', Oliver Davies, *Theology of Compassion* (London: SCM, 2001), p. 158. However, Tillich's emphasis on the ambiguity and partiality of all religious theory and practice under the conditions of existence perhaps insulates him from the criticisms of today's radically suspicious discourse.

exists that the same exercise could be repeated with an entirely different religious tradition.

In this section of the book a specific example of 'revelation' through encounter with human cultural creation will be subjected to analysis. Tillich's theory, as found in his systematic theology, will be employed to build up a general account based on this specific example. Tillich's own experience of the Botticelli painting, which he recognizes as both existentially and theoretically important, is the source of the concrete experience from which the general account is developed.

Tillich is characteristically slippery and opaque in the way he relates his Botticelli experience to revelation. In the account 'One Moment of Beauty' from *AA*, which was quoted in full above and was used extensively in the empirical research, Tillich refers to the experience as both comparable with and analogous to religious revelation. 'I compare it with what is usually called revelation in the language of religion [...] I believe there is an analogy between revelation and what I felt.'[59] In other accounts, for example in a lecture on 'Art and Human Nature', he refers to it as an experience of 'revelatory ecstasy' (*AA*, 12). In spite of this ambiguity, both the autobiographical statements about the importance of this experience for his concept of revelation as breakthrough and the exposition of his theory that will follow demonstrate that this experience does cohere at all points with his understanding of the possibility of revelation through culture.

There are two reasons for using this experience to organize this engagement with Tillich's thought. First, it facilitates navigation through the systematic theology, allowing the discussion to remain focused on the central interests of the hypothesis without being enveloped in the complex circularities of Tillich's method. Second, this is precisely the kind of experience which was envisaged when the intellectual puzzle that elicited this study came into being and developed. It therefore bridges the gap between the lay interest in the possibility of revelatory experiences and the theoretical account of the theology of revelation.

This methodological decision does have theoretical implications. First, it was noted above that the emphasis on the communal, on extended periods of time, and on culture as a whole that characterized Tillich's early, German works is transmuted to a focus on the individual, the moment, and the particular artwork. In part this refocusing reflects the change in Tillich's own approach noted above, his increasing pessimism with regard to the possibility of positive societal change, and increasing emphasis on existentialism. However, using another facet of Tillich's thought or biography as an organizing principle would result in a different construal. For example, George

---

[59] Tillich, 'Beauty', p. 235.

Pattison in his book *Art, Modernity and Faith* focuses his discussion of Tillich on the essay 'Mass and Personality'; its emphasis on 'mass' in the sense of the 'crowd' allows for the subsequent discussion to retain a communal dimension.[60]

Second, the foregrounding of this experience emphasizes the mystical nature of the experience of revelation through art, an emphasis that might appear to be at odds with a theological approach that is generally seen as immensely intellectual, rational, and philosophical. However, it may be argued that this mystical element is an essential component of Tillich's thought. The religious studies scholar John Thatamanil, for example, in his book *The Immanent Divine* which compares Tillich's thought with the eighth-century Hindu teacher Sankara, can write: 'Tillich's theology amounts to a twentieth-century distillation of the history of Christian mystical theology.'[61] This mystical element is also noted by Roman Catholic commentators. A quote by Thomas Franklin O'Meara from his essay 'Paul Tillich in Catholic Thought: The Past and the Future' is representative:

> Mysticism is faith and grace in the intuitive key. Tillich's interest in art and psychology showed his attraction to the intuitive, the mystical, as did his preference for the Platonic strain in the history of Christianity, his work on Schelling and Boehme, and his European acquaintance with spirituality and monasticism.[62]

Tillich's essay 'The Two Types of Philosophy of Religion' provides an example of a mystical approach in a primary text. Here Tillich differentiates between two types of philosophy of religion: the cosmological type and the ontological type. While the cosmological type, which he associates with St Thomas, is dependent on human reasoning and the authority of Scripture, the ontological type, associated with St Augustine, is developed from immediate awareness of the ground of Being. Tillich's choice is for the ontological type. In the opening paragraph of the essay he writes:

> One can distinguish two ways of approaching God: the way of overcoming estrangement and the way of meeting a stranger. In the first way man discovers *himself* when he discovers God; he discovers something that is identical with

---

[60] George Pattison, *Art, Modernity and Faith* (London: SCM, 1998), pp. 100–17.
[61] John J. Thatamanil, *The Immanent Divine: God, Creation, and the Human Predicament* (Minneapolis, MN: Fortress Press, 2006), p. 9.
[62] Thomas Franklin O'Meara, 'Paul Tillich in Catholic Thought: The Past and the Future', in Raymond F. Bulman and Frederick J. Parrella, eds, *Paul Tillich: A New Catholic Assessment* (Collegeville, MN: The Liturgical Press, 1994), pp. 9–32. See also Julia A. Lamn, '"Catholic Substance" Revisited: Reversal of Expectations in Tillich's Doctrine of God', in Raymond F. Bulman and Frederick J. Parrella, eds, *Paul Tillich: A New Catholic Assessment* (Collegeville, MN: The Liturgical Press, 1994), pp. 48–72, especially 51; Gustave Weigel, 'The Theological Significance of Paul Tillich', in *Cross Currents* 6.2 (1956), pp. 141–55, especially 144; and J. Heywood Thomas, 'Foreword', in *Paul Tillich in Catholic Thought*, especially p. vii.

himself although it transcends him infinitely, something from which he is estranged, but from which he never can be separated. In the second way, a man meets a *stranger* when he meets God. The meeting is accidental. Essentially they do not belong to each other. They may become friends on a tentative and conjectural basis. But there is no certainty about the stranger man has met. He may disappear, and only *probable* statements can be made about his nature. (*TC*, 10)

Importantly, it is only the ontological type of philosophy of religion that can overcome the 'destructive cleavage' and 'fateful gap' between religion and culture, 'thus reconciling concerns which are not strange to each other but have been estranged from each other' (*TC*, 10 and 29).

Having commented upon the individual and the mystical emphases implied by the focus on Tillich's experience of the *Madonna with Singing Angels*, the analysis will now proceed through six aspects of Tillich's theory of revelation: the individual, who is the recipient; the artwork, which is the medium; the mechanism of the event; the content of revelation; the effect of revelation; and the relationship of revelation to Jesus as the Christ. The theoretical exposition will be supplemented where appropriate by insights gleaned from Tillich's other writings of the period, including his collected sermons and *The Courage to Be*, and by occasional reference to theologians of other traditions treating the same subjects.

The Individual Tillich's ontological–existential analysis presents the human individual as open to revelation and, indeed, as actively seeking revelation. The causes of this quest are analyzed in different sections of *Systematic Theology* under the rubrics of being, existence, and reason.

The second part of Tillich's system, 'Being and God', opens with a discussion of 'finitude'. 'It is the finitude of being which drives us to the question of God' (*ST1*, 184). Finitude is being in the presence of non-being. 'There can be no world unless there is a dialectical participation of non-being in being' (*ST1*, 208). The question of God *must* be asked because of this threat of non-being, which humanity experiences as anxiety; anxiety drives humanity to the question of being conquering non-being and of courage conquering anxiety (*ST1*, 231). Thus, even in its essential state, human being is finite and is driven to the question of God. But for Tillich it is important to discuss being as we experience it under the conditions of existence, and so from 'essential finitude' we move to 'existential disruption'. This leap corresponds to the move from part two to part three of the system where the analysis is of humanity's existential condition (rather than ontological or essential nature) (*ST2*, 3–4).

The 'transition from essence to existence' can be equated with the traditional symbol of the Fall, which therefore takes on the characteristics not of a one-time historical event but of an expression of the human person's finite freedom, that is, freedom within limits.

> Creation is good in its essential character. If actualized it falls into universal estrangement through freedom and destiny [...] The state of existence is the state of estrangement. Man is estranged from the ground of his being, from other beings, and from himself. The transition from essence to existence results in personal guilt and universal tragedy. (*ST2*, 44–5)

Estrangement is Tillich's preferred term to denote the 'traditional concept of sin' (*ST2*, 45). It unites the universal tragedy of estrangement from one's self, from God, and from the world with a sense of personal freedom, choice, and responsibility. This is achieved through recognizing that 'Sin is a universal fact before it becomes an individual act, or more precisely, sin as an individual act actualizes the universal fact of estrangement' (*ST2*, 76–8). Estrangement entails 'despair' traditionally represented in the symbols of the 'wrath of God' and 'condemnation':

> Despair is the state of inescapable conflict. It is the conflict on the one hand, between what one potentially is and therefore ought to be and, on the other hand, what one actually is in the combination of freedom and destiny. The pain of despair is the agony of being responsible for the loss of the meaning of one's existence and of being unable to recover it. (*ST2*, 75)

Despair is not entirely negative because it is despair that leads to 'The Quest for the New Being' (*ST2*, 78). 'Actually, even the awareness of estrangement and the desire for salvation are effects of the presence of saving power, in other words, revelatory experiences' (*ST2*, 86). Having noted that in its essential finitude humanity initiates a quest for being-itself (symbolically named as God) and in its existential estrangement recognizes the need for New Being, it is now necessary to consider the third rubric—'reason'.[63]

Tillich distinguishes between two kinds of reason: 'technical reason' and 'ontological reason'. Technical reason effectively refers to 'capacity for reasoning'; it is an 'instrument' for practical and scientific use (*ST1*, 81–2). Ontological reason surpasses the purely cognitive interests of technical reason; it is 'effective in the cognitive, aesthetic, practical, and technical functions of the human mind' (*ST1*, 80). The structure of ontological reason can be divided into its objective and subjective sides, where objective reason refers to the rational structure of reality and subjective reason refers to the rational structure of the mind that engages with reality. In theological language, concepts like 'creation through the Logos or of the Spiritual presence of God in everything real' designate the objective side of ontological reason, while the

---

[63] I have inverted the structure of Tillich's system here, moving from part two, to part three and now back to part one. But Tillich himself was adamant that all parts relied on the others and that the placing of epistemological questions of reason at the start was a purely pragmatic rather than material choice. See for example *ST1*, 181, where Tillich states that while his epistemology was placed first, ontology and analysis of existence are actually primary.

'image of God' present in humanity and allowing for the grasping and shaping of the world designates the subjective side of ontological reason (*ST1*, 84).

Ontological reason points beyond itself and even beyond the structures of reality that it engages. 'Reason in both its objective and subjective structures points to something which appears in these structures but which transcends them in power and meaning' (*ST1*, 88). This 'something' can only be referred to by use of metaphorical language. It is that which 'precedes' reason: 'being-itself', 'ground' or 'abyss'. It is the '"infinite potentiality of being and meaning" which pours into the rational structures of mind and reality, actualising and transforming them' (*ST1*, 88). This is the goal of reason: in the cognitive realm 'truth-itself'; in the aesthetic realm 'beauty-itself'; and in the legal 'justice-itself' (*ST1*, 88).

However, the finitude of being leads to ambiguity, and the estrangement experienced under the conditions of existence leads to conflict. The quest of reason for this 'potentiality' which precedes reason becomes the quest for revelation.

> Being is finite, existence is self-contradictory, and life is ambiguous. Actual reason participates in these characteristics of reality. Actual reason moves through finite categories, through self-destructive conflicts, through ambiguities, and through the quest for what is unambiguous, beyond conflict, and beyond bondage to the categories [...] This is a quest for revelation. Reason does not resist revelation. It asks for revelation, for revelation means the reintegration of reason. (*ST1*, 90, 104)

In summary: theoretical analysis of the finite being of the human person estranged under the conditions of existence identifies ontological anxiety, existential despair, and actual reason's pursuit of the unambiguous as the factors that initiate the quest for revelation.

Tillich's best-selling book, *The Courage to Be*, moves the analysis from abstract theory to concrete human experience and psychology. He identifies and describes different types of anxiety—of fate and death, emptiness and meaninglessness, and guilt and condemnation—that are widely experienced and lead to a quest for 'courage to be'.[64] This salvific courage can only be found through the revelatory experience of the power of being transcending non-being.[65] In theory and in practice Tillich believes the human individual is not merely open to but actually searching for revelation.

The Artwork Tillich's theology of culture, discussed above, sees culture as a medium of religious revelation. Part IV of the systematic theology, Life and the Spirit, provides the most complete exposition of the theoretical work that underpins this contention. To understand culture as a medium of revelation it

---

[64] Tillich, *Courage*, pp. 40–54.   [65] Ibid., pp. 155–6.

is necessary to understand 'spirit' as the distinctively human dimension of life which is manifest in the spheres of morality, culture, and religion.

Tillich is unhappy with the common practice of dividing 'life' into hierarchical levels: inorganic, organic, animal, human, and divine, for example. Instead we should think of life in terms of different 'dimensions' which intersect with one another without conflict. While all forms of life have the potential for all dimensions, only in humanity are all dimensions of life actualized (*ST3*, 15-17). It is 'spirit' that is 'the particularly human dimension of life' (*ST3*, 21). 'Spirit' should not be equated with reason; while it has a rational structure it also includes passion and imagination (*ST3*, 24). The dimension of spirit is used 'to denote the unity of life-power and life in meanings, or in condensed form, the "unity of power and meaning"' (*ST3*, 22).

There are three functions of spirit which carry this unity of power and meaning in humanity; they are morality, culture, and religion. In their essential state these three functions would manifest themselves in perfect unity and in unambiguous meaning and power (*ST3*, 44). However, under the conditions of existence, 'The manifestations [of the spirit] are ambiguous in so far as they not only reveal but also conceal' (*ST3*, 29-30). Only in that which transcends them—the new reality, the divine Spirit—can their essential unity and their essential power of the revelation of meaning be restored (*ST3*, 44).[66] So, life under the conditions of existence in the dimension of spirit has a quest that is correlative with the quest of finite life for being-itself and estranged life for New Being. Life in the dimension of spirit desires the divine Spirit or Spiritual Presence.

To understand the relation of this quest to culture, Tillich's contention that the religious function is actually a 'quality' of the other two (rather than a truly independent function) must be emphasized. This is close to what was seen in the early, German writings. 'Meaning [in either the moral or the cultural function] cannot live without the inexhaustible source of meaning to which religion points' (*ST3*, 96-8). That culture can transmit this 'inexhaustible source of meaning' without recourse to the explicitly religious sphere is the key to this argument.

Tillich argues that humanity 'cultivates' everything, making something new out of a 'universal triad of elements'. First, the subject matter, chosen from encountered objects. Second, the form imposed upon the subject matter to give it its characteristics as an essay, or painting, or law or prayer. The third element, the substance, is not autonomously chosen by the human cultivator; it is, rather, 'the soil out of which it [the cultural creation] grows [. . .] giving

---

[66] Once again Tillich enters at this point into ontological analysis that outdistances the interests of this thesis. A good summary of the relation of the functions of spirit to the ontological structures previously discussed by Tillich can be found in *ST3*, 96-8.

the passion and driving power to him who creates and the significance and power of meaning to his creations' (*ST3*, 60).

This cultivation is an act of *theoria*, the grasping action of ontological knowledge. It 'is the act of looking at the encountered world in order to take something of it into the centred self as a meaningful structured whole' (*ST3*, 62). Cognitive creative acts of theoria produce concepts. Aesthetic creative acts of theoria produce images (broadly conceived to include music, ornaments, poems, and plays). This allows Tillich to proffer a broad definition of truth that can cover science, religion, and the arts, 'the fragmentary reunion of knowing subject with the known object in the act of knowledge' (*ST3*, 64). For the aesthetic function, truth is not as important as the expression of deeper 'qualities of being'. Thus aesthetic creations should not be judged by either their truth or their beauty, but by 'expressive power'; their authenticity increases with their expressivity. They are inauthentic in as much as they present the surface alone, but authentic when they uncover the hidden quality of a piece of the universe, and thereby of the universe itself (*ST3*, 64).

By way of a particular example, in a sermon entitled 'Nature, Also, Mourns for a Lost Good', Tillich tells the story of a Chinese emperor who asked a great artist to paint him a picture of a rooster. For year after year the emperor waited as the artist tried not just to perceive the surface of the rooster's nature but to penetrate to its essence. 'Finally, after ten years of concentration on the nature of the rooster, he painted the picture—a work described as an inexhaustible revelation of the divine ground of the universe in one small part of it, a rooster.'[67] This ability to transcend the finite is the religious element in culture.

> The religious element in culture is the inexhaustible depth of a genuine creation. One may call it substance or the ground from which culture lives. It is the element of ultimacy which culture lacks in itself but to which it points [...] self-transcendence cannot take form except within the universe of meaning created in the cultural act. (*ST3*, 95)

This is still the broader of Tillich's two understandings of religion, the 'larger concept of religion as experience of the unconditional [...] in the depth of culture' (*ST3*, 101–2). The human desire for self-transcendence, for contact with the unconditional, inexhaustible depth, the substance or the ground, is the quest for 'unambiguous life' (*ST3*, 109–10). The three symbols of unambiguous life are Spirit of God, Kingdom of God, and Eternal Life (*ST3*, 107). Thus a human cultural creation, or artwork, as a manifestation of human spirit expressing depth, can mediate the revelation of divine Spirit or Spiritual Presence.[68]

---

[67] Tillich, *Shaking*, pp. 79–80.

[68] Etienne Gilson, *Painting and Reality* (Princeton: Princeton University Press, 1968) offers a superficially similar but substantively different account of the 'being' of art, particularly painting,

A Theology of Revelation through Culture

The third stage of analysis turns to the event which unites the individual and her quest for revelation with the artwork which is expressive of power and meaning, and mediates revelation.

The Event 'Event' is preferable to 'experience', because Tillich is clear that revelation is not merely a subjective experience but also has an objective element (*ST1*, 123–4).[69] Therefore, in order to discuss the event of revelation, both 'sides' must be addressed, the subjective through discussion of Tillich's understanding of 'ecstasy', and the objective through Tillich's understanding of 'miracle'.

Tillich recognizes that 'ecstasy' needs to be 'rescued from its distorted connotations and restored to a sober theological function' (*ST1*, 124). To do this he returns to its meaning as 'standing outside one's self' where 'the mind transcends its ordinary situation' (*ST1*, 124). He goes on to identify three characteristics of ecstasy. First, ecstasy transcends reason because it is beyond the subject–object structure of reason. 'Ecstasy occurs only if the mind is grasped by the mystery, namely, by the ground of being and meaning [...] there is no revelation without ecstasy' (*ST1*, 124). Ecstasy is 'the form in which that which concerns us unconditionally manifests itself within the whole of our psychological conditions. It appears through them. But it cannot be derived from them' (*ST1*, 125–6). Second, ecstasy reflects the polar character of that which concerns us unconditionally; the ecstatic state involves the experience of both the ground and the abyss of being. The experience of the ontological shock of non-being corresponds to the abyss, while the ground corresponds to an experience in which 'reason is grasped by the mystery of its own depth and of the depth of being generally' (*ST1*, 126). Finally, ecstasy 'does not destroy the rational structure of the mind' (*ST1*, 126). Emotional, cognitive, and ethical functions are all involved but are all driven beyond themselves. Speaking specifically of the cognitive function, ecstasy might be called 'inspiration', but this must not be confused with a general creative mood on the one hand or with a state which mediates 'knowledge of finite objects or relations [adding] to the complex of knowledge which is determined by the subject–object structure of reason' (*ST1*, 127).

---

and of art's ability to provide a point of contact with 'Being' itself. Gilson writes as a philosopher recently persuaded of the truth of the Thomist tradition (ix–xi) and stresses the continuity between the realms of nature and of grace that Tillich explicitly rejected in his choice of a method of correlation. Thus for Gilson there is a more direct, uncomplicated relation between the being of the finite artwork and the Being of the infinite which it can invoke (106–16, 299); there is no need for Tillich's distinction between surface and depth, form and substance, or any requirement for 'ecstasy' and 'miracle' to make the event of revelation possible.

[69] The importance of the concept of 'event' in relation to revelation resonates throughout twentieth-century thought. For a brief but apposite discussion see Rudolf Bultmann, *Jesus Christ and Mythology* (London: SCM, 1960), pp. 70–3. He speaks of the move (post WWI) from a primarily psychological and subjective account of God's action in the human person (*Erlebnis*) to one which emphasizes the objectively real, event nature of such action (*Ereignis*) or event.

'Miracle', referring to the objective side of the revelatory event, is also in need of rehabilitation from its superstitious meaning as an event that contradicts the laws of nature. Instead, in its capacity as the 'giving side' of a revelatory experience, it would be better to speak of 'sign-event' (*ST1*, 128). Tillich states: it is 'possible to change the words describing miracle and those describing ecstasy. One can say that ecstasy is the miracle of the mind and that miracle is the ecstasy of reality' (*ST1*, 130). Thus miracle too has a negative side which engenders numinous dread or numinous astonishment in the subject of every truly revelatory experience. However, it is also 'an event which points to the mystery of being, expressing its relation to us in a definite way [...] and an occurrence which is received as a sign-event in ecstatic experience' (*ST1*, 130).

At this, the pivotal moment of the event of revelation, a sentence from Tillich's consideration of miracle affords an opportunity to weave together the strands of analysis that have been pursued separately thus far. Tillich writes: 'The sign-events in which the mystery of being gives itself consist in special constellations of elements of reality in correlation with special constellations of elements of the mind' (*ST1*, 130). Thinking of a human subject contemplating an artwork, Tillich's theory makes it possible to intuit something of the contents of the two constellations that are in play in the event of revelation. In the mind of the individual, anxiety (experienced as alienation or estrangement), despair, and confusion have initiated a quest for the revelation of the ground of being and meaning. In the artwork the aesthetic, creative cultivation of finite material in the dimension of spirit has produced a cultural creation where particular form and particular subject matter may become transparent to the depth of being and meaning that inhere in them in a moment of breakthrough. In the meeting of these two constellations the artwork becomes a sign-event and the individual experiences ecstasy as the power of being and meaning flows into her. As quoted above, when Tillich described his own experience of Botticelli's *Madonna with Singing Angels*, he put it this way:

> In the beauty of the painting there was Beauty itself [...] something of the divine source of all things came through to me. I turned away shaken [...] That moment has affected my whole life, given me the keys for the interpretation of human existence, brought vital joy and spiritual truth. I compare it with what is usually called revelation in the language of religion.[70]

The Content But what is the content of revelation with regard to knowledge and specifically knowledge of God in Tillich's system? The sections on 'The Mystery of Revelation' and 'The Knowledge of Revelation' are helpful starting places.

---

[70] Paul Tillich, 'Beauty', pp. 234–5.

In discussing mystery, Tillich defines revelation as 'a special and extraordinary manifestation which removes the veil from something which is hidden in a special and extraordinary way'. If the revelation is of a 'mystery' in the true sense of the word, then even the removing of the veil cannot 'solve' the mystery (*ST1*, 120). An essential mystery precedes the subject–object dimension and is impossible to express in human language (which arises out of the subject–object dimension). 'God' is such a mystery, and this is the paradox of religion and theology, that 'God has revealed himself and that God is an infinite mystery for those to whom he has revealed himself' (*ST1*, 121). Tillich does not want to imply that there is no 'cognitive element' to revelation. In revelation something more is known of the mystery—its reality and its relation to us, for example. But this does not 'add anything directly to the totality of our ordinary knowledge, namely, to our knowledge about the subject–object structure of reality' (*ST1*, 121).

Turning to the second discussion, 'The Knowledge of Revelation', we see that in part this is because the knowledge of revelation can never be separated from the situation or event of revelation; 'it cannot be introduced into the context of ordinary knowledge as an addition, provided in a peculiar way, yet independent of this way once it has been received' (*ST1* 143). What implications does this have for knowledge of God as the possible content of revelation?

Tillich writes, 'The knowledge of revelation, directly or indirectly, is knowledge of God, and therefore it is analogous or symbolic' (*ST1*, 145). Before moving from the first to the second part of the system in order to understand this statement more completely, it is worth turning away from *Systematic Theology* to consider Tillich's most concise discussion of symbol in an essay entitled 'The Nature of Religious Language', published in *Theology of Culture*. Parts of this discussion also have relevance for the aspect of the theory of revelation through culture which relates to Jesus as the Christ.

For Tillich, 'The first step in any clearing up of the meaning of symbols is to distinguish it from the meaning of signs' (*TC*, 54). Signs point without participating, for example the word 'desk' designates the particular kind of table at which the writer sits but in no way participates in the reality which it describes. Symbols participate in the reality to which they refer, and symbolic language, for example poetry or liturgy, has a more than merely referential purpose. Indeed, the main function of symbols is to open up other levels of reality to mediate something which cannot be reduced to merely descriptive words. Characteristically taking an example from the visual arts, Tillich speaks of a landscape by Rubens: 'What this mediates to you cannot be expressed in any other way except through the painting itself' (*TC*, 57). The same is true of symbolic language, again poetry and liturgy: 'If one uses philosophical or scientific language, it does not mediate the same thing which is mediated in the use of really poetic language without a mixture of any other language' (*TC*, 57).

As might be expected, given the discussion of revelation and ecstasy and the two constellations of revelation above, the efficacy of a symbol is a 'two-sided' function. It requires the opening up of the soul even as the symbol itself opens up deeper levels of reality. This two-sidedness allows Tillich to develop the theory that symbols either flourish or wither and die, not on the basis of their truth in the usual scientific or empirical sense of the word, but on the basis of their efficacy (expressiveness in the discussion of the event of revelation, above). Thus, religious symbols are not susceptible to scientific historical or textual criticism, but they can die as the context in which they function changes. For example, the importance of Mary declines in Protestantism not because any particular doctrinal formulation has been proved false but because within Protestantism universal access to God is promised to all and Mary therefore becomes redundant. In other words, 'Their truth is their adequacy to the religious situation in which they are created, and their inadequacy to another situation is their untruth' (*TC*, 66).

Returning to *Systematic Theology* and to the question of God, Tillich opens his discussion of 'The Reality of God' with a phenomenological description:

> 'God' is the answer to the question implied in man's finitude; he is the name for that which concerns man ultimately. This does not mean that first there is a being called God and then the demand that man should be ultimately concerned about him. (*ST1*, 234)

To describe God as that which concerns humanity ultimately is one thing; it is quite another to talk of the actuality of God. This is because 'The ultimate can become actual only through the concrete, through that which is preliminary and transitory' (*ST1*, 242). This mediation through the finite world gives the 'idea' of God a history. However, 'Historical conditions determine the existence of the idea of God, not its essence; they determine its variable manifestations, not its invariable nature' (*ST1*, 244). This means that whenever we speak of the actuality of God we speak symbolically.[71] 'There can be no doubt that any concrete assertion about God must be symbolic, for a concrete assertion is one which uses a segment of finite experience in order to say something about him' (*ST1*, 266).

It is a matter of debate as to whether Tillich finally allowed for any non-symbolic statements about God. At this point in *Systematic Theology 1*, 'God is being-itself is a non-symbolic statement' (*ST1*, 265–6). However, as early as the Introduction to *Systematic Theology 2*, where Tillich addresses some of the questions and criticisms directed at Volume 1, he seems to say that no

---

[71] It is important to note that Tillich does not consider symbolic language to be in anyway inferior to literal or non-figurative language. See, for example, *ST1*, 61, 145–6.

statement beyond the expression of ultimate concern as a quest for God is allowable as non-symbolic (*ST2*, 9–10).

Participation is the basis upon which we can talk about the finite or concrete being the basis for an assertion about the infinite, ultimate, or absolute, 'because that which is infinite is being-itself and because everything participates in being-itself' (*ST1*, 277). Participation allows Tillich to make innovative use of the idea of *analogia entis*. 'In this sense *analogia entis*, like "religious symbol," points to the necessity of using material taken from finite reality in order to give content to the cognitive function in revelation' (*ST1*, 145–6). So, symbol requires the participation of the finite in the infinite. It also requires the transparency of the finite.

Tillich discusses nature, history, groups, individuals, and words as possible media of revelation. Their participation in the ground of being fits them to be revelatory; but they are not revelatory on the basis of their finite characteristics, so much as on the basis of their ability to become transparent to the ground of being (*ST1* 131–9). Jumping forward to another discussion of the media of revelation in *Systematic Theology 3*, we see the logical conclusion that, because everything participates in the ground of being and everything can potentially become transparent to the ground of being, there are an unlimited number of 'religious and cultural documents' which can be revelatory (*ST3*, 124–5).

In summary, the content of revelation is of the absolute, of the abyss of reason, and the ground of being. It is of that which precedes the subject–object structure of reality and therefore cannot be described literally in human language; nothing is added to the complex of knowledge of our world. As the content of revelation is of that which concerns humanity, ultimately it is possible, but by no means necessary, to speak of this given-ness as 'God'. But any knowledge of God coming through revelation also comes through the mediation of the finite and is therefore symbolic rather than literal knowledge.

Transferring this conceptualization to the specific instance of revelation through an artwork, it is possible to infer that the content of the revelatory experience might be expressed in two ways. First, and primarily, it might be recounted as an experience of that which concerns the subject ultimately, being-itself.[72] This experience does not take the form of a personal encounter, nor of a transfer of knowledge or information, but as an antidote to the problems of anxiety and despair. Any later references to the event that use religious language (if, for example, the subject of the revelatory experience were to begin to use the language and conceptualities of his own religious

---

[72] It can be noted that in Tillich's own account he refers to beauty-itself, but this is simply one facet of being-itself, that facet grasped by the aesthetic pole of *theoria*; the cognitive pole of *theoria* would identify being-itself as truth-itself.

tradition), or even simply refer to the experience as 'religious', must then be taken to be second-order re-conceptualizations.

Such re-conceptualization is entirely appropriate, but must be subject to Tillich's conviction that all explicit religion, under the conditions of existence, is ambiguous. 'In so far as religion is based on revelation it is unambiguous; in so far as it receives revelation it is ambiguous. But no religion is revealed; religion is the creation and distortion of revelation' (*ST3*, 104). No specific dogmatic claims, doctrines, or ecclesial structures based on revelation can be ultimate; any such claim to ultimacy or universality is demonic.

Whether this concept of the content of revelation is adequate will be considered in the discussion of the critical reception of Tillich's theory in the next section. It will be revisited and examined in greater detail in the final chapter, in response to some of the findings of the empirical research. Nonetheless, once it has been settled that revelation does not equal the giving of a message, or even knowledge more generally construed, the following quote provides a useful link to the next stage of analysis:

> The quest for unambiguous life is possible because life has the character of self-transcendence. Under all dimensions life moves beyond itself in a vertical direction [...] The answer to this quest is the experience of revelation and salvation; they constitute religion above religion, although they become religion when they are received [...] both quest and answer become matters of ambiguity if expressed in the terms of a concrete religion. (*ST3*, 109–10)

The Effect Reading a section on Revelation and Salvation from *Systematic Theology 1* alongside the discussion of the three symbols of unambiguous life in Volume 3—Spiritual Presence, Kingdom of God, and Eternal Life—allows the following comments on the relation between revelation and salvation. This draws together a number of the observations made in the first four stages of analysis.

Tillich rejects two false conceptions of the relation between revelation and salvation. First, he discounts an overly intellectualized (and therefore non-existential) understanding of revelation as 'information about "divine matters," which is supposed to be accepted partly through intellectual operations, partly through a subjection of the will to authorities' (*ST1*, 161, also *ST3*, 104f.). Second, he discards an over-realized understanding of salvation as 'either complete [ultimate fulfilment beyond time and history], or not salvation at all' (*ST1*, 162). Having disposed of these limited understandings, Tillich presents his own: it is better to see that 'the history of revelation and the history of salvation are the same history. Revelation can be received only in the presence of salvation, and salvation can occur only within a correlation of revelation' (*ST1*, 160–61). Even more emphatically: 'Where there is revelation there is salvation! [or] Where there is salvation there is revelation [...]

Therefore, by speaking of universal (not 'general') revelation, we have spoken implicitly of universal salvation' (*ST3*, 362).

Speaking existentially, salvation is 'a creative and transforming participation of every believer in the correlation of revelation' (*ST1*, 162). Turning to the three symbols of unambiguous life, Tillich shows that this 'participation' relates to the symbol of the Spiritual Presence; faith and love are seen as the manifestation of the divine Spirit in the human spirit (*ST3*, 129). Whenever the Spiritual Presence is manifest within history, it creates the idea of the history of salvation represented symbolically by the Kingdom of God. Nonetheless, within history (under the conditions of existence) revelation and salvation remain fragmentary and/or ambiguous (*ST1*, 162).

> Salvation and revelation are ambiguous in the process of time and history. Therefore, the Christian message points to an ultimate salvation which cannot be lost because it is reunion with the ground of being. This ultimate salvation is also the ultimate revelation, often described as the 'vision of God' [. . .] One can only be saved within the Kingdom of God which comprises the universe. But the Kingdom of God is also the place where there is complete transparency of everything for the divine to shine through it. In his fulfilled kingdom, God is everything for everything. This is the symbol of ultimate revelation and ultimate salvation in complete unity. (*ST1*, 163)

The Kingdom of God beyond the ambiguities of temporal and historical process can be equated with Eternal Life. Here, for the first time, we see the compelling coherence of Tillich's whole theory. Eternal Life ultimately unites revelation and salvation in the 'vision of God'; participation and transparency are perfected and communicate the bliss of the divine presence.

Again, application to the example of revelation through experience of an artwork is required. It is obvious that in the experience salvation must accompany revelation, albeit in a fragmentary and ambiguous way. David Kelsey offers a helpful summary: 'According to Tillich, revelation is not a disclosure of special information which gives us new knowledge. Rather, it is a mediation of power that gives ontological "healing" or "salvation."'[73] For the individual, the experience of revelation through art brings limited but important healing. The Spiritual Presence empowers the individual, bringing faith to overcome essential anxiety and existential despair, and love to overcome estrangement and broken and damaged relationships. In Tillich's own words: 'Revelation is an ecstatic experience of the ground-of-being that shakes, transforms or heals' (*ST2*, 166–7), Given that Tillich has rejected an over-realized understanding, there is no reason why this cannot be identified as salvation.

---

[73] David H. Kelsey, *The Fabric of Paul Tillich's Theology* (London: Yale University Press, 1967), p. 25.

As this is immensely important to the whole structure of the empirical research project, it is worth noting the wide range of ways in which Tillich allows this understanding of healing and salvation to be developed. The relation to psychological or existential healing in the face of existential anomie assumed in the book *The Courage to Be* and Tillich's interest in psychoanalysis have been discussed above. There are other examples, which suggest a link between the experience of revelation and salvation and physical or medical healing.[74] Further references address the way the fragmentary salvation encountered in an ecstatic experience can work its effect out into the whole of the individual's life.[75]

Up to this point, and mirroring Tillich's own method, Christianity as a specific religious expression has been present in the background, but has remained without concrete exposition.[76] Yet, in the introduction to *Systematic Theology 3* Tillich states: 'Certainly, these three books would not have been written if I had not been convinced that the event in which Christianity was born has central significance for all mankind, both before and after the event' (*ST3*, 4). So, it is both in faithfulness to Tillich and with an ear to the debate engendered by his theology that the analysis turns to Tillich's treatment of Jesus as the Christ as the final revelation.

Revelation and Jesus as the Christ With regard to methodology, Tillich is open about the inherent circularity of theological practice.[77] In order to describe 'revelation' phenomenologically and uncover its universal meaning, he needs a criterion of what 'revelation' is, that is, an absolutely concrete and absolutely universal example of revelation. Thus an existential–critical decision must be made before the intuitive–descriptive method of phenomenology can begin (*ST1*, 118–20). Tillich elects 'Jesus as the Christ' as his criterion and final revelation—but on what basis can he do this?

> The first and basic answer theology must give to the question of the finality of the revelation in Jesus as the Christ is the following: a revelation is final if it has the power of negating itself without losing itself. This paradox is based on the fact that every revelation is conditioned by the medium in and through which it appears. The question of the final revelation is the question of a medium of revelation which overcomes its own finite conditions by sacrificing them, and itself with them. (*ST1*, 148)

---

[74] Tillich, 'Religion and Art', pp. 37–8.
[75] For an interesting discussion of this, see Thatamanil, 'Tillich on Therapy: Salvation as Ecstatic Healing', in *The Immanent Divine*, pp. 149–63.
[76] It is relatively late in his discussion of revelation that Tillich moves to the particularities of Christianity; see *ST1*, 147.
[77] For Tillich's discussion of the inevitability of circularity in a systematic theology, see, for example, *ST1*, ix and 14.

Here we see that the general theory and the criterion are correlative. In this description, the criterion of revelation is a perfect symbol as defined by the general theory. This is yet more clearly seen by returning momentarily to the more programmatic essay about symbols, 'The Nature of Religious Language', which was discussed above in relation to the content of revelation.

> Religion is ambiguous and every religious symbol may become idolatrous, may be demonized, may elevate itself to ultimate validity although nothing is ultimate but the ultimate itself; no religious doctrine and no religious ritual may be. If Christianity claims to have a truth superior to any other truth in its symbolism, then it is the symbol of the cross in which this is expressed, the cross of the Christ. He who himself embodies the fullness of the divine's presence sacrifices himself in order not to become an idol, another god beside God, a god into whom the disciples wanted to make him. And therefore the decisive story is the story in which he accepts the title 'Christ' when Peter offers it to him. He accepts it under the one condition that he has to go to Jerusalem to suffer and to die, which means to deny the idolatrous tendency even with respect to himself. This is at the same time the criterion of all other symbols, and it's the criterion to which every Christian church should subject itself. (*TC*, 66–7)

A perfect symbol would require perfect participation of its finite material in the ground of being (or God), and also the perfect transparency of its finite material to the mystery. Jesus' participation is perfect because he is 'essential man' who 'by his very nature represents God [...] essential humanity includes the union of God and man' (*ST2*, 93). The perfect transparency is evident in the event of the cross. It is this negation that allows Christianity to witness to the final and universal revelation without heteronomously asserting its own finality. 'A Christianity which does not assert that Jesus of Nazareth is sacrificed to Jesus as the Christ is just one more religion among many others' (*ST1*, 150). Because of this sacrifice, all of Jesus' teachings, traditions, piety, 'rather conditioned worldview and ethics', can be separated from what is essential (*ST1*, 149). 'In the picture of Jesus as the Christ we have the picture of a man who possesses these qualities [of perfect participation and perfect transparency], a man who, therefore, can be called the medium of final revelation' (*ST1*, 148).

The question now becomes soteriological: how is this final revelation received by us or mediated to us? In fact, the two sides—revelation and reception—cannot be separated. 'Christianity was born, not with the birth of the man who is called "Jesus," but in the moment in which one of his followers was driven to say to him, "Thou art the Christ"' (*ST2*, 97). Any attempt to find the 'real' Christ behind 'Jesus as the Christ' is bound for failure. 'The reports about Jesus of Nazareth are those of Jesus as the Christ given by persons who received him as the Christ' (*ST2*, 102).

Roman Catholic theologian Gustave Weigel has suggested that Tillich's Christology is merely exemplary.[78] In his published response to Weigel's essay, Tillich denied this:

> You say that I think that Christ's redemption was exemplary and not juridical nor ontological. I agree with you that I do not interpret it in juridical terms but the term, 'New Being', which is at the centre of all my theology proves that I have an ontological doctrine for atonement.[79]

So, the 'concrete' aspect of the coming of the New Being is still important. 'Without the concreteness of the New Being, its newness would be empty. Only if existence is conquered concretely and in its manifold aspects, is it actually conquered' (*ST2*, 114). Therefore, we need the New Testament and particularly the gospel pictures of Jesus as the Christ.

> There is an *analogia imaginis*, namely, an analogy between the picture and the actual personal life from which it has arisen. It was this reality, when encountered by the disciples, which created the picture. And it was, and still is, this picture which mediates the transforming power of the New Being. (*ST2*, 115)

'Picture' suggests another question to Tillich: what kind of picture is best suited to the task? Historical research would like a photograph; religious sensibility would appreciate a picture in the style of idealist art; but the best and most revelatory style is expressionist. And this is precisely the kind of picture that Tillich believes the New Testament presents to us. Contemplation of such a picture allows us vicariously to follow the original artist, to plumb the 'deepest levels', and to participate 'in the reality and the meaning' of Jesus as the Christ (*ST2*, 115–16).

Participation, or existential involvement, is central to Tillich's understanding of revelation, as can be seen in his discussion of original and dependent revelation (*ST2*, 140–2). In the context of Jesus as the Christ, the original revelation was Peter's while the dependent revelation is that of the church through history. Therefore:

> The original miracle, together with its original reception, is the permanent point of reference, while the Spiritual reception by following generations changes continuously. But if one side of the correlation is changed, the whole correlation is transformed [. . .] No ecclesiastical traditionalism and no orthodox Biblicism can escape this situation of 'dependent revelation'. (*ST1*, 140)

This discussion of Jesus as the Christ is the fitting end-point to this reading of the theology of revelation through culture of Paul Tillich. Here revelation through the products of artistic creation, in the kinds of experiences described

---

[78] Weigel, 'Contemporary Protestantism and Paul Tillich', pp. 193–4.
[79] Tillich's response quoted in Weigel, 'Protestantism', pp. 201–2.

A Theology of Revelation through Culture

by the evangelical authors in the Introduction and by Tillich in his autobiographical accounts, is translated from a peripheral anomaly to the centre of the revelatory constellation. In Tillich's theory of revelation, the distinction between special and general revelation is dissolved. Both forms of revelation are mediated through culture (whether through the expressionist gospel accounts or expressionist paintings);[80] both forms rely on the same mechanism of ecstasy and miracle; both forms offer the same possibilities and suffer the same limitations of content; both forms bring salvation; both forms witness (although not necessarily explicitly) to Jesus as the Christ as the criterion of all revelation.

2.2.4 Debate engendered by Paul Tillich's theology

The purpose of this section of the book is to develop a strong account of the possibility of revelation through culture that can then be grounded through empirical research of the actual experiences of filmgoers. It is this empirical data, rather than the debate among academic theologians, that will provide the primary resources for critical engagement with Tillich's theory in this project. A lengthy analysis of the critical reception of Tillich's theology by academic theologians is, therefore, not necessary. However, there are two, closely related, points at which the academic debate addresses issues of great import to the wider project and these will both be considered briefly here and then revisited in the final chapter.

First, there is the question of whether the relation between philosophical system and Christian doctrine is managed by Tillich in an appropriate way. In Kenneth Hamilton's book *The System and the Gospel: A Critique of Paul Tillich*, he argues that the philosophical system is primary and that its relation to the Christian faith is only secondary. Interestingly, he suggests that the desire to reconcile the irreconcilable at this point is at the root of Tillich's much-discussed opacity.[81] Concerns of this type surface regularly in the wider literature. Reinhold Niebuhr asks whether Tillich's 'ontological speculations have not, despite the great precision of his thought, falsified the picture of man as the Bible portrays it, and as we actually experience it'.[82] David Kelsey suggests that the method of correlation might result in the clothing of secular theories in pious language, 'translating the content of Christian faith without

---

[80] For reference to the Bible as cultural creation, see *ST3*, 196; for comments on the way even our experience of nature is mediated through culture, see Tillich, *Shaking*, pp. 79–80.

[81] Kenneth Hamilton, *The System and the Gospel: A Critique of Paul Tillich* (London: SCM, 1963), pp. 36 and, for example, 79–81.

[82] Reinhold Niebuhr, 'Biblical Thought and Ontological Speculation', in C. W. Kegley and R. W. Bretall, eds, *The Theology of Paul Tillich* (New York: Macmillan, 1961), pp. 216–27, especially 218.

remainder into the deepest convictions of the secular culture it attempts to address'.[83]

Inevitably, the greatest concern is centred on Tillich's Christology. Alistair McGrath, in his monograph *The Making of Modern German Christology*, says that for Tillich, Jesus' significance lies in his being the 'historical manifestation of New Being' under the conditions of existence.

> In other words, the significance of Jesus of Nazareth resides in his being the historical manifestation of a self-sufficient existential principle, which may be discussed without any reference to that original manifestation, save that it actually took place.[84]

This concern has been raised in this book in reference to the apparent circularity of Tillich's concept of symbol and his portrayal of Jesus as the Christ as the perfect symbol. For example, Donald Dreisbach argues that it is only in his theory of symbols that Tillich offers any account of why and how religion or culture can mediate salvation.[85] In line with the reading generated in the present monograph, he concentrates on Tillich's Christology as an exposition of Jesus as the Christ as a perfect symbol and as the criterion of all revelation. However, he notes that in order to make the claims for Jesus as the Christ, Tillich 'appears not only to be moving beyond his earlier position, but to be unaware that he is doing it [. . .] he is either abandoning the doctrine of symbols or imposing on it a burden it was not designed to bear'.[86]

Nonetheless, it is clear at least that Christology is of absolutely central importance for Tillich. This centrality is recognized by Gustave Weigel:

> For Tillich Christianity is a religion different from all others, and it is the true religion. Moreover, it is Christ that makes Christianity what it is. We are saved by Christ. Christ is the Son of God. Christ is the absolute centre of history, the end of the beginning and the beginning of the end.[87]

The relation of Tillich's Christology to an underlying philosophy must remain an open question which will be addressed again in the next chapter with reference to Tillich's writings on Schelling's positive philosophy.

Perhaps the most potentially devastating question directed at Tillich's theory is that asked by Michael Palmer, editor of the second volume of

---

[83] Kelsey, *Tillich*, pp. 98 and 100.
[84] Alistair E. McGrath, *The Making of Modern German Christology: From the Enlightenment to Pannenberg* (Oxford: Blackwell, 1986), p. 145.
[85] Donald Dreisbach, *Symbols and Salvation: Paul Tillich's Doctrine of Religious Symbols and his Interpretation of the Symbols of the Christian Tradition* (London: University Press of America, 1993), p. xii.
[86] Dreisbach, *Symbols*, pp. 149 and 157.
[87] Weigel, 'Protestantism', p. 193.

Tillich's works, *Writings in the Philosophy of Culture*. Palmer wonders if a tautology is hidden at the heart of Tillich's entire project:

> There remains also the purely philosophical point that, if the claim 'all culture is *gehaltlich*' is true—if a religious import is *entailed* in all cultural activity—then this proposition is a necessary one and is [...] applicable to any state of affairs whatever [...] The awesome possibility exists that at the heart of Tillich's theology of culture stands a tautology.[88]

This extreme charge might not take enough account of the fact that, for Tillich, there are different levels of adequacy in the ways in which different cultures and different cultural creations within a given culture manifest the *Gehalt*. However, it does helpfully raise the question of discernment. On Tillich's account, what basis is there for distinguishing between revelatory or non-revelatory experiences? This is very closely tied to Tillich's contention that communication of information or knowledge about the world is not a property of revelation.

A very thoughtful engagement with Tillich's understanding of art and culture and their revelatory potential is found in Jeremy Begbie's *Voicing Creation's Praise: Towards a Theology of the Arts*.[89] Begbie addresses Tillich's use of symbol and proffers three main criticisms. First, he argues that Tillich does not recognize the difference between discursive symbolism appropriate to language and presentational symbolism appropriate to the visual arts. In fact he privileges the latter, preferring an immediate grasping of meaning as a single whole (a single gestalt) to the more sequential discursive revelation where the meaning is delivered in a series of units over time.[90] Second, because Tillich believes that 'God', or being-itself, lies beyond the subject–object distinctions of cognition, therefore all *language* about God 'is necessarily symbolic; to treat it literally is to fasten upon its surface meaning and so to miss its real point'.[91] But even a 'symbolic statement must have some non-symbolic criterion or criteria of truth', states Begbie, if it is not to be meaningless.[92] Finally Begbie asks, even if Tillich's dismissal of *literal* language about God is justified, is there not room for *figurative* language (in metaphor and analogy) that communicates meaning and truth?[93] Begbie concludes:

> Deprived of any literal correlates to the statement 'God is being-itself', it is very hard to know how we can talk meaningfully at all about the disclosure of ultimate reality in art. How can we maintain at one and the same time that art discloses

---

[88] Palmer, *Writings*, pp. 30–1.
[89] Jeremy Begbie, *Voicing Creation's Praise: Towards a Theology of the Arts* (Edinburgh: T&T Clark, 1991), pp. 68–72.
[90] Begbie, *Voicing*, pp. 68–9 and 71.
[91] Ibid., p. 69.   [92] Ibid., p. 69.   [93] Ibid., p. 70.

ultimate reality and that there are no non-symbolic means for assessing the effectiveness of this supposed disclosure?[94]

It can be briefly shown that the broader academic consideration of Tillich expresses similar concerns. David Kelsey states, 'There has been considerable controversy whether "religious symbol", as Tillich understands it, has cognitive import.'[95] Discussing Tillich's category of 'ecstatic reason' in her essay 'Epistemology and the Idea of Revelation', Dorothy Emmet asks, 'How much cognitive value has it?'[96] She wonders if it can express only 'numinous astonishment' but not 'factual assertions'.[97]

Similar concerns are expressed by a number of Roman Catholic theologians who are particularly interested in the way in which Tillich draws parallels between his ontological philosophy and the traditional concept of the *analogia entis*, yet is far less willing to admit that either approach can yield valid information about God. Both Gustave Weigel, in his essay 'The Theological Significance of Paul Tillich', and George F. McLean, in his essay 'Symbol and Analogy: Tillich and Thomas', agree that although the *analogia entis* can never speak univocally, there is positive content based upon a relationship of 'proportionality' between the finite and the divine.[98] Tillich is, therefore, too negative. 'Our age has conditioned Professor Tillich. Where Thomas clung to the affirmatives in the paradoxical grasp of God, Tillich stresses the negative.'[99] In his reply Tillich agrees, explaining: 'I am more worried about the idolic character of traditional theology and popular beliefs about God than you are.'[100]

Having considered these two questions about Tillich's theology, it is worth briefly relating them to the analysis of Tillich's theory of the possibility of revelation through culture that has been developed above. Dorothy Emmet provides an interesting link when she writes, 'By what he calls his *method of correlation*, Tillich holds that every form of intellectual enquiry puts a question

---

[94] Ibid., p. 71. It might be that Begbie neglects Tillich's emphasis on the importance of the word. For example, in two sections addressing 'Sacramental Encounters and the Sacraments' and 'Sacrament and Word' (*ST3*, 120–6),Tillich is at pains to point out the importance of verbalization, 'because language is the fundamental expression of spirit' (*ST3*, 124).

[95] Kelsey, *Tillich*, p. 99.

[96] D. M. Emmet, 'Epistemology and the Idea of Revelation', in C. W. Kegley and R. W. Bretall, eds, *The Theology of Paul Tillich* (New York: Macmillan, 1961), pp. 198–214, especially 211.

[97] Emmet, 'Epistemology', pp. 212–13.

[98] George F. McLean, 'Symbol and Analogy: Tillich and Thomas', in T. A. O'Meara and C. D. Weisser, eds, *Paul Tillich in Catholic Thought* (London: Darton, Longman and Todd, 1965), pp. 145–83, especially 183.

[99] Weigel, 'Significance', p. 153.

[100] Tillich's reply quoted in Weigel, 'Significance', p. 155.

to which there may be a theological answer, the *form* [emphasis mine] of the answer being dependent on the way the question is asked.'[101]

In light of the reading developed above, I believe that Tillich would be unconcerned by the questions considered here, because he would readily agree that the *form* of all of his theology is dictated by the questions of philosophy; but then he would ask, why does that matter if it is only the 'import' or 'substance' which precedes both question and answer that is of ultimate concern? Tillich is primarily concerned with the way the event of revelation mediates salvation. In the course of the reading developed above, 'salvation' has been identified with the ground of being and of meaning; as courage to be; as New Being; as healing; as the absolute; as God; as Spiritual Presence; as the Kingdom of God; and as Eternal Life. All of these, with the possible exception of the last, are encountered within history and experienced in the event of revelation. Thus, in response to the criticisms, Tillich might contend that the substance of salvation is unaffected whether it is described using the *form* of philosophical language, relating to the questioning side of the correlation, or using the *form* of doctrinal language, relating to the answering side of the correlation; and symbols do not need cognitive content because, for so long as they are living and functioning as symbols, salvation comes in the revelatory event in which they become transparent.

Once again, the assessment of whether Tillich's is an adequate response must be, for now, deferred. The relation between revelation and salvation will be vital to the design and enactment of the empirical research project that is intended to ground Tillich's theology of revelation through consideration of the experiences of filmgoers. However, before proceeding to the empirical research, it is necessary to address some problems that arise when the attempt is made to apply Tillich's theology of revelation through culture to the possibility of revelation through the particular cultural medium of film.

---

[101] Emmet, 'Epistemology', p. 210.

3

From High Culture to Popular Culture and Film

Tillich was very much a theologian of high culture with little interest in, or respect for, popular or low culture. His dismissive attitude to popular media calls into question the appropriateness of utilizing his theology in an account of the possibility of revelation through film. The task of this chapter is to argue that the gap between Tillich's theology and film can be bridged.[1]

The first section of the chapter will consider the move from Tillich's focus on high culture to application of his theology to popular culture. Tillich's thought is frequently appropriated by contemporary theologians writing about popular culture, but the most common approach is to treat his theology, and particularly his method of correlation, as too positivist with respect to revelation and too biased towards the religious side of the religion–culture engagement. This interpretation of Tillich's theory and method is in direct conflict with the account of his theology of revelation through culture developed in this monograph. I will argue that the common approach is based upon neglect or ignorance of the presence of two meanings of 'religion' in Tillich's work. This first section of the chapter concludes with a more positive appraisal of Kelton Cobb's utilization of Tillich's thought. I will suggest that Tillich's position actually mediates between the traditional academic predilection for high culture and contemporary interest in popular culture.

The second section of the chapter will consider the application of Tillich's theology of revelation to film. It will begin with a survey of religion–film scholars' relations to Tillich's thought, noting a shift in approach over time from positive application to critical revision of his theology. The final part of

---

[1] In light of an essay like Walter Benjamin's 'The Work of Art in the Age of Mechanical Reproduction', in *Illuminations*, ed. Hannah Arendt and tr. Harry Zohn (London: Fontana, 1973), pp. 217–52, where film is considered almost as the archetype of art divorced from the religious 'aura', such a task may seem doomed to futility. Nonetheless, theologians such as George Pattison continue to engage Benjamin's account while still considering film as a potential site of 'strange miracles', in *Thinking About God in an Age of Technology* (Oxford: Oxford University Press, 2005), pp. 229–39.

the chapter takes the form of an extended thought experiment which suggests that the unique characteristics of film, in particular its intimate relation to the pro-filmic world, give it precisely the kind of breakthrough potential that Tillich associated with his most favoured art form, expressionist painting.

3.1 PAUL TILLICH: THEOLOGIAN OF POPULAR CULTURE?

3.1.1 On the meaning of 'culture'

Before discussing the different ways in which Tillich's theory and method are utilized by contemporary theologians of popular culture, it will be helpful to consider briefly what is meant by 'culture', 'high culture', and 'popular culture'.

Terry Eagleton has stated that culture is 'one of the two or three most complex words in the English language'.[2] It is best seen in the light of a brief historical survey.[3] First, in the classical world writers such as Cicero used agricultural cultivation as an analogy for the cultivation of the human person.[4] This sense of the word was appropriated in Germany at the start of the nineteenth century and linked with their term *Bildung*—the intentional formation of the human being into a certain image or *Bild*.[5] Friedrich Schiller's letters *On the Aesthetic Education of Man* provide the classic example. It is education in the fine arts and in the appreciation of beauty that facilitates the requisite harmony and balance between Enlightenment rationalism and Romantic sensibility.[6] As a corollary of this, culture came to be identified with 'the best that has been known and said in the world' (Matthew Arnold's oft-quoted phrase); today we might consider this 'high culture'.[7]

However, the developing science of anthropology led to the recognition that 'culture' and 'civilization' were not synonymous, and recent theory has focused on ways of interpreting the variegated plurality of cultures or 'ways of life' present in the world. Clifford Geertz writes, 'man is an animal suspended in webs of significance he himself has spun, I take culture to be those webs, and

---

[2] Terry Eagleton, *The Idea of Culture* (Oxford: Blackwell, 2000), p. 1.
[3] Three recent works have been helpful: Eagleton, *Idea*; Timothy J. Gorringe, *Furthering Humanity: A Theology of Culture* (Aldershot: Ashgate, 2004); and Gordon Lynch, *Understanding Theology and Popular Culture* (Oxford: Blackwell, 2005).
[4] Gorringe, *Humanity*, p. 3.
[5] See George Pattison, *A Short Course in Christian Doctrine* (London: SCM, 2005), pp. 127–8.
[6] Friedrich Schiller, *On the Aesthetic Education of Man: In a Series of Letters*, tr. R. Snell (Bristol: Thoemmes Press, 1994), see particularly Letters 6:45; 9:51, and 18:87.
[7] Arnold, *Culture*, p. 5.

the analysis of it to be therefore not an experimental science in search of a law but an interpretive one in search of meaning.'[8] With this latter understanding has come an increasing emphasis on mass or popular culture, no longer understood as a necessarily derogative comparison to high culture, but as 'the study of the environment, practices and resources of everyday life'.[9]

3.1.2 Problematic appropriations of Tillich's theology

Gordon Lynch's book, *Understanding Theology and Popular Culture*, addresses many of the issues raised by theological engagement with the popular culture of the contemporary world. He is quick to acknowledge Tillich's contribution. 'Interest in studying the religious dimension of culture was originally given a significant impetus in the twentieth century through the work of the theologian Paul Tillich.'[10] However, in his focal methodological chapter, 'Developing a Theological Approach to the Study of Popular Culture', his engagement with Tillich is critical and revisionary.[11] He states, 'the particular conversational model that I want to explore further [...] is the revised correlational approach'.[12] Tillich's correlational approach requires revision because it is too positivist with respect to revelation and too biased towards religion. Lynch implies that Tillich considers 'truth and goodness' to be 'the sole possession of one particular religious tradition or world-view'.[13] In contrast:

> A revised correlational approach advocates a more complex conversation between questions and answers offered both by religious tradition and popular culture. This approach also raises the possibility that popular culture may inform and challenge the beliefs and practices of religious tradition in the same way that theological norms may challenge popular culture.[14]

Other theologians considered in this monograph offer an identical reading of the weaknesses of Tillich's method of correlation and a similar revision of his approach.[15] In fact, it has also been picked up in recent writing on the methodology of theology and film with Deacy and Ortiz commending and utilizing this 'dialogical' approach in their *Theology and Film*.[16] As this is such

---

[8] Clifford Geertz, *Interpretation of Cultures: Selected Essays* (London: Fontana, 1993), p. 5.
[9] Lynch, *Popular*, p. 19; for his wider discussion, see pp. 1–19.
[10] Ibid., p. 29.
[11] Ibid., pp. 93–110.
[12] Ibid., p. 105.
[13] Ibid., p. 105.
[14] Ibid., pp. 109–10.
[15] For example, Clive Marsh, who is discussed later in this chapter, and John Swinton and Harriet Mowat, who are discussed in Chapter 4.
[16] Deacy and Ortiz, *Challenging*, p. 68.

a popular move its genealogy will be traced back through the work of the practical theologian Don Browning and the Roman Catholic theologian David Tracy.

In *A Fundamental Practical Theology*, Don Browning advocates a 'critical correlational approach to fundamental practical theology' and acknowledges that he has been 'assisted greatly by the revisionist view of theology found in the work of David Tracy'.[17] Browning writes, 'Tillich believed that theology is a correlation of existential questions that emerge from cultural experience and answers from the Christian message.'[18] However, in the revised correlational approach, 'Christian theology becomes a critical dialogue between the implicit questions and the explicit answers of the Christian classics and the explicit questions and implicit answers of contemporary cultural experiences and practices.'[19]

David Tracy had developed this approach in a chapter, 'A Revisionist Model for Contemporary Theology', in *Blessed Rage for Order* (1975).[20] Here, he argued that there are two possible sources for theology: first, 'common human experience and language'; and, second, 'Christian texts'.[21] Tracy identifies these two sources with the terms 'the situation' and 'the message' respectively, in Tillich's theology.[22] For Tracy, 'The Theological Task Will Involve a Critical Correlation of the Results of the Investigations of the Two Sources of Theology' (the title of his second thesis in this chapter).[23]

To identify the correct procedure for correlation, Tracy attempts 'a clarification through contrast' with 'the best known method of correlation in contemporary theology, Paul Tillich's'. While praising Tillich's project and stating that his method is still 'fundamentally sound', Tracy argues that Tillich's method does not call for a critical correlation of the results of one's investigations of the 'situation' and the 'message'. Rather, his method affirms the need for a correlation of the 'questions' expressed in the 'situation' with the 'answers' provided by the Christian 'message'. But, says Tracy, 'if the "situation" is to be taken with full seriousness, then its answers to its own questions must also be investigated critically'. Tracy concludes, 'Tillich's method does not actually correlate; it juxtaposes questions from the "situation" with answers from the "message"'. Thus, Tillich's positive bequest to modern theology

---

[17] Don Browning, *A Fundamental Practical Theology* (Minneapolis, MN: Fortress Press, 1991), p. 44.
[18] Browning, *Practical*, p. 46.
[19] Ibid., p. 46.
[20] David Tracy, *Blessed Rage for Order: The New Pluralism in Theology* (New York: Seabury Press, 1975), pp. 43–63.
[21] Tracy, *Rage*, p. 43.
[22] Ibid., pp. 43–4.
[23] Ibid., p. 45.

is his articulation of the need for correlation rather than the provision of a method for correlation.'[24]

This is already a slightly better reading of Tillich because it recognizes from the outset that both present situation and Christian texts are 'sources' for theology as far as Tillich is concerned; the only question is over the way they are 'correlated'. By contrast, Lynch and Browning seem to imply that Tillich considers only the texts or revelations of the Christian tradition as sources. It is also important to note that in his later book, *The Analogical Imagination* (1981), Tracy offers another reading of Tillich, placing him squarely within a tradition in the history of theological ideas that explicated the Christian faith from the perspective of an *a posteriori* phenomenological account of religious experience and with a strong negative and dialectical moment that would undercut any simplistic account of 'answers' found solely in Christian texts. This reading in many ways mirrors the analysis that will be offered below, where it is argued that there are two construals of 'religion' at play in Tillich's thought and writings: one which might be identified with the foundational religious experience and the second with a particular tradition.[25]

There is no doubt that Tillich's own language and terminology invite and to some extent authorize the simple reading offered by Lynch and Browning. However, the previous chapter has made it clear that Tillich believed that the same fundamental dimension underlies both cultural expression and religious expression. Therefore, both questions and answers can arise on either side of the secular–religious divide. On the questioning side, it is necessary to read the style of ecclesial culture as well as scientific or artistic culture in order to understand a given society. And, on the answering side, a secular painting can be more religiously meaningful and potent than a painting with religious subject matter.

In order to develop this counter-reading without rehearsing work already done, I will first consider essays collected in the volume *Theology of Culture* and then return to the earliest of Tillich's works of scholarship, his dissertation on Schelling's philosophy of religion.

In the essay 'Aspects of a Religious Analysis of Culture', which is a shorter update of the early lecture *On the Idea of a Theology of Culture*, Tillich writes:

> The confrontation of the existential analysis with the symbol in which Christianity has expressed its ultimate concern is the method which is adequate both to the message of Jesus as the Christ and to the human predicament as rediscovered in contemporary culture. The answer cannot be derived from the question. It is said *to* him who asks, but it is not taken *from* him. Existentialism cannot give the answers. It can determine the form of the answer, but whenever an existentialist

---

[24] All quotes in this paragraph from Tracy, *Rage*, p. 45.
[25] David Tracy, *The Analogical Imagination: Christian Theology and the Culture of Pluralism* (London: SCM Press, 1981), for example, pp. 188 n. 66 and 418–19.

artist or philosopher answers, he does so through the power of another tradition which has revelatory sources. To give such answers is the function of the Church not only to itself, but also to those outside the Church. (*TC*, 49)

Although at first reading this statement appears to substantiate the positivist charge levelled by Browning and Lynch at Tillich's method of correlation, it must be seen in its context in this essay. First of all, and as discussed in Chapter 2, it is the sacrifice of Jesus of Nazareth to Jesus as the Christ that gives Christianity its universality. In other words, the historically conditioned worldview and teachings of Jesus are made transparent (*TC*, 40). Further, the essay has earlier presented the foundational and broader understanding of religion introduced above.

> We can say that religion is being ultimately concerned about that which is and should be our ultimate concern [...] Such a concept of religion has little in common with the description of religion as the belief in the existence of a highest being called God, and the theoretical and practical consequences of such a belief. (*TC*, 40)

This means, 'A second consequence of the existential concept of religion is the disappearance of a gap between the sacred and the secular realm [...] In all preliminary concerns, ultimate concern is present, consecrating them' (*TC*, 41). Recently theologians have become more sensitive to the different meanings of 'religion' in Tillich's writings. For example, Russell Re Manning distinguishes between 'explicit religion', which is related to concrete traditions of revelation; and the broader sense of religion, which is related to the universally accessible 'fundamental revelation'.[26]

Another of Tillich's essays, 'Religion as a Dimension of Man's Spiritual Life', attempts to mark out a middle way between the revelation–positivism of conservative theologians and the reductivism of the social scientists.

> As soon as one says anything about religion, one is questioned from two sides. Some Christian theologians will ask whether religion is here considered as a creative element of the human spirit rather than as a gift of divine revelation. If one replies that religion is an aspect of man's spiritual life they will turn away. Then some secular scientists will ask whether religion is to be considered a lasting quality of the human spirit instead of an effect of changing psychological and sociological conditions. And if one answers that religion is a necessary aspect of man's spiritual life, they turn away like the theologians, but in an opposite direction. (*TC*, 3)

Tillich reserves his harshest criticism for the conservative theologians who 'begin their message with the assertion that there is a highest being called God,

---

[26] Russell Re Manning, *Theology at the End of Culture: Paul Tillich's Theology of Culture and Art* (Leuven, Belgium: Peeters, 2005), pp. 107–12.

whose authoritative revelations they have received. They are more dangerous for religion than the so-called atheist scientists' (*TC*, 5). Once again, religion understood in the broad sense cannot be separated from the wider, secular sphere of culture. 'It is at home everywhere, namely, in the depth of all functions of man's spiritual life. Religion is the dimension of depth in all of them. Religion is the aspect of depth in the totality of the human spirit' (*TC*, 7).

At the very least, these essays show that the picture is far more complex than the simple juxtaposition of cultural questions and religious answers. It is at least clear that even if the answers are considered religious, this certainly does not mean they are 'authoritative revelations'. The broad view of religion can be traced all the way back to Tillich's earliest academic writings on the positive philosophy of F. J. W. Schelling.[27] In his introduction to his own translation of these writings, Victor Nuovo offers a reading of Tillich's theology and his method of correlation that differs radically from that of Marsh, Lynch, and Browning.

To justify his understanding of the importance of Schelling's thought for the whole of Tillich's *oeuvre*, Nuovo opens with a quote from Tillich: 'what I learned from Schelling became determinative of my own philosophical and theological development'.[28] Nuovo continues, 'In all his works, Tillich displays a remarkable continuity of thought [. . .] his thought underwent no radical transformation [. . .] The abiding deep structure of Tillich's thought is [Schelling's] system of the potencies.'[29] The potencies will be considered below, but it is first helpful to see how different Nuovo's understanding of correlation is from that of the authors considered above:

> Through the method of correlation and the reinterpretation of Christian doctrine by means of philosophical concepts that originate in Idealism and Existentialism, Tillich attempted to free theology from heteronomy and to develop within it an openness to other creative spiritual realizations; he sought to liberate Christian consciousness from an external bondage to tradition so that the spiritual and universally human import of its content might be comprehended anew.[30]

Here correlation, rather than being doctrinal answers to the philosophical questions of culture, is the means by which Christian consciousness might be freed from the bonds of tradition.

---

[27] For Russell Re Manning's exposition of Schelling's writings as 'the philosophical foundations of Tillich's project of a theology of culture', see Manning, *Theology*, pp. 57–103, especially 102–3.

[28] Victor Nuovo, 'Translator's Introduction', in Paul Tillich, *The Construction of the History of Religion in Schelling's Positive Philosophy: Its Presuppositions and Principles*, tr. Victor Nuovo (London: Associated University Presses, 1974), pp. 11–32, especially 11.

[29] Nuovo, 'Introduction', p. 23.

[30] Ibid., p. 26.

Tillich's dissertation on Schelling was written in 1912. He defines his task as 'to present the construction of the history of religion as the focal point of Schelling's positive philosophy'; his purpose is clearly to present Schelling's concept of philosophical religion, which can incorporate history and particularly the Christ event, as superior to the older rational or moral religion that was restricted to universal and atemporal truths.[31] However, to accomplish this task Tillich must consider the 'epistemological and metaphysical principles of the whole system. Without the doctrine of the potencies one cannot even set foot in the positive philosophy.'[32]

There are two points of interest in this very complex dissertation: the first relates to the relation between the potencies and the Trinity, while the second relates to the nature of revelation. Nuovo offers a brief definition of the potencies as 'the highest metaphysical concepts, comprehending both the operations of nature and the actions of freedom'.[33] The three potencies 'constitute the Trinitarian nature of God'.[34] The first potency, identified with the Father, is potential being, the ground of all; the second potency is actual, necessary being, the formal and efficient cause of all (Nuovo frequently refers to Christ as 'the supreme manifestation of the second potency');[35] the third potency is the unity of the first two, seen in personality, consciousness, intellect, i.e. in spirit and Spirit.[36]

Tillich uses slightly different terminology both to define the potencies: 'Whereas the first potency is what can be, and the second is what must be, the third is the goal, what ought to be or what shall be';[37] and to describe the relation of the potencies to the persons of the Trinity: through Christ 'the tensions of the potencies have been dissolved in God himself and the unity of all has been realised with absolute perfection'.[38] In instances like this, it is almost impossible to unpick the relationship between metaphysical speculation and Christian doctrine. To what extent are terms like 'potency' simply the application of philosophical language to doctrine, and to what extent has doctrine been reconstituted and made subservient to philosophical concepts? The questions that were raised towards the close of the last chapter, with respect to the relation between Tillich's Christology and his philosophical system, continue to circulate.

Revelation is also interrelated with the theory of the potencies. Tillich argues that in Judaism and Christianity revelation 'signifies the supernatural

---

[31] Tillich, *Schelling*, pp. 41 and 158.
[32] Ibid., p. 41.
[33] Nuovo, 'Introduction', p. 16.
[34] Ibid., p. 17.
[35] For example, Nuovo, 'Introduction', pp. 17, 24, 26, and 28.
[36] Ibid., p. 17.
[37] Tillich, *Schelling*, pp. 53-4.
[38] Ibid., p. 112.

efficacy of the second potency in contrast to its natural efficacy in paganism'.[39]

> Because the free, personal God is the God who reveals himself, therefore revelation is will and act, and is opposed to reason. For reason lives in the necessary, and therefore in the natural. It is not the organ of the supernatural [...] Experience is the organ of revelation. Therefore it is deceitful to speak of revelation when what is meant is only a truth of reason that may be known even without revelation [...] Since revelation is act it cannot be conceived as instruction [...] But revelation is an act by which God enters into a new relation with man, not instruction about something always present.[40]

So here, in this very early work, there are a number of concepts which have been seen to run through Tillich's whole project. First, there is the importance of history and particularly of the Christ-event within history. Second, there is a complex entanglement of metaphysical speculation and Christian doctrine. Third, there is an understanding of revelation that emphasizes its effectual power over any knowledge content. Even in this the earliest of Tillich's works, it is salvation that is of primary concern. 'In Schelling's concept of revelation, the rationalistic antithesis of revelation and redemption is overcome.'[41]

Something very similar to Schelling's conception of philosophical religion is at play in the later essays collected in *Theology of Culture*. The presence of this understanding will be the final piece needed to state clearly why Lynch and Browning's readings of correlation are unhelpful. The 'mystical' bent of Tillich's theology has been discussed above with particular reference to the essay 'The Two Types of Philosophy of Religion'. In addition to this, the essay 'Existential Philosophy: Its Historical Meaning' most clearly shows the persistence of the approach first seen in the Schelling dissertation. While this is a long and complex essay which, as its title states, is concerned with philosophy rather than theology, there is a clear link between the analysis of various philosophers and Tillich's own thought. Here again, the reader encounters the mystical-type religious experience that is the substance or depth underlying any particular tradition; the contention that revelation is content-less as far as propositional knowledge is concerned; and the idea that the particular religious (or philosophical) vocabulary (the forms) used to describe this experience are incidental.

> Like many other appeals to immediate experience [existential philosophy] is trying to find a level on which the contrast between 'subject' and 'object' has not arisen. It aims to cut under the 'subject–object distinction' and to reach that stratum of Being which Jaspers, for instance, calls the '*Ursprung*' or 'Source'. But in order to penetrate to this stratum we must leave the sphere of 'objective' things

---

[39] Ibid., p. 135.
[40] Ibid., pp. 137–8.
[41] Ibid., p. 139.

and pass through the corresponding 'subjective' inner experience, until we arrive at the immediate creative experience or 'Source'. (*TC*, 92)

The focus on the level at which the subject–object distinction has not arisen negates even the possibility of the communication of information.

> The Existential thinker cannot have pupils in the ordinary sense. He cannot communicate any ideas, because *they* are *not* the truth he wants to teach. He can only create in his pupil by indirect communication that 'Existential state' or personal experience out of which the pupil may think and act. (*TC*, 90)

The implication of this approach is that the vocabulary used to speak of these experiences is a matter of personal choice.

> The Existential thinker needs special forms of expression, because personal Existence cannot be expressed in terms of objective experience. So Schelling uses the traditional religious symbols, Kierkegaard uses paradox, irony, and the pseudonym, Nietzsche the oracle, Bergson images and fluid concepts, Heidegger a mixture of psychological and ontological terms, Jaspers uses what he calls 'ciphers', and the Religious Socialist uses concepts oscillating between immanence and transcendence. (*TC*, 91)

To return to the statement from the essay 'Aspects of a Religious Analysis of Culture' which introduced this section of discussion, a deeper understanding of Tillich's contention that 'whenever an existentialist artist or philosopher answers, he does so through the power of another tradition which has revelatory sources' is possible. It does not necessarily mean that answers are the preserve only of the church, although 'to give such answers is the function of the church', or that answers are accessible only through Christian doctrine. Rather, Tillich believes that the power of all answers is predicated upon 'immediate experience' or revelation of the 'source'. The vocabulary used to express these answers is incidental. As Russell Re Manning puts it, in his essay on 'Tillich's Theology of Art':

> The engagement between theology and art, therefore, is correlational, but not in the simple sense of providing theological answers to cultural questions, but in the more robust sense of the reciprocal relation of religious and cultural expressions of the fundamental revelation of meaningfulness and ultimate concern.[42]

3.1.3 A more compelling appropriation of Tillich's theology

Kelton Cobb, author of *The Blackwell Guide to Theology and Popular Culture*, has spent a large proportion of his career studying Tillich, and as a result he is

---

[42] Russel Re Manning, 'Tillich's Theology of Art', in idem, ed., *The Cambridge Companion to Paul Tillich* (Cambridge: Cambridge University Press, 2009), pp. 152–72, especially 156.

more successful in his application of Tillich's thought to popular culture.[43] Importantly, he identifies and distinguishes between the two uses of 'religion' in Tillich's thought, which he designates religion1 and religion2; and he also addresses the issue of Tillich's negative attitude to contemporary culture. In Cobb's work, appropriation of Tillich is not limited to a reductive utilization of correlation but instead focuses on Tillich's understanding of the relation of religious substance to cultural forms, and on certain Tillichian concepts as effective tools for the probing of culture to find this substance.

Cobb begins by explaining why he believes popular culture is important:

> The media world is the shelter where the vast majority of those of us who live in the West dwell and from which we draw the material out of which we make sense of our lives. It is under the canopy of the media that we imbibe, speculate about and negotiate the meaning of love, friendship, beauty, happiness, truth, hope, pain, grace, luck, work, sacrifice, and death. The mediated world of electronic images, sounds and printed words provides us with our most broadly shared symbols, icons, myths and rituals—the signs with which we enlighten ourselves, search for consolation, and establish our bearings.[44]

And, precisely because he believes it is important, he writes:

> I am convinced that it is worthwhile to resume Paul Tillich's efforts to interpret cultural artefacts for the religious substance that rumbles in their deeper regions. As he proposed and argued repeatedly, beginning with his groundbreaking 1919 essay, 'On the Idea of a Theology of Culture': while religions depend upon the cultures in which they find themselves for their forms of expression, cultures draw the meaning that they hold for those that inhabit them from an underlying substrate of religious faith. Without this there is little passion for the culture's achievements and aspirations.[45]

There are two prongs to Cobb's method of engagement. First, he draws on cultural studies: 'a discipline for investigating popular culture already exists, and hoping to stand on its shoulders in the investigation that is undertaken in this book, I turn first to examine the field of cultural studies in its various paths'.[46] The second prong of his analysis is theological and this is funded, in Chapters 3 and 4, by engagement with Paul Tillich. While I will briefly

---

[43] Kelton Cobb, *The Blackwell Guide to Theology and Popular Culture* (Oxford: Blackwell, 2005); Cobb's PhD thesis addressed the theology of culture of Troeltsch, Tillich, and Ricoeur, and he has published other articles on Tillich, for example, 'Reconsidering the Status of Popular Culture in Tillich's Theology of Culture', *Journal of the American Academy of Religion*, LXIII/1 (1995), pp. 53–84.
[44] Cobb, *Theology*, p. 72.
[45] Ibid., p. 5.
[46] Ibid., p. 25.

consider his general reading of Tillich, I am most interested in the section that considers Tillich in light of his relation to the Frankfurt School.[47]

Cobb places his analysis of Tillich's theology of culture within a wider framework that identifies two possible approaches to culture. The first approach is negative and focuses on 'popular culture's defects'. It finds expression in a line of tradition that descends from Tertullian's *De Spectaculis*. The second approach is more positive, and addresses 'popular culture's religious vitality'. It is exemplified in Augustine's *City of God*.[48] Tillich is placed in a line of descent that comes down from Augustine, through Luther, onto Schleiermacher with his 'feeling of absolute dependence', and (even) Calvin with his understanding of common grace:

> The fundamental insight which each of these thinkers has handed on is that even the most common productions of human creativity can be interpreted theologically as indicating the presence and activity of God in the midst of human existence.[49]

Turning to Tillich's theology of culture, specifically the 1919 lecture 'On a Theology of Culture', and the experience of 'revelation' through the Botticelli painting that preceded it by just a few months, Cobb makes the helpful distinction (insufficiently considered by the theologians considered above) between religion1 and religion2. Religion1 is religion as the substance and depth of all culture, while religion2 is religion as institution, sets of beliefs and cultic worship.

In Tillich's early writings on this subject he appears positive: through careful analysis of the various spheres of culture—art, science, ethics, politics—he expressed the hope that theonomous revelation might occur. However, Cobb notes that a change occurred after Tillich's forced emigration to the US and, especially, after the second terrible war of the century. By 1946, Tillich was describing his earlier theology of culture as 'too romantic'.[50] He came to see secular culture as 'the place where the doubts and anxieties of human existence rise to the surface [he investigated culture] for its more revealing expressions of its own deepest absences, its raw ends seeking reconnection with some kind of meaning-giving substance'.[51]

While Cobb believes that this post-war pessimism did thaw slightly over the years, he nonetheless argues that:

---

[47] Ibid., pp. 97–100.
[48] Ibid., pp. 75–80 and 80–6.
[49] Ibid., p. 90.
[50] Quoted by Cobb, *Theology*, p. 95, with quotation taken from Tillich, 'Religion and Secular Culture' (1946) in *The Protestant Era*.
[51] Cobb, *Theology*, p. 94.

Although Tillich remained more attentive to culture than most theologians—and this continues to be his legacy—over time his expectations contracted regarding culture's power to express its own meaning-giving depths. He moved from expecting these depths to arise like artesian waters through the aquifer of cultural forms, to expecting, at best, a lucid expression of the dryness of the human spirit—and thereby its demand for waters of meaning from outside of itself— by the most gifted and honest artists, thinkers, and community leaders.[52]

The chronology itself hints at one important insight into the understanding of Tillich's rejection of popular culture: its use as a manipulative tool of propaganda in the hands of the Nazis. Cobb quotes Tillich, writing in 1945 in 'The World Situation': 'it must be recognised that standardized communication through radio, movies, press, and fashions tends to create standardized men who are all too susceptible to propaganda for old or new totalitarian purposes'.[53]

Cobb draws attention to the often unremarked links between Tillich and the famous Frankfurt School of cultural studies. First, Tillich was himself a professor in Frankfurt, where he supervised Theodor Adorno and was influential in the appointment of Horkheimer. Second, both Tillich and the Frankfurt philosophers, 'sharing the honour of being among the first academics expelled by the Nazis', all relocated in the early 1930s to New York City, where they worked across the street from one another: Tillich at Union Seminary and the others at Columbia University.

It is, therefore, helpful to look at Cobb's summary of the position of the Frankfurt School.[54] Their work was generated by their struggle with a very particular question: why did the proletariat masses not revolt if society was as inherently unstable as Marx had suggested? Their answer, that the masses were quiescent because they imbibed the false-consciousness of the ruling ideology through the ruling class's control of the 'culture industry', led them to a number of conclusions: that popular culture, *Kitsch*, was inherently conservative; that only radical avant-garde art had the resources and the power to revolutionize the consciousness of the masses; and that mass culture was inherently bad, driven as it was by the big business of the ruling class, while folk culture was good because it arose from below, from the masses themselves. Cobb writes:

> Understanding Tillich's relationship with the Frankfurt theorists provides an important key to his writings on culture [...] They had all worked out their thinking on these matters in conversation with each other, and reached many of the same conclusions. Taken together, these elements of critical theory help to explain Tillich's dismissal of popular culture as material that deserves to be taken

---

[52] Ibid., p. 95.   [53] Ibid., p. 98.   [54] Ibid., p. 45–52.

seriously for its religious content. His aversion toward popular culture was one constant in Tillich's theology of culture in both its early and later phases.[55]

Thus Cobb can draw certain conclusions that are of great import and relevance to the intention of this monograph, which is to apply Tillich's theory of revelation through culture to the medium of film. First, it must be recognized that all those who study religion and culture in the present climate are, whether they acknowledge it or not, indebted to Tillich; second, his aversion to popular culture doesn't mean that his method cannot be applied to it; in fact, 'it might be necessary to transcend Tillich's *prejudice* against popular culture by applying Tillich's own *method*'.[56]

Cobb's argument, along with the more general observation that theologians, and scholars in many other disciplines, are increasingly valuing academic engagement with popular culture, suggests that Tillich's aversion to popular culture was primarily a question of historical context. Tillich was embedded in a German milieu that glorified high culture as an essential part of an education that maintained the appropriate harmony between Enlightenment rationalism and passionate romanticism. More specifically, Tillich was closely connected to the Frankfurt School with its pessimistic view of mass culture. Popular culture was clearly not to Tillich's taste. However, in principle at least, there is no reason to suppose that its products lie outside the circle of things susceptible to his theoretical account of the relation between culture and religion, or of the revelatory potential of culture. Indeed, there are grounds for arguing that Tillich's contention (discussed in the last chapter in relation to his work *The Religious Situation*) that the theologian of culture must consider all spheres of culture—science, economics, politics, arts, and religion—in his analysis in some ways prefigures contemporary interest in everyday life. Nonetheless, this still leaves a second, but closely related, problem: is it appropriate to apply theories that Tillich developed in relation to the medium of painting to the medium of film?

3.2 PAUL TILLICH: THEOLOGIAN OF FILM?

It was noted in the previous chapter that Tillich's theology has been central to programmatic essays in the most important volumes of the last forty years of religion–film writing. Here I will consider these writings, noting the way the earliest essays are essentially positive and utilise Tillich's theology *in se*, while later appropriation tends to be more critical, adapting his methods prior to their utilisation in much the same way as the theologians considered in the last

---

[55] Ibid., p. 97.   [56] Ibid., pp. 98–100, especially 99.

section. It is of particular interest that the early essays' reliance on Tillich allows them to argue for something broadly analogous to revelation through film, conceived, for example, by Carl Skrade in terms of 'symbols of renewal' that arise from the depths, and by Michael Bird in terms of 'hierophany'.

3.2.1 Use of Tillich's theology in writing on film

Carl Skrade was a professor of religion at Capital University, Columbus, Ohio, when he wrote 'Theology and Films', and his concern for improved communication between church and society in general, and between the teacher of religion and his students in particular, pervades this essay.[57] It is to a Tillichian account of the role of art in mediating between a culture's self-understanding and religion that Skrade turns; 'the theologian is rewarded by looking into the arts, for there he can read the fundamental man-questions, obviously one of the basic poles of all meaningful theological talk'.[58]

Skrade looks first at the genres of war films and westerns, suggesting that at their best these examples of films 'ask us anew those questions which can be seriously asked only out of an awareness of the dimension of depth'.[59] Skrade then considers Michelangelo Antonioni's *Red Desert* (1964), which portrays a wife's social isolation and psychological alienation, against a visual backdrop of industrial pollution and decay. He says of this film: 'I cannot conceive of a more powerful, gripping, unrelenting illustration and experience of Tillich's analysis of the sources and reality of contemporary man's dilemma than Antonioni's *The Red Desert*.'[60] 'Like Psalm 90 and the Book of Job, like Paul Tillich, Antonioni says of man that "his place does not know him anymore". There is no home and no healing, no salvation.'[61]

However, Skrade's argument does not end once he has given examples of films that can ask the existentially important questions and highlight the emptiness of much of contemporary culture. Instead, he asks whether films can do more than 'accentuate and articulate the negative. Of what positive value are films in the face of the awesome questions?'[62] Drawing yet more heavily on Tillich's thought and vocabulary, he goes on to argue for an affirmative answer to his own question. Skrade believes that contemporary film can break through the surface to the dimension of depth and offer the world symbols of renewal. Films can go beyond 'serious and honest examination of the sacred void'; 'they can help us to break down the walls between the sacred and the secular, can help us realise once again that "the whole world is God's monastery"'.[63]

---

[57] See, for example, Skrade, 'Theology', pp. 1, 3, 16–17, and 22.
[58] Ibid., p. 2.   [59] Ibid., pp. 10–13.
[60] Ibid., p. 8.   [61] Ibid., p. 9.   [62] Ibid., p. 14.   [63] Ibid., p. 15.

Skrade underwrites this contention by reference to Tillich's theory of symbols, which was discussed in the last chapter:

> Is it true that our age is without its own symbols of renewal with their message of healing? In fact, may it not be that such symbols are to be found within some of our contemporary films? I believe that some of our contemporary films do contain such affirmations in the midst of the emptiness of our times.[64]

The two films that Skrade cites in this context are *Blow-Up* (1966), another Antonioni film, this time about a society photographer in fashionable 1960s London; and Stuart Rosenberg's *Cool Hand Luke* (1967), about an irrepressible prisoner in a US penitentiary. *Blow-Up* offers a 'spare symbol of renewal set amidst the mountain of decay' while Luke is himself 'a filmic symbol of renewal'. Luke offers 'a source of new being' that contrasts with the pathetic caricature of the human that is the prison governor or the 'powerful filmic image of non-being' that is the sunglass-wearing guard the prisoners have named 'No-eyes'.[65] 'Luke is the one who has brought home the meaninglessness and made possible a meaning; he is the filmic Christ-figure par excellence.'[66]

At the conclusion of the essay, Skrade writes:

> I believe that there is evidence that the filmic media not only can talk meaningfully about modern man's predicament but also can break through the surface of our illusions and disillusions and can, via the grammar peculiar to the film, force a new consideration of the possibilities of renewal. Certainly, consciously or unconsciously, contemporary film-makers force their audiences not only to examine the structures of destruction and peer into the depths of the human predicament, but they also offer filmic forms of symbols of renewal. Perhaps these artists can minister to us all by breaking through into the realm out of which symbols are born.[67]

The second essay under consideration is Michael Bird's 'Film as Hierophany'. Bird begins with Mircea Eliade's concept of hierophany as 'the *act of manifestation* of the sacred [...] precisely through the material of reality'.[68] He proceeds to consider at some length the particular nature of film's relation to reality that makes it capable of being 'the locus of a hierophanous manifestation'.[69] To develop this line of argument Bird engages with the phenomenologist philosopher Mikel Dufrenne, realist film theorists André Bazin and Siegfried Kracauer, and illustrates his argument with reference to Robert Bresson's *Diary of a Country Priest*. To give his account its theological character he relies upon Paul Tillich.

---

[64] Ibid., p. 17.   [65] Ibid., p. 20.   [66] Ibid., p. 21.   [67] Ibid., p. 21.
[68] Bird, 'Hierophany', p. 3.   [69] Ibid., p. 3.

In a familiar trope, Bird gives short shrift to explicitly religious subject matter, 'the tangible manifestation of a particular religious cultus'.[70] However:

> If art cannot give a direct representation of the dimension of the holy, it can nonetheless perform an alternative religious function: art can disclose those spaces and those moments in culture where the experience of finitude and the encounter with the transcendent dimension are felt and expressed within culture itself.[71]

Bird suggests it is Tillich who gives the best analysis of the way in which culture can point to the transcendent; in particular, he picks up on Tillich's term 'belief-ful realism', used in *The Religious Situation* and in *The Protestant Era*. This concept allows for a combination of the finite and the transcendent that mirrors Eliade's understanding of the relation of the sacred to the profane in his discussion of hierophany. As a theology 'from below', it rejects both idealism and supernaturalism which, in their different ways, both overwhelm the natural and material reality. '"Belief-ful realism" represents, then, a religion-and-culture typology which is at once "realistic" and "self-transcending," which in its seeking of the Unconditioned focuses upon the concretely finite, which perceives culture both as surface and as transparent to its religious depth.'[72]

In a section called 'From Art-and-Reality to Film-and-Reality', Bird moves to the realist film theorists. Formalist theorists based film's claim to be 'art' on its transformation of its source material, but the realists located film's worth precisely in its closeness to reality. 'For Bazin, as well as for Kracauer, the unique opportunity available to film is the proper disclosure of reality, not its reinterpretation.'[73]

> If film is understood to possess a continuity with the world it represents, then in order for cinema to have a means by which it can open us to the dimension of the sacred, this means would have to be directed to the discernment of the *holy within the real*, rather than leading away from the real as in the case of art that abolishes reality.[74]

Bird turns to the films of Robert Bresson, particularly *Diary of a Country Priest*, to illustrate how this might work in practice. This film combines great simplicity of cinematic style with exceptional emphasis on material physicality; and, paradoxically, it is precisely this realism that 'seems to produce [...] transcendence [...] a translucence to another world underlying surface appearances'.[75] In these sections much is made of the way in which reality, when subjected to this intensity of gaze, becomes transparent to a depth

---

[70] Ibid., p. 4. [71] Ibid., p. 4. [72] Ibid., pp. 6–7.
[73] Ibid., p. 12. [74] Ibid., p. 13. [75] Ibid., p. 19.

beneath the surface: 'a "depth of being" is encountered by the long, steady stare at reality'.[76]

Although Bird does not explicitly reference Tillich at this point, this is very similar to Tillich's understanding of the way symbols function: the finite material of which they are formed becomes transparent to the infinite depth of the reality they symbolize. In fact, earlier in the essay, in his discussion of belief-ful realism, Bird has quoted Tillich as saying, 'The power of a thing is, at the same time, affirmed and negated when it becomes transparent for the ground of its power, the ultimately real.'[77] Bird concludes his essay:

> In its intensification of those movements and spaces where reality is seen to be straining in its anguish, its void, its divisions, toward its boundary-situation, at which the dimension of depth breaks in, cinema becomes at least the witness for and frequently the agent of 'the manifestation of something of a wholly different order, a reality that does not belong to our world.' [Eliade] At such points film becomes hierophany.[78]

The appropriation of Tillich's theology in this monograph bears a close resemblance to the positive utilization of Tillich's thought in these two early religion–film essays. In particular they have highlighted important concepts such as the need for film art to have the potential to break through from surface to depth if it is to be revelatory, and the relation of this potential to realism. These concepts will be discussed in what remains of this chapter. However, in the more recent past there has been a notable change of approach with regard to utilization of Tillich's theology.

Paul Tillich is the most referenced theologian in the important British volume *Explorations in Theology and Film* that Clive Marsh co-edited with Gaye Ortiz in 1997. David John Graham is interested in the experiential impact of film, 'experiencing the religious through media [...] the sacred through the secular'.[79] 'Culture, media and technology can all be potent sources which provoke religious experience and theological reflection. In the words of Paul Tillich: "everything that expresses ultimate reality expresses God whether it intends to do so or not".'[80] Stephen Brown, writing on 'Feelgood Movies: The Capra Connection', draws upon Tillich's concepts of ultimate concern, New Being, Spiritual Presence, and Spiritual Community, to re-describe the journeys of Capra-characters like George Bailey.[81]

---

[76] Ibid., p. 21 (see also p. 14 for more on this transparency).
[77] Paul Tillich, quoted in Bird, 'Hierophany', p. 6.
[78] Bird, 'Hierophany', pp. 21-2.
[79] David John Graham, 'Uses of Film in Theology', in Clive Marsh and Gaye Ortiz, eds, *Explorations in Theology and Film: Movies and Meaning* (Oxford: Blackwell, 1997), pp. 35-43, especially 36.
[80] Graham, 'Uses', p. 37.
[81] Stephen Brown, 'Optimism, Hope and Feelgood Movies: The Capra Connection', in Clive Marsh and Gaye Ortiz, eds, *Explorations in Theology and Film: Movies and Meaning* (Oxford: Blackwell, 1997), pp. 219-32, especially 228-9.

However, while Tillich continues to be the theologian of choice when writers wish to construct a theological foundation for their engagement with film, his theory is approached more critically, and used heuristically rather than functionally (as it was in the 1970s and early 1980s). This reflects both the reception history of Tillich's theology and the fact that as time passes there is, inevitably, a greater gap between the cultural situation that Tillich addressed and our own. Clive Marsh quotes John Clayton: 'By incorporating the present cultural situation into his methodology, Tillich gave to his theology a planned obsolescence which precludes his system's having direct relevance for any but the cultural context in which and for which it was constructed.'[82]

Indeed it is Marsh, an editor of *Explorations in Theology and Film*, whose essay is most representative of the way in which Tillich's theology is typically appropriated in contemporary engagements with culture. In fact, it closely mirrors the approach of Lynch and Browning discussed at length in the last section of this chapter. Marsh's purpose is to 'discuss ways in which Christian theology must be understood if it is to make creative use of the medium of film'.[83] For Marsh, theology, at the most basic descriptive level, is 'God talk'. Assuming that 'God' is not, purely, a human construct, and that 'theology cannot comprise merely human conceptualising', different theological positions are ranged around the question of the extent to which theology is 'talk *about* God' or 'talk *from* God'. In contrast, Marsh believes that culture *is* a purely human construct and, as is common, he draws upon Geertzian-sounding language to describe it as 'the whole web of interpretive strategies by which human beings make sense of their experience'.[84]

Marsh believes that Tillich's method of 'correlation' must be refined at a number of key points: first, the system must not be allowed to overwhelm the autonomy of art; second, culture should not be read as uniform and undifferentiated; and third, popular or 'low' culture should not be excluded from the dialogue.[85]

> At its simplest, Tillich's whole theological system [...] can be regarded as a work of Christian apologetics. Tillich sought to 'read' Western culture in order to identify its key concerns, in relation to which he could then present Christian responses appropriate for the present.[86]

The problems inherent in this reading of Tillich have been discussed above. Here it is only necessary to note that the approach of the earlier authors seems to problematize Marsh's assertion. Skrade and Bird explicitly stated that they believed that films could do more than ask the questions. They did not believe that they were breaking with Tillich when they argued that contemporary

---

[82] John Clayton, quoted in Marsh, 'Film', p. 33.
[83] Marsh, 'Film', p. 21. [84] Ibid., p. 24.
[85] Ibid., pp. 31–2. [86] Ibid., p. 30.

films which made no reference to religion, let alone to the particular Christian traditions that might be considered 'responses', could provide symbols of renewal and revelations of transcendence.

3.2.2 From expressionism in painting to realism in film

It is only in engagement with empirically researched accounts of specific experiences of particular films that this monograph will tease out the way in which the possibility of revelation, as theorized by Tillich, can be related to film. However, here the task is to argue for the suitability of Tillich as a theorist of revelation through film. So, it is important at least to sketch the *possibility of the possibility* of revelation through film in a way that accords with his theory. In this sense, what follows should be considered a thought experiment rather than a part of the development of a grounded account of revelation through film, which is the principal task of this monograph. This thought experiment will evolve in relation to 'realist' theorists of film, a move already noted in relation to Bird's essay. However, before making the somewhat unexpected turn to realism, an initially far more promising but ultimately futile path must be considered—that of expressionism in film.

Expressionist cinema: Stranded on the surface Tillich used a number of different typologies of art to aid his analysis but the simplest, and here the most useful, was to distinguish between naturalism, idealism, and expressionism.[87] He defined naturalism as 'based on the direct encounter with naturally given objects' and idealism as 'anticipatory [...] it brings into the open the potential perfection and beauty in persons and things which in existence are indifferent or distorted'.[88] The third, and most important, style is that of expressionism.

In the early stages of Tillich's work, expressionism was identified in a narrow, art-historical sense with a particular German art movement that flourished between 1905 and 1920 and had bases in Dresden (the *Die Brücke* group) and in Munich (the *Blaue Reiter* group).[89] However, later in his career, for example in his essay 'Contemporary Arts and the Revelatory Character of Style', Tillich broadened his typology from reference to specific art movements to a wider sense, whereby expressionism could incorporate 'the style of the primitives, of the Asiatic, the later ancient, the medieval cultures' (*AA*, 132). Thus for Tillich any work of art is expressionist when it breaks through the surface form to the depths of substance beneath. In the case of the German

---

[87] Dillenberger 'Introduction', pp. xxii–xxiii.
[88] *AA*, 131.
[89] Dietmar Elger, *Expressionism: A Revolution in German Art* (Köln, Germany: Taschen, 1994), pp. 7–15.

expressionists, this 'breakthrough' was the result of a deliberate emphasis on distortion and horror, but Tillich recognized that other art movements had their own routes to the depths: denial of the 'block reality of objects' through deliberately perspective-less two-dimensional images, or the move towards greater and greater abstraction (AA, 135–7). What all 'expressionist' movements have in common is a challenge to the idealistic beauty or merely imitative naturalism of the surface; some kind of problematizing of the view of the surface reality that has the potential to allow a glimpse into the depths. In 'Reality and Faith' (originally published in 1929), he writes that:

> Expressionism was a revolution against the realism of the nineteenth century [...] things were interpreted by the expressionist painters in their cosmic setting and their immeasurable depth. Their natural forms were broken so that their spiritual significance could become transparent. Colours expressing divine and demonic ecstasies, broke through the gray of the daily life.[90]

What is of great import is the fact that, on Tillich's account, it is the substance found in the depths rather than the form found on the surface that matters. If the surface form of a work of art is capable of enabling the breaking through the surface to the depths, then it should be considered religious and potentially revelatory regardless of its content or subject matter.

Given Tillich's predilection for German expressionist painting, there is one obvious starting place for this quest for the revelatory potential of film: German expressionist cinema. In the very year and the very city (Berlin, 1919) in which Tillich's first major presentation and publication on the relation between religion and culture ('On the Idea of a Theology of Culture') took place, a film was released that would come to be considered the 'archetype of all [...] postwar [German] films'[91] and, simultaneously, the archetype of all expressionist cinema: *The Cabinet of Dr Caligari*. However, against what might be expected, I will argue here that expressionist cinema, exemplified by *The Cabinet of Dr Caligari*, fails to escape the surface and break through to the religious depths.

To help make this point, I turn to Siegfried Kracauer, a German film critic and theorist whose biography closely mirrors Tillich's. Their lives spanned the same epoch (Kracauer 1889–1966; Tillich 1886–1965). Both came of age in the cataclysmic upheaval of World War I, lived through the tumultuous post-war period in Berlin, were forced to leave Germany under Nazi rule and build new

---

[90] Tillich, *Protestant*, pp. 66–7. Theodor W. Adorno thought it was the move to American that 'de-provincialised' Tillich; quoted in Anton Kaes, 'German Cultural History and the Study of Film: Ten Theses and a Postscript', in *New German Critique*, 65 (1995), pp. 47–58, especially 47.
[91] Kracauer, *Caligari*, p. 3.

careers in a new language in New York in the latter halves of their lives. Both were friends of Theodor Adorno.[92]

Kracauer was commissioned to write a book about German cinema soon after his arrival in the US. *From Caligari to Hitler: A Psychological History of the German Film*, financed by the Museum of Modern Art Film Library and the Rockefeller and Guggenheim Foundations, is the most referenced account of the German cinema of the Weimar period. But, in spite of its fame, it is considered a flawed book: too essentialist in its reading of the German psychological character and too determinist in its tracing of the trajectory from Weimar Republic to Nazism. However, it was also remarkably ahead of its time in its examination of films not as stand-alone artefacts (artistic or industrial) but as innately related to a particular historical, social, and psychological context.[93]

In the first section of the book, Kracauer treats what he calls 'The Archaic Period' of German cinema, 1895–1918. Here he identifies the seeds of the expressionist style in both the films that were produced, like Paul Wegener's *The Student of Prague* of 1913, and in the 'progressive German film theories of the time' which prioritized 'fantastic worlds full of chimerical creatures [. . .] rendering not so much existing objects as products of pure imagination'.[94] *The Student of Prague*, for example, tells the story of the eponymous youth whose life seems cursed by a malevolent antagonist. However, it soon becomes clear to both character and audience that the antagonist is none other than the student's alter ego, a product of his split personality. For Kracauer, this preference for the psychological explanation of the character's problems over a social explanation was, at root, a means of displacement or sublimation for the German middle classes. It reflected 'the profound aversion of all German middle-class strata to relating their mental dilemma to their ambiguous social plight. They shrank from tracing ideas of psychological experiences to economic and social causes after the fashion of the communists.'[95] They chose 'retreat into the depth of the soul' rather than face the 'catastrophic breakthrough of social reality'.[96]

This essentially conservative and reactionary impulse in German cinema of the period only increased as the cinematic apparatus became more closely linked to the organs of the Weimar state through the genesis of a state cinema institution (UFA, or Universum Film AG) whose 'official mission [. . .] was to

---

[92] It appears highly likely that Tillich and Kracauer would have met, but I have not found any textual evidence for such a meeting.

[93] For Kracauer's understanding of his task, see his 'Introduction' in *Caligari* (especially pp. 3–8); and for a helpful summary of the reception history of this work, see Kaes, 'German', pp. 48–50.

[94] Kracauer, *Caligari*, p. 28.

[95] Ibid., pp. 30–1.

[96] Ibid., p. 31.

advertise Germany according to government directives. These asked not only for direct screen propaganda, but also for films characteristic of German culture and films serving the purpose of national education.'[97]

It is with this background in mind, and also the knowledge of the total defeat of German forces in World War I and the subsequent 'revolution' of November 1918 (which Kracauer describes as 'abortive' but still a 'cataclysm'[98]) that we turn to *The Cabinet of Dr Caligari*. The film is an early example of the 'horror' genre. A small town is terrorized by a zombie-like somnambulist who murders at the behest of his master, the evil fairground magician, Dr Caligari. Today, the most remarkable aspect of the film is its *mise en scène*: fantastical painted sets, canted at impossible angles and with impossible dimensions, bearing a very obvious resemblance to expressionist paintings of the era.

The crux of Kracauer's interpretation of the film's role in German society pivots around the contention that the original script, produced by Hans Janowitz and Carl Mayer, was a subversive and revolutionary critique of German authoritarianism. Kracauer believed that the original script ended with the revelation that the demonic Dr Caligari was actually the respected head of a psychiatric hospital; and that with this dramatic and unexpected unmasking, 'reason overpowers unreasonable power, insane authority is symbolically abolished'.[99] The expressionist sets, created by three artists—Hermann Warm, Walter Rohrig, and Walter Reimann who were members of the *Sturm* magazine group of Berlin—were 'animated by the same revolutionary spirit that impelled the two scriptwriters to accuse authority—the kind of authority revered in Germany—of human excesses'.[100]

However, Kracauer, drawing primarily on a manuscript written by Janowitz, believed that the studio powers, in collaboration with director Robert Wiene, subverted the revolutionary and critical nature of the screenplay and *mise en scène* by bracketing the central narrative in a framing storyline that implies that the narrator himself is the madman. The shocking discovery that the evil Dr Caligari is actually the authority figure in charge of a respectable institution is thus reduced to the fiction of a deranged mind. 'In the film *Caligari* the expressionism seems nothing more than the adequate translation of a madman's fantasy into pictorial terms.'[101] The radical edge, which for Tillich made expressionism capable of breaking through from surface to depth, had been domesticated.

While Janowitz's version of events, and therefore Kracauer's, has been undermined by the recent discovery that the earliest scripts also contained a framing device, theorists and commentators nonetheless concur with Kracauer's general diagnosis that in Weimar cinema the radicalism and power of

[97] Ibid., pp. 36, also 45. [98] Ibid., p. 43. [99] Ibid., p. 65.
[100] Ibid., p. 70. [101] Ibid., p. 70.

painted expressionism became merely a tame aesthetic device.[102] The art historian Lotte Eisner writes in her book *The Haunted Screen* that in the cinema the goal of the expressionist artist to delve beneath the surface of 'momentary accidental form [to] the *eternal, permanent meaning*' (original emphasis), and to make the world 'permeable' so that 'Mind, Spirit, Vision and Ghosts seem to gush forth', has been devalued by recourse to bland romantic sentiment.[103] Early film theorist Bela Balazs in his *Theory of the Film* recognizes that 'The camera did nothing but photograph [. . .] *The Cabinet of Dr Caligari* was a film-painting, the picture of a picture, not primary but secondhand.'[104] Jean Mitry, writing on cinema in *The Concise Encyclopedia of Expressionism*, is more positive about expressionism in cinema, but recognizes that it does frequently degenerate into mere 'Caligarism'.[105] Kracauer himself believed that expressionism of this sort was powerless, stating: 'Owing to their stereotyped character, these settings and gestures were like some familiar street sign—"Men at Work", for instance. Only here the lettering was different. The sign read: "Soul at Work".'[106]

It appears then that these expressionist films were unable, for historico-contextual, psychological, and aesthetic reasons, to perform the function of 'breakthrough' from surface to depth that Tillich associated with the related expressionist art form of painting. Socially, they were tied to a state-serving cinematic apparatus that was always likely to undermine radical or revolutionary impact. Psychologically, the turn to the interior world was a useful tool for displacement and sublimation of anxiety rather than for revelation of the religious depth, the abyss of being and meaning. Aesthetically, cinematic expressionism seemed to ignore the peculiar nature of the film medium, resorting instead to second-hand pictorial effects borrowed from painting. Tillich would appear to have been justified in ignoring the religious and revelatory potential of these films, but the question remains, is film ever capable of breaking through the surface form to the religious substance of the depths? If so, what might it be that gives film this potential?

Jean Mitry and Siegfried Kracauer both make suggestive comments on the importance of film's relation to 'reality'. Kracauer notes the German studios'

---

[102] See Leonardo Quaresima, 'Introduction to the 2004 Edition: Rereading Kracauer', tr. Michael F. Moore, in Siegfried Kracauer, *From Caligari to Hitler: A Psychological History of the German Film*, revised and expanded edn (Oxford: Princeton University Press, 2004), pp. xv–xlix, especially xliii–xlvii.

[103] Lotte H. Eisner, *The Haunted Screen: Expressionism in the German Cinema and the Influence of Max Reinhardt*, tr. Roger Greaves (Oxford: University of California Press, 1973), pp. 11–17.

[104] Bela Balazs, *Theory of the Film: Character and Growth of a New Art* (London: Dennis Dobson, 1952), pp. 104–6, especially 106.

[105] Jean Mitry, 'Cinema', in Lionel Richard, ed., *The Concise Encyclopedia of Expressionism* (Seacaucus, NJ: Chartwell, 1978), pp. 213–42, especially 217–18.

[106] Kracauer, *Caligari*, p. 71.

and directors' preference for 'the command of an artificial universe to dependence on a haphazard outer world'.[107] He writes:

> Since reality is essentially incalculable and therefore demands to be observed rather than commanded, realism on the screen and total organization exclude each other. Through their 'studio constructivism' [...] the German films revealed that they dealt with unreal events displayed in a sphere basically controllable.[108]

Mitry proceeds to argue that if expressionism is to retain its power in the film medium, it must turn from simply attempting to copy painting and pay attention to film's own particular properties. For Mitry, (silent) film cannot move towards abstraction in the way that painting can because its symbols are far more tightly linked to objects in the 'real' world. This means that while expressionist painting is able to pierce the surface reality through the introduction of abstraction, film must make the same move by different means:

> The expressionism of dynamic images was no longer the refusal, the negation of literature or pictorial expressionism, but the attempt to reach, thanks to a contrary step, an identical result—or purpose: to express that which cannot be expressed, to suggest what lies beyond the world and things—the beyond was in fact an *infra*.[109]

The idea, already introduced in the discussion of Bird's work, that it is the special relation of film to reality that creates the possibility for revelation in this particular medium will now be developed.

Realist cinema: A luminous impression of the surface Film-making and film theory have been divided between the formalists (which would include the makers of expressionist films) who hold that film's artistic potential lies in the language that is born of its technical *manipulation* of the image, and the realists, who hold that the essence of film's art lies precisely in its intimate relation to and exceptional representation of 'reality'. Thus those writing on the earliest days of the film medium tend to characterize Auguste Lumière as a realist film-maker who depicted everyday life; and Georges Méliès as a formalist whose signature method was to use technical 'tricks' to present impossible and fantastical storylines. Over the years the usefulness of this typology has been contested and the account has become far more nuanced; nevertheless, its persistence suggests that it helpfully highlights an interesting dichotomy in our understanding of the nature and potential of film.[110] Having deemed formalism, represented by expressionism, unsuited to the revelatory breakthrough, I will now proceed to consider the other option: realism.

---

[107] Ibid., p. 74. [108] Ibid., p. 76.
[109] Mitry, 'Cinema', p. 220. [110] Stam, *Theory*, p. 75.

André Bazin, often considered the father of the French New Wave, argued that ignorance of the importance of 'reality' or the 'real world' to cinema made the failure of German expressionism inevitable.[111] It is Bazin who offers perhaps the most celebrated account in film history of cinematic realism. He begins with the close relation that links cinema to photography; both are dependent on the image created when light passes through a lens and triggers a chemical reaction on a strip of celluloid. Commenting on the relation between the photographic image and the reality it depicts, he offers this remarkable metaphor: 'The photograph proceeds by means of the lens to the taking of a veritable luminous impression in light—to a mould.'[112]

Nonetheless, Bazin is convinced that the cinema did not come about primarily as a result of technological advances. In an essay entitled 'The Myth of Total Cinema' he outlines a view of the genesis of cinema that emphasizes the chronological and theoretical priority of the imaginative concept (the primordial myth) over the technological apparatus capable of realizing it. He writes:

> The cinema is an idealistic phenomenon. The concept men had of it existed so to speak fully armed in their minds, as if in some platonic heaven, and what strikes us most of all is the obstinate resistance of matter to ideas rather than of any help offered by techniques to the imagination of the researchers.[113]

The goal, the 'guiding myth', has always been total realism: 'the reconstruction of a perfect illusion of the outside world in sound, colour and relief'.[114] In 'The Evolution of the Language of the Cinema', Bazin re-states the basic formalist–realist dichotomy between 'those directors who put their faith in the image (formalists) and those who put their faith in reality (realists)'.[115] In an example of his favoured rhetorical style, he proceeds to offer an excellent account of formalism, recognizing the importance and power of the image constructed through the utilization of shot and montage, before deconstructing this point of view, arguing instead for a cinematographic art where 'the image is evaluated not according to what it adds to reality but to what it reveals of it'.[116] The directors Orson Welles (*Citizen Kane*, 1941) and Jean Renoir (especially *The Grand Illusion, The Human Beast, The Rules of the Game*, 1937–9) are the pioneers who 'uncovered the secret of a film form that would permit everything to be said without chopping the world up into little fragments, that would reveal the hidden meaning in people and things without disturbing the unity natural to them'.[117]

---

[111] Bazin, *Cinema I*, p. 108.   [112] Ibid., p. 96.
[113] Ibid., p. 17.   [114] Ibid., pp. 20 and 21.
[115] Ibid., p. 24.   [116] Ibid., pp. 24–6 and 28.
[117] Ibid., p. 38.

Bazin considered the greatest exponents of cinematic realism to be the Italian neo-realists of the post World War II period. In *The Oxford Guide to Film Studies* Simona Monticelli introduces the social context and the aesthetics of Italian neo-realism:

> In the immediate post-war years, Neo-Realist films provided an immediate response to the desire to wipe out the material and ideological legacies of fascism. They denounced the horrors of the war and/or dealt with themes central to the agency of Reconstruction such as poverty, unemployment, shortage of housing and social strife [. . .] Location shooting and use of available light resulted in more naturalistic photography, closer to the documentary than the studio-made fiction film. In addition, the contemporary topicality of the subject-matter, the focus on the lower-class milieux, and the casting of unglamorous minor stars, or even unknown non-professional actors, further distinguished the films from both indigenous studio productions and those of Hollywood.[118]

Before proceeding, the development of this thought experiment up to this point will be summarized. First, it has been reiterated that for Tillich all cultural creations, regardless of the surface of subject matter or form, have a depth of religious substance. Therefore, revelation through culture is possible whenever a breakthrough occurs that allows a movement from the cultural surface to the religious depth. While the universality of the form–substance relation means that this potential is inherent in all cultural products, Tillich believed that certain art forms and certain styles within these art forms are more successful at engendering this breakthrough than others. The common characteristic shared by these forms and styles is the potential to disturb or disrupt the surface to facilitate access to the depths. With regard to the painting art form, Tillich believed that the expressionist style is the most suited to the revelatory breakthrough. Cinematic expressionism therefore seemed an obvious place to begin to look for this revelatory capacity in film. However, after studying the archetypal expressionist film, *The Cabinet of Dr Caligari*, it was concluded that for social, psychological, and aesthetic reasons this style of film-making was not particularly suited for producing the breakthrough from surface to depth. Having discounted formalist expressionism, the turn was made towards realism and the Italian neo-realist movement.

The purpose of this thought experiment is to sketch a way in which film might be capable of mediating the kind of revelatory event that Tillich's theory describes. This final section will continue to draw upon the writings of two of the great realist theorists of film, André Bazin and Siegfried Kracauer, in order to argue that it is precisely film's close relation to reality that provides it with

---

[118] Simona Monticelli, 'Italian post-war cinema and Neo-Realism', in John Hill and Pamela Church Gibson, eds, *The Oxford Guide to Film Studies* (Oxford: Oxford University Press, 1998), pp. 455–60, especially 455.

From High Culture to Popular Culture and Film 109

the resources needed to break through from the cultural form to the religious depth.

3.2.2.3 From realism to revelation: The rupture of the surface

Tomás Gutiérrez Alea was a Cuban film director who had received a 'drenching in neo-realism' when he attended the 'Centre for Experimental Cinematography' in Rome.[119] In an essay on 'The Viewer's Dialectic', he outlines his understanding of the way in which 'looking *through*' filmic fictions is 'a revealing operation' that uncovers 'deeper, more essential layers of reality' by way of 'a moment of rupture'.[120] To understand the mechanism by which this occurs, it is necessary to consider more closely the difference between film, particularly realist film, and painting. In Bazin's essay 'Painting and Cinema' he describes the difference between the picture frame and the movie screen, arguing that the primary role of the frame is to emphasize the 'discontinuity between the painting and the wall, that is to say between the painting and reality'.[121]

> Just as footlights and scenery in the theatre serve to mark the contrast between it and the real world so, by its surrounding frame, a painting is separated off not only from reality as such but, even more so, from the reality that is represented in it [. . .] The essential role of the frame is, if not to create at least to emphasise the difference between the microcosm of the picture and the macrocosm of the natural world in which the painting has come to take its place.[122]

This means that the framed painting 'offers a space the orientation of which is inwards, a contemplative area opening solely onto the interior of the painting'.[123]

It is mistaken, however, to think of the outer edges of the movie screen as a kind of frame that emphasizes the difference between the intra- and extra-diegetic worlds. Rather, screens 'are the edges of a piece of masking that shows only a portion of reality'. 'The picture frame polarizes space inwards. On the contrary, what the screen shows us seems to be part of something prolonged indefinitely into the universe. A frame is centripetal [i.e. it sucks us into its

---

[119] Stephen M. Hart, *A Companion to Latin American Film* (Woodbridge, Suffolk: Tamesis, 2004), p. 8.
[120] Tomás Gutiérrez Alea, 'The Viewer's Dialectic', in Michael T. Martin, ed., *New Latin American Cinema, Volume I: Theory, Practices and Transcontinental Articulations* (Detroit, MI: Wayne State University Press, 1997), pp. 108–31.
[121] Bazin, *Cinema I*, p. 165.
[122] Ibid., p. 165.
[123] Ibid., p. 166.

world], the screen centrifugal [i.e. it constantly presses us out into a wider universe of reality].'[124]

Jean Mitry also draws attention to the characteristics that separate film from painting. Writing on the differences between expressionist painting and the expressionism of 'dynamic images' (that is, the moving pictures of the cinema), he argues that film cannot successfully move towards abstraction in the way that painting can because its symbols are too closely tied to objects in the 'real' world. If it wishes to achieve an 'identical result', that is 'to express that which cannot be expressed, to suggest what lies beyond the world and things', then it must do this 'thanks to a contrary step'.[125]

Placing Bazin's observation alongside Mitry's, it becomes clear that expressionist painting, constrained by its frame but with no necessary link or responsibility towards realist representation, can most effectively disrupt the surface and break through to the depth by the distortion or abstraction of its subject matter. Conversely, cinema is limited by its more immediate relation to reality. But because it is unconstrained by a frame, it remains, in some sense, continuous with the world it portrays. It is this continuity with the *wider* world that makes possible its own unique mechanism for breakthrough.

Turning now to Kracauer, whose most explicitly theoretical work is *Theory of Film: The Redemption of Physical Reality*, it is notable that he also emphasizes this continuity. He suggests that both (still) photographic and moving cinema media 'probe an inexhaustible universe whose entirety forever eludes them [...] It is therefore inevitable that they should be surrounded with a fringe of indistinct multiple meanings.'[126]

Kracauer contrasts the 'recording functions' of film, which relate to the surface and to the representational aspects of the image produced, with 'revealing functions', which allow 'things normally unseen', 'phenomena overwhelming consciousness', and 'special modes of reality' to be 'discovered'. These revealing functions rely on the 'Inherent Affinities' of the cinematic medium, which are: 'endlessness'; 'the indeterminate'; and 'the flow of life'.[127] Thus, the realism of film, establishing its close relationship to the endless universe of reality, necessarily produces indeterminacies, multiple meanings, ambivalence, and heterogeneity.

In her introduction to a recent paperback edition of Kracauer's book, Miriam Bratu Hansen offers a precis of the German scholar's position:

Films may *try* to direct our attention more forcefully than a play or a novel, but they may also afford us an opportunity to meander across the screen and away from it, into the labyrinths of our own imagination, memories, and dreams. The process takes the viewer into a dimension beyond—or below—the illusory depth of the diegetic space, beyond/below even the 'intersubjective protocols' and

---

[124] Ibid., p. 166. [125] Mitry, 'Cinema', p. 220.
[126] Kracauer, *Theory*, p. 20. [127] Ibid., pp. 41 and 46.

particular kinds of knowledge that govern our understanding of narratives, into the slippery realm of experience.[128]

It is because the neo-realist directors deliberately eschew the attempt to 'direct our attention' that Bazin considers the movement particularly powerful. For example, speaking of Roberto Rossellini's film *Paisa* (1946), a film of six chapters each presenting a short story related to the Allied liberation of Italy during World War II, he contrasts the typical film-maker's approach with Rosselini's:

> The [typical] film maker does not normally show us everything. That is impossible—but the things he selects and the things he leaves out tend to form a logical pattern by way of which the mind passes easily from cause to effect [...] with Rossellini the viewer has to work harder to make the leaps, there is more ambiguity [...] the mind has to leap from one event to another as one leaps from stone to stone in crossing a river. It may happen that one's foot hesitates between two rocks, or that one misses one's footing and slips. The mind does likewise.[129]

Bazin later describes this hesitation, ambiguity, or slippage as producing 'lacunae' in reality.[130] At this point it is finally possible to essay a complete description of the way in which realist film may be as successful as expressionist painting in creating the breakthrough from cultural surface to religious depth.

Film's relation to reality is far more immediate than that of painting because of its debt to the photographic process, which Bazin described as creating a mould in light. Film does not disrupt the surface through deliberate distortion or disruption, as expressionist painting does. Rather, the more perfectly it presents reality, the more closely it resembles Bazin's perfect cinema, the more it becomes continuous with the endless and indeterminate universe of which it presents just a small section. The continuity with a wider world gives film an inherent indeterminacy, ambiguity, and heterogeneity. The viewer's attention is challenged, there is hesitation and indecision, lacunae are produced, the surface is ruptured, and that which is beyond representation may be encountered in the depths.

Although it seems likely that Tillich's preference for expressionism would dispose him towards formalism, it has been noted above that he also expounded the value of belief-ful realism. For example, in a lecture on 'Art and Ultimate Reality' he can say:

> The realistic element in the artistic styles seems far removed from expressing ultimate reality. It seems to hide it more than express it. But there is a way in

---

[128] Miriam Bratu Hansen, 'Introduction', in Siegfried Kracauer, *Theory of Film: The Redemption of Physical Reality* (Chichester, UK: Princeton University Press, 1997), pp. i–xlv, especially xxxiii–iv.
[129] Bazin, *Cinema II*, p. 35.
[130] Ibid., p. 66.

which descriptive realism can mediate the experience of ultimate reality. It opens the eyes to a truth which is lost in the daily-life encounter with reality. We see as something unfamiliar what we believed we knew by meeting it day by day. The inexhaustible richness in the sober, objective, quasi-scientifically observed reality is a manifestation of ultimate reality, although it is lacking in directly numinous character. It is the humility of accepting the given which provides it with religious power. (AA, 147)

At the conclusion of this thought experiment, it only remains to note that both Bazin and Kracauer contemplated the religious possibility of this revelatory potential. In his final chapter, 'Film in Our Time', Kracauer asks the provocative question: 'What is the good of film experience?'[131] He answers:

Film renders visible what we did not, or perhaps even could not, see before its advent [. . .] We literally redeem this world from its dormant state, its state of virtual non-existence, by endeavouring to experience it through the camera [. . .] The cinema seems to come into its own when it clings to the surface of things but it is wrong to contend that this affinity for material data interferes with our spiritual preoccupations [. . .] Perhaps the way to them, if way there is, leads through the experience of surface reality? Perhaps film is a gate rather than a dead end or a mere diversion?[132]

However, Kracauer finishes on an agnostic note: speaking of the films that 'redeem physical reality' he states that they do so because 'they all penetrate ephemeral physical reality and burn through it' but 'their destination is no longer a concern of the present enquiry'.[133]

André Bazin was more religiously committed. The film theorist Robert Stam has written:

According to Bazin, new approaches to editing and mise-en-scène, especially long-take cinematography and depth of field, allowed the filmmaker to respect the spatiotemporal integrity of the pro-filmic world. These advances facilitated a more thoroughgoing mimetic representation, one linked, in Bazin's thinking, to a spiritual notion of 'revelation,' a theory with theological overtones of the presence of the divine in all things. Indeed, Bazin's critical language—real presence, revelation, faith in the image—often reverberates with religiosity. Cinema becomes a sacrament; an altar where a kind of transubstantiation takes place.[134]

The next stage in this monograph is the enactment of the empirical research project that will generate the data, derived from the actual experiences of filmgoers, that will be used to ground Tillich's theology of revelation. This thought experiment has at least demonstrated that it might be in the very realism of cinema's depiction of the world that its own particular revelatory potential lies.

---

[131] Kracauer, *Theory*, p. 285.
[132] These quotations are taken from Kracauer, *Theory*, pp. 300, 285–6, and 287.
[133] Kracauer, *Theory*, p. 311.
[134] Stam, *Theory*, p. 76.

Part III

The Empirical Research

BLOW-UP, DIR. BY MICHELANGELO ANTONIONI (1966)

On 30 July 2007 the Italian director Michelangelo Antonioni died peacefully, aged 94. In the English-speaking world he is best known for the enigmatic film *Blow-Up*, set in 1960s London and trailed in cinemas with the tagline, 'Sometimes reality is the strangest fantasy of all'.[1] Through innovative use of narrative, visual style, and soundtrack, Antonioni probes the complex impact of subjectivity and technology upon human perception of the world.

The film's central character, unnamed but traditionally known as Thomas, is a successful but misogynistic (even misanthropic) fashion and art photographer. One morning, tired of the business of fashion photography and jaded even to its erotic charge, Thomas escapes his studio and eventually wanders with his camera into a quiet London park. He seems rejuvenated by the beauty of the early morning light and becomes fascinated by a couple he chances upon. While remaining out of sight, Thomas shoots a roll of film of the beautiful young woman and the older, but clearly distinguished, gentleman. When the woman notices his presence she is visibly upset, chasing him, pleading with him, and eventually becoming violent in her efforts to recover the images. Thomas, claiming a kind of artistic licence, refuses to hand over the film.

Later, Thomas develops the pictures and obsesses over the question of whether the photographs reveal the presence of a sinister figure lurking in the bushes. As he studies the images more closely, he is confronted by the possibility that one of the final shots shows the distinguished older gentleman lying dead under a tree. The title of the film relates to this sequence as he 'blows up' the images and makes prints at greater and greater levels of magnification. However, he has reached the limits of his undoubtedly impressive skills. In spite of the clarity of the original negatives and the dexterity with

---

[1] Michelangelo Antonioni, *Blow Up—Original Trailer*, available to view at <http://uk.youtube.com/watch?v=-mDpxq689EM> (accessed 25 September 2008).

which Thomas manipulates his technological apparatus, the blow-ups prove inconclusive. A figure with a gun lurking in the bushes could also be foliage moving in the wind. A body lying on the grass could also be a dappling of shadow caused by sunlight passing through leaves. Nonetheless, in a sequence that deliberately brings to mind the storyboarding and editing work of film-makers, we watch as Thomas rearranges the images until they appear to reveal the narrative of a murder. Whether this is a process of discovery or of construction remains unresolved.

There are two further scenes in the park. First, Thomas returns there alone, at night, and seems to discover a body lying under the tree. Ironically, Thomas is without his camera. In the absence of a technological, photographic record, he seeks human corroboration by trying to get his friend Ron to the park to witness the body. But he fails to persuade Ron.

In the last sequence of the film, Thomas returns to the park at first light but the body has gone. Seemingly bewildered and uncertain, he watches a group of counter-culture youth as they embark upon a mimed game of tennis on a municipal court. As Thomas watches, one of the mimes pretends to hit the ball far into the air and out onto the grass. It appears that the film's director, Antonioni, accepts the mimes' version of reality because the camera follows the flight of this imaginary object and the shot comes to rest framing an empty patch of grass just as if it were following a real ball.

For the first time in the film Thomas appears to demonstrate a degree of empathy; he bends to collect the invisible ball and mimes throwing it back onto the court. Suddenly the soundtrack registers the impossible sound of a non-existent object being hit back and forth. Then, as the camera pulls back into the sky to offer a final, god's-eye view, Thomas disappears. Antonioni inverts reality/fantasy.

Colin Gardner, Assistant Professor of Art Theory and Criticism at the University of California, has summarized the usual reading of Antonioni's film:

> Michelangelo Antonioni's *Blow Up* [...] questions the possibility of perceiving 'reality' non-reflectively; active signification, semiotic interpretation and conceptual meaning-production necessarily interject between the perceiving subject and the perceived object. By this reading, the true meaning of the events in the park in *Blow Up* can only be brought to light through the mediating function of Thomas's (David Hemmings) photographs, and their reconstitution in the form of a semiotic narrative. In this way, brute reality must first be textualised (through representations) before it can offer up meaning.[2]

---

[2] Colin Gardner, 'Antonioni's *Blow Up* and the Chiasmus of Memory', <http://artbrain.org/journal2/gardner.html> (accessed 12 September 2008).

In many respects, Antonioni's interests in *Blow-Up* parallel those of contemporary scholars engaged in empirical research of film audiences. Many methodologists probe the interaction between the researcher's subjectivity and the research techniques in much the same way that Antonioni probes the interaction between the photographer's subjectivity and photographic technology. The next chapter will consider the fact that Tillich's theoretical account of the possibility of revelation through film, the respondents' accounts of their film-watching experiences, and even (or especially) my readings of this theory and empirical data are all constructed, already interpretive, accounts of reality.

Seymour Chatman is of the opinion, expressed in his book *Antonioni: Or, the Surface of the World*, that Thomas's problem is hubris. 'It is not too fanciful to see *Blow Up* as an Antonionian version of the Faust legend. Thomas's mastery of technology lures him into a Mephistophelian bargain.'[3] This reading is substantiated by Antonioni's own opinion that the film demands humility in the face of the attempt to capture reality.

> In [*Blow-Up*] I said that I do not know what reality is. Reality escapes us, changes constantly; when we believe we have grasped it the situation is already otherwise [...] The photographer in *Blow Up*, who is not a philosopher, wants to see things more closely. But he discovers that, in enlarging too much, the object itself decomposes and disappears. Thus there is an instant in which reality comes forth, but then immediately thereafter it vanishes.[4]

At the start of an empirical research project, the warning against hubris provided by this film is salutary. No matter how technically proficient the researcher, no matter how well formed the instruments, 'reality' (let alone divinity) is elusive.

---

[3] Seymour Chatman, *Antonioni: Or, the Surface of the World* (London: University of California Press, 1985), p. 142.

[4] Michelangelo Antonioni, quoted in Chatman, *Antonioni*, p. 141.

# 4

Researching Filmgoers' Experiences

This monograph develops a reading of Paul Tillich's theology of revelation and then researches the experiences of filmgoers in order to develop a grounded account of the possibility of revelation through film.

The first section of this chapter surveys the history of research into the relationship that exists between film and viewer in order to identify the research paradigm best suited to the generation of the kind of data required to ground the theoretical account. The qualitative research paradigm will be introduced. Consideration of appropriate methodology will address the relationship between the two components of the hypothesis (the theoretical account and the empirical research) in light of previous attempts to integrate empirical research into theology.

The second section of the chapter will present and discuss key issues in the design and enactment of this research project. Frequent reference to published discussions of qualitative methods and to particular examples of successful and respected research demonstrate how this project attempts to replicate best practice in the field.

Theses and monographs published in the disciplines of sociology or cultural studies frequently seem light on the kind of discussion undertaken in this chapter. I have dedicated a substantial amount of space to this task because my approach is novel with respect to both the religion–film and the systematic theology discourses. In contrast, sociological or cultural studies theses are delivered into an academic context where there is already a large body of common knowledge and procedural precedent. However, even in these disciplines experts warn of the dangers of not taking enough time over methodology, suggesting that when theory and method remain implicit they become a kind of 'cultural capital' accessible only by those already 'within the club', thus limiting the value of the research.[1]

---

[1] Johnson et al., *Practice*, pp. 3, also 17 and 77.

4.1 SELECTING A RESEARCH PARADIGM AND DEVELOPING A METHODOLOGY

4.1.1 A history of the audience in film studies and film theory

In Chapter 1, I drew attention to the way the religion–film discourse frequently ignores the interdependence of film text and film audience, passing over the difference between the professional critic or theorist and the wider audience or particular viewer.[2] Here, a brief account of the history of those studies that have intentionally discriminated between the (detached) observer–writer and the individuals who compose the rest of the audience will proceed through three stages: from empirical research motivated by concern about the effects of film on vulnerable audiences; to the highly technical theory of the constructed 'spectator', sutured into the film-watching experience through the shot-reverse-shot technique; and finally, to recognition of the need for more sensitive empirical, and ideally qualitative as well as quantitative, research.[3] It is important to note that this is not a set of discrete, chronologically differentiated approaches; all persist, albeit in variously mutated and subdivided forms, into the present.

The first approach developed in the 1920s and may be related to the period of moral panic within the religious establishment that was noted in Chapter 1. It was assumed that the audience was passive, particularly when young or working class (i.e. uncultured), and was susceptible to immoral messages transmitted through the medium of film and the wider apparatus of the cinema. Here the writer's detachment from the 'audience' was evidenced by the tone of paternal concern adopted. In America, the Payne Fund supported a series of studies into the 'effects' of cinema upon young audiences, concluding:

> [Film] has unusual power to impart information, to influence specific attitudes toward objects of social value, to affect emotions either in gross or microscopic

---

[2] Patrick Phillips draws attention to the importance of 'cinema practice': the process of socialization into a particular manner of film-watching; 'Spectator, Audience and Response', in Jill Nelmes, ed., *Introduction to Film Studies*, 4th edn (London: Routledge, 2007), pp. 143–71, especially 152.

[3] To construct this narrative I will be drawing on a number of sources: Ina Bertrand and Peter Hughes, *Media Research Methods: Audiences, Institutions, Texts* (Basingstoke: Palgrave Macmillan, 2005), pp. 35–106; Will Brooker and Deborah Jermyn, *The Audience Studies Reader* (London: Routledge, 2003); David Buckingham, ed., 'Introduction' to *Reading Audiences: Young People and the Media* (Manchester: Manchester University Press, 1993), pp. 1–23; Jancovich and Faire, *Place*, pp. 1–29; Phillips, 'Spectator', pp. 143–71; and Roy Stafford, *Audiences: An Introduction* (London: British Film Institute, 2003).

proportions, to affect health in minor degree through sleep disturbance, and to affect profoundly the patterns of conduct of children.[4]

The studies that are typical of this approach were empiricist and positivist and required 'researchers to conduct their work on the assumption that mass culture was inevitably crude and unsubtle, while its consumers were little more than undiscriminating dupes'.[5] This approach dominated through the period of the two World Wars, perhaps strengthened by reflection on the power of propaganda films.

The theoretical basis for the criticism of mass communication that underwrote this approach reached its zenith of complexity and influence in the writings of the Frankfurt School, which has already been discussed in Chapter 3. In *Dialectic of Enlightenment* (1947), Theodor Adorno and Max Horkheimer portrayed their task as 'the discovery of why mankind, instead of entering into a truly human condition, is sinking into a new kind of barbarism'.[6] They blamed the 'candy-floss entertainment [that] simultaneously instructs and stultifies mankind'.[7] In the 'culture industry', enlightenment thought has regressed to ideology which 'expends itself in the idolization of given existence'.[8]

They expand upon this theme in the chapter on 'The Culture Industry: Enlightenment as Mass Deception'. Considering the production and consumption of industrialized society, they see in everything from new housing developments through 'automobiles, bombs, and movies' the subjection of the common person to a de-humanizing ideology. Thus, for example, the telephone which at least allows its user some measure of autonomy is followed by the radio which subjects everyone to the authority of mass-produced and universally broadcast programmes.[9] Within cinema, the move to sound in films has allowed the medium 'intensely and flawlessly [...to] duplicate empirical objects [...] Real life is becoming indistinguishable from the movies.'[10] The de-humanizing powers of the movies are thus inherent in their essential features and the audience cannot resist:

> The stunting of the mass-media consumer's powers of imagination and spontaneity does not have to be traced back to any psychological mechanisms; he must ascribe the loss of those attributes to the objective nature of the products themselves, especially to the most characteristic of them, the sound film.[11]

---

[4] W. W. Charters, *Motion Pictures and Youth*, quoted by Andrew Tudor, 'Sociology and Film', in John Hill and Pamela Church Gibson, eds, *The Oxford Guide to Film Studies* (Oxford: Oxford University Press, 1998), pp. 190–94, especially 190.

[5] Tudor, 'Sociology', p. 191.

[6] Theodor W. Adorno and Max Horkheimer, *Dialectic of Enlightenment* (London: Verso, 1997), p. xi.

[7] Ibid., p. xv.   [8] Ibid., p. xvi.   [9] Ibid., pp. 121–2.

[10] Ibid., p. 126.   [11] Ibid., p. 126.

Over time approaches to the power of cinema evolved and grew in subtlety, often remaining fixed upon the message transmitted by the text but taking a more positive view of the independence of the audience. In particular, recognition of an 'active audience' is associated with 'uses and gratifications' research. Studies rooted in sociological disciplines tended to look to the way audiences used film and the gratifications they received from it, while studies drawing upon psychological resources emphasized the cognitive apparatus that made the experience of making meaning from films possible. While a film might intend the audience to take one interpretive position, audiences were capable of constructing alternative or resistant positions of identification for their own ends.[12]

The second approach, perhaps the most influential of all throughout the period of academic film theory and film studies, is that of spectator theory. Here, the film text, which is parasitic upon the powers at work in the wider social context, produces the subjectivity of the spectator. Cinema, which reflected the dominant ideological positions of the day, sutured the spectator into a particular interpretation of the text. The most celebrated piece of writing in this style is Laura Mulvey's 'Visual Pleasure and Narrative Cinema', published in 1975. She begins:

> This paper intends to use psychoanalysis to discover where and how the fascination of film is reinforced by pre-existing patterns of fascination already at work within the individual subject and the social formations that have moulded him. It takes as starting point the way film reflects, reveals and even plays on the straight, socially established interpretation of sexual difference which controls images, erotic ways of looking and spectacle [...] Psychoanalytic theory is thus appropriate here as a political weapon, demonstrating the way the unconscious of patriarchal society has structured film form.[13]

Drawing on Freudian and, more particularly, Lacanian descriptions of the psyche, Mulvey argues that the conventional narrative film is structured around mechanisms intended to give pleasure to the male viewer. She identifies two structures of looking: first, the scopophilic pleasure derived from looking at another person as an erotic object; second, the narcissistic identification of the viewer with the screen protagonist as the 'more perfect, more complete, more powerful ideal ego'.[14]

Both of these structures are intended for male pleasure. The male screen protagonist drives the narrative and the male viewer identifies with him 'as the active one [...] forwarding the story, making things happen'.[15] The male

---

[12] For a brief overview, see Buckingham, *Audiences*, pp. 8–10; for an extended example of this approach in action, see Runions, *Hysterical*.
[13] Mulvey, 'Pleasure', p. 833.
[14] Ibid., pp. 836–7 and 838.
[15] Ibid., p. 838.

screen protagonist gazes upon the erotic spectacle of the female actress and the male viewer copies his look. 'For instance, the device of the show-girl allows the two looks to be unified technically without any apparent break in the diegesis. A woman performs within the narrative, the gaze of the spectator and that of the male characters in the film are neatly combined without breaking narrative verisimilitude.'[16]

Mulvey's critique of male domination of cinematic production codes and structures, and her contention that these codes must be challenged and dismantled, are important. However, with regard to this book, what is relevant is the way in which this article exemplifies spectator theory's assumption that the viewer is directed into a particular subjectivity by the controlling codes and structures of the film text. In spite of the power of this particular essay, spectator theory is now criticized for being overly deterministic and for conflating the 'inscribed' viewer, constructed by the text, with real viewers. Barbara Creed argues that the theory constructs an ahistorical, monolithic, ideal spectator immune to the influence of class, colour, race, age, or sexual preference and, thus, its readings have a tendency to become totalizing and repetitive.[17] Criticism of spectator-type accounts has been driven not only by the development of rival theories but also by a return to empirical research.

It is this less positivist and more reflexive movement of empirical study that forms the third stage in this narrative of audience research. Richard Morley's work, which focused on the audience of the popular British television programme *Nationwide*, is particularly important. While film theory and film studies emerged out of the humanities, and retained a close relationship to literary theory, television and media studies have their roots in the social sciences. Television studies developed not just 'differently from film studies, but as a criticism of its key trends'.[18]

In *The Nationwide Television Studies*, Morley makes a radical move to a new research trajectory that had been developing for some time, 'albeit in a minor key'.[19] The paradigm shift was towards anthropological and ethnographic methods.[20]

> It seems that media and film studies are still subject to [a] kind of oscillation [. . .] At one moment the field is dominated by a theory (such as 'uses and gratifications' in recent years) which holds the media to have little or no direct 'effect' on its audiences, and at the next moment the pendulum swings towards the dominance of a theory (such as that developed in *Screen* more recently) of the near

---

[16] Ibid., p. 838.
[17] Barbara Creed, 'Film and Psychoanalysis', in John Hill and Pamela Church Gibson, eds, *The Oxford Guide to Film Studies* (Oxford: Oxford University Press, 1998), pp. 77–90, especially 86–7.
[18] Jancovich and Faire, *Place*, p. 5.
[19] Morley and Brunsdon, *Nationwide*, p. 6.
[20] Ibid., p. 10.

total effectivity of the text, in their terms, in the 'positioning of the subject' [spectator theory]. In order to escape from this oscillation we need to develop a theory which gives due weight to both the 'text' and 'audience' halves of the equation.[21]

Spectator theory's mistake then is the 'conflation of the reader of the text with the [theoretically derived] social subject'.[22] Morley believes that his empirical research, using ethnological, qualitative approaches, is the only way to overcome this oscillation.

> Crucially, we are led to pose the relation of text and subject as an empirical question to be investigated, rather than an *a priori* question to be deduced from a theory of the ideal spectator 'inscribed' in the text. It may be [. . .] that analysing a film within a determinate social moment in its relation to its audience 'has nothing to do with the counting of heads' but this is a point of methodological adequacy, not of theoretical principle [. . .] the challenge is the attempt to develop appropriate methods of empirical investigation of that relation.[23]

In recent years, the goal has been to develop methodologies that allow description of the ways in which particular audiences or audience members relate to films. This shift is widely acknowledged but variously denoted: from theoretical deduction to ethnographic investigation (Morley, above); from 'spectatorship to ethnography' (Jancovich and Faire);[24] from theoretical supposition to 'situated audiences' (Buckingham);[25] or from 'speculative constructions' to 'empirical studies' (Brooker and Jermyn).[26] I will refer to this as a move to the qualitative research paradigm.

4.1.2 Introducing qualitative research

Qualitative research has its roots in anthropology (where it is frequently named ethnology) and in the social sciences, particularly in studies like that of William Foote Whyte referenced in the Introduction.[27] It has been particularly influential in the development of cultural studies. The descriptive term *qualitative* defines this research paradigm over and against *quantitative* research. In their *Handbook of Qualitative Research*, Norman Denzin and

---

[21] Ibid., p. 271.
[22] Ibid., p. 283.
[23] Ibid., p. 286.
[24] Jancovich and Faire, *Place*, pp. 6–8.
[25] Buckingham, *Audiences*, pp. 13–16.
[26] Brooker and Jermyn, *Reader*, pp. 127–32.
[27] Arthur J. Vidich and Stanford M. Lyman, 'Qualitative Methods: Their History in Sociology and Anthropology', in Norman K. Denzin and Yvonne S. Lincoln, eds, *Handbook of Qualitative Research*, 2nd edn (London: Sage, 2000), pp. 37–84.

Yvonne Lincoln state: 'Quantitative researchers use mathematical models, statistical tables, and graphs, and usually write about their research in impersonal, third person prose.'[28] Later, they offer an extended definition of qualitative research which highlights the contrasts:

> Qualitative research is a situated activity that locates the observer in the world. It consists of a set of interpretive, material practices that make the world visible. These practices transform the world. They turn the world into a series of representations, including field notes, interview, conversations, photographs, recordings and memos to the self. At this level, qualitative research involves an interpretive, naturalistic approach to the world. This means that qualitative researchers study things in their natural settings, attempting to make sense of, or to interpret, phenomena in terms of the meanings people bring to them.[29]

The emphasis on the situated-ness of the activity requires careful consideration of the context in which the research takes place and within which the researched subjects live and the researched phenomena occur. There will be an extended presentation of the relevant characteristics of the context of this research in Chapter 5. The second part of Denzin and Lincoln's definition highlights the importance of the variety of research methods employed in qualitative research.

> Qualitative research involves the studied use and collection of a variety of empirical materials—case study; personal experience; introspection; life story; interview; artefacts; cultural texts and productions; observational, historical, interactional, and visual texts—that describe routine and problematic moments and meanings in individuals' lives.[30]

Two of the key strengths of this research paradigm, which are relevant to this project, may be introduced through brief consideration of two successful and widely referenced studies.

Mark Jancovich and Lucy Faire have conducted a study that considers the way in which film consumption has changed over time in a given geographic area—Nottingham, UK. In line with what has been reported above, they believe that previous scholars tended to 'elide any concern with actual audiences [. . .] they are not concerned with socially situated viewers but with an abstract and hypothetical construct—the audience—which is considered to have a single and unitary response to a text'.[31]

The strength of Jancovich and Faire's approach is their recognition that it is not merely the film text that is responsible for the impact of the viewing

---

[28] Norman K. Denzin and Yvonne S. Lincoln, eds, *Handbook of Qualitative Research*, 2nd edn (London: Sage, 2000), p. 10.
[29] Ibid., p. 3.
[30] Ibid., p. 3.
[31] Jancovich and Faire, *Place*, p. 6.

experience, but also the physical and social location. Therefore, they widen the scope of their study by considering the broader category of film consumption. This requires study of the social context, the mechanism and apparatus that underlies the exhibition of films, and the literal, geographical situation of the cinemas and the audience.[32]

To achieve their aim they draw upon a wide variety of data sources. Textually they make reference to films, contemporary reviews, and other published and archive data. They also construct and enact their own empirical study. After making contact with local consumers of film through the local press and street interviews, they use questionnaires, semi-structured interviews, and focus groups to incorporate the life-experiences of audience members into their account. They comment: 'While most forms of analysis can only deduce the reception of films, the strength of ethnographic research is that it can test this deduction.'[33] With respect to this book, their key finding is the extent to which both the social context and the cinematic context (in their words, the 'space, place and city') impact upon the film-watching experience.[34]

Annette Hill is the author of *Shocking Entertainment: Viewer Response to Violent Movies*. She began the study because she believed that the enjoyment she derived from watching violent films had not been sufficiently well represented or explained, neither in the academy nor in the, frequently sensationalizing, news media. She surmised, and later demonstrated, that even those studies that attempted to engage with actual viewers derived their assumptions from discredited effects-style research.

In her own work, Hill initially employed the text-based approaches typical of most film studies and film theory, but found this methodology unsatisfactory. Eventually she moved to empirical research in the hope of developing a more nuanced understanding that took account of actual viewers' reasons for watching violent films. She built up her sample of respondents through snowballing, street interviews, and telephone surveys, and then she used focus group discussions and in-depth interviews to generate her primary data.[35]

This focus on empirical research of actual viewers resulted in her developing an account of the viewing experience that pointed to the importance of what she called 'portfolios of interpretation'. She drew the metaphor from the portfolios that art students carry around, which contain a range of previous work, sketches, and images of famous art. She used this metaphor because it allowed her to draw attention to the fact that some portfolio contents were

---

[32] Ibid., pp. 6–26.
[33] Ibid., p. 6.
[34] Ibid., p. 16.
[35] 'Snowballing' is a term commonly used in empirical research, meaning that an initial contact provides the researcher with further contacts among their friends and acquaintances, thus producing an exponential growth in potential participants. For a brief definition, see Mason, *Researching*, p. 103; also Hammersley and Atkinson, *Principles*, p. 135.

common to all, while others were highly personal and carried by just one individual. These contents, widely held or deeply personal, correspond to 'what moviegoers bring to the viewing environment [...] waiting to be activated'.[36] The research carried out in this monograph corroborates Hill's account of the importance of such 'portfolios'.

All of the research methods utilized in these two studies (with the exception of focus groups) will play a part in the empirical research project undertaken in this monograph. The sensitivity that Jancovich and Faire showed to the social context in which viewing experiences take place will be reflected in my project through attention to history and social structures. These are investigated through reference to published texts, archive research, and engagement with human sources. Extended interviews with particular filmgoers will allow for the development of an understanding of the particular portfolio of interpretation that each individual brings to the viewing experience.

4.1.3 Articulating the hypothesis: A methodology of priority without privilege

At this stage it is essential to reflect carefully upon the nature of the relationship between the two major bodies of research data in this project: that derived from the theoretical, theological account, and that which will be generated by the empirical project (which, it must be noted, is itself dependent upon this theoretical account).

First, a note of caution should be sounded with regard to the danger of assuming that qualitative research generates data in an unproblematic way and can simply insert the filmgoer's voice into the research. David Buckingham has pointed out that:

> Researchers have often adopted an empiricist approach, in which audience data—and particularly talk—is often taken at face value, as 'evidence' of how people think or behave. In some instances, data is reduced to the level of illustration, and the connections between theory and the evidence are asserted rather than developed through a close analysis of the material itself.[37]

Jancovich and Faire quote a scholar who has 'argued that ethnographic research [...] provides no more access to the audience than textual analysis: the ethnographer has simply replaced the film text with the audience text'.[38] Jan Jagodinski uses Lacanian psychoanalytic theory to problematize any assumption that ethnographic, anthropological, or qualitative research places

---

[36] Hill, *Shocking*, pp. 107–8.
[37] Buckingham, *Audiences*, p. 211.
[38] Jane Feuer, quoted in Jancovich and Faire, *Place*, p. 28.

the researcher in straightforward 'contact' with the audience member.[39] The voices that are heard, even when speaking of personal experiences, are still secondary and indirect sources of data; their accounts are mediated through memory, which 'is not simply a record of the past, but a reconstruction of that past, a text whose meanings require interpretation'.[40] Furthermore, there are inevitably 'reactive effects' where the very presence and action of the researcher influences the data generated.[41]

Nonetheless, Buckingham, Jagodinski, and Jancovich and Faire all persevere with this method of research, convinced that if it is used sensitively and reflexively it has the potential to fill a void that disfigured previous studies. I am similarly convinced that empirical research should be used to ground an account of the possibility of revelation through film. However, the question still remains, how can the empirical data, generated by research of specific filmgoers seen against a particular cultural background, be related to a *theological* theory, such as an account of revelation? To answer this question it is necessary to turn to previous work which has attempted to incorporate empirical research into theology.

In his essay 'Through the Glass Darkly' in *Cinema Divinité*, William Telford offers a simple approach to the relation of religious and non-religious data. He enumerates six 'lenses' through which film can be studied. Three are drawn from film studies and film theory (including one which is empirically based) and three from religious studies and theology. When speaking of the deployment of these lenses, Telford mixes (or at least changes) his metaphors by referring to golf. Telford believes that just as a golfer selects the appropriate club from the range he carries with him in his bag, so the religious film-writer should select the appropriate club/lens/critical tool for the task in hand.[42] The structure of the essay assumes that these various lenses will function in harmony, but this may be overly simplistic.

A discussion of the etymology of 'method' and 'methodology' by Paula Saukko, a cultural studies scholar, highlights a problem with Telford's approach. She notes that the addition of the Greek word *logos* in the second term highlights an important difference: 'whereas methods refer to practical "tools" to make sense of empirical reality, methodology refers to the wider package of both tools and a philosophical and political commitment that come with a particular research "approach"'.[43] The thrust of her book is to show that

---

[39] Jan Jagodinski, *Youth Fantasies: The Perverse Landscape of the Media* (Basingstoke: Palgrave Macmillan, 2004), pp. 9–13.
[40] Jancovich and Faire, *Place*, p. 29.
[41] Pawluch et al., *Ethnography*, pp. 26–7.
[42] William R. Telford, 'Through a Lens Darkly: Critical Approaches to Theology and Film', in Eric S. Christianson, Peter Francis, and William R. Telford, eds, *Cinema Divinité: Religion, Theology and the Bible in Film* (London: SCM Press, 2005), pp. 15–43, especially 24.
[43] Saukko, *Research*, p. 8.

methods and methodologies are inherently related and, *contra* Telford, she argues that methods cannot be mixed and matched at will.[44] Other theologians have considered the relation of theological and empirical data more carefully.

John Swinton and Harriet Mowat, in their book *Practical Theology and Qualitative Research*, are far more intentional than Telford in their treatment of the relation between theological theory and empirical data. Recognizing that on the basis of some theological accounts—they reference John Milbank's work—the relationship between theology and the social sciences is always going to be contested, they state: 'The book provides a model of Practical Theology and an approach to qualitative research and examines the way in which these two disciplines can be brought together both at a conceptual and at a practical level.'[45]

In considering the merits of their approach, it is important to note that theological concepts and language—Trinity, conversion, hospitality, and sanctification—are used to order the engagement.[46] In other words, the theological account is prioritized. In the reading of their work that follows, I will argue that this *prioritizing* of theology, which I consider to be entirely legitimate in a work written primarily for theologians desiring to use qualitative methodologies, soon becomes a *privileging* of theology that I believe to be unhelpful.

This move from prioritization to privilege is based on a strong account of revelation as a possession of the Christian church. Thus, in the opening chapter which lays out Swinton and Mowat's understanding of practical theology, we find that the discipline is:

> Located within the uneasy but critical tension between the script of revelation [. . .] and the continuing, innovative performance of the gospel as it is enacted in the life and practices of the Church as they interact with the life and practices of the world.[47]

Here we see a bifurcated view of the situation. Revelation is distinguished from the concrete situation and the church is distinguished from the world. Again:

> This is *not* to suggest that human experience is a locus for fresh revelation (a new script), that will counter or contradict the script provided by Scripture, doctrine and tradition. It is however to recognise that the questions that we ask of Scripture and theological traditions *always* emerge from some context.[48]

The implication of this stance is that Swinton and Mowat are concerned to bring the methods and data generated by qualitative research under the

---

[44] Ibid., p. 9.
[45] Swinton and Mowat, *Practical*, p. viii.
[46] See, for example, ibid., pp. ix and 80-9.
[47] Ibid., p. 5.
[48] Ibid., p. 7.

judgement of theology authorized by revelation—'the essential message of the gospel'.[49]

> Because Scripture, tradition and church communities are not ahistorical, they are often profoundly impacted by aspects of society and culture which stand at odds with the essential message of the gospel. Part of the practical theological task is to discern such discrepancies in the practice of the Church and the world and to point to more authentic alternatives.[50]

It is unsurprising, therefore, that after a chapter which very helpfully describes qualitative research as it is practised in non-theological settings, Swinton and Mowat move in their third chapter to look at how qualitative research can be converted from its non-foundational, non-realist epistemology towards a tool that can be used by theologians. They ask, 'What kind of conceptual structure will allow the two disciplines to come together in a way that prevents one from collapsing into the other?'[51]

Swinton and Mowat's answer is to set out the correct relation carefully between the two dialogue partners. The engagement of the two strands of research—the situation (in the world or church) as investigated using the tools of qualitative research, and theology (as derived from the 'script' of revelation)—is articulated on the basis of Barth's reading of the Chalcedon description of the two natures of Christ. Thus there is indissoluble differentiation, inseparable unity, indestructible order, and, most importantly, a logical priority on the divine/theological side.[52]

This relation between qualitative research and theology is described in terms not only of hospitality but also in terms of conversion. Qualitative research, if used in theology, must recognize the foundation of all that it describes in God and recognize the precedence of the theological description of the world derived from revelation.

It is important to note, in mitigation of the arrogation of authority by theology in this book, that Swinton and Mowat place a great deal of emphasis on the provisional nature of all Christian practice, and therefore employ a 'hermeneutic of suspicion' with regard to the received Christian understanding of revelation and divine providence.[53] Other theologians working with empirical data are not so circumspect.

For example, an earlier attempt to incorporate qualitative or ethnographic research into theology was published in the *Scottish Journal of Theology* in 2000 by Nicholas Adams and Charles Elliot. Their title is provocative:

---

[49] Ibid., p. 11.
[50] Ibid., p. 26.
[51] Ibid., p. 73.
[52] Here Swinton and Mowat draw upon the work of Deborah van Deusen Hunsinger, *Practical*, pp. 83–7.
[53] For example, Swinton and Mowat, *Practical*, pp. 10 and 88–9.

'Ethnography is Dogmatics: Making Description Central to Systematic Theology'.[54] They arrive at their title by way of Karl Barth's contention that dogmatics is ethics and Michel Foucault's declaration that ethics is description (ethnography). 'We have taken these two ways of thinking together and excluded the middle term: ethics. This has yielded the abbreviated form: ethnography is dogmatics.'[55]

Adams and Elliot are admirably forthright. They recognize that their qualitative and ethnographic descriptions are less than professional. They also acknowledge the precedence and privilege afforded to theological assumptions in their work.[56] They declare that 'our descriptions are anything but neutral', rather, they 'are what an eschatologically oriented description of the world expects to see'.[57]

At one level their justification for their method is compelling. They 'insist' that, regardless of who is doing the research, 'ethnography is dogmatics because *description already includes a metaphysic* [...] To use something as an illustration already implies an agenda.'[58] If this is the case, they argue, there is no a priori reason why that metaphysic or agenda shouldn't be a Christian one.

However, the problem with their approach, at least as far as this project is concerned, is suggested by their revealing reference to the description as (merely) illustrative. In such a schema, the data derived from the qualitative or ethnographic investigation has no power to act upon, or to ground, what they term a metaphysic (and I term the theoretical/dogmatic account).

Thus, although Adams and Elliot acknowledge that the two cases they describe are exceptional (they have chosen to investigate and describe the stories of two Indian indigenous movements who have managed to overcome the powerful interests of state government and multinational corporations in a 'miraculous' manner), they can state that 'miracles [are] unexpected events which Christians nonetheless expect'.[59] The obvious corollary of this is that the vastly more numerous counter-examples that they could have given are allowed no power to change dogmatic presuppositions. Rather, Adams and Elliot explain, 'We do not yet have a strong enough hold on this idea to show how it might work out in situations of radical failure, and for that reason descriptions of cases which fail await a future occasion.'[60]

---

[54] Nicholas Adams and Charles Elliot, 'Ethnography is Dogmatics: Making Description Central to Systematic Theology', in *Scottish Journal of Theology*, 53:3 (2000), pp. 339–64.
[55] Ibid., p. 339.
[56] Ibid., p. 362. The Chipko movement is described pp. 347–53 and the Narmada Dam project is described pp. 353–8.
[57] Adams and Elliot, 'Ethnography', pp. 360 and 359.
[58] Ibid., p. 363.
[59] Ibid., p. 358.
[60] Ibid., pp. 359–60.

Although Swinton and Mowat's practice is more nuanced than that of Adams and Elliot, it is still the case that the order of the process they advocate, moving from 'the situation' to 'cultural contextual analysis' onto 'theological reflection' and finally 'revised practice', clearly privileges the theological account. Coming after the qualitative research and analysis, theology is allowed to sit in judgement over the situation.[61]

Overall, I believe that their approach is inappropriate for the project described in this monograph, for two reasons. First, it effectively neuters the qualitative strand of research because the process insulates 'theology' from critique by restricting the function of the qualitative research to description of the situation. There is no opportunity for the empirical research to 'ground' the theoretical account. Second, if this approach is enacted in research that uses personal testimony as its principal source of data, then it is, in fact, very *inhospitable* to those who graciously offer to share their experiences. Their experiences will be 'judged' after the event on the basis of theological commitments that the respondents may not share.[62]

Another approach is demonstrated by Martyn Percy in his book *Engaging with Contemporary Culture: Christianity, Theology and the Concrete Church*. Here qualitative research methods are used to develop thick descriptions of certain aspects of the concrete church. For example, with regard to a study of the continued state of the Toronto Vineyard Church entitled 'Adventure and Atrophy in a Charismatic Movement', Percy outlines his methodology with reference to 'three distinctive, but closely related, tactical trajectories':

> The first is drawn broadly from anthropology, the second from ethnography and the third from 'congregational studies'. Each focus their attention upon first-hand accounts of *local* practices and beliefs, rather than solely being concerned with 'official' texts [...] it is through a matrix of conversation, interviews, observation and the savouring of representative vignettes that one can begin to piece together a more coherent picture of what it is like to belong to a group, to be a pilgrim and to believe.[63]

---

[61] Swinton and Mowat, *Practical*, pp. 94-7. It is remarkable, then, that Swinton and Mowat replicate the typical practical theology utilization of Tillich's theory of correlation, deeming it too positivist with regard to the revealed answers of Christian theology that was criticized in Chapter 3 of this book.

[62] Two earlier attempts to combine theological and empirical data were published in the *Scottish Journal of Theology* and demonstrate similar weaknesses. Nicholas Adams and Charles Elliot explicitly refuse to allow their qualitative descriptions to challenge their dogmatic presuppositions, 'Ethnography is Dogmatics: Making Description Central to Systematic Theology', in *Scottish Journal of Theology*, 53:3 (2000), pp. 339-64, especially 358-60; and Christian Batalden Scharen remains at the level of problematizing the notion that an ideal, theoretical description is the best description without proceeding to challenge any particular theoretical account: '"Judicious Narratives", or ethnography as ecclesiology', in *Scottish Journal of Theology*, 58:2 (2005), pp. 125-42.

[63] Percy, *Engaging*, p. 161.

Percy recognizes that the different disciplines, from which he is drawing tools to *'listen deeply* and *well'* to the church in contemporary culture, are underpinned by conflicting views of reality; there is no neutral research position. 'Sociology assumes that religion is social; anthropology that it is cultural; and theology assumes that it is "real" and "irreducible".'[64] But, for the purposes of his study, Percy is willing to step outside the circle of a theology that holds these ontological commitments. Instead, he adopts another standpoint closely related to George Lindbeck's 'cultural–linguistic understanding of Christianity'.[65]

> In my own research, I have tended to treat religion as a complex cultural system. That is not to say that I, in any way, ignore or reject any idea of revelation, divinity or 'genuine' religious experience. Theologically I expect such things to be treated seriously, and I expect their reality to have some sort of impact on any empirical study. But I do not think that 'religion' is only the repository for revelation. I regard it as a complex system of meaning: a mixture of description and ascription; or deduction and induction.[66]

Here we see a far more nuanced account of the relation between revelation and culture, church and world, than that offered by Swinton and Mowat. For the purposes of 'practical theology' as it is practised by Percy, there is nothing other than the 'complex cultural system' that is religion. It is not possible to separate out culture and revelation and to reflect upon one on the basis of what is known by the other.

> To see the issue of religion and culture as something that requires refraction is to rescue it from 'simply' being *reflected* upon [...] there can be no substitute for separating out the constituent issues and disciplines, allowing them to interpermeate (pass through one another) and, in so doing, find their own proper density.[67]

Interestingly, this appears to be an almost perfect example of an approach that Paula Saukko characterizes as based upon a methodology metaphorically denoted by the prism. Such methodologies have an ontological commitment to 'fluid reality', an epistemology of the 'social construction of reality', and their goal is to describe multiple realities as accurately as possible.[68]

It appears that, on Percy's account, sociology, anthropology, and theology per se are considered to be based upon conflicting basic assumptions; while practical theology, which construes Christianity in a cultural–linguistic sense, is free to draw upon the tools of the social sciences in order to develop a thick and compelling description of the concrete church. While this is a more subtle approach than that of Swinton and Mowat, it is still not entirely satisfactory.

---

[64] Ibid., p. 8.　[65] Ibid., p. 8.　[66] Ibid., p. 163.
[67] Ibid., pp. 11–12.　[68] Saukko, *Research*, pp. 23–33.

Percy's decision to work within a cultural–linguistic conception of religion, thus conveniently bracketing out all questions of ultimate reality, seems slightly disingenuous. If, as he suggests, he believes in the reality of religious experiences and even expects these to impinge upon the empirical study, then it seems he would be better served by an account that is capable of incorporating these phenomena.

Nonetheless, I believe Percy's approach is more helpful than work that proceeds in the same key as that of Swinton and Mowat who, in spite of their recognition of the constant need to re-examine our interpretation of the complex of revelation, appear to privilege theology to an unhelpful degree. Drawing once again on Saukko's analysis, it seems that they provide a good example of empirical research conducted under the canopy of the myth of scientific objectivity. Here the appropriate metaphor is the magnifying glass. There is an ontological commitment to a fixed reality that, with the correct tools, can be uncovered to reveal the truth.[69]

So, it has not yet been possible to identify an approach that is suited to the needs of this project. One method seems to insulate the theory, in this case the theological account, from criticism; while the other seems unhelpfully to bracket out any questions regarding the reality or genuineness of religious experiences. As the appropriate interrelation of the theoretical and empirical parts of this monograph is so important, it is worth expanding the investigation to look a little more carefully at the way in which the discipline of practical theology manages the relation between the empirical and the theological.

Swinton and Mowat's process, as discussed above, is clearly a particular variation of the 'pastoral cycle' which is widely utilized within practical theology.[70] Interestingly, given the focus of the empirical part of this project on Latin America, at this point the methods of practical theology owe a great deal to liberation theology. Duncan Forrester writes: 'Christian practical theology [...] believes that realities need to be transformed, transfigured, revolutionised, converted, transfigured.' He goes on to quote Gustavo Gutiérrez: 'The praxis that transforms history is not a moment in the feeble incarnation of a limpid, well-articulated theory, but [...] the place where human beings recreate their world and shape themselves.'[71]

Within liberation theology, the empirical data is generated not so much through academic investigations as through life lived alongside the poor. As Jon Sobrino and Ignacio Ellacuria pithily put it in their book on systematic

---

[69] Saukko, *Research*, pp. 23–33.

[70] Duncan B. Forrester identifies the book *Social Analysis: Linking Faith and Justice* written in 1983 by Joe Holland and Peter Henriot as the point of origin of this method: Forrester, *Truthful Action: Explorations in Practical Theology* (Edinburgh: T&T Clark, 2000), p. 30.

[71] Forrester, *Truthful Action*, p. 27.

theology: 'Anyone hoping to do an adequate theology of liberation has to be willing to "take a qualifying exam" in union with the poor.'[72] This involvement with the reality of the contemporary context provides the starting point for what liberation theologians typically refer to as the hermeneutical circle. One of the most important writers on this subject was the Uruguayan theologian Juan Luis Segundo. In his book *The Liberation of Theology* he wrote:

> It is the continuing change in our interpretation of the Bible which is dictated by the continuing changes in our present-day reality, both individual and societal [...] And the circular nature of this interpretation stems from the fact that each new reality obliges us to interpret the word of God afresh, to change reality accordingly, and then to go back and reinterpret the word of God again, and so on.[73]

Importantly, the approach to practical theology that is developed from liberation theology also assumes that God is at work in the world and that this will impinge upon both our description and our understanding of the context. Forrester writes:

> The issues that are central to liberation theology arise out of the conviction that the God with whom we are engaged is the living God, active in today's world. One who can only be encountered in particular contexts and is to be responded to in quite specific ways. God is implicated in history and it is there, in the world, as well as in Scripture and worship, that we meet him.[74]

So, does a practice of practical theology that is rooted in the approach of liberation theology provide an 'off the peg' solution to the question of the appropriate articulation of the two halves of this research project? It certainly allows, even assumes, that God is active in the world and in ways which are susceptible to identification and description. And, as has been seen, any methodology derived from the approach of liberation theology will be committed to the re-interpretation of theoretical assumptions and theological positions on the basis of engagement with the way in which God is at work in the world. However, the usefulness of this approach for this project is limited by the focus of both liberation theology and practical theology upon action.

As Gerben Heitink construes it in his book *Practical Theology: History, Theory, Action Domains*: 'The word *practical* in "practical theology" refers to action.' Thus, he treats 'practical theology as a theory of action'.[75] In his

---

[72] Jon Sobrino and Ignacio Ellacuria, *Systematic Theology: Perspectives from Liberation Theology* (London: SCM, 1996), p. 11.
[73] Juan Luis Segundo, *Liberation of Theology* (Maryknoll, NY: 1976), p. 8.
[74] Forrester, *Truthful Action*, p. 29.
[75] Gerben Heitink, *Practical Theology: History, Theory, Action Domains*, tr. Reinder Bruinsma (Cambridge: Eerdmans, 1999), p. 6.

chapter on 'Practical Theology as a Theological Discipline', Heitink very helpfully surveys a wide range of different practices and notes that even within the 'hermeneutical approach', which he favours, there are 'distinctive streams'.[76] He differentiates between these streams by helpfully drawing upon a range of figures developed by their proponents. While some figures clearly ascribe a 'normative' role to tradition and Scripture,[77] and others are more radical,[78] in all cases the figures demonstrate that the focus and the goal is always action, a new praxis. 'Practical theology has the task to lead in this process of change [from 'unsatisfactory praxis'].'[79] 'The discipline has both a descriptive and a normative character, with the improvement of action as its main goal.'[80]

The goal of the present project is not action but the development of a grounded theoretical account of the possibility of revelation through film. Practical theology, especially in its use of a hermeneutical spiral or pastoral circle derived in part from the work of liberation theologians, has the resources to ground theory through consideration of empirical data. However, its desired and focal output is action, specifically new and improved praxis; its goal does not replicate the goal of this monograph.

So, the question as to the appropriate articulation of the two parts of the research project remains. On the basis of what has been discussed above, I believe that there are two equal and opposite dangers which, like Scylla and Charybdis, must be carefully negotiated. First, there is the danger of treating the theory with too much respect. As has been seen, this is especially true when the theory in question is theological in nature and might be considered to have a particular kind of authorization through revelation and therefore be viewed as invulnerable to contradiction by mere empirical data. However, as Buckingham and others have argued, it is also possible to treat the data generated by empirical research with too much respect, as if empirical study gives on to an unmediated and undistorted substratum of pure fact.

In response to these dangers, neither data source will be considered privileged in this research project. Both will be treated as humanly constructed discourses intended to explain human experiences which may, or may not, be experiences of divine revelation. Thus Paul Tillich is viewed as a human being who, in an act of *theoria* (his own term), offers a personal, interpretive account of the way in which human cultural creations might be revelatory of a dimension of depth or of the ground of being. Similarly, the qualitative research seeks to provide a rich description of a particular context in which

---

[76] Ibid., pp. 122–3.
[77] See, for example, figure 8, ibid., p. 122.
[78] See, for example, figure 4, ibid., p. 114.
[79] In relation to figure 4, ibid., p. 113.
[80] In relation to figure 8, ibid., p. 121.

certain individuals, also in acts of *theoria*, offer to the researcher personal, already interpretive, accounts of particular experiences which are to some degree congruent with Tillich's theory. The fact that one account is theological, highly technical, and universal in the scope of its description, while the other is presented by 'ordinary' individuals in their own language, and in response to particular experiences, is not considered to confer on either a greater or lesser access to the 'truth'. (Even this is not the end of the process, because both acts of *theoria* appear in this monograph re-read and re-interpreted by me, the researcher/writer.)

In contrast to Percy, there is no need to be restricted to an account, like the cultural–linguistic account, that brackets out the ultimate or divine. Rather, it is assumed that both the personal and the theological accounts may contain helpful descriptions of experiences of the divine or, more specifically, of revelation. Inevitably, the vocabulary and the conceptual schema utilized to describe such experiences will vary.

The fact that this study is primarily a work of systematic theology does require that the theological account be prioritized in two ways. First, theology is prioritized chronologically; the monograph begins with a theological question; and a reading of Tillich's theology has taken place prior to the empirical research. Second, theology is prioritized methodologically; and the account derived from the reading of Tillich's theory will be used as a heuristic lens actually to structure and organize the empirical research. In other words, the fact that this project is intended to develop theory rather than to result in action means that both the entry point *to* and the exit point *from* the hermeneutical spiral are different from those of practical theology. The manner in which this *priority* without *privilege* is maintained will be seen in what remains of the monograph.

4.2 THE METHODS AND INSTRUMENTS OF THE QUALITATIVE RESEARCH

In the first half of the last section, the history of film studies and film theory's engagement with the audience was considered. It was suggested that the recent shift from spectatorship to ethnography, from theoretical supposition to situated audiences, and from speculative constructions to empirical studies, represented a move to the kind of research paradigm that suited the particular goals of this project. This research paradigm is best described as qualitative research, and examples of this paradigm in action were given. The methodological stance which will determine the way the two parts of the project will

136   Part III The Empirical Research

interact was also discussed and the decision was taken to allow the theoretical and theological account priority without affording it undue privilege.

The aim of this second section is to lay out the research process for assessment and to demonstrate how the application and utilization of qualitative research methods and instruments in this particular project consistently aim to imitate best practice. To this end, the research procedure is evaluated against three different types of published qualitative research literature: first, there are general introductions to the practice of qualitative research;[81] second, there are books addressing particular aspects of qualitative research;[82] third, there are the papers and monographs published to report upon actual qualitative research projects. These publications may be subdivided into: general examples of good practice; examples of qualitative research concerning film; examples of qualitative research concerning religion; and examples of qualitative research concerning religion and film.[83]

4.2.1 Using qualitative research to produce a *grounded account*

The meaning of 'grounded account' in this project can best be established through consideration of the 'pre-eminent' and 'most widely used and popular qualitative research method'—grounded theory.[84] In the paragraphs that follow I will set out the ways in which my project resembles but also diverges from typical grounded theory research. Christina Goulding has written:

> The main thrust of [the grounded theory] movement was to bridge the gap between theoretically 'uninformed' empirical research and empirically 'uninformed' theory by grounding theory in data. It was part of a reaction against

---

[81] A number of these have already been referenced: Mason, *Researching*; Johnson et al., *Practice*; Saukko, *Research*; Pawluch et al., *Ethnography*. In this category, I will also draw upon the lecture notes prepared by Dr Gabriella Elgenius for the *Qualitative Research Methods Seminar*, Oxford University Department of Sociology, Hilary Term 2007 (unpublished material).

[82] For example, on questionnaire design, A. N. Oppenheim, *Questionnaire Design, Interviewing and Attitude Measurement*, new edn (London: Continuum, 1992); on interviewing, Hilary Arksey and Peter Knight, *Interviewing for Social Scientists* (London: Sage, 1999); and on data analysis, Miles and Huberman, *Analysis*.

[83] For example: Good practice—Gambetta and Hammil, *Streetwise*; Film—Faire and Jancovich, *Place* and Hill, *Shocking*; Religion—David Hay, 'Religious Experience Amongst a Group of Post-Graduate Students: A Qualitative Study', *Journal for the Scientific Study of Religion*, 18.2 (1979), pp. 164–82; and Gordon Lynch and Emily Badger, 'The Mainstream Post-Rave Club Scene as a Secondary Institution: A British Perspective', in *Culture and Religion*, 7.1 (2006), pp. 27–40; Religion and film—Jack Gabig, *Youth, Religion and Film: An Ethnographic Study* (Haverhill, Essex: YTC Press, 2007); and Lynn Schofield Clark, *From Angels to Aliens: Teenagers, the Media and the Supernatural* (Oxford: Oxford University Press, 2003).

[84] Kathy Charmaz, *Constructing Grounded Theory: A Practical Guide Through Qualitative Analysis* (London: Sage, 2006), p. 5; and Antony Bryant and Kathy Charmaz, 'Grounded Theory Research: Methods and Practices', in *The Sage Handbook of Grounded Theory*, ed. Antony Bryant and Kathy Charmaz (London: Sage, 2007), pp. 1–28, especially 1.

extreme empiricism, or 'Grand Theory', a term coined by Mills (1959) to refer pejoratively to sociological theories couched at a very abstract conceptual level. Mills similarly criticised abstracted empiricism or the process of accumulating qualitative data for its own sake.[85]

From this quote it may be seen that the aims and objectives of grounded theory closely mirror those of this project. This monograph foregrounds and analyzes a particular theory of revelation through culture to avoid the pitfalls of abstracted empiricism. By grounding that theory in empirical data it develops a more nuanced account than that offered by 'grand' theories.

Grounded theory research began with Barney Glaser and Anselm Strauss's *The Discovery of Grounded Theory: Strategies for Qualitative Research*, published in 1967.[86] In the book, they criticized the dominant 'logico-deductive method' of theory construction, arguing that this approach was prone to fanciful and quickly discredited proposals. In its place they proposed 'grounded theory'.

> Theory based on data can usually not be completely refuted by more data or replaced by another theory. Since it is too intimately linked to the data, it is destined to last despite its inevitable modification and reformulation [...] In contrast, logically deduced theories based on ungrounded assumptions, such as some well-known ones on the 'social system' and on 'social action' can lead their followers far astray in trying to advance sociology.[87]

Central to Glaser and Strauss's project was the desire to *create* theory; their goal was 'generation' of new theory, not 'verification' of existing theory.[88] In their 'general comparative method', data are considered and analyzed until the researcher begins to discern 'conceptual categories and their conceptual properties', these in turn leading towards 'hypotheses or generalized relations among the categories and their properties'.[89] Further research then tests, refines, and develops these hypotheses until theories may be constructed.[90] If the theory is restricted to the particular interaction and context of the original research, it is considered a 'substantive theory'; if, however, further research suggests that the theory has validity across a wide range of contexts

---

[85] Christina Goulding, *Grounded Theory: A Practical Guide for Management, Business, and Market Researchers* (London: Sage, 2002), p. 41.

[86] It should be noted that over the course of this development Glaser and Strauss have developed divergent and, to some extent, mutually exclusive practices. For commentary see, for example, Goulding, *Grounded*, pp. 46–8; and Charmaz, *Constructing*, pp. 8–9.

[87] Glaser and Strauss, *Discovering*, p. 4.

[88] Ibid., pp. 8 and 12–15.

[89] Ibid., p. 35.

[90] It is at this point that the divergence between the approaches of Glaser and Strauss (mentioned in n. 527) is most pronounced. Strauss developed elaborate systems and processes for coding which Glaser felt almost constituted a logico-deductive theory in their own right. See Goulding, *Grounded*, pp. 47–8.

and interactions, it becomes a 'formal theory'.[91] At this point the similarities between this project and grounded theory might appear to dissolve because this project *begins* with a fully elaborated theory.

However, it would be naïve to assume that grounded theory is not itself theory-laden. With respect to the systemic level, Adele Clarke explains, in a Prologue entitled 'Regrounding Grounded Theory', that her task is to make 'the theoretical groundings of grounded theory in early-20th-century Chicago School sociology, in pragmatist philosophy, and in post-World War II symbolic interactionism explicit'.[92] Theory is also implicit in each and every grounded theory research project. Commentators have questioned grounded theory's assumption of a *tabula rasa*, arguing 'that their suggestion that researchers should ignore the theoretical literature on an area of study and avoid presuppositions or prior conceptualisation [. . .] is exceedingly difficult for researchers to achieve'.[93]

Indeed, uncovering and highlighting theoretical baggage has been one of the main preoccupations of recent writing on the methodology of qualitative research. It is a central tenet of the qualitative research paradigm that pre-existing assumptions, whether they be fully articulated theoretical accounts or simply the biases inherent in the researcher's particular worldview, are inevitable. In weak research, the pre-existing assumptions remain hidden and their, potentially pernicious, impact upon the research design, results, analysis, and conclusions are ignored. Conversely, the best research demonstrates its 'reflexivity' by systematically uncovering and foregrounding these, previously hidden, assumptions and carefully tracing their effect throughout the project.[94]

Secondly, I would argue that this project differs substantially from what Glaser and Strauss refer to as projects of 'verification of theory'.[95] For Glaser and Strauss a project of verification is essentially a quantitative project. It would involve the reduction of Tillich's theory to a series of propositions which can then be tested in a binary verification/falsification through the use of large-scale surveys.[96] In contrast, the goal of this project is not merely to prove or disprove certain propositions but to develop Tillich's theory and even to develop new theory as respondents speak of their experiences. As discussed

---

[91] Glaser and Strauss, *Discovering*, pp. 32–5.
[92] Adele E. Clarke, *Situational Analysis: Grounded Theory After the Postmodern Turn* (London: Sage, 2005), p. xxxiii.
[93] Burgess, *Field*, p. 181.
[94] See, for example, Hammersley and Atkinson, *Ethnology*, pp. 16–21; Johnson et al., *Practice*, pp. 52–6.
[95] Glaser and Strauss, *Discovering*, pp. 10–18.
[96] See, for example, Matthew Miles and Michael Huberman, *Qualitative Data Analysis: An Expanded Sourcebook*, 2nd edn (London: Sage, 1994), p. 17, for an account of how empirical research can be designed for verification, or, in their words, to be 'confirmatory' of an existing theory.

above, while Tillich's theory is used to organize the empirical research, and is in that sense prioritized, the goal is to allow equal privilege to the respondents' accounts.

In concrete expression of this methodology, Chapter 6 is actually divided into two parts. In the first part the analysis is theory-driven: the data are considered with reference to categories and concepts derived directly from Tillich's theory of revelation through culture (particularly the six aspects of the revelatory experience). However, in the second part of the chapter the analysis is data-driven: the data are considered in their own right and a completely new and unexpected way of conceptualizing the possibility of revelation through film emerges. At this point, although the theory's role in organizing the research must never be forgotten, both the procedures utilized and the results obtained resemble quite closely those of grounded theory.

This kind of hybrid, theoretical/empirical approach is far from unusual in qualitative research. Glaser and Strauss themselves note that 'the *source* of certain ideas, or even "models", can come from sources other than the data [...] But the generation of theory from such insights must then be brought into relation with the data, or there is a great danger that theory and empirical world will mismatch.'[97] Annette Hill's research into the consumption of violent films (considered above) reflects this duality. She writes: 'this study tests certain hypotheses of my own about the process of viewing violence by conducting qualitative research in this area [but] I soon discovered that the nature of the participants' insights generated hypotheses as much as tested them'.[98] Similarly, Diego Gambetta and Heather Hamill enact a qualitative research project that begins with a theoretical account and a number of hypotheses and proceeds not only to test, or verify, these but also to develop new hypotheses and theories.[99]

I would argue, therefore, that this research project does, in fact, resemble grounded theory in many ways. However, in light of the real differences, and especially to highlight the importance of the fully developed theoretical account which acts as a heuristic lens structuring and organizing the qualitative research, I have chosen to refer to a grounded account rather than to a full grounded theory.[100]

---

[97] Glaser and Strauss, *Discovering*, p. 5.
[98] Hill, *Shocking*, p. 7.
[99] Diego Gambetta and Heather Hamill, *Streetwise: How Taxi Drivers Establish their Customers' Trustworthiness* (New York: Russell Sage, 2005), pp. 1–18.
[100] A very similar move is made by Gabig who opts for 'grounded qualitative research': *Youth*, p. 83.

4.2.3 Data sources and data generation

The goal of this monograph is the development of a grounded account of the possibility of revelation through film. In order to achieve this, Tillich's theory of the possibility of revelation through culture is grounded through empirical research into the experiences of actual filmgoers. Therefore, filmgoers are the primary data sources and their accounts of their experiences are the primary data. For reasons set out in the Introduction, the research focuses on Latin American cinema and filmgoers.

In the final research project, after piloting in the UK had demonstrated the weaknesses of various initial approaches to data generation, the plan involved three separate stages.[101] First, contact was made with as many potential respondents as possible using 'intercept techniques'.[102] An initial 'filter question' was presented to identify filmgoers who had had particularly powerful and memorable film-watching experiences.[103] Second, these filmgoers were then invited to respond to a questionnaire which mapped the general features of their experiences, allowing for a preliminary judgement about the degree of congruity between their accounts and Tillich's theory and the potential usefulness of each respondent's data.[104] Finally, semi-structured, qualitative interviews were carried out with a small sample of these questionnaire respondents. The interviewees were selected on the basis of two qualitative research sampling strategies intended to ensure that data was generated that had the potential not merely to confirm but also to challenge and develop Tillich's account. These three principal stages of data generation were supplemented by the researcher's own 'participant observation' and by text-based and archive research into the films referenced and the socio-political and cultural context of the respondents.[105] The questionnaires, the semi-structured interviews, and the sampling strategies will be discussed in detail in separate subsections below. Here, I will consider questions relating to the size of this research

---

[101] Most importantly, piloting showed the weakness of trying to make initial contact through non-personal text- or web-based media. Other researchers have experienced similar problems: see, for example, Gambetta and Hamill, *Streetwise*, p. 21. These approaches can work when it is possible to achieve saturation of the target audience or when there is no time constraint; for example, the Alister Hardy Research Centre has had a question (discussed below) in general circulation for nearly 40 years and their database has grown slowly but steadily as the solicited accounts arrive. See, for example, D. Hay and A. Morisy, 'Reports of Ecstatic, Paranormal, or Religious Experience in Great Britain and the United States: A Comparison of Trends', in *Journal for the Scientific Study of Religion*, 17.3 (1978), pp. 255–68, especially 257.

[102] Arksey and Knight, *Interviewing*, p. 79.

[103] For a brief account of 'filter' questions, see Oppenheim, *Questionnaire*, pp. 110–12.

[104] This idea was first suggested by Dr Heather Hamill of the Department of Sociology, University of Oxford, personal meeting, 19 January 2007.

[105] For an account of participant observation, see Robert G. Burgess, *In the Field: An Introduction to Field Research* (London: Routledge, 1984), pp. 78–100, especially 98.

project and the appropriateness of combining various methods of data generation.

The research carried out in this project generates data through 100 questionnaires and 10 long, semi-structured interviews. These numbers would be insufficient in a quantitative research project but are appropriate for qualitative research. Glaser and Strauss write:

> Since [statistically] accurate evidence is not so crucial for generating theory, the kind of evidence, as well as the number of cases, is also not so crucial [...] A single case can indicate a general conceptual category or property; a few more cases can confirm the indication.[106]

Miles and Huberman write: 'Qualitative researchers usually work with *small* samples of people, nested in their context and studied in-depth—unlike quantitative researchers, who aim for larger numbers of context-stripped cases and seek statistical significance.'[107] In his introduction to the qualitative research paradigm, John Creswell introduces five research 'traditions' and illustrates these through reference to five different research projects, presented in full, that provide examples of excellence. These five research projects include a 'biographical' project which, by definition, focuses on one subject; a 'grounded theory' project which is based on interviews with eleven women; work in the 'phenomenological' tradition that is based on ten interviews; and an 'ethnography' which combines initial questionnaires with five interviews.[108] While it is obvious that Creswell chose these studies precisely because they are small and concise, it also demonstrates that small projects can be highly effective.

Creswell's ethnography, which includes both questionnaire and interview data, is not unusual; the combination of techniques is common in qualitative research, which is always an iterative process.[109] For example, Arksey and Knight write: 'Rather than seeing interviews and questionnaires in opposition, it might be better to see them as complementary; within a multi-part study [questionnaires] can also be used as a quick-and-dirty way of getting a sense of issues to be explored in interviews.'[110] There are many studies that incorporate this hybrid approach. Martin Baker's study of fans of the magazine *2000AD* develops his data by moving in a step-by-step fashion from a large number (250) of short questionnaires to a small number (less than 10) of in-depth interviews.[111] Kate Hunt, in 'Understanding the Spirituality of People Who

---

[106] Glaser and Strauss, *Discovering*, pp. 29–30.
[107] Miles and Huberman, *Analysis*, p. 27.
[108] Creswell, *Traditions*, pp. 257–69, 271–95, 297–321, 323–56.
[109] Elgenius, *Methods*, l.1.
[110] Arksey and Knight, *Interviewing*, p. 33.
[111] Martin Barker, 'Seeing how far you can see: on being a "fan" of *2000AD*', in Buckingham, *Reading Audiences*, pp. 159–83.

Do Not Go to Church', utilized a similarly iterative structure—in her case from intercept questionnaires, to focus groups, to qualitative interviews.[112] The whole alignment of a qualitative research project frequently shifts as early stages of research uncover interesting and unexpected data.[113]

4.2.4 Creating reliable instruments (I): The questionnaire

This subsection will consider the design of one of the two 'instruments' used to elicit theoretically useful data from the selected data sources (the other instrument being the interview guide). The focus will be upon the relationship between Tillich's theoretical account and the questions asked.[114] The whole questionnaire (reproduced just in English in the Appendices) was developed in response to the key findings of the reading of Tillich's theology of revelation through culture. To demonstrate the relationship between Tillich's theory and the questionnaire, I will consider the questions with respect to the six aspects of a revelationary experience as these were expounded in Chapter 2.[115] The techniques utilized to minimize the various unwanted 'effects' that can undermine the reliability of questionnaire-generated data will be discussed as they arise.[116] Throughout the questionnaire design process, ideas and techniques were drawn from: Hilary Arksey and Peter Knight, *Interviewing for Social Scientists*; A. N. Oppenheim, *Questionnaire Design*; and Seymour Sudman and Norman Bradburn, *Asking Questions: A Practical Guide to Questionnaire Design*.[117]

The first and last sections of the questionnaire may be seen as an attempt to elicit basic information about 'the individual'. The opening section contains general questions intended to obtain information about the respondent's film-watching habits and to gauge the 'seriousness' of her engagement with cinema. The final section contains some very basic 'demographic' questions regarding the respondent's age, sex, profession, nationality, and religious commitments.

---

[112] Kate Hunt, 'Understanding the Spirituality of People who Do Not Go to Church', in Grace Davie, Linda Woodhead, and Paul Heelas, eds, *Predicting Religion: Christian, Secular, and Alternative Futures* (Aldershot: Ashgate, 2003), pp. 159–69, especially 160.

[113] See Gambetta and Hamill, *Streetwise*; and, for example, the fascinating study by Lynn Schofield Clark, *Angels*, especially p. 18.

[114] Oppenheim, *Questionnaire*, p. 6 for the necessary relation between overall research design and questionnaire design.

[115] To create a natural flow and avoid confusing the respondent with thematic jumps, the questions did not progress in the same order as the theoretical account. The importance of the development of 'rapport' between researcher and respondent is widely referenced in the literature; see, for example, Arksey and Knight, *Interviewing*, p. 38.

[116] See, for example, Pawluch et al., *Ethnography*, pp. 26–7.

[117] Only Seymour Sudman and Norman Bradburn, *Asking Questions: A Practical Guide to Questionnaire Design* (London: Jossey-Bass, 1982) has not been previously referenced.

Perhaps the most important question was the 'filter', intended to identify respondents who had had particularly powerful film-watching experiences that were at least minimally congruent with Tillich's account. Given that the central finding of my reading of Tillich's theory was the identification of revelation with (partial) salvation, it seemed appropriate to filter respondents on the basis of the perceived impact of a film-watching experience on their lives. The question 'Has a Latin American film ever changed your life?' was suggested.[118] However, this terminology provided no particular link with Tillich's theory of revelation through culture.

Appropriate vocabulary is a perennial problem in researching religious experience, and David Hay, a seasoned academic researcher of this topic, has spoken of 'a hornets' nest of definitional problems'.[119] After much thought it was decided that the filter question could best be derived from the short quote taken from *Systematic Theology* and discussed above in reference to the relation of revelation to salvation, where Tillich states: 'Revelation is an ecstatic experience of the ground-of-being that shakes, transforms or heals' (*ST2*, 166–7).

Extensive piloting led to a series of adjustments to both the wording and the manner of presentation of the filter question. First, references to 'ecstasy' and 'ground of being' were omitted as there seemed no way of translating these terms into lay vocabulary without completely losing the Tillichian meaning. Second, the filter was 'embedded' in the wider series of questions about film-watching practices, as this habituated the respondents to giving both positive and negative answers. Third, the level of intensity of experience implied by the question was heightened by speaking of 'one exceptionally memorable occasion'. Finally, the answer 'No' was placed before the answer 'Yes' (a technique utilized to mitigate the impact of interviewer effect on the respondent).[120] The final form of the question was:

---

6. Looking back upon your life, is there one exceptionally memorable occasion when a Latin American film shook, transformed or healed your life?

No	Yes
☐	☐

---

[118] Personal meeting with Dr Pete Ward, 9 January 2007.

[119] Hay, 'Experience', p. 165.

[120] Sudman and Bradburn, *Questions*, p. 38. For a more general discussion of 'interviewer effects', see Lucy Suchman and Brigitte Jordan, 'Interactional Troubles in Face-to-Face Survey Interviews', in Nigel Fielding, ed., *Interviewing, Volume 1* (London: Sage, 2003), pp. 191–216, especially 192.

A second group of questions were intended to generate data about the films with which the respondents' experiences were associated; these questions relate to 'the artwork' in Tillich's account. Here, simply asking for the title of the film can generate a large volume of data that can be accessed by the researcher at a later date through viewing the films themselves alongside consideration of textual evidence for academic, critical, and public reception. Follow-up questions then probed the theoretically important issue of the perceived cause of the film's impact. For example, question 10 asked: 'Which of the following characteristics of the film were important—Narrative/Plot; Cinematography; Music; Characters; General Setting; Particular Scene; or Message/Theme?'

The largest numbers of questions were intended to interrogate the third aspect in my account of Tillich's theory, 'the event' of revelation. These questions first probed the context of the experience. For example, question 8: 'Where did you see the film: cinema; home; friend's house?' Or question 9: 'Who did you see the film with: alone; with friend(s); with partner; with family?' Further questions went on to probe the actual nature of the experience. For example, question 13: 'How would you describe the onset of the experience: immediate (during the film); gradual (after the film)?' Or question 14: 'How would you describe the nature of the experience: intellectual; emotional; aesthetic; spiritual?'

It is important to note that with respect to question 14 respondents were free to respond affirmatively to more than one of the suggested answers. One of the reasons for including this question in this form was the belief that an experience that was reported as being simultaneously intellectual, emotional, aesthetic, and spiritual was as close as common vocabulary could get to Tillich's description of an ecstatic experience.

Another question, still related to 'the event', attempted to discern more clearly the extent to which the experience differed from the respondent's other film-watching experiences and from their daily lives. Question 15 asked: 'At any point during the experience did you sense a presence or a power (it doesn't matter whether you would call it God or not) that is distinct from your everyday life?' This question was developed by the Alister Hardy Research Centre, and David Hay, in particular, has used it over many years and in many different studies.[121] I felt that the question was simple enough to be understood but also ambiguous enough not to foreclose on any of the various construals of revelation or religious experience allowed by Tillich's theology.[122] Once again, the positive response that might be

---

[121] See Hay, 'Experience'; and Hay and Morisy, 'Reports'. Other questions were considered, for example one utilized by Lynch, in *Understanding*, pp. 175-6, which is derived from William James's four criteria of mystical experience.

[122] The practice of using existing questions in research design is a common one, as previous use in successful and respected research is a good indicator of validity and effectiveness: Sudman and Bradburn, *Questions*, p. 13.

considered theoretically desirable was deliberately placed in the least salient and least popular position among the list of possible answers.

The responses to this question were also considered in relation to answers to the demographic questions about religious commitments which closed the questionnaire. Taken together, these two pieces of information made it possible to intuit whether the respondents' answers might be the result of a conventional religious commitment, perhaps even to Jesus as the Christ, the sixth aspect of Tillich's account of revelation through culture, or whether they were given in spite of more materialist or atheist commitments.

Another group of questions aimed to generate data relevant to Tillich's concept of the two constellations of revelation by probing the respondents' understanding of the relation between the film-watching experience and their daily lives. For example, question 11: 'Was there any particular connection with your life, did you identify with—a particular character; the setting; a specific event?' Or question 16: 'Was the experience in any way related to what was going on in your life at the time?'

As stated above, the filter question is linked to the theoretical discussion of the effect of revelation and its relation to salvation. Question 17 aimed to interrogate more accurately the kind of impact the respondents felt they had experienced. 'Was there an impact on your life: no, there was no impact; yes, there was a positive impact; yes, there was a great positive impact; yes, there was a negative impact?'

Once the overall shape of the questionnaire had been developed, drafts were refined. Dr Gabriella Elgenius looked at the format and content of the questionnaire from the perspective of a sociologist with much experience of qualitative research methods. Correspondence with a Latin American theologian, Dr Alberto Roldán, who has published on Tillich's theory of revelation, helped with regard to the translation of specific Tillichian terms into Spanish.[123] Finally, the questionnaire was emailed to a number of Latin Americans who offered suggestions and comments about vocabulary and comprehensibility.[124]

4.2.5 Sampling and selection

As explained above, questionnaire respondents were contacted using simple 'intercept' techniques which involved approaching filmgoers at film festivals in

---

[123] Alberto Roldán, 'El concepto de revelacion en la teologia de Paul Tillich', *Teología y cultura*, 2.3 (2005), <http://www.teologiaycultura.com.ar/arch_rev/a_roldan_revelacion_tillich.PDF> (accessed 31 August 2008).

[124] There was only one obvious problem. On the advice of Alberto Roldán, '*sanación*' was used to translate 'healing'. However, a number of respondents commented that *sanación* carried overtones of faith-healing. So the more common form of the verb *sanar* (to heal) was used in Montevideo.

a random fashion. This resulted in 100 questionnaires being completed. In this subsection I will present the sampling strategy that was utilized to select the 10 respondents for the long semi-structured, qualitative interviews.[125] An explicit and intentional sampling strategy greatly increases the chance that theoretically relevant data will be generated and, simultaneously, reduces the likelihood that the relationship between the theoretical starting point and the empirical research will be elided or ignored. In particular, a sampling strategy helps to avoid 'exampling'.

Glaser and Strauss define 'exampling' as the claim that conclusions are based on empirical research when the empirical component is actually only finding 'examples for dreamed-up, speculative, or logically deduced theory after the idea has occurred'.[126] The underlying error is to fail to notice that 'since the idea has not been derived from the example, seldom can the example correct or change it (even if the author is willing), since the example was selectively chosen for its confirming power'.[127]

Of course, all studies are dependent upon respondents possessing the experiences or knowledge that fits them to answer the research questions. John Creswell makes this point in a discussion of the phenomenological tradition within qualitative research: 'The participants in the study need to be carefully chosen to be individuals who have experienced the phenomenon.'[128] Likewise, Hammersley and Atkinson state: 'The aim will often be to target those people who have the knowledge desired and who may be willing to divulge it.'[129] In fact, all the qualitative studies referenced in this monograph select respondents on the basis of their experience of the phenomenon under consideration.[130]

Quantitative research typically uses 'statistical sampling' or 'random sampling' which facilitate the generalizability of research results across a population because the sample was chosen precisely so that it could stand as a representative microcosm of the wider macrocosm.[131] In contrast, qualitative research is not, primarily, interested in generalizability but in illumination,

---

[125] The most helpful discussions of sampling strategy are found in Mason, *Researching*, pp. 83–97; Miles and Huberman, *Analysis*, pp. 27–30; and also Elgenius, *Methods*, l.2.
[126] Glaser and Strauss, *Discovering*, p. 5.
[127] Ibid., p. 5.
[128] John W. Creswell, *Qualitative Inquiry and Research Design: Choosing Among Five Traditions* (London: Sage, 1998), p. 55.
[129] Hammersley and Atkinson, *Principles*, pp. 133–7, especially 137.
[130] For example, Gambetta and Hamill require taxi drivers who take part in situations congruent with the 'trust game' as it is developed in their theory and hypothesis, *Streetwise*, pp. 3–5 and 20–3; Clark interviews teenagers with experiences of the supernatural mediated through televisual media, *Angels*, p. 18; and Hill searches out filmgoers who enjoy the horror genre, *Shocking*, pp. 12–15.
[131] For a brief discussion of this, see Thomas R. Black, *Doing Quantitative Research in the Social Sciences: An Integrated Approach to Research Design, Measurement and Statistics* (London: Sage, 1999), pp. 110–11.

achieved through thick description of a particular research puzzle.[132] To ensure that it is capable of generating these descriptions it engages in 'theoretical' or 'purposive' sampling. Miles and Huberman explain: 'Choices of informants, episodes and interactions are being driven by a conceptual question, not by a concern for "representativeness".'[133] Mason concurs, 'if you are making a non-representative sample with the aim of making key comparisons and testing and developing theoretical propositions, then what you are likely to be doing is some form of *theoretical sampling* or *purposive sampling*'.[134]

However, to avoid the danger of 'exampling', theoretical sampling selects respondents in a controlled, accountable, and scientific way: 'it is important to make the criteria employed as explicit and systematic as possible'.[135] In this research project the sampling strategy proceeded in two steps. First, a group of respondents were sampled and selected for interview on the basis of the congruity that existed between their questionnaire answers and Tillich's theoretical account of the possibility of revelation through culture. This is known as a 'critical case sample [...] the instance that "proves" or exemplifies the main findings'.[136] Clearly this must be supplemented if 'exampling' is to be avoided. Jennifer Mason writes:

> You must ensure that you do not simply pick those sampling units which will support your argument and disregard those inconvenient ones which do not. You can and should make sure that you sample in a way which will help you not only to develop your theory or explanation, but also to test it, and you need to build in a mechanism for doing this [...] In other words, you should use your sampling strategy not simply to acquire units from which you will generate data which support your analysis or explanation, but also to show that you have rigorously looked for cases or instances which do not fit with your ideas or which cannot be accounted for by the explanation which you are developing.[137]

Therefore, in addition to selecting for interview those respondents most closely resembling the theoretical ideal, I also incorporated a 'maximum variation' sampling strategy. '*Maximum variation* [...] involves looking for outlier cases to see whether main patterns still hold [...] Searching deliberately for *confirming and disconfirming cases, extreme or deviant cases*, and *typical cases* serve to increase confidence in conclusions.'[138] This meant inviting to interview not only those who had experiences which appeared to

---

[132] Elgenius, *Methods*, l.1.
[133] Miles and Huberman, *Analysis*, pp. 27–9, especially 29.
[134] Mason, *Researching*, pp. 93, also 100–4. As discussed above, the most influential account of theoretical sampling is found in Glaser and Strauss, *Discovering*, especially pp. 45–76. See also Hammersley and Atkinson, *Principles*, pp. 42–5; and Burgess, *Field*, pp. 54–6.
[135] Hammersley and Atkinson, *Principles*, p. 46.
[136] Miles and Huberman, *Analysis*, p. 28; also Elgenius, *Methods*, l.2.
[137] Mason, *Researching*, p. 94.
[138] Miles and Huberman, *Analysis*, p. 28.

resemble revelation on Tillich's account, but also respondents who stated they had never had 'shaking', 'healing', or 'transforming' experiences; respondents who claimed that such experiences had had a 'negative' impact upon their lives; and respondents whose answers appeared to challenge the theoretical construal.

The human dimension and the logistical difficulties inherent in field-based qualitative research make deviations from the perfect sample almost inevitable.[139] In this research project the final roster of interviewees deviated from that demanded by the sampling strategy because of difficulties in contacting some of those selected; this meant that no respondent was finally interviewed who declared that an experience had had a negative impact. However, the situated nature of qualitative projects can also have a positive impact on the research. In this case the *Cinemateca* club in Montevideo offered a great deal of assistance, presenting credentials and providing premises for questionnaires and interviews. The club acted as what qualitative research typically refers to as a *gatekeeper*, and this allowed for the research to develop in new and unexpected directions.[140]

4.2.6 Instruments (II): The interview guide

The semi-structured, qualitative interview was the primary instrument of data generation in this research project. Writing on the subject by Arksey and Knight, *Interviewing for Social Scientists*, and by Nigel Fielding and Hilary Thomas, 'Qualitative Interviewing', was particularly helpful in the construction of the interview guide and in the interview process.[141]

Both Arksey and Knight and Fielding and Thomas locate the semi-structured (or semi-standardized) interview at the midpoint in a typology that runs from the structured, survey interview through to the unstructured (or non-standardized) interview. In the semi-structured interview, 'the interviewer asks major questions the same way each time, but is free to alter their sequence and probe for more information. The interviewer can thus adapt the research instrument to the level of comprehension and articulacy of the respondent.'[142] These major questions or 'relevant topic areas and themes'

---

[139] On the importance of logistical factors and their impingement on the research process, see Mason, *Researching*, pp. 32–3; Hammersley and Atkinson, *Principles*, pp. 53–5; Johnson et al., *Practice*, pp. 64–8; and Arksey and Knight, *Interviewing*, pp. 70–2, especially 71.

[140] Burgess, *Field*, pp. 48–9; Hammersley and Atkinson, *Principles*, pp. 63–7; and Arksey and Knight, *Interviewing*, p. 64.

[141] Nigel Fielding and Hilary Thomas, 'Qualitative Interviewing', in Nigel Gilbert, ed., *Researching Social Life*, 2nd edn (London: Sage, 2001), pp. 123–44.

[142] Fielding and Thomas, 'Interviewing', p. 124.

are typically used to create a 'loosely structured' interview guide.[143] In this project the interview guide was based upon the questionnaire, but there was one major addition which will be discussed below.[144]

The first section of the interview guide asked general questions about the respondents' lives and their experiences of living in Montevideo: 'Could you tell me a little more about your life?' (in addition to the demographic information supplied for the questionnaire); and 'How does it feel to be a Uruguayan (from Montevideo) in 2007?' These were then followed up, as necessary, by various prompts and probing or clarifying questions.[145] As discussed above, the attempt to locate respondents within a wider socio-economic and cultural context is typical of qualitative research.

The second section took a more personalized approach to the filmgoers' film-watching habits, covering the same ground as the initial section of the questionnaire. Reflecting the difference between questionnaire and qualitative interview, a more conversational tone was employed:[146] 'Since when have you been interested in cinema?'; 'What importance does cinema have in your life?'; 'Are there other arts, recreational activities or cultural practices that have (greater or lesser) importance in your life?' Further questions addressed the respondents' opinions of the cinema's importance and power: 'Does it seem to you that the cinema is an important art / cultural product?'; 'Do you think that the cinema has a particular kind of power? What is it? How does it function? What is its effect? How do you feel its power in your own life?' In general the respondents seemed animated by the opportunity to discuss these questions, and their responses ranged from the personal and anecdotal to the abstract and highly theoretical.

The third section was explicitly presented to the respondents as a 'return' to the questionnaire, but the questions were reordered to allow for a better and more natural flow of conversation.[147] Every respondent named the same film in the follow-up interview as they had named in the questionnaire (one respondent required a prompt). The respondents were then simply invited to speak about the film and their experience of it in their own words: 'Let's talk a little more about that film and your experience... take your time and tell me what happened.' The respondents were given space and time to contribute as much information as possible before follow-up questions were used to probe particular areas of interest. Inevitably, the successfulness of this

---

[143] Arksey and Knight, *Interviewing*, p. 7.
[144] See ibid., pp. 85–6; and Fielding and Thomas, 'Interviewing', pp. 131–3 for basic introductions to the construction of an interview guide.
[145] A good definition of prompting and probing questions is found in ibid., pp. 128–9.
[146] Arksey and Knight, *Interviewing*, p. 39.
[147] Mason, *Researching*, pp. 44–5; Fielding and Thomas, 'Interviewing', p. 132; Arksey and Knight, *Interviewing*, p. 98.

150 Part III The Empirical Research

approach was dependent both on the intensity of the respondent's experience and on each individual's personality and loquacity.

At the close of the interviews there was a major addition to the questionnaire structure. Respondents were presented with two handouts. The first handout introduced Tillich's thought with regard to the possibility of revelation through culture. The second offered Tillich's description of his encounter with Botticelli's painting. (The handouts are reproduced just in English in the appendices.) The decision to disclose the theoretical framework that underpins the research, albeit in a highly abbreviated form, is, perhaps, the most radical and innovative aspect of the empirical research undertaken in this project.[148] Once again, this move is motivated by the desire to prioritize but not to privilege the theoretical theological account, and, more specifically, it is justified by the unique religious climate in Uruguay (which will be discussed in detail in Chapter 5). In a cultural context such as that of present-day Uruguay, where religious understandings, beliefs, and commitments are likely to be under-reported, the introduction of religious categories as a way of giving 'permission' for the respondents to speak in these terms may be wholly appropriate.[149] In any case, Johnson et al. have written that too slavish a following of accepted 'how to' practices and methods tends to lead to 'modest, safe efforts'; while risk-taking can lead to 'research of pleasure, significance and originality'.[150] Nonetheless, there are legitimate questions that should be addressed.

The primary cause for concern would be that such a disclosure could influence the respondents' answers. For example, those well-disposed towards the researcher might attempt to embroider their stories in order to please or, conversely, to withhold contradictory information in order to avoid giving offence. More generally, introducing theory into the conversation would be likely to contaminate the respondents' descriptions of their experiences with alien concepts and vocabulary. The very real weight of these concerns made it obvious that the disclosure should only take place at the very end of the interview process so that data generated prior to the introduction of Tillich's thought and experience could legitimately be taken to reflect the respondents' own understandings, vocabularies, and conceptual categories. Data generated after the introduction of the handouts was treated separately and its weight was clearly differentiated in the analysis that followed data collection.

After reading the first handout, which introduced Paul Tillich and offered a very brief account of his interests and his understanding of revelation through

---

[148] However, it is not without precedent; for another example of an explanation of the purpose and intent of the research see Hay, 'Experience', pp. 65 and 182.

[149] Hammersley and Atkinson discuss the occasionally helpful use of leading questions, *Principles*, pp. 129–31.

[150] Johnson et al., *Practice*, p. 62.

culture, respondents were asked: 'What do you think of the theory that art, especially cinema, can function as "revelation":—transforming, shaking, or healing our lives?'; and 'Would you be happy to describe some of your experiences, like the ones we have discussed, as revelatory?' After reading the second handout, Tillich's own account of his experience of the Botticelli painting, the respondents were asked: 'What do you think/feel?' 'Have you ever experienced anything similar?'[151] The interview guide continued with prompting and probing questions: 'Does it seem to you that art/cinema is a solely human activity and its power is solely human or do you think there might be a power or presence (it doesn't matter whether or not you would be happy to call it God or Beauty or Life or Nature) that challenges us, makes demands of us, transforms, shakes or heals through the cinema?' 'Would you say that a film has ever: given you the keys to interpret human existence; brought you a joy full of vitality; shown you a spiritual truth?' In practice, these follow-up questions were rarely needed.

4.2.7 Data analysis

This research project uses a combination of data generation methods. Questionnaires produced a body of data that was broad but shallow, and this was utilized in order to select respondents for semi-structured, qualitative interviews on the basis of a defined qualitative sampling strategy. In addition, in Chapter 5, the questionnaire data will be used to contextualize the empirical research, providing a route into description of the particular socio-political and cultural location of the interview respondents. However, the principal instrument of data generation was the semi-structured, qualitative interview, and this subsection will address the way in which the data arising from the interviews were analyzed.

The first stage in the analysis of the interview data is already underway as the recorded interviews are transcribed.[152] Arksey and Knight note that: 'Even the way that the transcription is done reflects the research purpose and design and is also effectively a part of the data analysis.'[153] In fact, word-for-word transcription using specialized equipment was the most time-consuming phase of analysis, with six hours of transcription for every hour of interview

---

[151] The only change I made to Tillich's account was to omit the word 'chaplain'. I felt that this was justified as it didn't obscure the religious element in the account—for example, the word 'divine' was retained—but it did avoid the risk of awakening the very powerful sense of anti-clericalism that pervades the sector of Uruguayan society from which the respondents came and which will be discussed at greater length in Chapter 5.

[152] For general discussions of the transcription process, see Arksey and Knight, *Interviewing*, pp. 142–6; and Fielding and Thomas, 'Interviewing', pp. 134–7.

[153] Arksey and Knight, *Interviewing*, pp. 147–8; also, Mason, *Researching*, p. 53.

recording being a widely held rule of thumb.[154] In the quotations from the transcripts that will be found in the following chapters it will be noted that the attempt has been made to reproduce exactly the words of the respondents. In the English translations non sequiturs are retained, pauses are designated with ellipses, and there is no attempt to rearrange the respondents' speech into more coherent sentences.[155] In this process I followed the protocols laid down by Blake Poland in his article 'Transcription Quality'.[156] Once complete transcripts were available, a qualitative research software package (MAXQDA) was utilized in the analysis of the interview data.[157]

In Chapter 6, the analysis of the interview data is presented in two major sections. The first section is theory-driven analysis. Every effort is made to attend closely and fairly to the data, and to note points where it challenges and contradicts the theoretical account as well as points where it appears to validate or substantiate the theory. Nonetheless, analysis is driven by questions arising out of the theoretical account, and its presentation is structured by concepts derived from the theoretical account. In this research project the account is, once again, organized with respect to the six aspects of the revelatory experience.

The second section of analysis is data-driven. Here it is important not to overlook the role played by theory which, even when it is relegated to the background, remains the heuristic lens through which the entire empirical project is focused. Nonetheless, in this stage of analysis the attempt is made to allow the data to lead in new directions. The concepts and categories that arise are those suggested by the data and are only secondarily related to the theoretical account. What takes place in this section is much closer to a genuine grounded theory projected as presented by Glaser and Strauss.

Both of these sections are further divided into two separate analytical approaches.[158] First, each section is introduced by way of an *illustrative vignette* which focuses on the experience of one particular respondent whose account is particularly illuminating.[159] Mason considers the analysis of particular, individual cases to be 'non-cross-sectional'.

---

[154] Fielding and Thomas, 'Interviewing', p. 136.

[155] Qualitative research theses and monographs do not typically incorporate full versions of either data recordings or transcripts, even when there are multiple languages involved; for example, Gambetta and Hamill, *Streetwise*, p. 24.

[156] Blake D. Poland, 'Transcription Quality', in Jaber F. Gubrium and James A. Holstein, eds, *Handbook of Interview Research* (London: Sage, 2001), pp. 629–50, especially 641.

[157] For a brief introduction to MAXQDA, see Ann Lewins and Christina Silver, *Using Software in Qualitative Research: A Step-by-Step Guide* (London: Sage, 2007), pp. 252–7.

[158] These are helpfully introduced in Mason, *Researching*, pp. 107–33.

[159] These might also be considered 'case studies', but as these are not full case studies I prefer to follow Martyn Percy (*Engaging*, p. 161) in his use of the term 'vignette'; also, Miles and Huberman, *Analysis*, pp. 81–3, on the nature and usefulness of vignettes.

This means that the researcher begins by analysing the holistic 'unit', or case study, to try to produce an explanation of processes, practices, or whatever, within that unit. This might, for example, involve an analysis of someone's biography [...] Instead of moving on to examine another unit (or biography) and to compare its features as though they were like for like with the first unit, the researcher compares the *explanation* of the first unit with the *explanation* of the second.[160]

In this project, the 'explanation' offered with respect to the particular respondent account is compared with the wider field of data.

This wider field of data is approached using 'cross-sectional' or 'categorical' analysis. Miles and Huberman describe the process of cross-sectional or categorical analysis as beginning with the application of 'codes', which is another name for 'tags or labels', to 'chunks' of data in the interview transcripts; these might be 'of varying size: words, phrases, sentences, or whole paragraphs'.[161] These are then organized into 'clusters' until 'identifiable themes [...] recur with some regularity'.[162] Mason refers to this as cross-sectional because once you have created a code or category, which might be an individual word, a concept, or a theme, you search for the code across the whole body of interview data. As you compile the various appearances of this code, you are creating a 'slice' across or through the whole range of data.[163]

To use the two approaches to analysis in the same project is not unusual. Mason notes: 'It is possible to approach the same substantive intellectual issues from these different analytical directions. Indeed, it is common to use both approaches in tandem, given the [...] interpretive and qualitative complexity with which qualitative researchers frequently want to grapple.'[164]

4.2.8 The validity of the gathered data

To think that any research project can produce 'pure' data or analysis is a grave mistake.[165] Schuman writes: 'No matter what method we use as sociologists we are always dealing with *data about* social reality, not with social reality itself. We are always drawing inferences, making interpretations, testing ideas.'[166] Data generation and data analysis within qualitative research are always simultaneous and interactive: researchers 'order and construct the

---

[160] Mason, *Researching*, p. 131.
[161] Miles and Huberman, *Analysis*, p. 56.
[162] Ibid., p. 57.
[163] Mason, *Researching*, p. 130.
[164] Ibid., p. 131.
[165] Hammersley and Atkinson, *Principles*, p. 131.
[166] Howard Schuman, 'Artifacts are in the Mind of the Beholder', in Nigel Fielding, ed., *Interviewing, Volume 1* (London: Sage, 2003), pp. 180–90, especially 188.

154   *Part III The Empirical Research*

social reality presented in their analyses. The lived experiences of respondents are refracted through the analyst's lens, never captured in any pure sense.'[167] In this context the 'truth' of the data is not a function of its factual accuracy.

In place of purity or factual accuracy, qualitative researchers tend to speak of the 'validity' of their data and analysis.[168] The most widely used method for demonstrating validity is 'triangulation'.[169] Triangulation is an adaptation of the methodology used by navigators and surveyors, who validate data obtained by observation and measurement by recourse not only to other instruments but by comparing it with data drawn from an entirely different source— the laws of geometry, specifically the geometrical properties of triangles.[170] In qualitative research, triangulation may occur by comparing data generated by different instruments, different sources, or different researchers. At the interpretive level it can be achieved by applying different theories to the same data to see which appears to have the greatest explanatory power.[171] In this project I use a form of 'triangulation' when, for example, I compare and contrast a respondent's questionnaire answers with their interview answers; or compare their memory, analysis, and interpretation of a given film with the reception history of the film as seen in archive data, or with my own viewing of the film.

However, triangulation is not a universally accepted method for establishing validity.[172] Overall I prefer to think that qualitative research can be validated only through the appropriate exercise of reflexivity. The goal of this methodological chapter, both in its consideration of the wider methodology appropriate to the correlation of theological theory and empirical research, and in its consideration of the methods and instruments utilized in that research, is helpfully summarized by Mason:

> In my view, validity of interpretation in any form of qualitative research is contingent upon [...] a demonstration of how that interpretation was reached [...] The basic principle here is you are never taking it as self-evident that a particular interpretation can be made of your data but instead that you are continuously and assiduously charting and justifying the steps through which your interpretations were made. If you do this effectively, it should enable you to show that you have understood and engaged with your own position, or standpoint, or analytical lens, in a *reflexive* sense.[173]

---

[167] Pawluch et al., *Ethnography*, p. 33; and Johnson et al., *Practice*, p. 74.
[168] For example, Burgess, *Field*, pp. 143-7; Mason, *Researching*, pp. 146-52.
[169] Burgess, *Field*, p. 144.
[170] Ibid., pp. 144-5.
[171] Ibid., p. 145.
[172] See, for example, Mason on the dangers of assuming that different methods can unproblematically validate one another: *Researching*, pp. 148-9.
[173] Ibid., p. 151.

4.2.9 The ethical question

Any research conducted with human participants must be carried out in an ethical manner and must be assessed and authorized by an institutional body.[174] Within Oxford University this role is carried out by CUREC—the Combined University Research Ethics Committee.[175] In order to obtain CUREC authorization for this project, a proposal had to be submitted and questionnaires assessing the potential risks and ethical issues that might be raised were completed. As the project involved only adults who participated on a purely voluntary basis and placed themselves at no physical or psychological risk, the process was straightforward and approval was gained on the basis of a commitment to conform to data protection requirements and to provide the opportunity for respondents to give their informed consent for their participation.

In the case of the questionnaires this consent was taken for granted if they agreed to go ahead after having the research briefly explained to them. At the beginning of the qualitative interviews the research project was explained to the respondents who were then asked for their signatures to confirm that they consented to take part. (Copies of these documents in English may be found in the appendices.)

---

[174] Pawluch et al., *Ethnography*, p. 26; Mason, *Researching*, pp. 29–31; also, Johnson et al. have a more philosophical discussion of the ethics of research in their chapter 'Method and the Researching Self', *Practice*, pp. 44–61.

[175] CUREC, *Research Ethics: Review of Research Using Human Participants*, <http://www.admin.ox.ac.uk/curec> (accessed 1 September 2008).

5

Contextualizing the Research Data

In this chapter the data generated by the questionnaire surveys will be utilized to map out the general features of filmgoers' experiences, and draw attention to key questions and preliminary hypotheses that will be revisited in the interview stage of research. The questionnaire data are considered with reference to the reading of Tillich's theology of revelation through culture developed in Chapter 2, but this pattern of engagement is often broken to allow for extended introductions to three important features of the research context. First, the nation of Uruguay will be introduced with basic demographic information and a representative account from one of the respondents of the life-experience of middle-class, educated members of Uruguayan society. Later, the recent political history and the unusual religious culture of the country will be considered in more detail. Second, there will be an overview of the development and contemporary reality of Latin American cinema. Finally, the *Cinemateca Uruguaya*, the cinema club that forms the specific social context from which the interview respondents were drawn, will be presented. Clearly, the goal of these sections cannot be an exhaustive cultural history. Rather, the purpose is to contextualize the empirical research, providing a background against which the data generated by the interviews may more clearly be seen.

5.1 ON EXPERIENCES RESEMBLING TILLICH'S THEORETICAL ACCOUNT

The last chapter discussed the genesis and formulation of the filter question that was presented to questionnaire respondents: 'Looking back upon your life, is there one exceptionally memorable occasion when a Latin American film shook, transformed or healed your life?' In Montevideo, 70 per cent of the questionnaire respondents answered this filter question affirmatively, named the relevant film, and answered questions about the associated experience. The extent of the film's impact was considered in a later question. However, it was noted in the last chapter that the filter question deliberately omitted reference to the concepts of 'ecstasy' and the 'ground of being' which were found in the original quote from Tillich's *Systematic Theology*. Therefore, merely answering the filter question affirmatively cannot be taken as evidence of an experience resembling the theoretical account.

A respondent was considered to have had an experience resembling the theoretical account of the possibility of revelation through culture only if their questionnaire answers demonstrated all of the following characteristics. First, they described their experience as irreducibly complex and were unable to differentiate between its intellectual, emotional, spiritual, and aesthetic characteristics; 34 per cent of respondents included all four categories. This was taken to be as close as the questionnaire answers could approach to a description of what Tillich named 'ecstatic' experience. Second, they described the experience as being one which included awareness of a 'presence or a power that was different to their daily lives' (they were not required to name this presence or power 'God'); 22 per cent answered 'yes' with a further 24 per cent answering 'perhaps'. This was taken to be as close as the questionnaire answers could approach to description of an experience of the 'ground of being'. Third, they noted a particular connection or identification with the films. This was taken as indicating the possibility that the two constellations of revelation described by Tillich had aligned in the experience. Finally, they were among the 74 per cent who described the experience as having had a '(great) positive impact' upon their lives.

A total of 11 questionnaires demonstrated all these characteristics. It is important to reiterate that the questionnaires do not form the primary data source and this result should not be taken as 'proof' of 11 respondents having had revelatory experiences. Rather, this information was used for the sampling strategy described in the last chapter. These respondents were taken to be the 'critical cases' whose experiences would be researched in far greater detail in the qualitative, semi-structured interviews.

5.2 ON THE SETTING FOR THE RESEARCH PROJECT: MONTEVIDEO, URUGUAY

Uruguay is a small country in the 'Southern Cone' of South America where it forms a wedge-shaped buffer between the much larger land masses and economies of Brazil to the north and Argentina to the south. Uruguay has a population of just 3,463,000, of whom nearly half (1,341,000) live in the capital city, Montevideo. Most Uruguayans are descended from Spanish, Italian, or other European immigrants. Literacy and life-expectancy are high for South

America, at 98 per cent and 75.3 years, respectively.¹ The country covers an area of 176,220 square kilometres.² The life-experience that lies behind these statistics can be illustrated by quotes from one of the interview respondents:

> I chose Uruguay voluntarily, nobody forced me to come here to Uruguay. I lived in Buenos Aires, I was born in the federal capital and [...] and I ... since I was 18, 20 years old, said that someday, when I could, I would come to live in Uruguay because it is a country where you can live a more tranquil life.

Later statements suggested that experience removed the rosy tint from this respondent's vision of Uruguay, especially with regard to its social, economic, and political character.

> But this is a fact, you have to have an income ... a decent one. Because ... this is a, my life, my conclusion after living twelve years in Montevideo, and having chosen it voluntarily, is that this is a beautiful country in which to live ... with a decent salary. [Laughs] The ideal, for Uruguay, is to generate your income abroad and then live here [...] The economy here has frequent depressions [...] there's a certain conception ... I believe an outdated one, that Uruguay is a peaceful country of educated, well-mannered people. I believe that has been deteriorating over time. Now it's not so peaceful, nor are the people so educated, nor is the state education what it was thirty or forty years ago. In fact ... the politicians, the businessmen, the successful professionals, they all send their children to private schools, not state schools. And that's a sign—that grabs your attention. Lamentably ... [Uruguay is] uhm ... governed by a corrupt political class, very corrupt, thirty or forty families that are the real owners of the country and, if nothing changes. And percentage, perhaps1 percent of the population, control the other 99 percent.

Nonetheless, there is still much to recommend Uruguay as a place to live.

> With regards to the rest, well, Uruguay is a, is a country that is blessed geographically with a good climate, it's well removed from the climatic disasters that other countries suffer, it doesn't have any border disputes with its neighbours. Here the army is ... practically just a symbol, because here they don't spend anything on defence, there's not even a special training for the soldiers because no one can imagine there being an armed conflict. And that's a very important part of the budget in the developed countries. This ... is a country that, generally, a country of geographical bounty, it has fertile lands, a lot of fresh water, a very important system of underground aquifers, that will be, according to the experts, a very important resource in the coming decades. The ... the crops don't require any particular care. The Spanish came here, they brought their horses, a few cows and, all on their own, they reproduced without any help. So,

---

¹ Instituto del Tercer Mundo, *The World Guide 2005/2006*, 10th edn (Oxford: New Internationalist Publications, 2005), p. 575.
² Ibid., p. 576.

let's say, geographically, geo-physically, let's say, Uruguay is a blessed country [...] That's my view of Uruguay.

5.3 ON ENGAGEMENT WITH LATIN AMERICAN CINEMA

Returning to the questionnaire data, the first set of questions relate to the individual, the recipient of revelation, the first of the six aspects of the revelatory experience considered in the reading of Tillich's theology. The questionnaires began by enquiring into the respondents' film-watching habits. These questions were initially intended simply to put the respondent at ease and to habituate them to giving a range of answers to non-confrontational questions. However, it became clear that these questions also provided a theoretically significant insight into the degree of 'seriousness' of the respondents' relationship with film.

To measure 'seriousness', points were awarded on the basis of frequency (for example, the number of films watched and the number of film-related activities engaged in) and intensity (for example, engagement with more 'difficult' film genres and less common film-related activities such as reading theory or writing about film). The usefulness of these questions was anecdotally validated by frequent correlations between high scores and a stated professional relation to film-making or film studies. Overall the qualitative interviews suggest that this initial sounding probably under-reported the seriousness of each respondent's engagement with film. For example, upon interview a respondent with a near average seriousness rating of 56 can say, 'Let's see. Let's put it on a scale. I would say the most important thing in my life is... first, my health; uhm, second, my work; ah, third, my family... and I would say that fourth is cinema.' This 'seriousness' is an unsurprising characteristic of a group of respondents accessed at a festival run by a cinema club, and suggests that rather than being mere filmgoers most of the respondents were serious film fans with extensive experience and knowledge of Latin American and world cinema.

Their discussion of film and its role in their life must be seen in light of this knowledge which, in Hill's terminology, forms part of the 'portfolio of interpretation' which they bring to the films they watch. Therefore, the more in-depth analysis of films and the respondents' interactions with them will be greatly aided by an introduction to the history of Latin American cinema. Here, a brief overview of its development through the twentieth century will progress through reference to pre-history; golden age; the movement known as 'New Latin American Cinema'; and finally, the 'qualified success story' of the most recent past. It will be suggested that seeing the latter three stages in Hegelian terms, as a process of thesis, antithesis, and synthesis, is a helpful means of picturing the development.³

Many commentators have noted the dangers and difficulties associated with speaking too glibly of a national or regional cinema. There are those, like David King, author of *Magical Reels*, who believe that any attempt to identify regional characteristics is misguided.⁴ It should therefore be noted that reference to *a* Latin American cinema and, further, to three stages in its development is a simplification of an extremely complex subject.⁵ Nonetheless, as King has pointed out, with reference to one of Latin America's most celebrated writers, 'To try to impose [an adequate] categorization on the whole of Latin America would be to risk moving into the world of Borge's cartographers, who produced a map of the empire the size of the empire.'⁶ In other words, simplification is necessary even though it is not entirely satisfactory.

Elena and López note that Latin American cinema is 'as old as the invention itself—the first film shows in the area took place in Rio de Janeiro on 8 July 1896, to be repeated in many other capitals before the end of the year'.⁷ King continues the story: 'From these [urban] centres, the itinerant film-maker/projectionists could follow the tracks of the railways which, in the interest of export economies, linked the urban metropolis to the hinterland, projecting in cafes and village halls or setting up their own tents (*carpas*).'⁸ This period of pre-history saw a 'cottage industry' of 'artisanal production' developing.⁹ From the first there was a strong realist tendency in Latin American films.

In his *Companion to Latin American Film*, Stephen Hart writes:

> The earliest films produced in Latin America aspired to what might be called the Lumière blueprint. Yet, even though they focused on the discourse of the quotidian, this proved in some cases to be rather more gripping than a film about a train entering a station packed full of commuters.¹⁰

For example, during the Mexican revolution, rebel General Pancho Villa was quick to agree lucrative financial terms with film-makers, granting unparalleled access to the lurid material provided by his campaigns, battles, and executions.¹¹ Documentary was also attractive, because its local focus broached subjects that did not interest the large international film

---

³ When available, bibliographic references will be given to English language versions of these texts; in all other cases, as elsewhere in the book, the translations are my own.
⁴ King, *Magical*, p. 4.
⁵ Alberto Elena and Marina Díaz López, eds, *24 Frames: The Cinema of Latin America* (London: Wallflower Press, 2003), pp. 10–11.
⁶ King, *Magical*, pp. 258–9.
⁷ Elena and López, *Frames*, p. 2.
⁸ King, *Magical*, p. 8.
⁹ Ibid., pp. 9 and 25.
¹⁰ Hart, *Companion*, p. 1.
¹¹ Ibid., p. 1; and King, *Magical*, p. 14.

competitors: 'football competitions, civic ceremonies, military parades, often organized into film "journals"'.[12] Unlike the New Latin American Cinema to which I will turn later, these documentaries were almost always filmed from the point of view of the powerful elites.[13]

As the financial motivation for making local documentaries to compete with the more generic international imports suggests, 'practices did not emerge as self-contained movements within Latin America: the subcontinent's culture has always evolved in a dynamic relationship of attraction and rejection with work produced in Europe and North America'.[14] Initially, European imports flourished, but the development of the classical Hollywood style, most importantly by D. W. Griffiths, and the strife in Europe over the period of World War I, meant that Hollywood dominated from 1916 onwards.[15]

> During World War I, the European film industry virtually closed down, not least because the same chemicals—that is nitrates—used to produce film celluloid were also used to manufacture explosives and gunpowder. A year after the conclusion of the war 90 per cent of all films screened in Europe were American [...] In Latin America the figure was even higher; by 1920, about '95 per cent of screen time in South America was taken up by U.S. films'.[16]

The impact of imports from the north was a major factor in the way that Latin American cinema developed through the twentieth century.[17] Even the coming of sound failed to disturb the northern hegemony: 'a major opportunity for autonomous development' was negated by elaborate strategies for the dubbing of Hollywood products.[18]

Nonetheless, the 1930s and 1940s did become a golden period (*epoca de oro*) of Latin American, and particularly Mexican, cinema. King writes, 'The success of Mexican cinema in the 1940s was due to a series of circumstances: the added commercial opportunities offered by the war, the emergence of a number of important directors and cinematographers and the consolidation of a star system resting on proven formulae.'[19] An important measure of this, 'the most dynamic decade of Mexico's film-making', is the rise in the number of local productions in the domestic market: from 6.2 per cent in 1941 to 24.2 per cent

---

[12] Ibid., p. 21.
[13] Ibid., p. 26.
[14] Ibid., p. 69.
[15] Ibid., p. 10.
[16] Hart, *Companion*, p. 4; see also, King, *Magical*, p. 11 (from which the 95 per cent quote is taken).
[17] King helpfully charts the complex relations between the geo-political intrigues and priorities of the times and the Latin American film industry in a section entitled 'Hollywood in Latin America', in *Magical*, pp. 31–6.
[18] Ibid., p. 54.
[19] Ibid., p. 47.

in 1949. A similar story may be told of both Argentina and Brazil, traditionally the other powerhouses in Latin American cinema.[20] However, as King's reference to 'proven formulae' suggests, this was not necessarily the most artistically productive of times. Hart writes:

> Both the *comedia ranchera* [Mexican musical melodramas] and the *chanchada* [a style of comedy-musical from Brazil] can be seen as symptoms of a culture struggling to find its voice beneath the pressure of acculturation from without. It is clear that the Mexican melodramas and the Brazilian *chanchadas*—in that they were successful re-vampings of the Hollywood idiom—led to commercial success but also to an artistic cul-de-sac. There were always going to be the poor cousins.[21]

If in the 1940s Latin American cinema could 'still find the energy to try to compete with the huge factory of dreams', it might be that they had sacrificed both their individuality and their artistic passions to do so; as a result, their defiance was soon snuffed out.[22] If this was the high period of the original thesis of Latin American cinema, what was to come was an almost perfect antithesis. The new movement broke with both the colonial powers of the old world and 'the *old* cinemas of Latin America'.[23] 'Theirs would be a lucid, critical realist, popular, anti-imperialist, revolutionary cinema which would break with neo-colonialist attitudes and the monopolistic practices of North American countries.'[24]

> A desire to unveil the conflicting realities of their own countries has led young directors in Latin America since the early 1950s to explore the political potential of the medium. [Film-makers in Argentina, Brazil, Cuba, Colombia, Chile, Uruguay, and Venezuela] sought committed ways to use film as an instrument of social awareness. By the end of the decade and through a concerted effort, these filmmakers sought to join diverse radical projects developed within specific national contexts into a broader ideological and cultural agenda capable of encompassing the territorial expanse of the continent. This ideological agenda was initiated and developed through a cinematographic movement known as the New Latin American Cinema.[25]

This was what Tillich might refer to as a *kairos* moment in the history of Latin American cinema. A moment of great 'optimism that a wave of social change could sweep through the continent' was serendipitously allied with a fresh model of film-making imported from Europe, particularly from Italy.[26]

---

[20] Ibid., p. 4.
[21] Hart, *Companion*, p. 5.
[22] Elena and López, *Frames*, p. 3.
[23] Zuzana M. Pick, *The New Latin American Cinema: A Continental Project* (Austin, TX: University of Texas Press, 1993), p. 190.
[24] King, *Magical*, p. 66.
[25] Pick, *Cinema*, p. 1.
[26] King, *Magical*, p. 67.

Indeed, the importance of the Italian model was magnified when a number of Latin American film-makers—including the Argentine Fernando Birri and the Cubans Gutíerrez Alea and García Espinosa—went to study at the Centre for Experimental Cinematography at Rome.[27] As Elena and López present it: 'certain realist and socially inspired traditions began to take shape which found themselves in tune with some of the most innovative aesthetic movements coming from overseas'.[28] The confluence of the streams of social change and aesthetic innovation is neatly brought out by Hart:

> Both Italian Neo-Realism and the French New Wave played a crucial role in the formulation of a new cinematic style in the work of Latin American film directors in the 1960s, for that was the decade in which Latin American film finally established its uniqueness and identity. It is arguable, though, whether these artistic experiments would have led to the formulation of a new cinematic movement were it not for the arrival in Latin America of a new political language, specifically that new political horizon which was provided by the Cuban Revolution.[29]

The founding documents of this movement were written at the Viña del Mar film festival in Chile in 1967, and from the first the goal was not merely to chronicle, nor simply to create, art, but to foment revolution and social change.

> The unfolding of the New Latin American Cinema as an ideological project and a cinematographic practice—is the result of its capacity to conceptualize the social and political impact of cinema as a cultural practice [...] What remains stable is the movement's resolve to use film as a tool for social change, a vehicle to transform national and regional expressions, support international differences, and assert regional forms of cultural autonomy.[30]

Such a politically motivated and practically focused cinema was always likely to result in as many manifestos and political statements as it was films. Two of the most important were written by the Cuban, Julio García Espinosa, and the Argentinians, Fernando Solanas and Octavio Gettino.

Espinosa describes how Latin American cinema must break from its previous slavish following of US and European customs and become more authentic. Mass culture, produced by the elite for the masses, must be replaced by folk art, produced by the people for the people.

> Nowadays perfect cinema—technically and artistically masterful—is almost always reactionary cinema. The major temptation facing Cuban cinema at this time—when it is achieving its objective of becoming a cinema of quality, one

---

[27] Hart, *Companion*, p. 8.
[28] Elena and López, *Frames*, p. 4.
[29] Hart, *Companion*, p. 7.
[30] Pick, *Cinema*, pp. 3–4.

which is culturally meaningful within the revolutionary process—is precisely that of transforming itself into a perfect cinema. [What is actually called for is precisely an] ... imperfect cinema.[31]

Solanas and Gettino, writing in 1969, are even more direct. They note that the most basic building blocks of cinema are already related to the oppressive powers, 'conceived not to gratuitously transmit any ideology, but to satisfy, in the first place, the cultural and surplus value needs *of a specific ideology, of a specific world-view: that of U.S. finance capital*'.[32] However, 'Real alternatives differing from those offered by the System [...] can be found in the revolutionary opening towards a cinema outside and against the System, in a cinema of liberation: the *third cinema*.'[33] This requires 'guerrilla film-making' with 'the camera as our rifle [...] The camera is the inexhaustible *expropriator of image-weapons*; the projector, *a gun that can shoot 24 frames per second*.'[34]

Solanas was forced into exile with the coming of military dictatorship to Argentina, and he lived in France from 1976 to 1983. Upon his return he continued his trajectory of political film-making, and in *La mirada: Reflexiones sobre cine y cultura* Solanas showed that his views had not mellowed. He angrily denied that there was any equivalence between the few dozen, or perhaps hundred, killed by left-wing guerrillas and the tens, or even hundreds, of thousands killed by the oppressive powers of the political right over the course of Argentina's history.[35]

In one particularly interesting strand of argument that weaves through the book, Solanas develops ideas that provide a bridge between the thought of Paul Tillich and the accounts of the interview respondents that will be considered in the next chapter. Solanas bases his thought in his own life-history, and the universal experience of the trauma, the 'exile', of adolescence, particularly the traumatic break away from the family home and the attempt to live your dreams.[36] He argues that the younger generation of artists must always act out a similar process if they are to create something relevant and new.

> I say: this is possible. I say it especially to the young. It is possible to create. Yes, it is possible, on condition that you leave behind the prisons, the reformatories, the educational establishments where they wish to inter us. *We have to leap walls and leave in order to create, we have to invent ourselves.*[37]

---

[31] Espinosa, 'Imperfect', p. 71.
[32] Fernando Solanas and Octavio Gettino, 'Towards a Third Cinema: Notes and Experiences for the Development of a Cinema of Liberation in the Third World', in Michael T. Martin, ed., *New Latin American Cinema, Volume I: Theory, Practices and Transcontinental Articulations* (Detroit, MI: Wayne State University Press, 1997), pp. 33–58, especially 41.
[33] Solanas and Gettino, 'Third', pp. 42–3.
[34] Ibid., pp. 49–50.
[35] Solanas, *Mirada*, pp. 232–3.
[36] Ibid., for example, pp. 16 and 227.
[37] Ibid., p. 230.

Here, Solanas appears to be advocating a cinematic equivalent of the 'Protestant Principle' and in this same context he also uses 'style' in a very similar way to Tillich. 'From there [the questioning and passion of the new generation] flows what we could call the new style, the style of a new generation or a new epoch.'[38] Solanas here describes the power of this new cinema in terms of 'opening' and 'breaking' that resemble those used by both Tillich and the interviewees:

> I am convinced that the function of the artist, of the creator, of the discoverer, is to open new perspectives upon life, on the relation that we have with life, with all creativity. *It has to do with the breaking of closed systems, to compare and evaluate one against the other, to examine the languages in their purest potency and specificity.*[39]

Given the revolutionary tone of such writings, it is perhaps ironic that it is frequently suggested that financial expediency was responsible for the synthesis that has recently sublated the old thesis of the golden age and the radical antithesis of the New Latin American Cinema.[40]

> In spite of its passions and its very real achievements in the Latin American context, there were problems that the New Latin Cinema was never able to overcome: there were drawbacks in the single-minded search for an ideology-laden language with which to record reality in which Latin American film directors were involved. It was clear, for example, that—in creating a politicised image—Latin American cinema was typecasting itself into a ghetto of Third World cinema, an image which it would with some difficulty cast off [...] the Latin American film directors of the 1960s and 1970s were producing films which were making waves in European film festivals but—in direct contradistinction to the Hollywood blockbuster—were not 'popular' in the sense of attracting large audiences in Latin America.[41]

Deborah Shaw has written two books that investigate the recent resurgence in the popularity and artistic merit of Latin American cinema. In her first book, *Contemporary Cinema of Latin America: 10 Key Films*, she notes that in the 1990s and early twenty-first century Latin American cinema has become stronger through use of international systems of funding and distribution. The fact that successful directors of recent years, many with a background in advertising, have greater understanding and respect for the commercial aspects of film-making is also important. Alejandro Gonzalez Iñárritu, creator of *Amores Perros* (2001)*, 21 Grams* (2003), and *Babel* (2006), has said that he and his producer 'loathe the government financed movie-making that seems

---

[38] Ibid., p. 226.
[39] Ibid., p. 229.
[40] Hart, *Companion*, pp. 12–14.
[41] Ibid., p. 10.

to operate by the maxim: "If nobody understands or nobody goes to see a movie it must be a masterpiece".[42] Nonetheless, there is a genuine synthesis: the commercial viability of the golden age has been grafted on to the social emphasis and politically committed film-making of the New Latin American Cinema.

Shaw draws upon work on Scandinavian film to fund her analysis of the Latin American phenomenon. 'Mette Hjort (2000) has applied literary critics Peter Lamarque and Steia Haugom Olsen's (1994) categories of perennial and topical themes to her analysis of Danish cinema, and these categories can be useful in assessing the success of the Latin American films selected in this book.'[43] Perennial themes are those that resonate across historical and cultural boundaries and are quasi-universal in their thrust, while topical themes arise within and are relevant to one particular historical and cultural context.

Central Station (1998) by Walter Salles is a very good example of this kind of film-making, uniting the perennial and the topical.

> The initial script and the later film version did not anxiously look for codes that might appeal in the international market, but instead told a universal story—a child's search for his father—within a very Brazilian context [...] These thematic concerns have been constant in Brazilian cinema since the earliest days of Cinema Novo, but they are given a fresh inflection in Salles's treatment.[44]

In her second book, *Contemporary Latin American Cinema: Breaking into the Global Market*, Shaw returns to this theme of the way the local and the universal, the commercial and the social, have been brought together. She argues that 'the most profitable films of recent times—*Cidade de Deus, Central do Brasil, Y tu mamá también*, and Walter Salles's *Los diarios de motocicleta* (*The Motorcycle Diaries*, 2004)' have retained their social conscience and socio-political agenda, but:

> Unlike more explicitly political filmmaking of the earlier era, this agenda is filtered through a personal, intimate, character-driven focus and shares high production values and an emphasis on an entertaining plot [...] The strength of some of the most successful films from Latin America, in contrast to many (but not all) of its Hollywood counterparts, is that high-quality entertainment is produced without the loss of a socially committed agenda.[45]

It might be that with this synthesis Latin American film-making has finally matured:

---

[42] Quoted in ibid., p. 12.
[43] Shaw, *Contemporary*, pp. 2–3.
[44] King, *Magical*, p. 273.
[45] Deborah Shaw, ed., *Contemporary Latin American Cinema: Breaking Into the Global Market* (Plymouth, UK: Rowman & Littlefield, 2007), pp. 4–5.

Amores Perros and *Cidade de Deus* have recourse to breathtakingly innovative filmic techniques which astounded even juries and audiences in Hollywood and Paris. It was when Latin American films made audiences around the world sit up and say 'how did they do that?', rather than 'authentic but the special effects aren't that good' that Latin American film had come of age, seemingly overnight.[46]

The intellectual/theological puzzle about the possibility of revelation through film that finally resulted in this research project came into being against the backdrop of this contemporary success in Latin American cinema, particularly its ability to marry social conscience with striking imagery, accessible characters, and gripping narratives.

Although Uruguay has a very small cinema industry, there is no doubt that it has participated in this renaissance. Writing on cinema in a volume of essays about the first twenty years of the return to democracy in Uruguay, Manuel Martínez Carril says: 'In 2003, the four Uruguayan films produced that year won almost seventy prizes in festivals, shows and competitions, which gives a coefficient of around 17, the highest, per film produced, in the whole of Latin America.'[47] As recently as August 2008, the British film magazine *Sight and Sound* chose a Uruguayan film, *El baño del Pápa*, as its film of the month.[48] The films which were mentioned in this context in the Introduction to this book—films like *25 Watts*, *Whisky*, and *Aparte*—are of this generation.

5.4 ON THE IMPORTANCE OF THE *CINEMATECA* FILM CLUB

Respondents who answered the filter question affirmatively were asked which film had been the focus of the shaking, transforming, or healing experience. Answers to this question generated data which have relevance for two of the six aspects of the theoretical account: the individual who is the recipient of revelation and the artwork that is the medium of revelation. In Montevideo, 50 respondents were able and willing to name a film which had shaken, transformed, or healed them. Across these respondents, 36 different films were named. (Similarly, in Mar del Plata, 26 respondents named 19 different films.) The large number of films listed hints at the great importance of the unique connections that link individual respondents to particular films, an issue which will be discussed further in the next chapter.

---

[46] Hart, *Companion*, pp. 13–14.
[47] Manuel Martínez Carril, 'El espejo del cine', in Gerardo Caetano, ed., *20 Años de democracia, Uruguay 1985–2005: Miradas múltiples* (Montevideo, Uruguay: Ediciones Santillana, 2005), pp. 551–71, especially 569.
[48] Michael Brooke, 'Bottom of the Heap', *Sight and Sound*, August 2008, pp. 50–51.

Considering the films listed in Mar del Plata against those proffered in Montevideo raises interesting questions with regard to the provenance and the subject matter of the films.

Table 5.1. Films by subject matter

	Mar del Plata (Argentina)	Montevideo (Uruguay)
Argentinean films	86%	41%
Uruguayan films	0%	10%
Political or social films	45%	76%

The first two lines of Table 5.1, which show a marked bias towards local films, suggest that, in these contexts at least, a strong affective association with the setting of the film is an important contributing factor to its impact. However, the third line of the table is, perhaps, of greater theoretical relevance. The Montevideo list is markedly more concerned with politics and social conscience than that of Mar del Plata.[49] Clearly, such differences could be a reflection of any one of a number of variables that distinguish the universe of potential respondents in Mar del Plata from that in Montevideo—age, class, professional status, for example—and my sampling techniques are not designed to shed light on this kind of variation. However, I will suggest below that the role of the *Cinemateca* film club in relation to the Montevideo respondents might best account for this difference.

The *Cinemateca* club was initially only peripheral to the research project: they happened to be running a festival at a convenient time. However, the club moved towards the centre of the project in two stages. First, their helpfulness in offering access to their members in their auditoriums and venues, along with the production of credentials to legitimate the researcher, and later their willingness to allow the interviews to take place on their premises and to open their extensive archives for examination, meant that the research project became far more closely associated with the club than had been anticipated. However, more important still was the recognition, which dawned as the research data were interpreted and analyzed, of the role played by the club in the lives of its members. As will be seen in the next chapter, this was intimately related to a new conceptualization of the revelatory potential of cinema that arose out of data-driven analysis of the interviews. For these reasons it is important to offer an introduction to the club's history, purpose, and current reality.

The *Cinemateca Uruguaya* was founded in 1952 at the zenith of cinema's popularity in Uruguay. The social historian Osvaldo Saratsola offers some remarkable statistics for cinematic attendance during this period. His data

---

[49] Remarkably, Argentina's most famous political film, *La hora de los hornos* (1968), receives three mentions in Uruguay but none in Mar del Plata.

state that in 1952 in Montevideo (pop. 814,561), there were 102 cinemas and a total spectatorship of 18,032,109; in other words, approximately 22 visits per annum for every member of the population. (By the last year in Saratsola's records, 2002, a population of 1,382,142 were making 2,368,089 visits to the cinema: less than two visits per person, per annum.)[50]

The organization's institutional documents state that: 'The purpose of the *Cinemateca* consists in contributing to the development of the cinematographic, and generally artistic, culture of wide sectors of society, and especially among the young, maintaining and preserving the heritage of motion-pictures, and giving the public access to the spiritual and creative values of *auteur* cinema.'[51]

To this end, the *Cinemateca* carries forward a number of related functions. Primarily, their role is the diffusion and exhibition of the best of non-commercial world cinema. Their 8,200 members pay a small monthly subscription (between £2 and £3) and then have free access to watch as many of the 453 screenings each month as they wish in any of the club's four cinemas. This primary undertaking is supplemented through the maintenance of a large archive of motion pictures; another archive of film-related texts; and a film school which has been running since 1972. On a smaller scale, the *Cinemateca* also acts a publisher and runs a small cinematic museum and a video library.[52]

The early years of the *Cinemateca Uruguaya* were precarious, but from the 1970s it flourished under the leadership of Manuel Martín Carril (who is still an executive director). The importance of its role in promoting independent cinema in Uruguay is clearly visible in another of Saratsola's statistics: of the 4,612 films that have been screened in Uruguay outside the commercial cinemas, *Cinemateca* is responsible for showing 3,800 of them.

The *Cinemateca* was caught up in the political struggles of the period of Latin American dictatorships. Indeed, the director Carril has written that in this period: 'The cinematographic culture, supposedly a glory of Uruguay since the early fifties [...] was confused with a form of cultural and political resistance [...] the artists, particularly the cinematographers, were perceived as the left, the opposition.'[53]

Today the *Cinemateca* struggles economically. The editorial of the handbook to the XXV Festival Cinematográfico Internacional del Uruguay (25th Uruguayan International Cinema Festival), at which the questionnaire research took place, states that this *Cinemateca*-run festival is 'the poorest in

---

[50] Osvaldo Saratsola, *Función completa, por favor: Un siglo de cine en Montevideo* (Montevideo, Uruguay: Trilce, 2005), pp. 300–1.
[51] *Cinemateca*, 'Documentos'.
[52] Ibid.
[53] Carril, 'Espejo', p. 551.

the world'.[54] In fact, during this very festival the paid employees of the club went on strike because negotiations chaired by the Ministry of Employment had broken down, with the *Cinemateca* simply unable to meet their obligations on pay.[55] (By the time the second stage of interview research took place in July 2007, *Cinemateca* had been forced to close three of its auditoria.)

Cinemateca documents consistently differentiate between two types of cinema:—the commercial and the artistic. In 2002 the editors wrote:

> [Hollywood] is a production-line entertainment factory with prefabricated products of proven commercial success [...] objects to use, consume and discard. The industry lives off these products that, in general, don't place the spirit among their priorities. But the cinema, like literature, is a medium within which there are *auteurs* that express themselves and communicate with an attentive and sensible spectator capable of appreciating other qualities. And it is these qualities which, incidentally, turn out to be more gratifying, more provocative for people, more capable of spiritual enrichment, than the predictable chases, the curvaceous blondes, the commonplaces of sentiment without sensibility.[56]

The idea that there is a distinction between two kinds of cinema is developed by many of the respondents during interview and is also present in the 2007 festival handbook:

> [It is these films] that guarantee that the cinema has been and continues to be an artistic expression and not a business industry which is what the centres of power, particularly Hollywood, want to make it. But as we suspected, not everything is Hollywood [...] For a quarter of a century 'The Uruguayan Festival of International Cinema' has remained firm in its intent to make known that cinema that is worth the effort, that justifies the continuing belief that the cinema is art and an expression of the spirit, of the talent, of the ever new creativity of the cinematic *auteurs*.[57]

Cinemateca continues to be held in great affection and to exercise an important role in the lives of its 10,000 members and the wider film-loving population of Montevideo. In a well-circulated advert, alongside a line drawing of a sexy, Tinkerbell-like fairy, *Cinemateca* offers transformation: 'We cast our spells against the plague of timidity, we help the repressed, we fight using the magic of the different and we struggle using the fascination of freedom. Warning: once you enter there's no turning back.'[58] There is some evidence that this is not a vain boast. On the 'Letters' page of the *Cinemateca* website,

---

[54] *Cinemateca, Boletín del XXV Festival Cinematográfico Internacional del Uruguay* (Montevideo, Uruguay: *Cinemateca*, 2007), p. 3.
[55] Anon., 'Conflicto: Empleados de *Cinemateca* reclaman aumentos', *El Diario*, March 2007.
[56] *Boletín de Cinemateca Uruguaya*, December 2002, quoted in Saratsola, *Función*, p. 209.
[57] *Cinemateca, Festival*, p. 3.
[58] Ibid., back cover.

one member states: 'I have been a member since I was sixteen years-old and without a doubt it has changed my life—for the better.'[59]

5.5 ON RESPONDENTS' USE OF RELIGIOUS LANGUAGE

Respondents were asked which characteristics of the films they mentioned had the greatest relevance to their experiences (Table 5.2).

Table 5.2. Film characteristic by its importance

Film characteristic	Great importance	Some or Great importance
Narrative	86%	100%
Message	78%	98%
Cinematography	56%	96%
Music	40%	82%
Setting	68%	96%
Particular scene	60%	74%

These results, which in recognition of the limitations of questionnaire-generated data must still be considered preliminary, present a potential challenge to Tillich's theory of what gives the artwork its revelatory potential. Respondents clearly consider the discursive elements of the films, for example the narrative and the message, to be of greatest importance in relation to their experiences. This will be discussed further in the next chapter in relation to the content of revelation.

Other groups of questions (Table 5.3) probe different elements of what was described in the reading of Tillich as the event of revelation. The first questions refer to the context of the experience, where it took place, with whom and when.

Table 5.3. Experience by location, companions, and time

Where?	Cinema	At home	Friend's house	Unknown
	78%	18%	0%	4%
With whom?	Alone	With friends	With partner	With family
	40%	38%	14%	8%
When?	Childhood	More than 5 yr	More than 1 yr	Less than 1 yr
	14%	42%	22%	22%

[59] *Cinemateca*, 'Cartas', <http://www.*Cinemateca*.org.uy/cartas.html> (accessed 17 June 2008).

The fact that 56 per cent of the experiences took place more than five years ago gives some credibility to the suggestion that these were exceptional and memorable events in the respondents' lives.

Another substantial variation between Montevideo and Mar del Plata emerges concerning the percentage of experiences that took place in a cinema and the percentage that took place while the respondent was alone. In Montevideo these percentages are 78 per cent in a cinema (against 62 per cent in Mar del Plata) and 40 per cent alone (against 23 per cent in Mar del Plata). Once again, it is likely that these differences relate to the Montevideo respondents belonging to a cinema club where, once the quota is paid, attendance is free and watching alone is socially acceptable.

The second group of questions, which relate to the event of revelation, address the nature of the experience: 60 per cent of respondents declared that the onset was 'immediate', occurring during the film-viewing; 26 per cent that it was 'gradual', occurring after the film had finished; and 13 per cent declared that it was 'both'. An interesting datum is generated when the answers to this question are correlated with the question about the nature of the experience. Overall, 56 per cent of respondents stated that their experience included an 'intellectual' component; 96 per cent an 'emotional' component; 50 per cent an 'aesthetic' component; and 48 per cent a 'spiritual' component. As noted above, 34 per cent declared that their experience was a mixture of all four of these, and 70 per cent that it was a mixture of at least three elements.

First, it may be noted that 100 per cent of those who said the onset of the experience was 'gradual' emphasized the intellectual aspect of the experience (as opposed to 73 per cent of those who said the onset of the experience was 'immediate'). Concomitantly, 100 per cent of those who described the onset as 'immediate' emphasized the emotional aspect of the experience (as opposed to 95 per cent of those who said the onset was 'gradual'). This statistical link between the manner of the onset of the experience and the nature of the experience will be discussed in greater detail below. Along with the question raised above, about the importance of the discursive aspects of films, it has implications with regard to the validity of Tillich's understanding of the relevant properties of an artwork and the way in which it creates its impact.

A preliminary hypothesis might suggest that the conceptual net cast by the questionnaire might be capturing two distinct types of experience: first, a mystical-type experience, associated with immediate onset, an emotional response and with the aesthetic characteristics of the film text; second, a cognitive-type experience, associated with gradual onset and intellectual engagement with the discursive characteristics of the film text.

In the last chapter triangulation was introduced as an occasionally useful means of establishing the validity and reliability of different data sources by checking results against data derived from other sources. At this point, triangulation of questionnaire and interview data uncovers a potentially important lack of clarity in reference to the term 'spiritual'. In particular, a number of the interview respondents found it hard to distinguish between the 'emotional' and 'spiritual' characteristics of their experiences. For example, 'And, and, and spiritual, yes. Spiritual in... I don't know what, what is the difference from emotional, no?' And again, 'Spiritual, I'm not sure... let's see... no, it would be a little mixed-up with the emotional.'

This does not appear to be a problem of translation. Spanish dictionaries differentiate clearly between the two terms in precisely the same way as English dictionaries, and Spanish–English dictionaries translate the terms with the expected English counterparts.[60] Moreover, some respondents clearly did associate 'spiritual' with religious belief. For example, one respondent answered 'No' for precisely this reason: 'I don't know, the thing is that for me... the word spiritual... uhm, makes me, makes me... I associate it with the Christian religion or with... or with conceptions... uhm, I don't know, from the middle ages.' As the documents considered above demonstrate that the term 'spiritual' is used by the *Cinemateca* club in contexts where a religious or mystical element is clearly not present, it may be that the Spanish word, at least in Uruguay, carries the broader meaning of, for example, the German *Geist*.

To avoid the temptation to read too much importance into the respondents' reporting of the complexity of their experience (which in the sampling, at least, was taken as an indicator of a possibly ecstatic experience), it should be noted that a number of respondents linked the complexity to the nature of the cinematic medium itself. This comment is illustrative of this widely felt opinion:

> They are categories that at times we establish in order to, to think through something [...] But I think that they all go together... you know that... that, that... the cinema is a, is an experience that incorporates... if it's well made, if the film is well made... uhm... it hits you, let's say, well, emotionally, intellectually, uhm, spiritually, or well, aesthetically or whatever.

It was for this reason that the sampling strategy used to select the critical cases required that a complex experience be coupled with an affirmative answer to the most explicitly religious or mystical question before the experience be taken to resemble the theoretical account. Overall, 46 per cent of respondents answered affirmatively with respect to a question that asked: 'At any point during the experience did you sense a presence or a power (it doesn't matter whether you would call it God or not) that is distinct from your everyday life?' A question of this nature may be understood variously by different respondents and a great breadth of interpretation is present in the

---

[60] Beatriz Galimberti Jarman and Roy Russell, eds, *The Oxford Spanish Dictionary* (Oxford: Oxford University Press, 1994).

interview data. For example, one spoke of theatre rather than film and related the presence or power to the 'energy' that builds between cast and audience.

However, most respondents did make the intended link from the question to religious-type experience, whether they considered this positive or negative: 'Ah, well, I'm Catholic'; 'Eh...uhm...well, really, I don't believe in God.' Two interview respondents who answered 'perhaps' had great difficulty articulating why they had answered in this way. The inarticulacy of one respondent, a trained psychologist, at this point is in marked contrast to his normally clear and coherent commentary:

> Eh...yes, I don't know, I, I...because...that question, well...yes, what happened is that it's formulated so, so...well, I understand that it wasn't intended in that way, no, no, no, no, well, well, well, and I don't remember it, don't remember, don't remember, don't remember it in that way.

Another respondent answered 'perhaps' and then struggled to explain her answer: 'Ah...it's that...No, I don't know...I can't, can't, can't explain to you. I don't know. No, no, no, I don't know. The truth is, I don't know.' However, it does appear, at least in this case, that the problem is not a lack of understanding of the meaning or the mystical/religious inference of the question. After her hesitant explanation, the respondent was asked whether she thought the question was a sensible or meaningful one. Her answer implies that she understands the question and can relate to it.

> No, no, no things have happened to me, well, things that, things that occasionally, I mean...I'm not a religious person...no. But no...but...well, I say...because I've never really engaged with that topic. But...I know that...there are people...[some garbled words]...and I'm not closed off in that position. Uhm...and well...I don't know, you see...I mean, occasionally, things have happened to me...it's, it's...as if, you feel that something more powerful than you...but...I wouldn't know...that's...it's a thing that's too much, that...

Consideration of the very prominent place of secularity in the Uruguayan worldview is an important part of the contextualizing task of this chapter.

Overall, 72 per cent of the Montevideo questionnaire respondents stated that they either had 'no religion' or were 'atheist'. (This compares with 44 per cent of the Mar del Plata respondents.) A short 'filler' article in the sports section of a national newspaper, which was published while the interview research in Uruguay was underway, provides a vivid example of how deeply the secular attitude is ingrained in the national self-consciousness. Commenting on the international football competition, the 'Copa America', the article was headlined, 'It appears that God is a fan'. Alongside a photograph of a Venezuelan goal-scorer with his face lifted heavenward, it was noted that 'Everybody thanks God in the Copa America matches...Except the Uruguayans of course!'[61]

Pablo da Silveira, Academic Vice-Rector of the Catholic University of Uruguay, writes in his essay 'Laicity: That Rarity': 'We, the Uruguayans, are so profoundly marked by the influence of the French culture that at times we fail to appreciate it.' In particular, he notes that the famous Uruguayan phrase regarding education that is 'lay, free and obligatory' was taken, word for word, from the texts of the French reformers of the nineteenth century.[62] Further, he argues that the Uruguayans should not be deceived into thinking that this form of laicism is the only, or even the most common, manner of establishing an appropriate distance between church and state in modern democratic societies, and they should also be aware that at the present time their form of laicism is more extreme even than that of its progenitors in France.

> The curiosity of the case is that that practice of laicism that the French have begun to debate is, in reality, far less rigorous than our own practice. The French have chosen in their papers the 'brutal separation' between the churches and the state but they have applied this decision in a pragmatic and relatively prudent manner. With regard to laicism (and forgive the use of this expression in this context) the Uruguayans are more popish than the Pope.[63]

Néstor da Costa, a doctor in Political and Social Sciences at the University of Bilbao and a founding member and secretary of UNESCO in Montevideo, offers a 'brief historical sketch of the place of the religious in Uruguayan society':[64]

> That process of secularization that allows us to affirm that, as Uruguayans, we are different in that which has to do with the religious, occurs through a series of long confrontations between groups within and without the churches, basically the Roman Catholic church, and the elite groups, who constructed the modern Uruguayan state.[65]

In the first instance, and following the French pattern, the disputes were over control of the 'public spaces' of national life—pre-eminently education.

> The debate between the Church and the State was one of the most radical aspects of the modernizing process and there was no part of the national life that did not reflect, at least in part, the 'religious question'. In effect, although there were

---

[61] Anon., 'Parece que Dios es hincha...', *El Observador*, 7 July 2007.
[62] Pablo da Silveira, 'Laicidad: esa rareza', in Roger Geymonat, ed., *Las religiones en el Uruguay: Algunas aproximaciones* (Montevideo: Ediciones La Gotera, 2004), pp. 183–213, especially 183.
[63] Ibid., p. 183.
[64] Néstor da Costa, 'Lo religioso en la sociedad uruguaya', in Roger Geymonat, ed., *Las religiones en el Uruguay: Algunas aproximaciones* (Montevideo: Ediciones La Gotera, 2004), pp. 62–70, especially 62.
[65] Ibid., p. 62.

privileged matters (teaching, for example), nothing appeared to lay outside of this debate, not even the public holidays, the names of streets and of towns, or of history textbooks.[66]

At times the confrontations were less than cordial and, indeed, deliberately provocative. Da Costa writes of how 'liberal anti-catholic groups' used to cook *asados* (barbecues) right in front of the doors of Roman Catholic churches on Good Fridays and advertise the free food to the general population through adverts in newspapers.[67] The complete victory of the state, most clearly evidenced in the separation of church and state in the Constitution of 1917, resulted in 'the church ceasing to fight for the public [arena], circumscribing itself within the arena of the private'.[68] Roger Geymonat argues that up until recently the, frequently dogmatic, assumption that Uruguay was a happily 'non-religious' society dominated academic discourse.

> This is clearly verifiable in the historical studies. In effect, the national historiography marginalised the analysis of the religious fact, starting from the foundation of considering it as a cultural manifestation practically devoid of any kind of significance in the social life of the country. The survival of cults and practices were seen as atavistic and superstitious remnants, or, at best, as expressions of folklore.[69]

The national pride in secularity, the weak, reactionary character of traditional Christianity, and the rise of unattractive expressions of extreme religious beliefs coalesce to create a climate where the intellectual middle classes are loath to admit to any religious belief or commitment. It seems likely that this would lead to under-reporting of religious explanations and of mystical-type experiences in the empirical research. In the words of one respondent who did express a religious commitment:

> And in this country there's also ... for Christians it costs them a great deal to say 'we're Christians' [...] At some points in my life, perhaps, it also cost me ... cost me a lot. I don't know that all those who told you that they were atheists really are atheists. Perhaps yes, perhaps not [...] in Uruguayan society the level [of religious belief] is low but it is less low than one might believe because of the way that it costs many people to profess [their faith].

A second Roman Catholic interviewee noted that this is particularly true among the intellectual strata of society from which the respondents were drawn. She asked, 'Where did you do the interviews? All of them at

---

[66] Roger Geymonat and Alejandro Sánchez, 'Iglesia Católica, Estado y Sociedad en el Uruguay del Siglo XX', in Geymonat, *Las religiones en el Uruguay*, pp. 11–38, especially 13.
[67] Da Costa, 'Religioso', p. 63.
[68] Ibid., p. 63.
[69] Roger Geymonat, 'Introducción', in Geymonat, *Las religiones en el Uruguay*, pp. 5–8, especially 6.

Cinemateca?' I replied, 'Yes, all of them.' She felt that this went some way to explaining the high levels of stated atheism. 'Of course, because here in the intellectual cadre the, or the people who belong to the intellectual classes... it seems to me that they hide a little. That's to say, that here they don't, let's say, intellectually it's not seen well to be a Christian.'

A third respondent, who does not consider himself a believer, offers a very similar account. He thinks the problem is especially acute because of the visibility of the more extreme forms of religious expression. He thinks that people don't like to talk about their religious beliefs because, 'well, to say that, is generally to be under suspicion, as if, well, uhm, uhm, uhm... as if those people are only a step away from lifting their hands in an old abandoned cinema [the type of meeting place used by the most successful of the Pentecostal-type cults]'.

In Uruguay as in other parts of Latin America, one expression of Christianity that is treated with respect is that which follows the lead of liberation theology. In the western academy Latin American liberation theology is sometimes considered only in the past tense, as 'merely a phase of modern political theology at a time when a critical Marxism, unfettered by the rigidities of its Eastern European manifestations, pervaded the social teachings of late twentieth-century Roman Catholicism, only to be snuffed out by a determined reaction from a more traditionalist papacy'.[70] However, its values and action on behalf of the poor are still celebrated in Uruguay and elsewhere. This is as apparent in the cinema of the region as in other cultural manifestations. One recent example of this tendency is seen in the film *El Crimen del Padre Amaro* (*Father Amaro's Crime*).

While this is probably not a great film, the director does cleverly use the physical beauty of the Mexican actor Gael García Bernal as a device to make his moral and ethical deterioration through the film's narrative all the more unexpected and shocking. Bernal plays an ambitious young cleric assigned to a rural parish in Mexico. There he follows in the footsteps of the older priests and proceeds to seduce a beautiful young girl. He later forces her to risk an ultimately fatal abortion in order to protect his good name and career. While Bernal's character and all the parish priests he works with are portrayed as venal and corrupt, the renegade priest who lives up in the mountains with the indigenous population, and whose liberationist views have brought him into conflict with the church hierarchy, is portrayed as entirely laudable.

This cinematic approval of liberation theology is unsurprising when the obvious close parallels between the New Latin American Cinema and

---

[70] Christopher Rowland, 'Epilogue: The Future of Liberation Theology', in Christopher Rowland, ed., *The Cambridge Companion to Liberation Theology*, 2nd edn (Cambridge: Cambridge University Press, 2007), pp. 304–7, especially 304.

liberation theology are considered.[71] In addition to the common concern with the plight of the poorest members of society, both movements were birthed in particular gatherings. If the New Latin American Cinema was born in Viña del Mar in 1967, liberation theology might be seen to have come to life at the Second General Conference of Latin American Bishops in Medellín, Columbia, in 1968. Alfred Hennelly writes: 'There can be little doubt that the Medellín conference marked a momentous watershed in the history of the church in Latin America.'[72] This conference, primarily intended to provide a setting for the discussion of the proceedings of Vatican II with respect to the Latin American context, ended with a series of papers that gradually came to be seen as the key foundational documents for liberation theology. They recognize the importance of cultural practices such as film-making. A statement 'On Justice' closes with the words: 'this conference urges all, but especially laypersons, to make full use of the mass media in their work of human promotion'.[73]

As the academics Roger Geymonat and Néstor da Costa have noted, even in Uruguay it is not just a token respect for some expressions of religion that persists; even in Uruguay the religious impulse has not disappeared. Geymonat writes, 'Today, the supposed "irreligiosity" of Uruguayan society does not seem to stand up to the judgement of the reality.'[74] He goes on, 'Today, the majority of the authors coincide in affirming that religiosity should not be sought only in its institutional manifestations [. . .] it should be understood as the capacity for transcendence that can impregnate with meaning the whole of a person's existence and can orient all its dimensions.'[75] Da Costa writes in a similar vein:

> Another characteristic of the epoch is the reappearance of what some authors have called the return of the religious, in synthesis, a thirst for contact with the numinous, a search for the transcendent that is carried through various currents and spaces at the same time as a certain religious indifference takes hold.[76]

Both the strongly anti-clerical context and also the thirst for, and openness to, a numinous or transcendent element should be borne in mind when the accounts of film-watching experiences offered by the interviewees are considered.

---

[71] For a brief introduction to liberation theology, see Rebecca S. Chopp and Ethna Regan, 'Latin American Liberation Theology', in David F. Ford with Rachel Muers, eds, *The Modern Theologians: An Introduction to Christian Theology Since 1918*, 3rd edn (Oxford: Blackwell, 2005), pp. 469–84.

[72] Alfred T. Hennelly, ed., *Liberation Theology: A Documentary History* (Maryknoll, NY: Orbis, 1990), p. 89.

[73] Medellín Conference, 'Document on Justice', in Alfred T. Hennelly, ed., *Liberation Theology: A Documentary History* (Maryknoll, NY: Orbis, 1990), pp. 97–105, especially 105.

[74] Geymonat, 'Introducción', p. 6.

[75] Ibid., p. 7, quoting Alicia Casas de Cesari, 'El proceso de secularización en el Uruguay'.

[76] Da Costa, 'Religioso', p. 64.

The questionnaire data is also relevant to the final aspect of Tillich's theology of revelation considered in the theoretical account, which was his contention that all revelation must be considered in light of Jesus as the Christ as the criterion of revelation. Of those professing a religious commitment of any kind, 83 per cent acknowledged either a spiritual dimension to the experience or an awareness of a presence or a power related to the experience (80 per cent of those professing Christian commitments) and 58 per cent recognized both of these qualities. However, of those who declared that they had no religious commitments, 66 per cent reported a spiritual dimension or awareness of a presence or a power and 32 per cent reported both. Clearly, there is a correlation between stated religious belief and affirmative answers to these questions, but it is not as emphatic as might have been expected. Perhaps this also reflects the unique religious situation in Uruguay, where a search for transcendence is increasingly divorced from traditional religious institutions and commitments.

5.6 ON THE RESPONDENTS AND THE FILMS: FOCUS ON DICTATORSHIP

There is a final group of enquiries on the questionnaires that is related to the event of revelation. These questions address the possibility of particular points of connection between the films and the respondents' lives. They relate to Tillich's account of the 'quest' of the individual and his conception of the two constellations of revelation (subjective and objective) that must come into alignment if a revelatory event is to occur.

Of the respondents, 20 per cent stated that there was a 'strong relation' to the film which linked it in a particular way to what was happening in their life at the time. A further 64 per cent stated that there was 'some relation'. More specifically, a high percentage, 72 per cent, of respondents identified with the setting of the films. Clearly this could simply reflect the fact that the research project was focused on Latin American cinema. Slightly lower percentages identified with other aspects of the film discussed: 56 per cent identified with a particular event and 42 per cent with a particular character. At interview it became clear that for many of the respondents one of the most important links to the subject matter and the characters of the films was the experience of living under a military dictatorship. In fact, this aspect of Uruguayan life is so prevalent in the interview-generated data that it is the last of the contextual factors to be considered here.

Uruguay enjoyed a social, cultural, and economic golden age in the mid twentieth century. The markets for its primary exports of processed meat and wool grew through the period of the two World Wars. Partly because of its wealth and partly as a result of the continent-wide popularity of its banks, Uruguay became known as the 'Switzerland of South America'.[77] However, by the late 1960s the country was in decline and experiencing a violent struggle between the political left and right.[78]

Virginia Martínez offers a day-by-day, present-tense account of the Uruguayan dictatorship that is derived from original documents and audio-visual archive material. She writes of this period: 'The pre-dictatorship Uruguay, dominated by political violence and social upheaval, presages the dark times that will come. The actions of the "guerrilla", the Death Squadron, assassinations and attempted assassinations, raids, all formed part of the daily life of the Uruguayans.'[79] The turmoil provoked the military.

> On the 27th of June 1973 the President Juan María Bordaberry—an estate owner, a politician without either personal or popular prestige and ex-director of the Federal League of Rural Action—dissolves Parliament by decree. The *coup d'état* is the culmination of a long process marked by statements that signal the increasing autonomy of the Armed Forces over against the political system. It has been said that the overthrow occurred in slow-motion; some authors speak of the longest *coup d'état* in history and say that the events of June were no more than the final act.[80]

Unfortunately, the military's intervention did little to bring peace to Uruguay. 'The coup crushed the country, kidnapped, tortured, made adults and children disappear, punished and impoverished the workers, sank the culture and tried to quash the young people.'[81] It is the memory of this repression that is most obviously still in the minds of the interview respondents. Through the period of dictatorship almost all social groups and gatherings were banned, tens of thousands of individuals were blacklisted and thousands were incarcerated in newly built prisons (including the ironically named Libertad [Liberty] which features in one of the films discussed in the next chapter). At times the military were detaining and torturing so many that they had to be held for months in a vast sporting arena and even a local refrigeration plant.[82]

Historiography of the period suggests that in 'the twelve years of the authoritarian regime three clearly distinguishable stages can be recognised': 1973–6, the 'commissarial dictatorship', where the military attempted to 'put the house in order'; 1976–80, the 'new foundations' attempt to create a fresh political order to the liking of the dictatorship; and 1980–5, the 'transition to

---

[77] Instituto del Tercer Mundo, *Guide*, p. 574.
[78] Virginia Martínez, *Tiempos de dictadura 1973–1985: Hechos, voces, documentos: La represión y la resistencia día a día*, 3rd edn (Montevideo, Uruguay: Ediciones de la Banda Oriental, 2005), p. 13.
[79] Ibid., p. 13.   [80] Ibid., p. 13.   [81] Ibid., p. 11.   [82] Ibid., p. 15.

democracy'.[83] The key factor which led from the attempt to create a new political order to the transition to democracy was a plebiscite held in 1980.[84] In spite of the 'oppressive and unequal' climate in which the debate was carried out, the impossible occurred. The people voted against the dictatorship by 869,100 to 635,022. As Martínez expresses it, 'The popular rejection of the dictatorial project has a wide repercussion in the press and in international public opinion. It is greeted as the first time that a dictatorship has called and lost a plebiscite.'[85]

Over the coming years the military dictatorship gradually made space for the political parties and groups that it had banned and repressed. In November 1984, presidential elections were held and in 1985 the civilian president Julio María Sanguinetti assumed power.[86] Later, on 2 March 1985, a law was passed stating that there were no longer any banned persons or organizations in Uruguay.[87]

However, although 22 years had passed since the fall of the dictatorship by the time this piece of research was undertaken, it will be clear from what follows that this period of dictatorship continues to loom large in the psyches of the respondents. Many of the respondents chose films which related to this period in some way, and many of the most powerful experiences discussed have a connection to life under a repressive regime.

---

[83] Gerardo Caetono and José Rilla, *Breve historia de la dictadura: 1973–1985*, 2nd edn (Montevideo, Uruguay: Ediciones de la Banda Oriental, 1998), pp. 13–15.
[84] Martínez, *Tiempos*, p. 131.
[85] Ibid., p. 132.   [86] Ibid., p. 237.   [87] Ibid., p. 238.

6

Grounding the Theoretical Account

This chapter presents and analyzes the data generated by the ten long, qualitative interviews, the largest and most important body of data in this research project. The chapter has two major sections. In the first, a theory-driven method of analysis will be utilized, which is to say that the approach to the data will be governed by the conceptual categories derived from Tillich's theoretical account of revelation. In the second section, a new way of looking at the possibility of revelation through film is introduced. As this new conceptualization arose unexpectedly out of the data, it can be described as the fruit of data-driven analysis.[1]

The sampling strategy discussed in Chapter 4 selected the interviewees on the basis of two different approaches. A critical case approach was responsible for the selection of six respondents who were chosen on the basis of the *congruity* between their questionnaire answers and Tillich's theory (see Table 6.1). The questionnaire answers of these respondents referred to an experience that had shaken, transformed, or healed; of a complex experience which at least left open the possibility of an ecstatic spiritual and mystical element; of an important connection between the film and their lives; and of a

Table 6.1. The interview respondents selected for congruity

Respondent	Sex	Age band	Nationality	Profession	Religion
Augusto	Male	18–30	Uruguayan	Systems engineer	Roman Catholic
Samuel	Male	50–65	Argentinean	Businessman	Atheist
Marta	Female	50–65	Uruguayan	Lecturer	Roman Catholic
Jorge	Male	31–50	Uruguayan	Psychologist	None
Lucilda	Female	50–65	Israeli	Casual worker	None
Fernando	Male	65+	Uruguayan	Retired	None

---

[1] Although this analysis does not begin with the theoretical account, it is essential not to lose sight of the fact that the theoretical account was used to organize the whole project and its influence cannot therefore be wholly eliminated.

Grounding the Theoretical Account 183

Table 6.2. The interview respondents selected for difference

Respondent	Sex	Age band	Nationality	Profession	Religion
Beau	Male	65+	Uruguayan	Retired	Atheist
Miguel	Male	18–30	Uruguayan	Actor	None
Pedro	Male	18–30	Uruguayan	Master of Arts	None
Gastón	Male	31–50	Uruguayan	Photographer	Jewish

notable impact. For the purpose of analysis the accounts of these respondents will be assumed to be accounts of revelatory experiences (as construed by Tillich) until evidence emerges to the contrary.

A maximum variation approach was then responsible for the selection of four more respondents whose stories *differed* in some important respect from Tillich's theoretical account (see Table 6.2). These respondents either denied a film had ever shaken, transformed, or healed them; discounted any spiritual or mystical element; or stated that there had been no appreciable impact on their lives. For the purpose of analysis the accounts of these respondents will be assumed *not* to be accounts of revelatory experiences (as construed by Tillich) until evidence emerges to the contrary.

6.1 THEORY-DRIVEN ANALYSIS: ON THE SIX ASPECTS OF THE REVELATORY EXPERIENCE

6.1.1 Samuel: An illustrative vignette

Samuel is in his early 50s and, having spent the first 38 years of his life in Buenos Aires, Argentina, he decided to immigrate to Montevideo, believing the smaller city to be safer and more peaceful. He is of Jewish descent, has two adult sons who live in Israel, and he left a failed marriage behind him in Buenos Aires. He is a successful businessman with a mobile-phone shop.

Cinema has great importance in his life. As a young man his passion led him to study at film school in Buenos Aires where he spent three years learning film-making while simultaneously pursuing a degree in engineering and working to earn a living. At the end of this process he wanted to pursue a career in film-making but eventually decided that this was impossible: 'a cinematic career in Argentina at that moment in time [. . .] came with three or four or five years of penury, of hunger'.

Samuel's questionnaire answers related to a film named *Tango feroz: La leyenda del Tanguito*, directed by Marcel Piñeyro and released in 1993. The film tells the story of a mythical figure from the earliest days of Argentinean rock music. In the late 1960s, in the midst of the foment of student protest, a singer–songwriter named Jose Alberto Iglesias (nicknamed Tanguito, a diminuitive form of Tango) began composing and performing what were considered to be the first indigenous Argentinean rock songs. *Tango feroz* is a musical biopic, more concerned with mood and emotional power than documentary reliability, which charts the romance, the rise and fall of this tragic hero. As the qualitative interview progressed, it became clear that Samuel had a very unusual link to this film. After finishing film school he and a group of friends and contemporaries scripted, directed, and produced a film:

> In some sense it was the embryo of *Tango feroz*. That was the seed that we planted, in order that... in a far more professional manner, headed up by... well, well-known directors and scriptwriters, uhm, the film would be taken, let's say, to the commercial [market].

This resulted in a profound ambiguity in Samuel's reception of the film. Positively, 'my relation to the film has a great deal to do with my life, as... as an adolescent and post-adolescent, of university education and of persecution, of repression, and of rebellion' but 'spiritually it didn't do much for me, but that is because I felt a little bit of annoyance... because it had been our screenplay originally and it became something very commercial'.

However, at interview Samuel spoke even more passionately of a European film—Federico Fellini's *Amarcord* (1973). There are a number of factors that closely align Samuel's account of his experience of this film with the reading presented in Chapter 2 of Tillich's theology of revelation. First, Samuel links the film-mediated experience with experiences mediated by nature in a manner reminiscent of the way Tillich himself associates childhood experiences of nature, especially the sea, with later cultural experiences of pictorial art. Second, the film that elicits the experience is made in a symbolic or surreal rather than classical Hollywood style, which would seem to suit Tillich's preference for difficult art with ambiguous meaning-content over readily accessible art with an obvious message. Third, Samuel's experience could be defined as mystical and his lack of language to describe it seems to imply a quality of ineffability. Finally, the impact of the film experience is certainly taken by Samuel to be one of healing, or what Tillich might refer to as partial salvation.

The most illuminating section of the interview came at the close when the handouts were introduced. Samuel considered the first handout, which offers a brief summary of Tillich's theory of revelation and art, to be: 'Very interesting. It seems to me a... a good approach.' However, he is wary of the term 'revelation' precisely because of its religious 'connotations'. 'Uhm... revelation is a word that has a lot to do with religion, it seems to me.' This hesitation and concern about the use of the word 'revelation' is surprising; it appears to be used more often in Spanish-language cinema reviews and related texts than in their English equivalents. A most striking example in the context of this particular interview is a banner headline relating to *Tango feroz* that describes the film as: 'The most recent revelation from Argentinean cinema'.[2]

In spite of his concern about the religious resonances he hears in the word 'revelation', Samuel links the text of the handout to his own film-watching experiences without any prompt or invitation. 'But the experience, uhm, well, the different possibilities that are suggested here [an experience that shakes, transforms or heals us; an experience of something ultimate] seem very valid to me, and in fact I have lived some of them with different films... My own experience, yes?'

When I read out the second handout, about Tillich's experience of the Botticelli painting, Samuel is entirely confirmed in his initial antipathy towards the religious connotations of the term 'revelation'. 'Ehm [sighs]... Well, this confirms a little what I'd said before. Eh... it has a lot to do with a religious meaning and... sentiment. He says it himself, it's explicit. Even the image has to do with something religious.' Samuel had already declared himself to be an atheist and at this point he elaborated on his view of religion.

> I have a concept... a very particular concept of religion, no? Well... I believe that religions were... created in the world by men... simply in order to divide humanity, never to unite... In order to divide humanity... and... I'm overwhelmed with examples, each religion, Holy Lands, Crusades... Pah! Etcetera, etcetera, etcetera. That's my... personal interpretation... of religion. Therefore, for me, the subject of religion... no.

As the conversation progressed, I attempted to redirect Samuel's focus from the abstract towards his personal experience.

> Interviewer: Would you say that at any moment of your life you have... you have experienced something similar, comparable... to that experience? But obviously not with a religious painting or with... but that moment of... I don't know what to call it, very powerful.
> Samuel: Revelation? [laughs]
> Interviewer: Yes, well, we've returned to revelation, it's true.

In spite of his profound misgivings about religion and the concept of 'revelation', Samuel began to speak at length of his experiences:

> Well... yes, there were many moments, not just one... I had many moments of, of revelation. In my contact... with the cinema I had them... in addition to the film we've been talking about [*Tango feroz*], I had... other moments of revelation. And not only with the cinema, I like nature a lot, in fact I'm a lover of fishing but fishing... ah... for the contact that signifies with nature. Ehm... I like to go and fish simply for the fact of observing... the phenomena, of removing myself

---

[2] M.P., 'La más reciente revelación del cine argentino', *Busqueda*, 8 July 1993.

from the noises, distancing myself and witnessing a little of... of the majesty of nature, no?

Clearly, it would be wrong to place too much weight on Samuel's use of revelation here, although his adoption of the term, in spite of his earlier antipathy towards it, is interesting. What's more important is the unsolicited linking of the experience of nature and the experience of film-watching. As he goes on, his normal vocabulary seems insufficient and he begins to lapse into silences and to leave sentences unfinished, particularly when he is about to name what it is that he encounters in these moments. 'For me the act of going fishing is, is, is the contact that I have with... [pause]. Those, for me, have been... revelatory moments on more than one occasion, and I often seek this, this type of contact.'

I prompted Samuel for one specific film-watching experience that fits this pattern and he responded with Federico Fellini's *Amarcord* (1973), which he had mentioned earlier in the interview when he stated that it was the film that he had viewed the most times in the cinema—at least fifteen. *Amarcord* is the director's semi-autobiographical account of growing up in the Adriatic seaside resort of Rimini in the 1930s. There is little plot or traditional narrative development, but instead the characters and the happenings of village life are exaggerated to create a surreal, bawdy, and carnivalesque film. Once again, with respect to this film, as with *Tango feroz*, Samuel's language is of encounter, but when it comes to naming the 'other' he falls silent. '*Amarcord* in some ways... ehm... it brought me a little closer to...'

It is at this point that Samuel begins to speak of the impact that the experience of watching *Amarcord* had upon his relationship with his parents, particularly his father. It is notable that he ascribes a direct causality to the film using the indicative mood and active voice—'it made me... reflect'; 'it brought me closer'.

> Yes, I saw *Amarcord* during the period of my adolescence when... I was a very rebellious adolescent, I had a lot of confrontations with my parents, very grave ones. Grave, no, let's say serious. And with a great deal of substance, and with much force... I was 15 years old and I left home, to live at my grandparents' house. Later I returned. Well... I wanted to quit my studies, I wanted to focus on chess, on cinema, and my father never permitted it. Well... I rebelled against that, no? Well, I even had two years living with my father but eating at different times and never greeting him. And... and the truth is that *Amarcord* made me... reflect on my stance. And well, afterwards, I approached him... he never reproached me about anything... And... well... *Amarcord* in some way, in the moment I was living through, brought me closer... to an affectionate relationship... paternal and maternal more than anything.

The final point of similarity with Tillich's account relates to the kind of film and the way in which it seems to have made its impact on Samuel. Samuel notes that the film affected him in spite of, rather than because of, its explicit portrayal of family life. He can only explain its effect through reference to a highly personal and idiosyncratic symbolic interpretation of certain aspects of the film. By this point he is happy to describe this as revelation and to reaffirm the powerful nature of its impact upon him.

> In spite of the fact... that in *Amarcord*, eh, the family relations are very hard and... but it's full of symbols [said with great emphasis], and well... for me a cow was my mother... and... the cow that was there, uhm, my mother, and my father was... another symbol, and well... They were revelatory experiences. Other people... they interpret it in another way, yes? Or... well, they wouldn't feel anything. But for me it's a film that... every time I see it... I, I'm moved by it... from the side of family... still today.[3]

Samuel's account, in both its reference to nature and film, bears a likeness to the kind of immediate, mystical apprehension of the ground of being discussed by Tillich in both his autobiographical writings and in essays like 'The Two Types of Philosophy of Religion'. Consideration of the six aspects of Tillich's account that have been in use throughout the research points to other ways in which Samuel's experience resembles the reading of Tillich's theology of revelation.

First, there is at least the implication that the individual in question is searching for a kind of healing, in this case of the paternal–filial relationship. As he himself admits, what he brings to the film, in terms of a yearning for this kind of wholeness, is perhaps more important than what the film itself presents—quite a dysfunctional and unattractive family life. This might be seen as the individual's 'quest', which results in the alignment of the two constellations of revelation as the subject's need meets its counterpart in the resources made available by the film.

Second, the film in question resembles the kind of product of cultural and artistic endeavour that Tillich would consider suited to the mediation of revelation. Its surreal atmosphere and limited narrative thrust have the potential to create precisely the kinds of fissures and aporia that the discussion of expressionism in painting and realism in film suggested might be related to the potential to mediate revelation.

Third, with respect to the event of revelation, Samuel's description of the way the film spoke to him, particularly the cow representing his mother, again resembles the kind of pre-cognitive, pre-communicative, ecstatic experience that Tillich's description might suggest. The similarity is further strengthened when it is noted that Samuel offered this story in direct response to Tillich's

---

[3] It is interesting to note that another film referenced in this thesis, *El lado oscuro del corazon* directed by Eliseo Subiela in 1992, has a scene where a cow speaks to the central character as if his mother.

experience of the Botticelli and that he associated the experience with an ineffable encounter that is often mediated through nature.

Third, again in congruence with Tillich's theory, the content of revelation is not a communication either of knowledge about our day-to-day subject–object world, nor of information about 'divine matters' (*ST1*, 161). Samuel was not taught about family life, nor was he persuaded to change by any moral or religious authority communicated in or through the film.

In fact, fourth, it is clear that it is more appropriate to speak of the effect of this revelatory experience than the content. Tillich considers the effect of revelation to be the conferring of a partial and limited salvation, which may be characterized as a shaking, transforming, or healing experience. Both healing and transforming would appear to be appropriate descriptions of the impact that Samuel recounted.

Finally, the last step is to consider the relation of this revelation to Jesus as the Christ as the criterion of revelation. As an atheist (and ethnically Jewish), Samuel has no time for this kind of language. However, this does not present a problem with regards to the resemblance of this account to Tillich's theory. Tillich was clear that the use of the religious language of any particular faith tradition to describe such events (the narrower definition of religion) must be seen as a second-order re-description of a fundamental experience (the broader and more basic definition of religion). For Tillich, Samuel's atheism and lack of religious vocabulary would not invalidate this experience as one of authentic revelation.

Having considered this one vignette, data will now be drawn from the other interviews in order to ground the theoretical reading of the six aspects of the experience of revelation.

6.1.2 The individual

In Chapter 2, Tillich's ontological–existential analysis was shown to present the human individual as open to revelation and, indeed, as actively seeking revelation. At the most basic level, the human experience of finitude and the concomitant threat of non-being create anxiety and desire for union with the ground of being or being-itself. At the social level, the universal tragedy of estrangement from one's self, from God, and from the world and its inhabitants, entails despair and a loss of meaning. The desire to escape anxiety and despair leads to a quest for wholeness that, for Tillich, is a quest for revelation. In fact, it was noted that awareness of finitude and estrangement and the desire for salvation is itself a revelatory experience, in that it is a step on the road towards the 'courage to be' and the revelation of New Being.

Many of the respondents selected on the basis of the critical case sample showed evidence that their film-watching experience was one element in a wider search for wholeness. The way they engaged with the subject matter of the films reflected this. Two of the female respondents showed this particularly clearly.

Lucilda is a middle-aged woman with two adult daughters whose life is, perhaps, harder than many of those interviewed. The film she spoke about treated the topic of the Uruguayan dictatorship, through focusing on the experiences of the inmates of a notorious prison for political detainees, ironically named 'Libertad' (Liberty). The film, *Les Yeux des Oiseaux*, was made in Europe by the French director Gabriel Auer in 1983 and was not released in Uruguay until democracy had returned. Lucilda's experience of the film focuses on a plot strand where a young girl goes to visit her father. She wants to give him a picture of a tree with doves in it but the censors believe that doves could be seen as a subversive and inflammatory symbol. They refuse to pass on the drawing. In the end, the little girl simply shows the eyes of the birds (*les yeux des oiseaux*, in French) peering out from among the foliage. With regard to the impact the film had upon her when it was finally released in Uruguay, Lucilda comments:

> And, well, because ... it's difficult to explain it but ... obviously if it was twenty years ago that, that film ... in some way, well ... its imprint remains, doesn't it? So ... and, a little, I don't know, I felt myself identified with all that frustration ... because you don't know how it was here, you couldn't open your mouth. Look, really, you couldn't open your mouth [...] I tell you, it was, was so powerful, for all of our generation—don't open your mouth, don't speak, don't say what you think [...] So that always you had to be distrustful of everyone, you couldn't open your mouth, it was horrific [...] So yes, it helped me. But ... it was as if that rage that I had [came out] through that little girl ... well, it was like making a bloopa-loopaloopa [here the respondent puts her hands to her face and waggles her fingers making the common children's sign of defiance; she then laughs].

Lucilda's generation, who grew up under the dictatorship, might be thought of as being on a quest for liberation from an oppression that persisted in their lives long after the political change had come. The young girl's clever victory over the forces of oppression in *Les Yeux des Oiseaux* apparently aligned with Lucilda's need for a symbol of defiance and freedom, making her experience of the film a profound and liberating one.

A second critical case respondent, Marta, spoke of the Cuban film *Fresa y chocolate* by Tomás Gutiérrez Alea (1994). This moving and provocative film tells the story of the growing friendship between a young heterosexual student, studying social sciences and committed to the communist ideology of Cuban society, and a cultivated, older homosexual man who is striving to be heard and appreciated in the face of harsh discrimination.

Marta is a middle-aged academic and a practising Roman Catholic; she explained that the film's impact, which will be discussed below, was like the final step in a process that had been underway in her life for some time. 'No, I was already breaking out [of a restrictively conservative worldview] but the film helped me to, exactly, to finish... dissolving them, no?'

These and other references appear to confirm the appropriateness of Tillich's suggestion that these possibly revelatory experiences are in some sense a response to a quest which is already present in the individual. The interviews provide further evidence which suggests that the particular meshing of the individual's need (the subjective constellation of revelation) and the artwork's resources (the objective constellation of revelation) is an important part of the process that results in what might be described as a revelatory event.

Indeed, there is a considerable quantity of data that shows exceptional links between the respondents and the films they found most powerful in their lives. The way Samuel was linked to *Tango feroz* by a connection to its thematic content, its geographical and temporal context, and its production history has already been noted. Marta explained that she was particularly moved by *Fresa y chocolate* because, through trips to Cuba, she had built up a strong affective link with the people and had visited many of the locations used in the film, notably the ice-cream parlour where the central characters first meet. Another respondent, whose experience will be considered below, Pedro, was linked to the characters of the film he selected, Eliseo Subiela's *El lado oscuro del corazon* (1992), by similarities between his own life and that of the central character. The film is a cinematic expression of magic realism with a blurred, porous and unreliable boundary separating events in the 'real' world from events of the central character's interior life. This character, Olivero, is a poet living in Buenos Aires. Supplementing his meagre income by doing occasional casual work for a friend's advertising company, he travels across the River Plate to Montevideo where he falls in love with a prostitute. The passion for creative writing and the life-experience of moving from the interior of Argentina to Montevideo are shared by the film's protagonist and my respondent Pedro. Other respondents stressed the importance of more general factors such as the Uruguayan setting (Gastón and *Whisky*); experience of childhood poverty (Beau and *Pizza, Birra, Faso*); and life under the dictatorship (Jorge and *Cabra marcado para morrer*).

6.1.3 The artwork

In line with the current mode of theory-driven data analysis, the next three aspects of the reading of Tillich's theology of revelation—those relating to the artwork, the experience, and the content of revelation—will be treated in turn. However, it should be noted that while the data relating to these aspects are separated out for the purpose of analysis, in the interview transcripts they tend to be intermingled. As a result, it is only at the end of the process that the overall relevance of the discussion of each individual aspect may be seen.

In Chapter 2, the artwork which is the medium of revelation was considered. To understand how a film, an artwork, or culture more generally, can be a suitable medium of revelation it was necessary to understand 'spirit' as the distinctively human dimension of life. Spirit, which incorporates reason, imagination, and passion, is the unity of power and meaning. All culture has a religious dimension because any cultural creation depends for its vitality upon the inexhaustible depth of power and meaning, which may be designated the ground of being, being-itself, or, in religious language, God. It is this substance that animates the creations formed by a human artist as she manipulates different permutations of subject matter and form in acts of *theoria*. A cultural creation, an artwork, or a film's power and authenticity are measured by the degree to which it is capable of allowing the viewer to delve below the surface to the depth or substance beneath. This rupture of the surface and contact with the depth or substance below is an experience of revelation, an experience of the unconditional and of unambiguous life.

When the questionnaire data were considered in Chapter 5, it was suggested that there might be two broad types of experience caught in the research net: a cognitive type and a mystical type. Samuel's experience of the film *Amarcord*, recounted above, would fit within the mystical category. Across the interview data, experiences which might be considered to be of the mystical type are characterized by limited reference to the plot or message of the film; tend to be immediate (although they may not occur on first viewing or might be repeated on subsequent viewings); are likely to be described as primarily spiritual or emotional experiences; and the difficulty encountered by the respondents when they attempt to describe them is an indication of their ineffability.

The two types of experience are considered in this section because there appears to be a correlation between the type or style of a film and the type of experience it engenders. In this research project, realist films predominated over formalist films. With respect to the films discussed at interview, the most striking examples include *Pizza, Birra, Faso* (or *Pizza, Beer, Pot*) by Adrián Caetano and Bruno Stagnaro (1998), which tells the story of a group of semi-delinquent young people on the streets of Buenos Aires and is in the mould of Italian neo-realism; and *Cabra marcado para morrer* (discussed at the beginning of this monograph), which is a documentary. Speaking of this latter documentary, Jorge said: 'the work is so well made that, well, it, it transcends obviously, uhm, the level of propaganda, no?' So, realism should not be considered a lack of artistry.

In Chapter 3, I presented a thought experiment which suggested that realist cinema was at least as well suited as formalist cinema to mediating revelation, so the possibility that experiences associated with these films might be revelatory need not be discarded out of hand. However, it does appear that realist films are more likely to engender cognitive-type experiences. In contrast to the mystical-type experience, these cognitive experiences are closely related to the explicit plot or message of the film; are frequently gradual in onset; are normally depicted as primarily intellectual in character; and can be described by the respondents with a reasonable degree of success. A number of the respondents selected for interview on the basis of the critical case sample described experiences of this cognitive type.

Augusto provides a theoretically interesting example of a cognitive-type experience that otherwise demonstrates all of the characteristics of a revelatory event. He is a young, successful executive in his late 20s. Between my conducting the questionnaire survey with him and my returning for the interview, he had moved jobs from a management role with a credit control company to become the head of operations for Uruguay's largest chain of multiplex cinemas. The interview was carried out at his office in the chain's flagship multiplex. Augusto spoke of a film written and directed by the director of *Tango feroz*. While *Tango feroz* was Marcel Piñeyro's debut after a career in advertising, *Cenizas del paraiso* (1997) is his third feature (the intermediate film being the acclaimed *Caballos salvajes*, 1995). *Cenizas del paraiso* is essentially a complex murder mystery set among the wealthy professionals of Buenos Aires. The film begins with two deaths. An elderly judge leaps, or is pushed, from the roof of his office block and a beautiful young woman is found dead of multiple stab wounds in her house. The job of the female judge assigned to investigate the case is made all the more difficult when all three of the dead judge's sons confess to the murder of the young woman. The truth is revealed gradually as the events leading up to the murders are seen from a number of different viewpoints in flashbacks and reminiscences.

Augusto's appraisal and description of the film is excellent, closely resembling the critical reception. He first locates the film within the context of a moment of resurgence in quality Argentinean film production: 'it was an epoch of... in which Argentine films... caused a storm here. Well, a number of films began to arrive... it was a good moment in Argentinean cinema.' Or, as the critic Huascar Toscano puts it, it was a moment of 'new rebirth in Argentinean cinema'.[4] Second, Augusto sees the complexity of the plot and the manner of its telling as central to the success of the film and of its careful positioning between commercial and art-house products. A review in *El Diario* concurs, calling it 'ambitious entertainment'.[5]

Augusto links the intellectual demands of the film with its impact; he is impressively consistent in this. 'It's a film that requires a great deal of mental attention, first. And that, second, is that it also tells a little, of, of the family relations that lie behind.' A couple of paragraphs later, having again spoken of

---

[4] Huascar Toscano, 'Cenizas del paraiso', *Sabado Show*, 1 November 1997.
[5] Alberto Postiglioni, 'Drama contemporáneo', *El Diario*, 2 November 1997, p. 11.

the screenplay and its intricacies, he speaks of the impact 'of the relation of the father with the sons [...] and of being struck by a story about fathers and sons that is, that is good, no?'

Augusto is able to link his experience to the narrative of the film and the discursive elements of particular scenes in a way which contrasts sharply with Samuel's idiosyncratic and symbolic interpretation. Asked if there was a particular scene, event, or character with which he identified, Augusto spoke of the oldest son and of certain scenes which he shared with the father. 'The way in which he... has... the deepest, most profound relationship with his father. How, how... he shares with his father a relationship that is more matey, more conspiratorial.' A little later he continues to speak of these scenes in greater detail:

> There are, in the film, two or three events, uhm... uhm, in which he... well, in which the father calls him apart and they... they speak in confidence, no? And there you see more how, how, how that relation, you see it in some... some scenes of the film, and, and, and... it's much more tangible, that depth of relationship that those two have. In one scene they are... they are at the table, there after drinking something, drinking wine, listening to music... I don't know, but it's clear that he... he has a relationship with his father... of much greater... much greater interiority than the rest of his brothers, and vice versa, no?

It is here that Augusto first really expands on the way in which he sees the impact of the film on his life.

> And well, uhm, I believe that yes, I... I lived my, my adolescence, well, with a relationship with my father that was very conflicted. And that... by the end of my adolescence and entering into young adulthood around 18 or 19... it changed radically and it was, it was a relationship of... of much greater depth and much more enjoyable. And, I don't know, from one side to the other, it's continued right up until today, and I believe that from that point that it was also the film, also how it... how it made me see, no? See how great it is... to have a, a relationship... uhm, that's profound and deep and at that level, with, with your father.

It is also clear that the film exerted its impact upon Augusto over an extended period. At the close of the interview I attempted to clarify the timeline of events. Augusto was 28 when interviewed in 2007, so the film would have been released in the cinema when he was about 13 years old. This would have been at about the time of the fracture of the relationship with his father, rather than at the time of its restoration. As Augusto remembers first seeing the film at the cinema, it seems likely that he saw it on its first release as an adolescent, but that the repeated viewings on television and video that followed this initial experience were at least as important, if not more important, than that first exposure.

This coheres with Augusto's description, in both the questionnaire and the interview, of the experience as one of gradual onset. 'It was a film that I saw two or three times afterwards [the first viewing], and each time it shows on cable... I, I, I watch it and I remain transfixed watching it because... And I think that in that sense, or from, or from that perspective. I told you that it was gradual, no?'

It might be argued that these cognitive-type experiences fall outside the bounds of a revelatory experience as construed on the basis of the Tillichian account. However, I believe it is more accurate and more fruitful to continue to view such experiences as revelatory, but to consider carefully the points at which they challenge and stretch the Tillichian account. For example, there are grounds for considering Augusto's experience to be revelatory. First, he was selected on the basis of the critical case sample, so his questionnaire answers demonstrated a degree of congruence with Tillich's theory. Second, there appears to have been a clear healing or transforming effect upon his life, one almost identical to that recounted by Samuel whose experience was of the mystical type. Perhaps most importantly, Augusto was the respondent who spoke most easily and most convincingly of the involvement of God in his experience. This will be discussed below when the final aspect of Tillich's account, the relation to Jesus as the Christ, is considered.

Thus far, in this analysis of the artwork that is the medium of the revelatory event, it has been noted that two types of experience—mystical and cognitive—might be related to two types of artwork—formalist and realist, respectively. A number of respondents suggested that a mystical-type experience was more likely to be engendered by listening to music than by watching films. It is worth pursuing this strand of data because it is pertinent to Tillich's emphasis on the non-discursive characteristics of art, and therefore on revelation as other than communication of knowledge. The comments about music arose in response to the question about a presence or a power, which clearly suggested a religious or mystical-type experience, and after the reading of Tillich's account of his Botticelli experience.

Miguel is a young actor chosen on the basis of the maximum variation sample because he claimed a film had never shaken, transformed, or healed him. After reading Tillich's Botticelli story to Miguel, I asked if he had experienced anything similar. He replied:

> Yes, uhm [there was a long pause, perhaps as he re-read the handout]... It happens to me a lot with music. There, well... when I listen to a certain type of music it... it... it... it arr-, it seems to me that I feel... as if, like a revelation. And I... I... I associate it with... I associate the revelation with change as well. With a change of direction, no? It's as if... it's like they say, 'where are we heading?'

Augusto, who has been identified as the most openly religious of the respondents, moves from speaking of the way music can bring him inner peace in the midst of troublesome situations, even move him to the 'state approaching ecstasy' of which Tillich spoke, to the direct involvement of God. 'Yes, yes, completely, I believe that... that, I also believe that God can speak through those things.'

Marta offers an explanation of why music is more conducive to mystical-type religious experience, suggesting that it has a kind of purity that is not found in film. Speaking of classical music, and giving Bach as her example, she says: 'it's like a more direct route to the transcendent. Uhm, and in film the image is already... is already burdened with another, with another sensuality... which the music doesn't have.' In this she sounds similar to Paul Schrader, whose theory of transcendental style in film, which involved the stripping away of all 'abundant' or material means, was discussed in the analysis of the contemporary religion–film discourse in Chapter 1.

In summary, it seems that in putatively revelatory experiences related to film art, discursive elements like plot, narrative, and characterization have a more important role than Tillich's theory would allow. While the research uncovered mystical-type experiences, like Samuel's and like those engendered by music, other experiences like Augusto's, which I am naming cognitive type, seem to bear sufficient resemblance to Tillich's theory to be considered revelatory. However, these experiences challenge Tillich's dismissal of the importance of the content or subject matter of the artwork and of the knowledge-content of the revelatory experience. This problem will be discussed further in the sections that follow and in the final chapter.

6.1.4 The event

In Chapter 2, analysis turned next to the event which unites the individual and her quest for revelation with the artwork which is expressive of power and meaning, and mediates revelation. 'Event' is preferred to 'experience' because, for Tillich, revelation is not a merely subjective experience but an objective reality. The subjective side may correctly be designated an 'ecstatic experience', where the cognitive, emotional, and moral faculties are all engaged but are also transcended. But the objective side is designated a 'miracle', a moment in which an element of reality, in this case a film, becomes a sign-event pointing to the mystery of being. This ecstatic, miraculous experience of the unconditional might be astonishing and life-affirming, or it might be dreadful, but in either case it is identified as revelatory. Tillich's analysis has highlighted the way in which the particularities of the subjective and objective constellations—the individual and the element of reality—must align and engage if the revelatory event is to occur.

Chapter 5 considered the way in which the questionnaire attempted to approach the possibility of an ecstatic and miraculous event by seeking out those respondents who viewed their experience as an irreducibly complex mix of intellectual, emotional, aesthetic, and spiritual elements. However, in the interviews respondents tended to relate the nature of these complex experiences to the particular way in which cinema functions. By utilizing a cross-sectional method of data analysis, it is possible to construct an account of how the respondents as a group understand the mechanism by which cinema creates an experience and generates its impact. In summary: first, the respondents see the cinema as the point of integration of many arts; second, as an immersive medium, where, in a unique kind of interaction between spectator and film text, the 'real' world is left behind; third, as a medium that continues to work on you after viewing; and finally, as an experience that engenders a breakthrough to a new way of seeing, thinking, or living. I will develop the first three stages of this account by drawing on the respondents' own words.

First, Marta, who at the time of the interview was teaching a university course on 'Cinema and Complexity', stated: 'I consider that the cinema is like, like a species of synthesis... a synthesis of all of the artistic modes.' 'In that sense it has a comprehensiveness that exceeds all the individual arts.' Similarly, Jorge says: 'The cinema integrates [...] If each thing, let's say... is, is well placed and is, is... then it [cinema] has a power... that is brutal. Really brutal.'

Second, this integration of many artistic modes and communicative potentialities results in a uniquely immersive experience that allows the spectator to leave the 'real' world behind. This is an aspect of the mechanism spoken of by nearly all (at least 8 out of 10) of the respondents. Spatial metaphors abound in their accounts: to penetrate, to be caught, to be placed, and to enter in. Samuel expressed this most representatively and concisely: 'Ehm... the act of attending a cinema where there are no noises, where the screen is big, where the music is loud, in some sense facilitates the spectator's access, his ability to make himself part, or to take part in the story, or to inhabit [*hacerse carne*—incarnate] some character, one of those within the story.'

The respondents were clear that this immersion, while related to the particular, synthetic attributes of the cinematic medium, was actually an interaction between the spectator and the film: there are, mostly intentional, acts of projection and identification. Using language very similar to that of Annette Hill in her work on violent cinema, Pedro speaks of the 'encyclopedia' which each spectator carries with them: 'the collection of knowledge [...] the cultural backpack [cf. Hill's portfolio] that that person has.' 'But there is a mediation, it's not, it shouldn't be confused, it's not the film that changes you. Because, don't forget... that... each person sees a different film. We could both see a film and yet we have different films.'

Third, the respondents commented on the fact that this interaction, between the viewing subject and the film text, continues after the actual experience of watching is completed. Beau says: 'When you go, when you exit the cinema, when you're on the bus, when you arrive home, you speak "na, na, na", and you go to bed or whatever... the film begins to be, within you it begins to transform itself or... and to show other facets.'

It is clear that these first three stages can be discussed without any reference to revelation. Divorced from the rest of the interview data, the discussion of mechanism generates no sense of an unaccountable surplus; and it is clear that here there is no need to resort to miracle and ecstasy to explain the irreducible intermingling of the intellectual, emotional, aesthetic, and spiritual aspects of the experience. Rather, this complex experience is simply a corollary of a complex medium.

However, as noted above, the fourth stage in the respondents' explanation of the nature of their experiences references a breakthrough to a new way of seeing, thinking, or living in the world. The extent to which this final stage suggests or authorizes a return to consideration of these experiences as revelatory will be considered below in relation to the fifth aspect of Tillich's theology: the effect of revelation. First, I will consider Tillich's theory with respect to the content of revelation in light of the interview data.

6.1.5 The content

In Chapter 2, when Tillich's understanding of the content of revelation was discussed, his definition of 'mystery' was found to be important. Even though revelation might, correctly, be understood as the unveiling of the ground of being (or God), the nature of the ground of being as a true mystery means that the content of revelation can never be rendered in human language. The function of the medium of revelation is, therefore, not discursive but symbolic. It is because the artwork participates in the ground of being that it is capable of playing a mediating role. Revelation occurs when the medium becomes transparent to that which underlies it and gives it its substance of power and meaning. Thus, the content of a revelatory experience is neither of a personal encounter, nor of a transfer of knowledge or information, but is an ineffable experience of the ground of being. Any later references to the event which use (religious) language must be taken to be second-order re-conceptualizations.

As the content of revelation is, in effect, a negative category in Tillich's theory, neither of the two major instruments of research directly interrogated respondents with respect to the noetic content of their experiences. However, it has already been noted that in cognitive-type experiences the discursive or narrative properties of film were very important and might be seen as supplying content to the experiences under consideration. For example, the previously discussed experiences of Augusto, Lucilda, and Marta were closely related to the content of the films which respectively depicted an attractive father–son relationship, a successful act of defiance of oppression, and a dismantling of prejudice.

Even if the decision is taken to continue to consider these to be revelatory experiences, the importance of the subject matter does not directly contradict Tillich's theory of revelation through culture. Clearly Tillich would not want to deny that artworks have subject matter and content; he simply argued that this must become transparent or must be ruptured at the moment of revelation in order to provide access to the religious depth or substance beneath. Both the reading of Tillich's theory of revelation through culture, and the qualitative research project that has been constructed on the basis of that reading, prioritize the effect of revelation over the content of revelation. However, in the examples under consideration here, there is an obvious connection between the content of the films and the nature of the effect of the experience. Augusto views a film that presents an attractive father–son relationship and is moved to repair the breach that exists in his own paternal–filial relationship. Lucilda views a film that shows an act of defiance against a military dictatorship and feels that something of the oppressive pall that has lain for so long over her and her generation is lifted. Marta views a film which portrays a character who overcomes prejudice against homosexuality and senses that some of her own prejudices, fruit of a conservative upbringing, are broken down. It would be disingenuous to claim that this link between the content of the films and the nature of the effect of the experience was incidental.

The final section of the final chapter will return to address the question of the content of revelation in far greater detail. In fact, it is around this question that the most fundamental discussion of the adequacy of Tillich's theory of revelation through culture is focused. In the final chapter, many of the strands of discussion which are to some extent artificially separated in the theory-driven analysis developed here will be re-woven as the nature of the artwork, the mechanism of the event, the content and the effect of revelation are all discussed together.

6.1.6 The effect

In the original discussion of Tillich's theory, his dismissal of the possibility that revelation was concerned with the transmission of a message or with a personal encounter led to consideration of the effect of revelation and the relation between revelation and salvation. In fact, the identification of revelation *as* salvation, albeit in a carefully proscribed sense of the word, was the key finding of the analysis of Tillich's theory of revelation through culture. The unity of revelation and salvation is seen perfectly only beyond the ambiguities of time and history in the perfect (beatific) vision of God in eternity. Here and now both revelation and salvation are fragmentary and ambiguous.

Nonetheless, revelation is the mediation of a power that brings limited but genuine healing. The experience of the ground of being brings courage and faith to overcome essential anxiety. The experience of New Being can banish existential despair. The experience of Spiritual Presence can generate the love needed to overcome estrangement and broken and damaged relationships.

One respondent, Jorge, spoke of the potency of film: 'it has a very, very great power, and it's something, well, almost, well... something almost 'magical' in quotation marks'. The question immediately arises, what is the effect of this 'almost magical' power, a power which the same respondent, Jorge, had previously described as 'brutal'?

The impact of two very different films upon Samuel and Augusto's relationships with their respective fathers has been discussed above. However, the majority of respondents spoke of the impact that films had on their thinking and feeling. Two examples of this have already been mentioned. Lucilda felt a weight of oppression lifted by her experience of *Les Yeux des Oiseaux* and Marta stated that *Fresa y chocolate* had played a part in dismantling certain aspects of a rigidly restrictive worldview. In relation to the various characteristics of his engagement with *Tango feroz*, Samuel says:

> Eh... perhaps the most interesting is the intellectual. The film somehow... let's say changed my vision a little bit with regard to the way I understood my... my political position. I... uhm, I repeat, well... I had always held to a centre right position, perhaps that was the position of my parents and grandparents, well... And the truth is that having seen the film, and having lived through that, and, and... coming to see it in a certain sense from the outside, to see my life from the outside... I was... I expanded my, my political outlook a little. Let's say, let's say... I allowed, eh, a little bit of... of the left to enter, and of... of a better social distribution... and of better understanding... Eh, so that's how it broadened my political horizon a little.

The approach to the data which, perhaps, sheds most light on the way the respondents as a whole understood the impact of their film-watching experiences was coding. Coding gathers all the words or phrases that the respondents used and files them under various thematically linked headings. In cross-sectional analysis the gathering together of conceptually or thematically linked packets of information, which could be individual words or short tropes, out of the interview transcripts is frequently referred to as *en vivo* coding.[6] This method generates a number of insights with respect to the impact of the experiences under consideration.

The phrase which arose most frequently across the interviews in reference to the impact of the experiences was '*me ha marcado*', which carries the same sense as the English phrase 'it has marked me'. This is indicative of an impact

---

[6] Miles and Huberman, *Analysis*, p. 58.

but, like Jorge speaking of the 'power' of film, it is neutral and not particularly descriptive of the nature of the impact. Also, it was used by the researcher in a number of the interviews and so, arguably, is not the respondents' own vocabulary. Similarly common, but slightly more interesting, especially in light of Tillich's focus on breakthrough, was the concept of the effect of a film-watching experience being the creation of an opening. For example, Samuel writes: 'The cinema can create an opening... more quickly and more directly... than other [artistic] manifestations.'

When the search parameters were broadened to include not only exact repetitions but also thematically linked words and phrases, a new category emerged carrying the sense of breaking out, expanding, or liberating. For example, 'Yes, it seemed to me to be liberating in that sense, no? Like a film that liberates from taboos, from, from, from prejudices.'

Perhaps the most condensed expression of this kind of language came from Pedro, who was chosen for interview on the basis of the maximum variation sample. His questionnaire responses were considered theoretically interesting because, while they resembled a critical case in many respects (the complexity and intensity of the experience and a great positive impact), he allowed absolutely no room for a mystical or spiritual dimension. The relation of this to his views on religion will be discussed below, but in light of his questionnaire answers and his interview it seems appropriate to include his experience with those that are possibly revelatory. When asked, in the interview, about the way the film he referenced had impacted on him, he said:

> I'll tell you again, I don't know if you've already guessed this because of my tone of voice... this isn't just a film that I like a lot, because there are mil-, millions of films that I like a lot. In fact, there are films that I... today I like a lot more than *El lado oscuro del corazon*, but... when one is... is vulnerable... uhm, uhm... that is, in a certain sense the film... attacks, attacks you or wounds you... in some... I don't mean that in a negative way. Uhm... certain... uhm, barriers that one has... when the barriers fall... and one is confronted... with... things that, they don't necessarily have to be sad, they could be sad, they could be situations of joyous emotion... uhm, that's part of the joy... that a film can suddenly bring, bring to you. And that's what happened to me.

For Pedro this very potent experience is intimately linked to his discovering and pursuing his vocation as an intellectual and a writer. Interestingly, the film didn't make a great impression on him when he first saw it as a young adolescent. At this point, aged 11 or 12, his primary interest was 'erotic'; he had heard that there was female nudity in the film and he was keen to see it. However, in the event the film merely frustrated and bored him. An uncle who was an admirer of the film mentioned it frequently but Pedro always replied, 'no, that's a boring film'.

Until I saw it one time and ... and ... it became very important to me in the sense that ... it was ... we spoke a moment ago of catharsis, no? Well, to see someone who shared certain similarities with me, or me with him ... and who lived a life that, by my criteria, was fantastic, incredible, that is, a writer who lived by writing alone.

Now living in Montevideo permanently, Pedro continues on this literary trajectory. He holds a Master's degree in literature, has published volumes of short stories and critical theory, and pays his bills by promoting cultural events. While there is no way of proving any causal or even influential relation between the film-watching experience and this vocational development, there is no doubt that in Pedro's own mind the two are related.

There is a temptation in this research project, on the part of the researcher and the researched, to attend only to positive experiences and to positive outcomes, but Pedro's choice of words is fascinating in that they are not univocally 'happy' terms. Although the overall impact was seen to be positive, he felt 'sad' and 'vulnerable', and the film 'attacked' and 'wounded' him before the 'barriers fell' and 'joy' was experienced. I noted in the previous chapter that I was unable to interview any of the small number of respondents who reported a negative impact. I did, however, select one respondent in the maximum variation sample on the basis of his stating that there was no impact in his life from the particularly memorable viewing experience that he discussed.

Gastón is a young photographer, and from the first his attitude at interview was more distant and less animated than any of the other interviewees. He spoke of a film called *Whisky* (2004), the second film of two young Uruguayan directors, Juan Pablo Rebella and Pablo Stoll. This film, winner of the Audience Prize at the Cannes Film Festival, is considered 'the most important feature film in the history of Uruguayan cinema'.[7] It is a very slow film of the blackest and driest humour and it concerns a middle-aged owner of a tiny sock-making factory, his long-time assistant, and his more successful and worldly brother. When the elder brother comes to visit, the sock-maker feels compelled to hide his loneliness by trying to pass his assistant off as his wife. This proves difficult even in familiar surroundings, but when the trio head off down the Uruguayan coast for a few days' holiday, maintaining the illusion becomes impossible.

For Gastón the film was about the pointless monotony of our lives and the impossibility of breaking out towards something better. He saw the endless running of the thread through the sock-making machines as a visual presentation of this mechanistic and meaningless existence. While Gastón's reading of the film might be challenged, I would certainly argue that for one of the

---

[7] Raúl Forlán Lamarque, 'Historia mínima', *La República*, 6 August 2004.

characters, at least, the end of the film intimates a new start and a new hope; the question is whether he is right to consider that the film had not had an impact on him. A critic speaks of the characters as having their 'existence shaken', and perhaps this might also be true of members of the audience.[8] If this is the case, and it would appear that Gastón answered the filter question in the affirmative because he recognized this film as a shaking experience, then it might well be true to say that for Tillich the film that makes you question the meaning, or meaninglessness, of life is precisely the most revelatory of art forms. For example, Tillich emphasized the negative aspects of the experience of revelation in miracle and ecstasy (*ST1*, 124–30) and argued that the very awareness of estrangement may be seen as revelation (*ST2*, 86).

In the concluding chapter I will return to consider the way in which immersion into the world of the film may result, upon return to the real world, in the discovery that certain barriers have fallen and a new way of seeing, of thinking, or of being is possible. In particular, I will suggest that there are theological accounts of revelation, particularly those based on the work of Rowan Williams and Paul Ricoeur, which resemble this mechanism more closely than does Tillich's. This discussion will again raise the question of the content of revelation. In particular, it will address the fact that the respondent accounts suggest a much closer link between the subject matter of the film, the content, and the effect of the experience.

6.1.7 Revelation and Jesus as the Christ

For Tillich, the religious categories, conceptualizations, and language that come to attach themselves to experiences of revelation are second order accretions. The primary experience of revelation, the experience of the ground and abyss of being, is ineffable. Nonetheless, the relation between revelation and Jesus as the Christ is fundamental for Tillich. Indeed, Jesus as the Christ is the criterion of all revelation, the absolutely concrete and absolutely universal example. Here the general theory and the particular instance are correlative. Jesus as the Christ is the theoretically perfect symbol. His participation in the ground of being is perfect because he is the essential man. His transparency to that ground becomes perfect in the event of the cross when all that is finite, material, and conditioned is sacrificed. It is in the individual's existential involvement with Jesus as the Christ, mediated through the expressionist word portraits provided by the gospel writers, that the most perfect occurrences of revelation and salvation occur.

---

[8] Jorge Traverso, 'Figuras en el paisaje', *El Observador*, 15 August 2004.

It has already been noted that Samuel (an atheist) and Augusto (a Roman Catholic) employed very different terminology and conceptualizations to speak of their experiences. Both responded positively, at least in the end, to Tillich's own account of his Botticelli experience, and, ironically, it was Samuel's story which appeared to have more of the mystical or religious about it. However, although Augusto's experience appeared more intellectual or cognitive, it was he who was happy to mimic Tillich's vocabulary and, indeed, to deploy religious categories of his own in speaking of his experience. He says:

> So, it's ... I don't know if ... it's not that I felt the presence of God in the film but, yes, that, at a personal level and ... in the life of faith the film made me, well, uhm ... also pray very much from that starting point, uhm ... question myself from that starting point, and share a lot from that place. So that ... when it happens that you have an experience that moves you from the intellectual, from the emotional, from the spiritual, it's impossible ... to ... at least the way I live, uhm, to not pass from there to God.

Prompted to elaborate on God's ability to 'speak through a film', he goes on:

> It's not that God speaks through a film but yes, I believe he takes advantage of that opportunity in order to ... in order to question us and in order to ... make us see things that ... or in order to ask us, or in order to ... I don't know, return things to us ... As I said to you, the ways of God are, are strange.

When Tillich's concept of revelation through culture was presented to Augusto he was receptive, although he was concerned that in the brief summary of Tillich's thought provided, these 'revelations' were too closely associated with external phenomena. For a devout Roman Catholic with concerns about the syncretistic distortions of the faith that are prevalent in South America, this might open the door to an unhealthy focus on appearances of the Virgin Mary or miraculous lights in the sky. However, having made this point he proceeds immediately to elaborate on the problems he had experienced in his relationship with his father, on the father–son relationship in the film, and on the way his relationship changed radically. He finishes, 'And in that sense I think that it was a ... a revelation that I lived, also, as a very powerful experience of God and a ... a very powerful experience with my father, well, for the better, no?'

In contrast, a non-religious respondent, Lucilda, tried to describe the kinds of experiences that had led her to answer the survey question about a presence or a power with 'perhaps', but struggled to find the language she needed:

> Yes, yes, yes, I said 'perhaps' to you because I have felt those experiences in the cinema. Uhm, well yes, occasionally, I'd say ... I'd say it's as if the film transmits to me, I'd say, and ... it's as if I'm completely and absolutely immersed and it's something beyond [*mas alla*—which often has superstitious or mystical

connotations] that which...uhm...look, beyond that which I am as pure rationality, no? But it's not something that I can ...

As when Samuel attempted to describe his experience of nature or of an 'other' in film, it seems that Lucilda has slipped towards the ineffable, beyond what her limited religious vocabulary allows her to communicate.

The rest of the data generated in the interviews similarly reflected the way in which, even when respondents describe very similar experiences, mechanisms, and impacts, there is a notable difference between the language used by those with religious commitments and those without. In some cases it is clear that it is not merely a difference in the language used after the event, but a difference in the actual seeing or reading of the film. One atheist respondent, whose wife had been a nun, describes the way in which they would watch a film together; but in travelling on the bus afterwards, or discussing it at home, it would become clear that she saw a 'spiritual dimension' that was absent for him. However, when the same respondent read the handout that presented a summary of Tillich's thought on revelation through art and, particularly, the sentence which states that the believer and the atheist would have different language for the same experience, he commented: 'Aha! Here I am with my wife. [Laughs] A shared experience, it's true.'

This resembles the general attitude of all the respondents when presented with the two Tillich handouts. While a number of the atheist respondents questioned the vocabulary of both handouts and the explicit link to religion in the Botticelli piece, this generally did not imply that they could not or would not relate to the actual experiences. For example, Pedro, in spite of atheist commitments, says: 'Uhm...I...perhaps everything that I've been speaking of with regard to that film [*El lado oscuro del corazon*], well, you could say it would enter into that category [of revelation].' It appears that Tillich's account, at least as presented in the two short handouts, was attractive to both believers and non-believers; members of both groups were willing, and indeed enthused by the possibility, to understand their experiences against Tillich's framework.

At the end of the theory-driven stage of the analysis, a number of questions have been raised that can only be answered by a return to critical engagement with Tillich's theology. In particular, there is a complex problem oriented around the question of the content of revelation, the relation of these experiences to any explicit religious frameworks, and the difficulty in distinguishing between positive aesthetic experiences and genuinely revelatory experiences on the basis of Tillich's theology of revelation as it has been developed in this monograph. It would be possible to argue that this problem would not exist if the qualitative research had incorporated a more rigorous filter and sampling policy: for example, by incorporating a far more stringent definition of 'ecstasy' and 'miracle'. However, this argument overlooks the way in which many respondents identified with Tillich's account of his encounter with the *Madonna and Singing Angels* painting, which in this monograph functions as the paradigmatic revelatory experience. Raising the threshold with respect to miracle and ecstasy so as to incorporate only those willing to describe their accounts in explicitly mystical or religious terms would also have done violence to Tillich's contention that these experiences are had even by materialists and atheists. Addressing this issue will be one of the main tasks of the concluding chapter of this book. However, I will first turn to data-driven analysis of the interviews to show how a completely new hypothesis about the way in which cinema might function in a revelatory manner emerges unexpectedly out of the data.

6.2 DATA-DRIVEN ANALYSIS: FROM INDIVIDUAL MOMENT TO COMMUNAL LIFE-PRACTICE

A number of different approaches to data analysis have already been utilized (non-cross-sectional analysis in the vignette; cross-sectional or thematic analysis of the whole corpus of interviews; and *en vivo* coding focusing on frequently repeated words or phrases) but the process has been guided consistently by the theoretical interests and concerns brought to the empirical research project from the reading of Tillich's theology of revelation through culture. However, as discussed in Chapter 4, an expectation of good qualitative research is that as well as testing hypotheses it should also generate new ones. In this project a fresh way of considering the revelatory potential of cinema arises directly out of the data.

As in the previous section, the method will be to proceed from non-cross-sectional analysis (i.e. an illustrative vignette) to cross-sectional analysis of the whole body of interview data to investigate how the other interviews confirm or undermine the provisional hypotheses drawn from the vignette. Once again, *en vivo* coding will be incorporated where appropriate. It was suggested in Chapter 5 that, perhaps, it was the influence of the *Cinemateca* club that led to the surprisingly high number of political films referenced in Montevideo. Closer consideration of this possibility in light of the interview-generated data provides the first hint of the new construal of the possibility of revelation through film.

It was a salient characteristic of the interview data that respondents repeatedly referred to good and bad films, and good and bad cinema. 'Now look, you have to know how to choose because there are all kinds of cinema.' 'All media technologies have that face ... ambiguous, bi-frontal, no? No, or ... that's to say that God ... who has two faces, no? Commercial cinema can also be the opium of the people. There are opiums all around, no?' This distinction between a commercial cinema of, at best, mere entertainment and another cinema of far greater merit was very widespread. The grounds upon which these decisions were made became increasingly intriguing.

It became clear that, as suggested by the questionnaire results, a very important role was being played by the *Cinemateca* club. As Marta puts it, 'But in general, if a film is selected by *Cinemateca* or by a trustworthy source then I ... I see it.' Similarly, Gastón, speaking of his involvement with *Cinemateca*, said, 'I realized that there is another ... another possibility for cinema that is ... that is something different.' Many respondents spoke of festivals and of other *Cinemateca* programmes that had had a profound effect upon them. It was reflection on the role played by *Cinemateca* that first raised the possibility that to see cinema-going and film experiences in a restrictively individualistic way might be to miss something important about the manner in which film functions as a site or medium of revelation.

6.2.1 Beau: An illustrative vignette

Beau is a 75-year-old retired teller in the state bank of Uruguay with a lifelong passion for the cinema. Indeed, he was named by his cine-projectionist father after John Barrymore's eponymous character in Harry Beaumont's *Beau Brummel* (1924). In middle age, Beau became an award-winning screenwriter and director. In short, he is a self-proclaimed 'cinephile'.

The qualitative research method in general, and the maximum variation sampling strategy in particular, require that close attention be paid to apparently anomalous data, to results which appear to contradict either the theoretical account that is being considered or the rest of the data set. Beau was selected for interview on the basis of the maximum variation sample because his answers to the questionnaire marked him out as the respondent with the most serious engagement with film; and yet his answers were not indicative of the kind of experience found in my reading of Tillich's theory. A respondent with a very high level of commitment to the cinema, whose experience did not resemble Tillich's account, was deemed worthy of investigation.

A second anomaly was noted after the interviews had been carried out when his transcript was considered alongside the others. In spite of his passion for film, he was the only interviewee who couldn't remember which film he had spoken of in the questionnaire survey. The transcript of his interview suggests that this is not merely forgetfulness but a reflection of the fact that he finds it almost impossible to isolate one particular film or memorable experience.

Beau is a non-dogmatic but confirmed atheist. He is married to a former nun and although he frequently discusses the 'spiritual' aspect of films with her, he has a tendency to congratulate himself on helping her to escape from the organized religion that he considers to have imprisoned her. However, he is the respondent who is most enthusiastically receptive of Tillich's theory of revelation through culture as it is presented at the close of the interviews.

He responds even before the end of the first handout. 'Perfect! Wonderful! Fantastic! Eh, it's revelation, of course!' When asked whether he thinks revelation is an appropriate way of speaking of cinema he cannot respond emphatically enough:

> Yes, yes, yes, yes, yes, it's true. Yes, that's it. It's a revelation, a, a . . . a very important thing in my life, and in that of all my family . . . It's a way of . . . it's a . . . like a lifebuoy on a ship. For me the cinema is a lifebuoy . . . of, of life, if you are . . . uhm . . . grab it in order to . . . in a good way, in order to survive but in the best way. Understand?

He is equally positive after reading Tillich's experience of the Botticelli painting:

> I see, I see myself . . . clearly . . . clearly reflected in all that it says here [. . .] With a great deal of the cinema that I see I leave . . . I walk away shaken [. . .] this thing about shaking, for me, the cinema shakes me a huge amount. Well, but it is . . . it's . . . a moment of beauty [the title of the handout], it's true. For me the cinema is a moment of beauty. So, if the film is . . . if it's good . . . this thing is a moment of beauty for me. It's fantastic.

I would like to draw attention to two key elements of Beau's account: first, the way in which the impact is primarily a result of a sustained life-practice rather than a momentary event related to one particular film; and, second, the way in which the experiences that result in the greatest impact have a strong communal dimension.

It soon becomes clear that Beau's strongest statements are not related to particular films. With regard to *Pizza, Birra, Faso*, the film which he discussed at the time of the questionnaire research, and to which he eventually returned in the interview, he says merely, 'That's . . . well, that's one that marked me.' However, when speaking more abstractly he can say, 'cinema has marked me extremely' or 'In my case cinema is . . . totally powerful.'

This ties in with what has been noted above, that cinema has always been an important part of his life: from childhood experiences, 'because we were very poor at home [we went to] a neighbourhood cinema [. . .] every Monday night it was cheap, they put on, for 15 cents, they put on three films'; through his own cinematic practice, 'when you see my film you'll realize [. . .] that it's *noir* cinema, very *noir*, it's the cinema of Humphrey Bogart'; and through to later generations, 'I've got two children . . . and, and my wife as well [laughs] I made her a cinephile, my wife and my children too'.

Family life is one of the two spheres where the communal nature of Beau's engagement with cinema is most apparent. 'We begin to speak of the cinema and we don't stop . . . it's fantastic, very good.' 'It's a reference, the cinema is a [point of] reference at home.' Whether speaking of the emergence of a hitherto unseen spiritual dimension when he discusses a film with his wife, or the more general sense in which the film 'begins to transform itself within you' when you converse about it later, both the mechanism and the impact of cinema are clearly communal on Beau's account. However, this communal dimension is most notable in a second sphere, relating to his involvement with *Cinemateca* through the period of the Uruguayan dictatorship.

Cinemateca's importance emerges early in the interview. 'I go to see all the films at *Cinemateca* [...] I'm very involved with *Cinemateca* [...] here *Cinemateca* is immensely valuable.' Beau explains that he first became involved with *Cinemateca* when he decided to study film-making in the earliest years of Uruguay's military dictatorship, in 1972 or '73. In this context he described *Cinemateca* as a 'refuge'.

> It was a big group and we had, it was a refuge because we spoke ... we spoke of politics, we spoke of what was happening ... of people who had disappeared, of people who had been tortured, of all the families that had had to flee into exile, of my family. My sister and my brother-in-law, with their four children, had to flee the country. They took me, they took me prisoner ... first, because I was a bank-teller [and after] the *coup d'état* we went on strike for 15 days [...] And that's why, it's a refuge because it was ... in the cinema I found a refuge, even in fiction films ... Living under a dictatorship ... it's like the best remedy that they can give you. It's like a vaccination [laughs] ... like a vaccination against the world. Understand?

For Beau, as this paragraph shows, the communal experience of the *Cinemateca* and the experience of films are curiously and beneficially intermingled. When he speaks, repeatedly, of the positive impact of cinema, these two aspects remain entwined.

> For example, in the dictatorship, when we lived the dictatorship and ... part of my family had to leave ... I was very sensitive to the cinema then, because what's more they never let you write anything in the newspapers, nor in the magazines, there was nothing of anything. Then in contrast the cinema came, with prize-winning films and all this ... renewed you ... Any film with any little theme, as it were, a character that was ... living what you were living, a time of dictatorship, or prohibition, of not being able to do anything. At the family level ... I, I didn't, I had, my children were little during the dictatorship ... and we never spoke to them about politics or about the dictatorship, not even about ... their aunts and uncles who had had to go into exile. So, in that period of dictatorship to go to the cinema was even more renewing for me than in a normal period.

In summary: Beau's interview data demonstrate his appreciation of Tillich's account of the revelatory potential of art; he is happy with the term 'revelation'; considers film's impact to be 'shaking'; and he identifies strongly with Tillich's article about his Botticelli experience; further, he describes the impact of cinema in terms which accord with Tillich's contention that the effect of revelation is partial salvation. He describes cinema as 'a lifebuoy', 'a refuge', a source of 'renewal', and a 'vaccination' against the vicissitudes of life.

However, this impact is not primarily associated with momentary experiences related to individual films. Beau's account demands that careful consideration be given to the communal element and the sustained practice of cinema-going over an extended period of time. The other interviews will now be examined to consider whether cross-sectional analysis of the whole field of interview data strengthens or undermines the emerging hypothesis that the possibility of revelation through film might be manifest as much through communal practices extended over time as through individual moments of ecstatic experience. I will consider cross-sections of data at two locations: instances of the greater importance of 'the community' over 'an individual'; and instances of the greater importance of 'the cinema' over 'a film'.

6.2.2 The greater importance of 'the community' over 'an individual'

As a group the respondents showed a highly positive attitude to cinema. This is almost inevitable given that they were 'intercepted' at a film festival. However, once Beau's account has opened new horizons and suggested that the categories 'communal' and 'life-practice' might be considered in place of 'individual' and 'momentary experience', the notion of 'a positive attitude to cinema' can be developed and refined.

Through consideration of the childhood experiences of the respondents, both the communal and the life-practice aspects of this analysis can be brought together. Most respondents reported cinema-going as a habit stretching back into their childhoods. It is a natural fact of childhood cinema-going that it is a communal undertaking, and a number of the respondents referred to particular family members with whom they habitually visited the cinema, specifically: a grandfather; an older sister; an uncle; and a mother. These accounts of childhood describe socialization into a practice of cinema-going that is always and already communal.

It is easy to ignore this communal element because most of the respondents offer a relatively individualistic description of the mechanism by which the cinema effects its 'magic' as the lights go down and the spectator is drawn into the world of the film. However, careful analysis of the interview accounts draws attention to the importance of the social setting that surrounds this individual moment of immersion.

The respondents' reaction to those with whom they share the cinema experience is not always positive. Lucilda perhaps expresses this ambiguity most succinctly: 'It depends on the companion [laughs]. Yes, yes, yes... when you have at your side a person who, a person at your side who, who, who... is capable of enjoying the film. If not, you're better off seeing it alone!' A number of other respondents agree that sometimes a companion or the audience more generally can distract and devalue the experience by their interruptions or their general lack of sensitivity.

However, far more common is a sense that a good companion or, more generally, the opportunity to discuss the film after the event is a very important and fruitful part of the process. Augusto, who was taken to the cinema by his grandfather as a young child, speaks of the communal practice of cinema-going by reference to a, perhaps romanticized, view of a former generation. This 'mature' Uruguayan 'lives' the cinema 'as a cultural event, as a cultural outing... uhm, there are still many people... who are of that old school, well, of going out to eat and to watch a film, then of having a coffee and a chat, discussing the film'.

The importance of *Cinemateca* as an arbiter of 'good' cinema has been established, but, as Beau suggested, the club also has an important social role. For example, the relatively low cost of membership makes the club a natural hub for the social life of university students, and Pedro described how it was his friends at the University who persuaded him to join. In fact, Pedro is so effusive in his praise of *Cinemateca* that he remarks that it might appear as if he was being paid to publicize the club.

Overall, the wider field of interview data adds weight to the hypothesis, initially derived from consideration of Beau's account, that the impact of film-going is frequently related to the location of a filmgoer within a wider social network of family or other relations. Marta's interview offers a good example of the profound impact of a communal cinema-going life-practice rather than an individual and momentary film-watching experience. Marta grew up in the 'interior' of Uruguay, far from the big cities, but came to Montevideo as a teenager to pursue her tertiary education. She said:

> When I came, one of the, one of the methods that I found to... to... well, to establish that I belonged in the city, because I felt very closely identified with the countryside, the interior. Right? The city tormented me with its noises, with its... So one of the ways that I found to establish my sense of myself [*asujetarme*] was the cinema. The cinema as it acted out city life for me, no? Because, uhm... it, it, it recreated a world for me, a world... that, that... I couldn't go back there again and again to my town, and so gradually... And so, that's to say, it, it, it saved me from the distress of living in the city.

In response to a question from the researcher about the exact meaning of '*asujetarme*', Marta went on to elaborate further on the role cinema had played.

> It helped me because I detached myself from my family in that activity. I had friends, we talked, afterwards we'd go and have a coffee and discuss the film. It

helped a lot to socialize me, no. The socialization that... because I was... was, was a kind of the kid from the other side of the tracks, I didn't have the same, I didn't move, I didn't know the streets very well. I got lost. So, uhm, the cinema helped me a lot. It educated me. It educated me a lot.

6.2.3 The greater importance of 'the cinema' over 'a film'

The wider group of respondents also reflect Beau and Marta in that they speak frequently not just of the effect of particular film-watching experiences, or even of particular films, but of cinema as a more general category.[9] One of the respondents remarked that the impact of cinema in her life was greatest when considered over a long period, like 'the little work of ants'. *En vivo* coding shows that, across the interview transcripts as a whole, phrases referring to the impact of cinema as a general category outnumber those related to specific films by nearly 2:1 (46:26).

There are two groups of these phrases that are of particular interest. First, those phrases that can be grouped together under the same thematic category as those considered above in the theory-driven analysis; that is, those phrases which convey a sense of breaking open, expanding, and liberating. Second, there are those phrases which explicitly address a mystical and spiritual dimension in relation to the cinematic experience. While some of these phrases arise before the explicit discussion of Tillich and revelation and some arise afterwards, there is enough continuity across these two moments of data generation to suggest that these are not concepts introduced by the researcher but are a genuine reflection of the respondents' own understandings.

A number of respondents spoke on multiple occasions of how the cinema, construed generally, 'creates an opening'. This terminology is similar to the way in which the political film-maker Fernando Solanas discussed the impact of authentically creative cinema in his book *La mirada*, discussed in Chapter 5. Jorge was the most consistent in seeing cinema as having this function. Throughout the interview he returned to this kind of phrasing on a number of occasions, saying 'it opens you up'; 'creates an opening in a number of senses'; 'it generates certain openings'. He then goes on to give slightly more form to this concept: 'it creates something like a broadening of the conscience'; 'it gives our lives a broader dimension'.

---

[9] It could be argued that the general understanding of cinema is simply a reflection of questions early in the interview guide that referred to 'cinema' or 'film' in this general sense. However, respondents frequently returned to this general sense even when the researcher's intention and questions were aimed at keeping them speaking of a particular film experience, so it seems likely that they owned this way of speaking.

In spite of having no religious commitments, Jorge also associates this power with what might be termed 'transcendence'. Cinema has 'to do with, with that kind of art that transmits something, that, that ... that touches on the incomprehensible, no?' Marta, a Roman Catholic, spoke explicitly of cinema's relation to 'transcendent topics'; 'questions that have to do with, with the absolute'; 'that move one to ... to feel the experience of the absolute'.

The analysis is now tending towards seeing the potentially revelatory power of film not in individual and momentary terms but in relation to community and to long-term life-practices. This suggests a return to consideration of the political sphere and of the function of cinema in Uruguay in the period following the collapse of the military dictatorship.

As previously noted, there are a remarkable number of references to the political sphere, and particularly to repression and dictatorship, in the respondent accounts. Samuel's experience of *Tango feroz* was intimately related to its portrayal of student life in the repressive 1960s, and he characterized its main impact as a broadening of his political stance and openness. Beau's experiences were also closely related to life under the dictatorship. He stated that it was in this context that he felt the saving and renewing power of the cinema most strongly. The film which Jorge discussed, *Cabra marcado para morrer*, was also related to the politics of repression and violence, this time in Brazil. Marta spoke of *Fresa y chocolate*, a film related to the negative attitude of revolutionary idealism towards homosexuality or other 'differences' in Cuban society.

Lucilda's experience of *Les yeux des oiseaux* is interesting because it illustrates how the wider social and political situation impinges on the individual's reception of a film. It was noted above that Lucilda saw the film very positively and described its effect as a kind of healing of the distorted subjectivity that had been imposed on her generation by the acutely repressive military regime.

However, this is at odds with the general reception history of this film. The film is clearly a denunciation of a brutal military regime. Contra Marta's interpretation, it makes its point precisely by highlighting the almost omnipotent power of the violent and manipulative prison officials. The film shows the utter powerlessness of the prisoners and their families.

The narrative is actually structured around the visit of an International Red Cross team who try to ensure there are no human rights abuses in the prison. While the prisoners and their families are depicted as noble but impotent, the Red Cross is shown to be self-serving and impotent. In fact, the release of the film in Uruguay resulted in a press release from the International Committee of the Red Cross, stating that they had not been consulted about the film's production and that they considered it a 'caricature [...] bearing no relation to reality'.[10]

---

[10] Elvio Gandolfo, 'Buenas intenciones', *Cine*, 15 February 1985.

It is clear that Marta's reading and experience of the film is only possible because of what was happening in Uruguayan society at the time of the film's release. If the film, described by one reviewer as 'a bitter message of fury, horror and pain', had been screened in Uruguay while the dictatorship was still in power, it would surely have exacerbated the sense of hopelessness and powerlessness.[11] However, when it reached the cinemas immediately after the return to democracy its very presence was a sign of hope and renewal. Germán Lago observes:

> The Uruguayans' interest in this matter is somewhat different [to the European reception], and arises above all from the emotional charge that the spectator brings to a topic that he feels as his own, and the fact that he is able to hear expressions and opinions that would have been unthinkable on a screen in our country just a few months ago.[12]

Consideration of the accounts of respondents like Lucilda, Marta, and Beau has suggested the importance of renewed attentiveness to the communal dimension of cinema-going, to cinema-going as a sustained life-practice, and to the relation of the film-viewing experience to what is happening in the wider social or political sphere. As the empirical research project was not set up to investigate this conceptualization, there is not enough empirical data available to develop the new theory further. However, this data-driven analysis has already developed far enough to suggest a return to facets of Tillich's theology of culture which were considered in Chapter 2. In particular, there were elements of Tillich's theory, seen clearly in the early German writings, which were set aside in later sections when the reading was organized around Tillich's experience of the Botticelli painting.

The facets of Tillich's theology that were set aside focused upon the task of reading the style not of a particular art object but of a whole culture, and considered the '*kairos* time' not in terms of seconds or minutes but as a period of years when change was a real possibility. In this context revelation was associated with the breaking of old heteronomous or autonomous cultural styles and the irruption of a more theonomous culture. In one section of the final chapter I will address the potential of considering the *Cinemateca Uruguaya* in terms of Tillich's understanding of a 'spiritual community'.

---

[11] Rodolfo Fattoruso, 'Un amargo mensaje de furia, espanto y dolor', *Vida cultural*, 7 February 1985.
[12] Germán Lago, 'Pese a todo el testimonio', *La Democracia*, 8 February 1985.

Part IV

Illuminations

NUEVE REINAS (NINE QUEENS), DIR. BY FABIÁN BIELINSKY (2002)

In the questionnaire research that was undertaken at the Mar del Plata film festival, no film was referred to by more respondents than Fabián Bielinsky's *Nueve reinas*. Indeed, one of the hottest tickets at the festival was a special screening of the film to celebrate it as one of the most nationally and internationally, commercially and critically successful Argentinean films of all time.

The film is a classic crime drama, in the style of a David Mamet or Alfred Hitchcock. The plot is about two small-time conmen whose paths cross, apparently serendipitously, in downtown Buenos Aires. Soon after the meeting, the chance of a lifetime appears to fall into the hands of the two swindlers when an ageing and ailing associate of the older of the two requests their help in selling a perfect forgery of the priceless *Nueve reinas* set of stamps. He can even put them in touch with a millionaire Spanish buyer who is already on his way to Buenos Aires.

The older of the two swindlers, Marcos, is played by Ricardo Darín, an actor who has risen from early work in the daytime soaps to become one of Argentina's most famous leading men. At first, he takes on a kind of mentoring relationship with respect to his younger partner, developing the kind of role that is typical of a certain kind of film and would perfectly suit a well-liked actor of Darín's standing. However, as the narrative unfolds, Darín's character becomes less and less likeable. He is no Robin Hood and is willing to swindle the poorest and most vulnerable, to cheat and manipulate his younger brother, and even to sell his own sister to the Spanish businessmen in order to get what he wants. As the film progresses, the audience members' loyalties are split and their desires become confused. Is it possible to go on willing this character to succeed even as he unhesitatingly uses and abuses everyone around him in the single-minded pursuit of his selfish goal? When Marcos finishes the film penniless and despairing, the audience finds it is hard to know whether to cheer or to commiserate with him.

It is only in the very final scene that the true nature of the events that have unfolded is revealed. As the younger conman passes through the entrance of a decrepit warehouse on a Buenos Aires backstreet, it is as though the curtain has been pulled back and the audience are allowed to look backstage. Gathered around a green beize card table are the ensemble cast of characters who have appeared through the film. Here is the old associate with forgeries to sell; the Spanish businessman desperate to buy; the art expert who authenticated the stamps; and a number of others who played incidental and apparently inconsequential parts in what transpired. All of them, as it turns out, were in the employ of the younger man who had been cleverly conning his partner throughout.

One of the great satisfactions inherent in this kind of a conclusion is found in the way the impact of the moment of revelation works backwards. The knowledge that throughout the film the younger man has been manipulating and playing his erstwhile mentor demands that you rewind your way back through the film's earlier scenes in your mind. A cascade of smaller revelations is released as each event is seen differently in light of the new understanding.

In the discussion of methodology and methods that took place in Chapter 4, it was noted that the goal of qualitative research is not to prove a particular theory, nor to provide statistical evidence for the presence or prevalence of a particular phenomenon in or across a population. Rather, its goal is illumination. It is to be hoped that in the final chapter of this book there will be some illumination as we reflect upon the way in which the findings of the empirical research interact with the theoretical account of revelation developed by Paul Tillich. In some sense the theoretical account should look different in light of the empirical data, in much the same way that the early parts of *Nueve reinas* look different in light of the revelations of the final scene.

However, it has been noted throughout this project that sometimes revelation is found precisely in the complexity that refuses to be separated into constituent parts and in the questions that resist easy answers. The thought experiment that addressed the revelatory potential of film suggested that it was the tensions, fissures, and aporia inherent in film's unique relation to the 'real' world that created the possibility of breakthrough. Respondents noted that 'difficult' films, where there was no obvious or simple resolution, often generated the most fruitful thought and discussion. Tillich was certain that a true mystery is never 'solved', even after the lifting of the veil.

Similarly, it is in the wrestling with a particular research puzzle or problem in a particular context that qualitative research aims to develop understanding and, metaphorically, to generate light. In this sense a grounded account will never be final or closed; rather than an end result, it is an ongoing process. Even in this final chapter, questions and mystery remain; it is to be hoped that, in and of themselves, as questions and mysteries, they are illuminating.

7

The Theory in Light of the Empirical Research

This monograph has moved towards a grounded account of the possibility of revelation through film through the combination of two bodies of research. A strong theoretical account was derived from a reading of Paul Tillich's theology of revelation. An empirical research project was then developed to ground this theoretical account in the experiences of a group of filmgoers by considering the ways in which their understandings of their experiences either confirmed or challenged the theory at key points.

The empirical component of the project was carried out in accordance with the precepts of the qualitative research paradigm which was introduced and defined in Chapter 4. As previously discussed, qualitative research is not overly concerned with the numbers of respondents contacted, questionnaires completed, or interviews recorded. Under ideal circumstances, a research project would continue until the researcher felt 'saturation' had been reached; in other words, no new relevant data were being generated and no new avenues for investigation of the central research questions were opening up. However, qualitative researchers recognize that, more frequently, it is practical issues or finite resources that dictate the end of the research process.[1] With respect to this project there is no doubt that research might have continued. In addition to simply interviewing more respondents, it would have been interesting to have had the resources to carry out a second study in the local multiplex. This might have addressed the question of whether the cinema somewhat dismissively labelled 'commercial' by *Cinemateca* and its members might itself be a medium of revelation. More importantly, the last section of the previous chapter introduced a new way of construing the revelatory potential of film but acknowledged that the original research project had not generated enough data to develop this idea further through qualitative analysis

---

[1] For a discussion of saturation and the role of practical considerations, see Mason, *Qualitative*, pp. 95–100.

techniques. Nonetheless, this new construal suggested a return to previously under-utilized aspects of Tillich's theoretical account.

The return to theory and consideration of the implications of the findings of the empirical research for a wider field is an important moment in the ongoing process of qualitative research. In this closing chapter, I consider Paul Tillich's theology of revelation in light of the empirical research undertaken in this project. In the first section of the chapter, the implications of the remarkable uniqueness of the film-viewer encounter evidenced by the empirical research are examined. Tillich's thought, whilst remaining firmly in the theoretical mode, is found to be highly sophisticated in its treatment of the interaction between particular viewer and particular artwork. Concomitantly, it is noted that there is a major methodological aporia in the wider religion–film discourse. It is suggested that religion–film writers should be far more attentive to the particular, individual nature of these encounters if their treatments of the possibly religious impact of film are to be suitably robust and compelling.

In the second section, the new conceptualization of the possibility of revelation through film which stresses the importance of sustained life-practice and the communal and social dimensions of film experience is revisited. I suggest that Tillich's theology has the resources at its disposal to offer a theoretical account of this conceptualization. The possibility is raised that it might be helpful to think of the *Cinemateca Uruguaya* as what Tillich names a latent spiritual community; a place where there is the impact of the Spiritual Presence in revelation and salvation.

In these first two sections Tillich's theory is viewed positively in light of the empirical research. His theory is attentive to the particularity of each encounter between individual and artwork and is well able to encompass the new conceptualization of the possibility of revelation through film. However, in the final two sections the results of the empirical research are seen to call into question aspects of Tillich's theoretical construal of the event of revelation and of the content of revelation.

The third section seeks to develop an account of the mechanism of the revelatory experience that is more attentive both to the understandings of the respondents and to the particularity of film as an art form which typically presents a narrative that unfolds over time. Tillich's approach is contrasted with an account derived from essays on revelation by Paul Ricoeur and Rowan Williams. This discussion leads, finally, to the fourth section. Here, it is the question of the content of revelation that is considered, in particular, whether it is appropriate to identify a closer link than Tillich allows between the subject matter of the artwork, the content, and the effect of revelation.

7.1 THE FILM-VIEWER ENCOUNTER IN LIGHT OF THE EMPIRICAL RESEARCH

The description and evaluation of religion–film writing undertaken in Chapter 1 noted that the discourse was moving towards greater consideration of the functional role of film in people's lives, particularly its religion-like character. However, the same chapter showed that such moves tended to rely upon the, potentially solipsistic, interpretations of religion–film academics and extrapolations from these readings to a putative impact in the lives of the audience more generally conceived. At best, religion–film writers have drawn upon some of the many theories of reception that were discussed in Chapter 4. The qualitative research undertaken in this monograph suggests that this might be a major methodological aporia. It appears that, at least for the most powerful of film-viewing experiences, the film-viewer relation is far more specific and radical than any general theory is capable of incorporating into its proposals.

In the empirical research, people spoke of films that were directly linked to their lives because of childhood experiences shared with the central characters; involvement in the actual production of the film; experience of the particular location or setting of the film; and experience of life in a dictatorship. Of these, only the last could possibly be predicted by any generalized methodology. With respect to the rest, their presence and their impact upon the experience and reception of the films could only be uncovered through direct engagement with the viewer. The research also showed that, in this group at least, the highly personal nature of each individual–film relation often led to highly idiosyncratic readings. On many occasions the most powerful aspects of the film for a given respondent were concerned with scenes and plot-lines only tangentially related to the main thrust of narrative or authorial intention: a father's relation to his oldest son; a chance encounter in the mist between a boy and a cow; a little girl's act of minor defiance; and a meeting in an ice-cream parlour. Again, these are beyond the reach of any generalized interpretive strategy.

Furthermore, the film *Tango feroz* provides an interesting example of the potential dangers of an 'expert' religious reading. *Tango feroz* received mixed reviews in both Argentina and Uruguay, some critics proclaiming it '*Bodrio* [Rubbish] *feroz*'[2] and others celebrating it as the best of Argentinean cinema.[3] However, its popularity was indisputable: 'It is the film with the biggest box office of the year and it's on its way to being one of the most-viewed films in the history of Argentinean cinema.'[4]

---

[2] Raúl Forlán Lamarque, 'Bodrio feroz', *El Día*, 19 September 1993, p. 27.
[3] Guillermo Zapiola, 'Buen cine argentino', *Guía del Ocio*, 8 October 1993, p. 15.
[4] Anon., 'Tango feroz', *Sabado Show*, 25 September 1993.

Tango feroz would appear tailor-made for treatment by the religion–film discourse. In its presentation of the legend of a marginalized young rock singer in the Buenos Aires of the tumultuous late 1960s, it taps into the power of a kind of archetypal struggle of youthful creativity and love against the dark powers of reactionary oppression. 'It's a perfect myth,' writes Ronald Melzer in *Brecha*.[5] The lead song on the best-selling soundtrack is entitled 'Love Is Stronger'. There is also reason to see a deliberate attempt on the part of the writer and director to allude to the Christ story and construct the central character, Tanguito, as something of a Christ figure.

The protagonist's surname is changed from the already religious 'Iglesias' (churches) to the yet more suggestive 'Cruz' (cross).[6] And Dardo Billotto notices that 'The film adopts the form of the *via cruces*: ascent, ephemeral glory, fall and definitive glory "*post-mortem*".'[7] Billotto is drawing upon an earlier essay by the Argentinean critic Marcelo Figueras, who ascribed the success of *Tango feroz* to the fact that 'Tango isn't Tango but rather Christ, and in the end he goes towards his death as if offering it for the sins of his own, the apostles who abandoned him in the final hour.'[8] Hugo Acevedo, who does not note the Christ connection, nonetheless summarizes the film in this manner: 'Beneath a drama with a sharply tragic profile, established by a torturous journey by the protagonist on route to a Dante-esque universe of degradation, lies the vital energy of love as the motor force and as the sustenance of all relationships and all hope.'[9]

The problem is that this subtext goes unnoticed by the respondent, Samuel, who described this film. While it might be possible to argue that a subconscious appreciation of this subtext is at work, it seems more likely that for Samuel, an atheist and ethnically Jewish, either conscious or subconscious appreciation would have alienated rather than attracted. While the religion–film writer might assume that it is this theological, or more broadly mythological, core that generates the film's impact, empirical research suggests that it was the way in which the film reflected Samuel's own life-experience that gave it its power. 'The impact was . . . seeing something reflected on the screen . . . that I had . . . lived just a few years earlier, yes?'

Tillich's work, whilst remaining firmly in the theoretical mode, is highly sophisticated in its treatment of the interaction between particular viewer and particular artwork. With respect to the aspect of Tillich's theory that treats the individual as the recipient of revelation, the empirical data appeared to substantiate Tillich's theory at two points. First, it was possible to identify a

---

[5] Ronald Melzer, 'Tango feroz', *Brecha*, 24 September 1993, p. 24.
[6] Lamarque, 'Bodrio', p. 27.
[7] Dardo Billotto, 'Morir para ser inmortal', *El Pais*, 19 September 1993.
[8] Billotto, 'Morir'.
[9] Hugo Acevedo, 'Tango feroz', *La Mañana*, 19 September 1993, p. 35.

sense of 'quest' in a number of the respondents' accounts. The recognition of a lack or brokenness in their lives preceded the film experience, even if it had not been brought fully to consciousness or articulated. For example, Lucilda's sense of an oppressed generation; Gastón's facing up to the possible meaninglessness of life; Marta's breaking down of restrictive thought patterns and assumptions; Samuel and Augusto's dissatisfaction with the fractured nature of their relationships with their fathers. All of these clearly preceded the film experience, yet were also definitely linked to it in the respondents' minds.

Second, the empirical research highlights the importance of Tillich's description of revelatory events as dependent upon the alignment of the objective constellation, represented by the artwork, and the subjective constellation, represented by the individual. One comment made by Tillich towards the close of his life shows his sensitivity to the uniqueness of each individual interaction.

In a lecture on 'Contemporary Visual Arts and the Revelatory Character of Style', Tillich offers a very interesting answer to a question from the floor relating to *Kitsch*. He reiterates his view that in an aesthetic, and potentially revelatory, encounter, there are two entities involved: the encountered art object and the encountering subject, these *entities* clearly correspond to what this monograph has referred to as the two constellations of revelation. Tillich states that the interplay of these two entities means that an art object that is not highly regarded with regard to 'quality' can still have a profound, and by implication revelatory, effect at the point of 'involved encounter' (*AA*, 132–3).

7.2 THE 'SPIRITUAL COMMUNITY' IN LIGHT OF THE EMPIRICAL RESEARCH

The second section of the last chapter detailed how a fresh understanding of the revelatory potential of film emerged when the theoretical account which had been used as a heuristic lens to construct and order the empirical research was set aside and data-driven analysis was allowed to take the place of theory-driven analysis. Allowing the data to speak in this way led from an emphasis on the momentary, individual event of revelation to the revelatory potential of cinema construed in a more general sense and correlated with a communal life-practice of committed cinema-going. It is possible to combine this new conceptualization with aspects of Tillich's theology in order to create what Glaser and Strauss would refer to as a new *grounded theory* of the possibility of revelation through film.

Chapter 6 considered Beau's description of his experience of *Cinemateca* during the Uruguayan dictatorship as a 'refuge' and a source of 'renewal'. His understanding of the power of cinema was seen to incorporate both a communal element and the power of the films themselves. By moving from this illustrative vignette to cross-sectional analysis of the other respondent accounts, evidence was uncovered which suggested that others understood their own experiences in a similar way. Marta told of the way in which cinema—conceived as both the films themselves and the social context that surrounded them—'saved her' from the pain of leaving behind her childhood home and country life.

The analysis also showed that many respondents used more potent words and phrases to describe the impact of the general life-practice of cinema-going than they used to describe particular film-watching experiences. Consideration of the data generated through the Montevideo interviews as a whole appeared to substantiate the new conceptualization initially suggested by Beau's story. The approach seemed to have strong explanatory potential and to be capable of incorporating large quantities of data within its conceptual framework.

The resources to offer a theological account of this fresh conceptualization are present within Tillich's early German writings, and also within the volumes of *Systematic Theology*, especially Part IV, 'Life in the Spirit'. In the reading of Tillich's theory of revelation through culture offered in Chapter 2, this part of *Systematic Theology* contributed to understanding the nature of the work of art as inherently capable of revelation due to its genesis in a spirit-filled act of *theoria*. The argument Tillich develops in this part of his theology also contributed to understanding of the identity of revelation and salvation. However, the reading presented in Chapter 2 did not address Tillich's concept of a 'Spiritual Community'. It is this concept that might provide a theological basis for the new conception of the revelatory potential of film developed out of the data-driven analysis. It also provides a link between the early German writings and *Systematic Theology*.

I will begin with a quote from this part of *Systematic Theology* that recapitulates the essential ground of this monograph, the relation of religion to culture as its depth or substance:

> The religious element in culture is the inexhaustible depth of a genuine creation. One may call it substance or the ground from which culture lives. It is the element of ultimacy which culture lacks in itself but to which it points. Religion, or the self-transcendence of life under the dimension of spirit, is essentially related to morality and culture. (*ST3*, 95)

It is this interrelation that causes a kind of revelatory potential to inhere in cultural creations, including film. This monograph has emphasized the way in which this potentiality awaits the moment when the subjective constellation of revelation in the individual who comes to watch the film is matched with the objective constellation that inheres in the particular work of art.

The data-driven analysis has highlighted the way in which these two constellations must also be seen as related to the broader cultural spheres of society and politics. The location of the individual and the artwork within a wider culture means that both specific events and the general political and social climate impinge upon the individual–artwork encounter.

> All creatures long for an unambiguous fulfilment of their essential possibilities; but only in man as the bearer of the spirit do the ambiguities of life and the quest for unambiguous life become conscious. He experiences the ambiguity of life under all dimensions since he himself participates in all of them, and he experiences them immediately within himself as the ambiguity of the functions of the spirit: of morality, culture and religion. The quest for unambiguous life arises out of these experiences; this quest is for a life which has reached that toward which it transcends itself. (*ST3*, 107)

The motivating force is the quest of the human race as a generalized whole under the conditions of existence, but also of the individual in the midst of the fragmentation, alienation, ambiguity, and distortion of her own life and society, for an experience of life that is not subject to this fallenness or brokenness. With regard to the aspect of the qualitative research under consideration here, it is possible to point to Beau's frustration under the heavy hand of the military government; Marta's alienation when she moved from countryside to cityscape; and the oppression felt by Lucilda's mute generation.

> The answer to this quest is the experience of revelation and salvation; they constitute religion above religion, although they become religion when they are received. In religious symbolism they are the work of the Spiritual Presence. (*ST3*, 109)

There is a sense, then, that in the meeting of artwork and questing individual the Spiritual Presence is manifest. For Tillich this is an effective, salvific presence. It is the active agent in any healing that takes place, whether that is a healing of fractured relationships, of the psyche, or of spiritual alienation. By turning to Tillich's idea of the 'Spiritual Community' it is possible to develop this account in a more social and less individualistic direction.

> The divine Spirit's invasion of the human spirit does not occur in isolated individuals but in social groups, since all the functions of the human spirit—moral self-integration, cultural self-creation, and religious self-transcendence—are conditioned by the social context of the ego–thou encounter. (*ST3*, 139)

It is clear that even an individual's encounter with a film in a darkened cinema must, in some sense, be considered social because the film is not the creation of the individual but of an 'other', and (perhaps especially in film-making) an 'other' community. The 'other' is present and active, albeit only as mediated through the artwork. However, Tillich intends something more than this.

Again, it is the connection between revelation and salvation that provides the link.

'The mark of the Spiritual Presence is not lacking at any place or time. The divine Spirit of God, present to man's spirit, breaks into all history in revelatory experiences which have both a saving and a transforming character' (*ST3*, 140). By implication, the shaking, healing, and transforming experiences recounted by the interview respondents may be considered marks of the Spiritual Presence in the particular geographic and historical location that is early twenty-first-century Montevideo.

In light of the fact that such revelations do not occur in isolated individuals but in social groups, Tillich continues: 'where there is the impact of the Spiritual Presence and therefore revelation (and salvation) there must also be the Spiritual Community' (*ST3*, 152). As the Spiritual Presence is not 'lacking in any time or place' and the divine presence 'breaks into all history', it follows that the Spiritual Community is not coterminous with, and cannot be reduced to, the church.

> The concrete occasion for the distinction between the latent and manifest church comes with the encounter of groups outside the organized churches who show the power of the New Being in an impressive way. There are youth alliances, friendship groups, educational, artistic, and political movements, and, even more obviously, individuals without any visible relation to each other in whom the Spiritual Presence's impact is felt, although they are indifferent or hostile to all overt expressions of religion [...] The churches represent the Spiritual Community in a manifest religious self-expression, whereas the others represent the Spiritual Community in secular latency. (*ST3*, 153)

There seem to be grounds for considering the *Cinemateca* as a secular and latent Spiritual Community. In fact, the new conceptualization of the revelatory potential of film that emerged from the data-driven analysis is entirely congruent with this strand of Tillich's theology.

A Tillichian theologian of culture might read the 'style' of Uruguayan society during the dictatorship in terms of its suffering under a crude and brutal expression of secular autonomy. Such an experience will lead to a quest for freedom, wholeness, and integration; but in a country like Uruguay, with its history of anti-clericalism, the goal of the quest would not be to replace secular autonomy with religious heteronomy, or even explicitly religious theonomy, but rather with an authentic but secular form of theonomy. In such a context, social groups like the *Cinemateca* club might be assumed to be imbued with this sense of quest, and therefore assumed to be actively, if unconsciously, seeking revelation and salvation. As the *Cinemateca* is a social group organized around a particular artistic expression, it would be unsurprising if these artworks were the media of revelation and salvation. When the objective constellation of revelation that is inherent in the artwork aligns with the subjective constellation of revelation that is related to the quest for healing and salvation in the individual, the event of revelation may occur. This in-breaking of the Spiritual Presence into the members of the *Cinemateca* creates a 'Spiritual Community' that brings with it the potential to create a more authentic theonomous life in the individual and society.

7.3 THE EVENT OF REVELATION IN LIGHT OF THE EMPIRICAL RESEARCH

In light of the findings of the empirical research, this section attempts to develop an account of the mechanism of the potentially revelatory event that is attentive both to the way the respondents expressed their understanding of their experiences, and to the particularity of film as an art form. In order to do this it is necessary to direct attention to the limitations of Tillich's account and to draw upon other theological resources.

Chapter 4 of this book finished with a thought experiment that explored one way in which Tillich's usual focus on painting, and in particular expressionist painting, might be developed in the direction of film. The thought experiment made the move from an emphasis on the formal (and possibly abstract) properties of painting towards the realism inherent in cinema's photographic depiction of what lies before the lens. Still more importantly, it was suggested that with respect to film the potential for the 'rupture of the surface' was due not only to the continuity between the filmic image and the real world but also to the inherent dynamism of the medium. For example, with reference to Rosselini's work, André Bazin spoke of the way a director could create 'slippage' and breakthrough potential through creating ambiguity by subverting the classical cause-and-effect style of narrative development.

The qualitative research has reinforced the importance of the way in which a film unfolds over time and has shown that in most cases viewers understand and describe their experiences in a way which focuses attention on film's ability to conjure a world and then invite the viewer to inhabit that world. In contrast to Tillich's emphasis on the timelessness of a painting, essays by Paul Ricoeur and Rowan Williams provide an account of the mechanism of revelation that emphasizes the importance of a narrative unfolding over time and thus allowing the reader/viewer to enter and dwell in the world of the artwork.[10] While it is important not to gloss over the fact that both Williams'

---

[10] Here Jeremy Begbie's criticism that Tillich fails to distinguish between discursive symbolism, appropriate to language, and presentational symbolism, appropriate to the visual arts, might be extended to film (discussed above in subsection 2.2.4). George Pattison also addresses the particularity of film as a medium incorporating time, light, and sound: *Technology*, p. 236.

and Ricoeur's essays are text-focused, not film-focused, for the purposes of this research the use of these essays is legitimated, primarily, upon the similarity of this construal of revelation to the respondents' accounts.

In his essay 'Trinity and Revelation', Rowan Williams wishes to find a new way of speaking of revelation. He believes that 'a model of truth as something ultimately separable in our minds from the dialectical process of its historical reflection and appropriation', a model often called upon to give revelation its authorizing power, is inadmissible because it leads all too frequently to heteronomy and a kind of 'intellectual totalitarianism'.[11] For Williams, the way to avoid this short cut to heteronomy is to pay close attention 'to the question of how [theology or the church] *learns* its own language'.[12] His first move is to an essay by Paul Ricoeur, 'Toward a Hermeneutic of the Idea of Revelation'. In this essay Ricoeur links the idea of revelation to the way in which a poetic text functions, 'inviting me into its world the text breaks open and extends my own possibilities'.[13] In such texts, truth is identified with manifestation rather than verification.

Ricoeur's intention is 'to recover a concept of revelation *and* a concept of reason that, without ever coinciding, can at least enter into a living dialectic and together engender something like an understanding of faith'.[14] To accomplish this, revelation must be rescued from an 'opaque and authoritarian' understanding by turning back from the carefully formulated dogmas of academic or ecclesial theology to consider the 'most originary level', that of the 'confession of faith', as it is found in Scripture.[15]

Ricoeur is acutely sensitive to the various genres of Scripture, arguing that these are not merely 'a rhetorical façade which it would be possible to pull down in order to reveal some thought content that is indifferent to its literary vehicle'. Rather, 'the confession of faith expressed in the biblical documents is directly modulated by the forms of discourse wherein it is expressed [they are] *per se* theologically significant'.[16] Thus, 'if the forms of religious discourse are so pregnant with meaning, the notion of revelation may no longer be formulated in a uniform and monotonous fashion which we presuppose when we speak of *the* biblical revelation'.[17]

The 'uniform' theology of revelation that arises out of an overemphasis or a sole emphasis on prophetic discourse, 'the double divine and human author where God is posited as the formal cause and the writer is posited as the

---

[11] Williams, 'Revelation', pp. 131–3, especially 132.
[12] This emphasis on the process of the learning of revelation can also be seen in the Uruguayan liberation theologian Juan Luis Segundo's book, *The Liberation of Dogma: Faith, Revelation, and Dogmatic Teaching Authority* (Maryknoll, NY: Orbis, 1992), where he develops the concept of 'divine pedagogy'; see especially pp. 40–1.
[13] Williams, 'Revelation', p. 133.   [14] Ricoeur, 'Hermeneutic', p. 1.
[15] Ibid., p. 2.   [16] Ibid., pp. 15 and 16.   [17] Ibid., p. 16.

instrumental cause',[18] is modulated and superseded by a more 'polysemic and polyphonic concept of revelation'.[19] Narrative, prescriptive, wisdom, and hymnic discourses show revelation to be not 'a body of truths which an institution may boast of or take pride in possessing',[20] but 'the possibility of hope in spite of',[21] the 'very formulation of our feelings that transcends their everyday, ordinary modalities'.[22]

Already, in the idea of entering another world and emerging with new 'hope in spite of' or a 'new formulation of our feelings' there are evident similarities with the respondents' words and phrases as they were presented in the last chapter. However, it is in the second part of his essay, when Ricoeur turns from revelation to reason, that these congruences are most clearly to be seen. This is especially true with regard to the mechanism by which the experience proceeds—immersion in a new world; and the effect of the experience—breaking down barriers and opening up new possibilities. Both of these closely resemble the language of the respondents.

Ricoeur has already taken on 'the unacceptable pretentious claim of the idea of revelation [...] that of a *sacrificium intellectus* and of a total heteronomy under the verdict of the magisterium'.[23] He now faces 'the opposed pretentious claim of philosophy [...] to a complete transparency of truth and a total autonomy of the thinking subject'.[24] Ricoeur's move is to poetics which 'does not designate one of the literary genres [of the Bible] but rather the totality of these genres in as much as they exercise a referential function that differs from the descriptive referential function of ordinary language and above all scientific discourse'.[25] On this account texts exercise their power as the reader enters their world and finds herself spoken to by a truth that redescribes reality.

> My deepest conviction is that poetic language alone restores to us that participation-in or belonging-to an order of things which precedes our capacity to oppose ourselves to things taken as objects opposed to a subject [...] And in this regard, the most extreme paradox is that when language most enters into fiction—e.g., when a poet forges the plot of a tragedy—it most speaks truth because it redescribes reality so well known that it is taken for granted in terms of the new features of this plot.[26]

Next Ricoeur develops the concept of truth as manifestation, not verification, which Williams picked up. 'What shows itself is in each instance a proposed world, a world I may inhabit and wherein I can project my ownmost possibilities. It is in this sense of manifestation that language in its poetic function is a vehicle of revelation.'[27] Returning to the specifically biblical revelation,

---

[18] Ibid., p. 17. [19] Ibid., pp. 16, also 3 and 8. [20] Ibid., p. 19.
[21] Ibid., p. 13. [22] Ibid., p. 15. [23] Ibid., p. 19.
[24] Ibid., p. 19. [25] Ibid., p. 23. [26] Ibid., p. 24. [27] Ibid., p. 25.

Ricoeur again speaks in terms reminiscent of both the language of the Montevideo respondents and of Paul Tillich: 'The proposed new world that in biblical language is called a new creation, a new Covenant, the Kingdom of God, is the "issue" of the biblical text unfolded in front of this text.'[28] 'The power to project this new world is the power of *breaking through* and of an *opening*.'[29] 'If the Bible may be said to be revealed this must refer to what it says, to the *new being* it unfolds before us. Revelation, in short, is a feature of the biblical world proposed by the text.'[30] (The italics used to emphasize these terms are my own insertion.)

It is worth exploring whether this new approach to the mechanism of the revelatory event might be re-integrated with the Tillichian account. Tillich's sensitivity to the two constellations of revelation might again be important. The engagement and alignment of the two constellations in the encounter between viewer-and-painting and viewer-and-film will necessarily not be identical, but they are not necessarily incompatible. The unique nature of film, which is a complex amalgam of different media and which unfolds over time, might also mean that the breakthrough occurs differently. For example, it might not occur immediately, as with the disruption of the surface of the painting as it is grasped as a conceptual whole in the moment of attention, but later as the viewer reflects on the film and attempts to resolve the tension between their experience of the film world and their experience of the real world. In other words, it might be possible to see the breakthrough as occurring primarily in a moment of crisis in the individual rather than in the artwork. If this is the case, then it might explain why the discursive or narrative content of the film is of far greater import in the respondents' stories than in the ungrounded version of Tillich's theory which is based primarily upon reflection on paintings. It is to the question of the content of revelation that we turn in the final section of this concluding chapter, specifically to consideration of the apparent tension between Tillich's notion of the importance of transparency and the respondents' accounts of the importance of the subject matter of the films.

7.4 THE CONTENT OF REVELATION IN LIGHT OF THE EMPIRICAL RESEARCH

It may be instructive to turn once again to Tillich's own account of his experience of Alessandro Botticelli's *Madonna with Singing Angels*, an account that stands at the very heart of this monograph both conceptually and

---

[28] Ibid., p. 26. [29] Ibid., p. 26. [30] Ibid., p. 26.

methodologically. With respect to the relation between the subject matter of the artwork and the content and effect of the revelatory experience, it should be noted that Tillich likened the way the painting impacted on him with the manner in which light passes through a stained-glass window.

> In the beauty of the painting there was Beauty itself. It shone through the colours of the paint, as the light of day shines through the stained-glass windows of a medieval church. As I stood there, bathed in the beauty its painter had envisioned so long ago, something of the divine source of all things came through to me. I turned away shaken.

It is a suggestive analogy. In many ways the explicitly religious films of the twentieth century were prefigured by stained-glass windows in purpose (didactic), content (biblical narratives), and technology (light passing through a necessarily translucent but pigmented membrane—glass or celluloid). In addition, the character of the painting itself makes the drift of Tillich's thought unsurprising. Botticelli's *Madonna* is the kind of image that would not seem out of place rendered in a cathedral window. Nonetheless, Tillich's reference to an almost exclusively religious medium is intriguing. It draws attention to an as yet unconsidered tension between the nature of this specific experience, and particularly the artwork that occasioned it, and Tillich's general, theoretical account of revelation. While Tillich's general theory states that the subject matter of the surface of the artwork is important only in as much as it is capable of producing a breakthrough, and, furthermore, that challenging, modern, secular, expressionist paintings that tend towards abstraction are best suited to the breakthrough from surface to depth, this particular painting is religious, representational and undoubtedly beautiful. Indeed, it is not hard to imagine that the effect of the peaceable beauty of the companionable young angels that surround the Madonna might have been to provide a powerful antidote to the sights of distressed, torn, and broken young men that Tillich undoubtedly encountered in the trenches.

This tension, or puzzle, which arises out of Tillich's own experience, elicits the question of whether it is actually possible or helpful to argue that there is no necessary connection between the subject matter of the artwork, the content of revelation, and the effect of revelation. Thus Tillich's own experience actually corroborates the fact, noted frequently in the preceding chapters, that the respondents' experiences were much more closely linked to the subject matter of the films than Tillich's theory would lead us to expect.

In Ricoeur and Williams, we encountered an approach that sees an analogy rather than an identity between the way poetic texts, generally conceived, and the various poetic genres of Scripture function in a revelatory way. At no point did they elide the distinction between the two. Both offer new worlds to the reader which can be inhabited in such a way that a new truth becomes manifest. But it is their unique *content* that differentiates the biblical texts and makes them *sui generis*. It is also obvious that, in contrast to Tillich, the approach of Williams and Ricoeur does not argue that the texts have to become transparent in order to be revelatory. In fact the opposite is true; it is precisely the uniqueness of the subject matter and discursive content of the texts that give the particular potency to the world that is conjured in front of the text.

Similarly, but working specifically on the medium of film, theologian Robert Johnston has written an essay on 'Transformative Viewing: Penetrating the Story's Surface', that finds the route to the depths to be precisely through the content of the film's narrative and images.[31] He develops this approach out of a reading of medieval interpretation which acknowledges that 'the text not only has a surface meaning but also embedded within that is a spiritual sense that invites our deepening gaze'.[32] This account more helpfully links the subject matter on the surface of the artwork with the transformative power of the spiritual depths, and also appears more congruent both with Tillich's own experience in front of the Botticelli painting and with the respondents' accounts of their film-watching experiences.

However, it is important not to be too quick to adjust the account of the possibility of revelation through film at this point. The idea that the artwork must become transparent to be revelatory, and that the subject matter of the work of art should not be too closely or necessarily linked to the content and effect of revelation, is not an incidental or superficial aspect of Tillich's theology. In fact, it is related to the deepest roots and the most important fruits of Tillich's thought. Indeed, this idea is vital to his understanding of what makes Christianity uniquely non-idolatrous, non-demonic, and potentially theophanous rather than merely heteronomous. For example, a passage from 'The Nature of Religious Language' which was quoted in Chapter 2 states that it is only in the perfect negation of the Christ on the cross that Christianity has 'a truth superior to any other truth' (*TC*, 66–7).

Moreover, for Tillich, it is the contention that in the moment of revelation the finite material becomes transparent to the substance or depth of the ultimate beneath, and that there is no communicable knowledge of the everyday world present in the content of revelation, that allows for a huge range of mediators of revelation, in fact a limitless range—actions, gestures, bodily, musical. and artistic expressions;[33] all cultural or religious texts, whether 'sublime, great, and dignified' or 'average, small, and profane' (*ST3*, 125); plus prophetic–political demands and scientific truth (*TC*, 28).

---

[31] Robert K. Johnston, 'Transformative Viewing: Penetrating the Story's Surface', in Johnston, *Reframing*, pp. 304–21.
[32] Johnston, 'Transformative', p. 307.
[33] Tillich, *Protestant*, p. 218.

This does not mean that language and the word are not important to Tillich. He believes that language is the 'basic cultural creation' and, indeed, that language is the most important of the three forms in which religion 'actualises itself' (the other two being art and philosophy) (*TC*, 42). However, it is clear that this process of actualization is the process of transition from the first understanding of religion to the second. It is the entirely necessary and natural, second-order re-description of the revelatory experience of the ultimate, or the ground and abyss of being, translated into the vocabulary of an existing (or even creating a new) religious tradition. Nonetheless, as discussed in Chapter 4, for Tillich neither a religious tradition, nor its component doctrines, can be considered 'revealed'. To repeat what was quoted above, 'no religion is revealed; religion is the creation and distortion of revelation' (*ST3*, 104).

As suggested at the close of Chapter 2, Tillich might argue that this discussion of the relation between the subject matter of the artwork and the content of revelation is actually unimportant: all that matters is the salvific effect of the revelationary experience. There is no doubt that this is one of the most deep-rooted, compelling, and attractive aspects of his theory.[34] And, certainly, segments of the qualitative research data would reinforce the prioritization of the effect of the experience over the noetic content of the experience when it comes to establishing the presence of revelation.

With respect to the respondents whose stories were considered in the previous chapter, it is clear that some experiences were judged on their effect rather than their content. For example, would it still have been possible to describe as 'revelatory' Gastón's life-shaking experience of the monotonous meaninglessness of life in his viewing of the film *Whisky* had it led him not to a positive re-evaluation and re-alignment of his life, conceivably even a religious one, but to suicide? In fact, suicide was precisely the decision taken by Juan Pablo Rebella, one of the young directors of *Whisky*, just a few years after its much garlanded release.[35] In such an instance, we would surely want to judge the experience based on its effect or outcome rather than on a discussion of the subject matter of the film or of Gastón's interpretation of the film.

Conversely, we cannot avoid the conclusion that for many respondents there appeared to be a very close link between the subject matter, narrative, or plot of the film and the content of the experience and the effect of the

---

[34] Interestingly, given the location of this project's research in Latin American, the approach of liberation theology to the relation between revelation and salvation is somewhat similar to Tillich's. Indeed, at a number of points they acknowledge their debt to Tillich. See, for example, Gustavo Gutiérrez, *The Truth Shall Make You Free: Confrontations*, tr. Matthew J. O'Connell (Maryknoll, NY: Orbis, 1990), p. 104, where he quotes from Tillich's sermons; and Leonardo Boff, *Jesus Christ Liberator: A Critical Christology for Our Times*, tr. Patrick Hughes (London, SPCK: 1980), pp. 41–3, where Boff discusses the hermeneutics of salvation history.

[35] María José Borges, 'La inercia de una cierta mirada', *El Observador*, 5 July 2007, p. 5.

experience. In Chapter 6, the cases of Augusto, Lucilda, and Marta were discussed and it was noted that it would be disingenuous to maintain that their experiences and the effects of their experiences were not closely related to the content of the films. It was precisely the attractive father–son relationship, the successful (if minor) act of defiance of oppression, and the example of dismantling of prejudice that the respondents perceived to have had an impact on their lives. This does not necessarily contradict Tillich's contention that the content of revelatory experiences is not *new* knowledge of the subject–object order, i.e. of the everyday world; after all, there is nothing new or unexpected about the benefits of a good father–son relationship, freedom from oppression, or dismantled prejudice. But these examples do contradict the supposition that the subject matter must become transparent and does not impact on the content or effect of the experience.

It might be necessary simply to settle for a stalemate at this point. However, I would like to suggest it is possible to hope for a way through the impasse grounded on the belief that the greatest strength of Tillich's theory is that, while it is not empirical in the sense of the research undertaken in this project, it is sensitive to the reality of observed human experience.

In *Systematic Theology 1* Tillich defends the importance of experience for theology, describing this as empirical or phenomenological theology (*ST1*, 43). The impact of Tillich's own life-experience on his theorizing has already been noted with reference to childhood contacts with nature, the Botticelli moment, and World War I and its aftermath. Christoph Schwöbel was quoted in Chapter 3 speaking of the 'personal, even autobiographical concretenes' of Tillich's work.[36] On a similar note, Donald Dreisbach suggests: '[Tillich's] treatment is not a deductive metaphysics, but a description, rooted in our common experience of ourselves.'[37] The fact that so many of the respondents were attracted by Tillich's theory, and identified with his autobiographical account of the Botticelli experience, is indicative of the success of Tillich's description of common human experience, including the revelatory potential of film.

In light of this sensitivity to human experience, I believe that Tillich might have been open to his theological, highly technical, and universal account being nuanced by the personal stories of particular experiences which were given by the respondents in this research. In such a situation he might have been willing to consider the possibility that, in the case of the particular art form of film, the revelatory potential might be more closely linked to the subject matter or narrative than was previously thought.

In any case, it is my hope that the experiences that were so graciously shared by the interview respondents might be recognized as examples of the

[36] Schwöbel, 'Tillich', p. 640.   [37] Dreisbach, *Symbols*, p. xii.

possibility of revelation through film, that is of the possibility of the gracious inbreaking of the Spirit of God into the human world in healing, shaking, and even saving power.

> Every good gift and every perfect gift is from above, coming down from the Father of lights with whom there is no variation or shadow due to change.
>
> James 1.17 (*ESV*)

APPENDICES

All the appendices are given in English. With the exception of the handout 'One Moment of Beauty', these are translations from the originals which were in Spanish.

1. *Research into Latin American Cinema*
   Montevideo Questionnaire (translated English version)
2. *Research into the Reception of Latin American Cinema*
   Informed Consent for Interview (translated English version)
3. *Guide for Montevideo*
   Qualitative Interview Guide (translated English version)
4. *Paul Tillich: Biography and Theory*
   Interview Handout 1 (translated English version)
5. *Paul Tillich: 'One Moment of Beauty'*
   Interview Handout 2 (original English version)

University of Oxford
Research into Latin American Cinema

This is a brief questionnaire that should take between five and ten minutes. The questions deal with your personal experiences as a cinema-goer. I'm a scholar from the University of Oxford and am doing these questionnaires as an important part of my research into Latin American cinema. All of your answers and details will be kept safe and will remain confidential. Your identity will not be made known in any publication of the results. Your collaboration is, of course, entirely voluntary.

Many thanks, I am immensely grateful for your cooperation.

If you wish to know more, the researcher can be contacted at:

1. How many films have you seen over the past year?
   (Mark the appropriate box)

More than one a week (>50)	☐
More than one a month (>12)	☐
A few over the year (<12)	☐
None during the year (0)	☐

2. How frequently have you seen the following types of film over the past year?
   (Mark one box in each line)

	Frequently	Occasionally	(Almost) Never
'Hollywood' films	☐	☐	☐
Independent films	☐	☐	☐
Classics (1900–1950)	☐	☐	☐
Documentaries	☐	☐	☐
Shorts	☐	☐	☐
Animated films	☐	☐	☐

3. How frequently have you watched the following genres of films over the past year?
   (Mark one box in each line)

	Frequently	Occasionally	(Almost) Never
Romantic	☐	☐	☐
Comedy	☐	☐	☐
Action	☐	☐	☐
Sci-fi / Fantasy	☐	☐	☐
Horror	☐	☐	☐
Drama	☐	☐	☐
Arthouse	☐	☐	☐

4. How frequently have you participated in the following activities over the past year?
   (Mark one box in each line)

	Frequently	Occasionally	(Almost) Never
Read film reviews	☐	☐	☐
Read film theory	☐	☐	☐
Discussed film with friends	☐	☐	☐
Solitary reflection on film	☐	☐	☐
Written about film	☐	☐	☐

Appendices

5. How many Latin American films have you seen over the past year?

More than one a week (>50)	☐
More than one a month (>12)	☐
A few over the year (<12)	☐
None during the year (0)	☐

---

6. Looking back on your life, is there one exceptionally memorable occasion when a Latin American film shook, transformed, or healed your life?

No	Yes
☐	☐

If you responded 'YES' to question 6:

Please continue with questions 7–17 concentrating on the memorable occasion and answering with respect to that specific experience.

If you responded 'NO' to question 6:

Please turn directly to the demographic questions on page 7.

---

7. With respect to the particularly memorable occasion, to which film was it related?
   (We require just enough information to identify the film.)

   Title: _____
   Director: _____
   Actor: _____
   Writer: _____
   Year: _____

---

8. Where did you see the film?

In the cinema	☐
At home	☐
At a friend's house	☐
I don't remember	☐

9. Who did you see the film with?
   (Mark all the appropriate boxes)

   Alone ☐
   With friend(s) ☐
   With a partner ☐
   With your family ☐
   Other comments [_____]

10. How important were the following characteristics of the film?
    (Mark one box in each line)

	Very important	Quite important	Not important
Narrative/Plot	☐	☐	☐
Cinematography	☐	☐	☐
Music	☐	☐	☐
Characters	☐	☐	☐
Setting	☐	☐	☐
A particular scene	☐	☐	☐
Message/Theme	☐	☐	☐

11. Was there any particular connection with your life? Did you identify ...?
    (Mark one box in each line)

	Yes	No	Perhaps
... with a particular character?	☐	☐	☐
... with the setting?	☐	☐	☐
... with a particular event?	☐	☐	☐

    Other comments [_____]

12. How long ago did the experience occur?

    It was a childhood experience ☐
    More than five years ago ☐
    More than one year ago ☐
    Less than one year ago ☐
    Less than one week ago ☐

13. How would you describe the onset of the experience?

Immediate (while watching the film) ☐
Gradual (after watching the film) ☐
Other comments

14. How would you describe the nature of the experience?
    (Mark one box in each line)

	Yes	No	Perhaps
Intellectual	☐	☐	☐
Emotional	☐	☐	☐
Aesthetic	☐	☐	☐
Spiritual	☐	☐	☐

15. At any point in the experience did you sense a presence or a power (it doesn't matter whether you would call it 'God' or not) that is distinct from your everyday life?

No ☐
Yes ☐
Perhaps ☐

16. How would you relate the experience to what was going on in your life at that time?

No relation ☐
Some relation ☐
Strong relation ☐

17. Was there an impact on your life? (Mark only one box)

No, there was no impact ☐
Yes, there was some positive impact ☐
Yes, there was great positive impact ☐
Yes, there was a negative impact ☐
I don't know ☐

DEMOGRAPHIC INFORMATION

Sex: Male ☐   Female ☐

Age: 18-30 ☐   31-50 ☐   50-65 ☐   65+ ☐

Profession: _____

Nationality: _____

Religion (or none): _____

Is there any other personal information that you think might be relevant to this research project?

_____

_____

_____

Would you be willing to participate further in this research project? (For example, later in the research process I would like to conduct a few interviews of greater length and depth.)

Yes: ☐   No: ☐

If you answered 'Yes', you will need to give contact details:

Name: _____

Address: _____

City: _____   Postcode: _____

And / Or

Email: _____

Once again, thank you very much for your cooperation with this research project. All your answers and personal details will be kept safe and confidential. Your identity will not be disclosed in any publication of the results.

University of Oxford
Research into the Reception of Latin American Cinema

This interview will take approximately one hour. The questions relate to your personal experiences as a film-goer. I am a scholar from the University of Oxford and am carrying out these interviews as an important part of my research into Latin American cinema. It is important that you understand:

- Your participation is entirely voluntary and you can withdraw from the project at any time
- After the interview I will be at your disposal and will give you any other information you consider necessary
- All of your answers and personal details will be kept safely and confidentially
- Your identity will not be revealed in any publication of the results
- This project is enacted under the oversight of *CUREC* (Central University Research Ethics Committee of Oxford University)

Many thanks, I am grateful for your participation.

Signature: _____ _____

Block capitals: _____ _____

                        Researcher   Participant

INTERVIEW GUIDE

Section 1 Introduction and background questions

It would be very useful to know a little more about you: I have some basic information from the questionnaire, for example... [read the information]... but perhaps you could tell me a little more about your life?
How does it feel to be a Uruguayan, Montevideo resident in the year 2007?

Section 2 Cinema, General

Are you a member of the *Cinemateca Uruguaya*?
For how long have you been interested in cinema?
Do you think that the cinema is an important art or cultural activity?
   Why? Why not?
Do you think that the cinema has a particular power?
   What is that power? How does it work? What effect does it have?
Do you think that the cinema can demand [or claim] a response [a change of behaviour or life-style or thinking] from the viewer?
What importance does cinema have in your life?
   How do you feel its power in your own life?
Are there other arts, recreational activities, or cultural passtimes that are important in your life?
   Would you say that these are more or less important than the cinema in your life?

Section 3 Return to the Questionnaire

When we met and spoke at the international cinema festival, I began with a number of questions that related to your habits as a film fan: the frequency that you watched films, the productions that most interested you etc. Then I asked you... 'Looking back on your life, is there one particularly memorable occasion when a Latin American film shook, transformed, or healed your life?' Can you remember how you responded at that time?

The Film

Can you remember the specific film that you spoke about?
Let's talk a little more about that film and your experience of it... take your time and tell me all about it.
Which aspects or characteristics of the film impacted on you most memorably?
   In the questionnaire you said that the [...] was very important. Would you like to add anything about that characteristic?

The Context

Do you think that there is a great difference between watching a film at the cinema and at home?
Do think that there is a great difference between seeing a film alone and with companions?

The experience that you spoke about in the questionnaire occured more than [...] years ago. Do you think that there are periods in people's lives when they are more open or more sensitive to the power of the cinema or to a specific film?

The Experience

In the questionnaire you described the way in which the experience occurred as [immediately] [gradually]. Do films typically impact on you in that way?
You described the experience as [intellectual] [emotional] [aesthetic] [spiritual]. Can you tell me a little more about your understanding of those categories?
   Do you think that you can distinguish between those categories easily?
   Why did you describe the experience as [intellectual] [emotional] [aesthetic] [spiritual]?
   Which of these categories was the most important, the most noticeable in the experience that we discussed?
In the questionnaire you said that you felt [didn't feel] a presence or a power (it doesn't matter whether you call it God or not) that is different to your daily life...
   Do you think that the question makes sense, that it's a valid and useful question?
   Can you explain a little more of what you meant by your answer?
Are there other experiences, circumstances, or moments in your life when you've experienced a presence like this?
Is there a link between your answer and your religious beliefs / your understanding of the world and of human life?

Connection to Life

You said that you identified [with a particular character] [with the general setting] [with a specific event] from the film...
   Can you tell me a little more about the identification, the connection you felt?
You said that there was [not] a [strong] link between the film and what was happening in your life at that time...
   Would you like to comment on the connection, the link to your life?
   Are there other films that have impacted on you because of their connection with your life?
You said that the experience had [no] impact [great positive] [positive] [negative] in your life...
   Could you tell me a little bit about the impact?
   Could you explain to me why that experience in particular had an impact?
   Are there other films which have had an impact on your life? Why or why not?

Section 4 The Concept of Revelation

We're left with one more section of questions. Before beginning, I would like to tell you a little bit about my research project, about the theory I've used and about the thinker (the philosopher) that I'm studying. I'm doing it because I would like to know what you think of the theory and to know if you find it an appropriate or useful way of describing your experience of cinema.
Read the first sheet.

What do you think of the theory that art, and specifically cinema, can function as 'revelation'—challenging, demanding, transforming, shaking, and healing?

Would you be happy to describe some of your experiences, like those we've discussed, as revelation?

We're now going to read an autobiographical account written by Paul Tillich. (You'll find it on the reverse of the sheet I gave you a few minutes ago.)

What do you think / how do you feel?

Have you ever experienced anything similar?

Do you think that art / cinema is a purely human creation and its power is purely human or do you think that there could be a power or presence (it doesn't matter if you call it God or Beauty or Life or Nature) that challenges, demands, transforms, shakes, or heals us through the cinema?

Would you say that on any occasion a film:

- has given you the keys to understand human life?
- has brought you a joy full of vitality?
- has shown you a spiritual truth?

PAUL TILLICH: BIOGRAPHY AND THEORY

Paul Tillich was a German thinker. In 1933 he had to flee from his country because his socialist ideas had offended the Nazi powers. He lived out the rest of his life in the US, studying, giving lectures, and writing. Before his retirement he was President of Harvard University and was featured on the cover of *Time* magazine.

He was interested in modern, Western, post-Christian culture, existential philosophy, and the fine arts, especially painting. (As professor of philosophy in Frankfurt he had been the supervisor of the doctoral thesis of the much more famous Theodor Adorno.)

My research focuses on one specific idea of Tillich's. He suggests that in a post-Christian world art can function like what the Christians of the past termed 'revelation'. Tillich was unconcerned as to whether a person was an atheist or a Christian—in the modern world both are reasonable choices for a sensible person. Obviously, an atheist would use certain words to describe their experience of revelation through art, while a Christian would use other words, but Tillich thought that beneath the differing words there was a shared experience.

In this space, the original handout showed a cover of *Time* magazine featuring Paul Tillich.

For Tillich 'revelation' can have different meanings:

- An experience that shakes, transforms, or heals us
- An experience that demands a change of lifestyle or of thinking
- An experience that directs us onto another path
- An experience of something absolutely essential or foundational

Paul Tillich: 'ONE MOMENT OF BEAUTY'

'Strangely, I first found the existence of beauty in the trenches of World War I. To take my mind off the mud, blood and death of the Western front, I thumbed through the picture magazines at the field bookstores. In some of them I found reproductions of the great and moving paintings of the ages. At rest camps and in the lulls in the bitter battles, I huddled in dugouts studying this "new world" by candle and lantern light. But at the end of the war I still had never seen the original paintings in all their glory.

In this space, the original handout showed Alessandro Botticelli's Madonna with Singing Angels.

'Going to Berlin, I hurried to the Kaiser Friederich Museum. There on the wall was a picture that had comforted me in battle: *Madonna with Singing Angels*, painted by Sandro Botticelli in the fifteenth century. Gazing up at it, I felt a state approaching ecstasy. In the beauty of the painting there was Beauty itself. It shone through the colours of the paint as the light of day shines through the stained-glass windows of a medieval church. As I stood there, bathed in the beauty its painter had envisioned so long ago, something of the divine source of all things came through to me. I turned away shaken.

'That moment has affected my whole life, given me the keys for the interpretation of human existence, brought vital joy and spiritual truth. I compare it with what is usually called revelation in the language of religion.'

Index of Films Referenced

Where a film is well-known by an English title, that title is given. In all other cases the original language title is given, with English translation in brackets if relevant.

21 Grams, dir. by Alejandro Gonzalez Iñárritu (2003).
25 Watts, dir. by Juan Pablo Rebella and Pablo Stoll (2001).
Alien, dir. by Ridley Scott (1979).
Amarcord, dir. by Federico Fellini (1973).
Amores perros, dir. by Alejandro Gonzalez Iñárritu (2001).
Aparte, dir. by Mario Handler (2002).
Babel, dir. by Alejandro Gonzalez Iñárritu (2006).
El baño del Pápa (*The Pope's Toilet*), dir. by César Charlone and Enrique Fernández (2008).
Beau Brummel, dir. by Harry Beaumont (1924).
Blow-Up, dir. by Michelangelo Antonioni (1966).
Caballos salvajes, dir. by Marcel Piñeyro (1995).
The Cabinet of Dr Caligari, dir. by Robert Wiene (1920).
Cabra marcado para morrer (*Guy Marked for Death*), dir. by Eduardo Coutinho (1985).
Central Station, dir. by Walter Salles (1998).
Cenizas del paraiso, dir. by Marcel Piñeyro (1997).
Citizen Kane, dir. by Orson Welles (1941).
City of God, dir. by Fernando Meirelles (2002).
A Clockwork Orange, dir. by Stanley Kubrick (1971).
Cool Hand Luke, dir. by Stuart Rosenberg (1967).
El crimen del Padre Amaro (*Father Amaro's Crime*), dir. by Carlos Carrera (2002).
Diary of a Country Priest, dir. by Robert Bresson (1951).
La dolce vita, dir. by Federico Fellini (1960).
Fresa y chocolate, dir. by Tomás Gutiérrez Alea (1994).
The Godfather Trilogy, dir. by Francis Ford Coppola (1972, 1974, and 1990).
The Gospel According to St. Matthew, dir. by Pier Paolo Passolini (1964).
The Grand Illusion, dir. by Jean Renoir (1937).
Los hijos de fierro, dir. by Fernando Solanas (1972).
La hora de los hornos, dir. by Fernando Solanas (1968).
The Horitz Passion Play, dir. by Walter W. Freeman (1896).
The Human Beast, dir. by Jean Renoir (1938).
King of Kings, dir. by Cecil B. DeMille (1927).

El lado oscuro del corazon, dir. by Eliseo Subiela (1992).
The Last Temptation of Christ, dir. by Martin Scorsese (1988).
Last Year in Marienbad, dir. by Alain Resnais (1961).
La Passion de Jeanne d'Arc, dir. by Carl Theodor Dreyer (1928).
Mean Streets, dir. by Martin Scorsese (1973).
Memento, dir. by Christopher Nolan (2000).
The Motorcycle Diaries, dir. by Walter Salles (2004).
Nueve reinas (*Nine Queens*), dir. by Fabián Bielinsky (2002).
Paisa, dir. by Roberto Rossellini (1946).
The Passion of the Christ, dir. by Mel Gibson (2004).
Pizza, Birra, Faso, dir. by Adrián Caetano and Bruno Stagnaro (1998).
Red Desert, dir. by Michelangelo Antonioni (1964).
The Rules of the Game, dir. by Jean Renoir (1939).
The Seventh Seal, dir. by Ingmar Bergman (1957).
The Student of Prague, dir. by Stellan Rye and Paul Wegener (1913).
Sur, dir. by Fernando Solanas (1988).
Tango feroz: La leyenda del Tanguito, dir. by Marcel Piñeyro (1993).
Tangos: El exilio de Gardel, dir. by Fernando Solanas (1985).
Taxi Driver, dir. by Martin Scorsese (1976).
The Ten Commandments, dir. by Cecil B. DeMille (1923).
The Trial of Joan of Arc, dir. by Robert Bresson (1962).
Walk the Line, dir. by James Mangold (2005).
Les Yeux des Oiseaux (*The Eyes of the Birds*), dir. by Gabriel Auer (1983).
Y tu mamá también, dir. by Alfonso Cuarón (2001).

Bibliography

(Short titles are used in the text and footnotes when books or articles are referred to on more than one occasion.)

ACEVEDO, HUGO, 'Tango feroz', *La Mañana*, 19 September 1993, p. 35.
ADAMS, JAMES LUTHER, *Paul Tillich's Philosophy of Culture, Science and Religion* (New York: Harper & Row, 1965).
ADAMS, NICHOLAS, AND CHARLES ELLIOT, 'Ethnography is Dogmatics: Making Description Central to Systematic Theology', in *Scottish Journal of Theology*, 53:3 (2000), pp. 339–64.
ADORNO, THEODOR W., AND MAX HORKHEIMER, *Dialectic of Enlightenment* (London: Verso, 1997).
ALEA, TOMÁS GUTIÉRREZ, 'The Viewer's Dialectic', in Michael T. Martin, ed., *New Latin American Cinema, Volume I: Theory, Practices and Transcontinental Articulations* (Detroit, MI: Wayne State University Press, 1997), pp. 108–31.
ALSTON, WILLIAM P., *Perceiving God: The Epistemology of Religious Experience* (London: Cornell University Press, 1991).
ANDERSON, R. S., 'Evangelical Theology', in David F. Ford, ed., *The Modern Theologians*, 2nd edn (Oxford: Blackwell, 1997), pp. 480–98.
ANKER, ROY M., *Catching Light: Looking for God in the Movies* (Cambridge: Eerdmans, 2004).
ANON., 'Conflicto: Empleados de Cinemateca reclaman aumentos', *El Diario*, March 2007.
ANON., 'Parece que Dios es hincha...', *El Observador*, 7 July 2007.
ANON., 'Tango feroz', *Sabado Show*, 25 September 1993.
ANTONIONI, MICHELANGELO, *Blow Up—Original Trailer*, available to view at <http://uk.youtube.com/watch?v=-mDpxq689EM> (accessed 25 September 2008).
ARKSEY, HILARY, AND PETER KNIGHT, *Interviewing for Social Scientists* (London: Sage, 1999).
ARNOLD, MATTHEW, *Culture and Anarchy*, ed. Samuel Lipman (London: Yale University Press, 1994).
BACH, ALICE, '"Throw Them to the Lions, Sire": Transforming Biblical Narratives into Hollywood Spectaculars', in *Semeia: An Experimental Journal in Biblical Criticism*, 74.1 (1996), pp. 1–13.
BAKER, BRIAN, 'Key Concepts in Film Studies', in Eric S. Christianson, Peter Francis, and William R. Telford, eds, *Cinema Divinité: Religion, Theology and the Bible in Film* (London: SCM Press, 2005), pp. 44–60.
BALAZS, BELA, *Theory of the Film: Character and Growth of a New Art* (London: Dennis Dobson, 1952).
BARNARD, TIMOTHY, AND PETER RIST, eds, *South American Cinema: A Critical Filmography 1915–1994* (Austin: University of Texas Press, 1998).
BARSOTTI, CATHERINE M., 'Películas: ¿A Gaze from Reel to Real?', in Robert K. Johnston, ed., *Reframing Theology and Film: New Focus for an Emerging Discipline* (Grand Rapids, MI: Baker Academic, 2007), pp. 179–201.

BAUGH, LLOYD, SJ., *Imaging Jesus in Film: Sources and Influences, Limits and Possibilities* (Canada: Campion College, 2007).

——*Imaging the Divine: Jesus and Christ Figures in Film* (Kansas City, MO: Sheed & Ward, 1997).

BAZIN, ANDRÉ, *What is Cinema? Volume I*, ed. and tr. Hugh Gray (London: University of California Press, 1967).

——*What is Cinema? Volume II*, ed. and tr. Hugh Gray (London: University of California Press, 1972).

BEAUDOIN, TOM, *Virtual Faith: The Irreverent Spiritual Quest of Generation X* (San Francisco, CA: Jossey-Bass, 2000).

BEGBIE, JEREMY, *Voicing Creation's Praise: Towards a Theology of the Arts* (Edinburgh: T&T Clark, 1991).

BENJAMIN, WALTER, *Illuminations*, ed. Hannah Arendt and tr. Harry Zohn (London: Fontana, 1973).

BERGESON, ALBERT J., AND ANDREW M. GREELEY, *God in the Movies* (London: Transaction Press, 2000).

BERTRAND, INA, AND PETER HUGHES, *Media Research Methods: Audiences, Institutions, Texts* (Basingstoke: Palgrave Macmillan, 2005).

BILLOTTO, DARDO, 'Morir para ser inmortal', *El Pais*, 19 September 1993.

BIRD, MICHAEL, 'Film as Hierophany', in John R. May and Michael Bird, eds, *Religion in Film* (Knoxville, TN: University of Tennessee Press, 1982), pp. 3–22.

BLACK, THOMAS R., *Doing Quantitative Research in the Social Sciences: An Integrated Approach to Research Design, Measurement and Statistics* (London: Sage, 1999).

BOFF, LEONARDO, *Jesus Christ Liberator: A Critical Christology for Our Times*, tr. Patrick Hughes (London, SPCK: 1980).

BORGES, MARÍA JOSÉ, 'La inercia de una cierta mirada', *El Observador*, 5 July 2007, p. 5.

BORDWELL, DAVID, *Filmguide to La Passion de Jeanne d'Arc* (London: Indiana University Press, 1973).

——*Making Meaning: Inference and Rhetoric in the Interpretation of Cinema* (Cambridge, MA: Harvard University Press, 1989).

BRATU HANSEN, MIRIAM, 'Introduction', in Siegfried Kracauer, *Theory of Film: The Redemption of Physical Reality* (Chichester: Princeton University Press, 1997), pp. i–xlv.

BRAUDY, LEO, AND MARSHALL COHEN, eds, *Film Theory and Criticism*, 5th edn (Oxford: Oxford University Press, 2004).

BROOKE, MICHAEL, 'Bottom of the Heap', *Sight & Sound*, August 2008, pp. 50–1.

BROOKER, WILL, AND DEBORAH JERMYN, *The Audience Studies Reader* (London: Routledge, 2003).

BROWN, STEPHEN, 'Optimism, Hope and Feelgood Movies: The Capra Connection', in Clive Marsh and Gaye Ortiz, eds, *Explorations in Theology and Film: Movies and Meaning* (Oxford: Blackwell, 1997), pp. 219–32.

BROWNING, DON, *A Fundamental Practical Theology* (Minneapolis, MN: Fortress Press, 1991).

BRYANT, ANTONY, AND KATHY CHARMAZ, eds, *The Sage Handbook of Grounded Theory* (London: Sage, 2007).

——'Grounded Theory Research: Methods and Practices', in Antony Bryant and Kathy Charmaz, eds, *The Sage Handbook of Grounded Theory* (London: Sage, 2007), pp. 1–28.

BUCKINGHAM, DAVID, ed., *Reading Audiences: Young People and the Media* (Manchester: Manchester University Press, 1993).
BULMAN, RAYMOND F., AND FREDERICK J. PARRELLA, eds, *Paul Tillich: A New Catholic Assessment* (Collegeville, MN: The Liturgical Press, 1994).
BULTMANN, R., *Jesus Christ and Mythology* (London: SCM Press, 1960).
BURGESS, ROBERT G., *In the Field: An Introduction to Field Research* (London: Routledge, 1984).
BURRIDGE, R. A., *Faith Odyssey: A Journey Through Life* (Oxford: Bible Reading Fellowship, 2003).
BUTLER, IVAN, *Religion in the Cinema* (London: Zwemmer, 1969).
CAETANO, GERARDO, ed., *20 Años de democracia, Uruguay 1985-2005: Miradas múltiples* (Montevideo, Uruguay: Ediciones Santillana, 2005).
—— AND JOSÉ RILLA, *Breve historia de la dictadura: 1973-1985*, 2nd edn (Montevideo, Uruguay: Ediciones de la Banda Oriental, 1998).
CARRIL, MANUEL MARTÍNEZ, 'El espejo del cine', in Gerardo Caetano, ed., *20 Años de democracia, Uruguay 1985-2005: Miradas múltiples* (Montevideo, Uruguay: Ediciones Santillana, 2005), pp. 551-71.
CASILLO, ROBERT, *Gangster Priest: The Italian American Cinema of Martin Scorsese* (London: University of Toronto Press, 2006).
CHARMAZ, KATHY, *Constructing Grounded Theory: A Practical Guide Through Qualitative Analysis* (London: Sage, 2006).
CHATMAN, SEYMOUR, *Antonioni: Or, the Surface of the World* (London: University of California Press, 1985).
CHOPP, REBECCA S., AND ETHNA REGAN, 'Latin American Liberation Theology' in David F. Ford with Rachel Muers, eds, *The Modern Theologians: An Introduction to Christian Theology Since 1918*, 3rd edn (Oxford: Blackwell, 2005), pp. 469-84.
CHRISTIANSON, ERIC, S., 'An Ethic You Can't Refuse? Assessing the Godfather Trilogy', in Eric S. Christianson, Peter Francis, and William R. Telford, eds, *Cinema Divinité: Religion, Theology and the Bible in Film* (London: SCM Press, 2005), pp. 110-23.
—— PETER FRANCIS, AND WILLIAM R. TELFORD, eds, *Cinema Divinité: Religion, Theology and the Bible in Film* (London: SCM Press, 2005).
CHRISTIE, IAN, AND DAVID THOMPSON, eds, *Scorsese on Scorsese*, updated edn (London: Faber & Faber, 1996).
CINEMATECA URUGUAYA, Boletín del XXV festival cinematográfico internacional del Uruguay (Montevideo, Uruguay: Cinemateca, 2007).
—— 'Cartas', <http://www.cinemateca.org.uy/cartas.html> (accessed 17 June 2008).
—— 'Documentos institucionales', <http://www.cinemateca.org.uy/institucional.html> (accessed 13 June 2008).
CLARK, LYNN SCHOFIELD, *From Angels to Aliens: Teenagers, the Media and the Supernatural* (Oxford: Oxford University Press, 2003).
CLARKE, ADELE E., *Situational Analysis: Grounded Theory After the Postmodern Turn* (London: Sage, 2005).
CLARKE, ANTHONY J., AND PAUL S. FIDDES, eds, *Flickering Images: Theology and Film in Dialogue*, Regent's Study Guides 12 (Oxford: Regent's Park College, 2005).
COBB, KELTON, *The Blackwell Guide to Theology and Popular Culture* (Oxford: Blackwell, 2005).

—— 'Reconsidering the Status of Popular Culture in Tillich's Theology of Culture', *Journal of the American Academy of Religion*, LXIII/1 (1995), pp. 53-84.

COOPER, JOHN C., AND CARL SKRADE, eds, *Celluloid and Symbols* (Philadelphia, PA: Fortress Press, 1970).

CORLEY, KATHLEEN, AND ROBERT WEBB, eds, *Jesus and Mel Gibson's The Passion of the Christ: The Film the Gospels and the Claims of History* (London: Continuum, 2004).

COWAN, DOUGLAS E., *Sacred Terror: Religion and Horror on the Silver Screen* (Waco, TX: Baylor University Press, 2008).

—— *Sacred Space: The Quest for Transcendence in Science Fiction Film and Television* (Waco, TX: Baylor University Press, 2010).

COWIE, PETER, *The Godfather Book* (London: Faber & Faber, 1997).

CREED, BARBARA, 'Film and Psychoanalysis', in John Hill and Pamela Church Gibson, eds, *The Oxford Guide to Film Studies* (Oxford: Oxford University Press, 1998), pp. 77-90.

CRESWELL, JOHN W., *Qualitative Inquiry and Research Design: Choosing Among Five Traditions* (London: Sage, 1998).

CUBITT, SEAN, *The Cinema Effect* (London: Massachusetts Institute of Technology Press, 2004).

COMBINED UNIVERSITY RESEARCH ETHICS COMMITTEE (CUREC), *Research Ethics: Review of Research Using Human Participants*, <http://www.admin.ox.ac.uk/curec> (accessed 1 September 2008).

DA COSTA, NÉSTOR, 'Lo religioso en la sociedad uruguaya', in Roger Geymonat, ed., *Las religiones en el Uruguay: Algunas aproximaciones* (Montevideo, Uruguay: Ediciones La Gotera, 2004), pp. 62-70.

DA SILVEIRA, PABLO, 'Laicidad: esa rareza', in Roger Geymonat, ed., *Las religiones en el Uruguay: Algunas aproximaciones* (Montevideo, Uruguay: Ediciones La Gotera, 2004), pp. 183-213.

DAVIE, DONALD, *A Gathered Church: The Literature of the English Dissenting Interest, 1700-1930* (London: Routledge and Kegan Paul, 1978).

DAVIE, GRACE, LINDA WOODHEAD, AND PAUL HEELAS, eds, *Predicting Religion: Christian, Secular, and Alternative Futures* (London: Ashgate, 2003).

DAVIES, DOUGLAS J., *Anthropology and Theology* (Oxford: Berg, 2002).

DAVIES, OLIVER, *Theology of Compassion* (London: SCM Press, 2001).

DEACY, CHRISTOPHER, *Faith in Film* (Aldershot: Ashgate, 2005).

—— 'Paradise Lost or Paradise Learned? Sin and Salvation in *Pleasantville*', in Jolyon Mitchell and Sophia Marriage, eds, *Mediating Religion: Conversations in Media, Religion and Culture* (London: T&T Clark, 2003), pp. 201-10.

—— 'Redemption Revisited: Doing Theology at *Shawshank*', in *Journal of Contemporary Religion*, 21.2 (2006), pp. 149-62.

—— *Screen Christologies: Redemption and the Medium of Film* (Cardiff: University of Wales, 2001).

—— AND GAYE WILLIAMS ORTIZ, *Theology and Film: Challenging the Sacred/Secular Divide* (Oxford: Blackwell, 2008).

DENZIN, NORMAN K., AND YVONNE S. LINCOLN, eds, *Handbook of Qualitative Research*, 2nd edn (London: Sage, 2000).

DETWEILER, CRAIG, AND BARRY TAYLOR, *A Matrix of Meanings: Finding God in Popular Culture* (Grand Rapids, MI: Baker Academic, 2003).
DILLENBERGER, JOHN, 'Introduction', in Paul Tillich, *On Art and Architecture*, ed. John Dillenberger and Jane Dillenberger (New York: Crossroad, 1987), pp. ix–xxviii.
DREISBACH, DONALD, *Symbols and Salvation: Paul Tillich's Doctrine of Religious Symbols and his Interpretation of the Symbols of the Christian Tradition* (London: University Press of America, 1993).
DULLES, A. R., *Models of Revelation* (Dublin: Gill and Macmillan, 1992).
—— *Revelation Theology: A History* (New York: Herder and Herder, 1969).
EAGLETON, TERRY, *The Idea of Culture* (Oxford: Blackwell, 2000).
EISNER, LOTTE H., *The Haunted Screen: Expressionism in the German Cinema and the Influence of Max Reinhardt*, tr. Roger Greaves (Oxford: University of California Press, 1973).
ELENA, ALBERTO, AND MARINA DÍAZ LÓPEZ, eds, *24 Frames: The Cinema of Latin America* (London: Wallflower Press, 2003).
ELGENIUS, GABRIELLA, *Qualitative Research Methods Seminar: Lectures 1–7*, Department of Sociology, University of Oxford, Hilary Term 2007 (unpublished material).
ELGER, DIETMAR, *Expressionism: A Revolution in German Art* (Köln, Germany: Taschen, 1994).
ELLIS, JACK C., *A History of Film*, 4th edn (Needham, MS: Allyn & Bacon, 1995).
EMMET, DOROTHY M., 'Epistemology and the Idea of Revelation', in C. W. Kegley and R. W. Bretall, eds, *The Theology of Paul Tillich* (New York: Macmillan, 1961), pp. 198–214.
ESPINOSA, JULIO GARCÍA, 'For an Imperfect Cinema', in Michael T. Martin, ed., *New Latin American Cinema, Volume I: Theory, Practices and Transcontinental Articulations* (Detroit, MI: Wayne State University Press, 1997), pp. 71–82.
ESV: English Standard Version Study Bible (Wheaton, IL: Crossway).
EXUM, J. CHERYL, 'Beyond the Biblical Horizon: The Bible and the Arts', in *Biblical Interpretation* 6:3/4 (1998), pp. 259–65.
FACKRE, G. J., *The Doctrine of Revelation: A Narrative Interpretation* (Edinburgh: Edinburgh University Press, 1997).
FATTORUSO, RODOLFO, 'Un amargo mensaje de furia, espanto y dolor', *Vida Cultural*, 7 February 1985.
FERLITA, ERNEST, AND JOHN R. MAY, *Film Odyssey: The Art of Film as Search for Meaning* (New York: Paulist Press, 1976).
FIDDES, PAUL, *Freedom and Limit: A Dialogue between Literature and Christian Doctrine* (Basingstoke: Macmillan, 1991).
FIELDING, NIGEL, ed., *Interviewing, Volume 1* (London: Sage, 2003).
—— AND HILARY THOMAS, 'Qualitative Interviewing', in Nigel Gilbert, ed., *Researching Social Life*, 2nd edn (London: Sage, 2001), pp. 123–44.
FLESHER, PAUL V. M., AND ROBERT TORRY, *Film and Religion: An Introduction* (Nashville, TN: Abingdon Press, 2007).
FORD, DAVID, WITH RACHEL MUERS, eds, *The Modern Theologians: An Introduction to Christian Theology Since 1918*, 3rd edn (Oxford: Blackwell, 2005).
FORRESTER, DUNCAN B., *Truthful Action: Explorations in Practical Theology* (Edinburgh: T&T Clark, 2000).
FRASER, PETER, *Images of the Passion: The Sacramental Mode in Film* (London: Flicks Books, 1998).

GABIG, JACK, *Youth, Religion and Film: An Ethnographic Study* (Haverhill, Essex: YTC Press, 2007).

GAMBETTA, DIEGO, AND HEATHER HAMILL, *Streetwise: How Taxi Drivers Establish Their Customers' Trustworthiness* (New York: Russell Sage, 2005).

GANDOLFO, ELVIO, 'Buenas intenciones', *Cine*, 15 February 1985.

GARDNER, COLIN, 'Antonioni's *Blow Up* and the Chiasmus of Memory', <http://artbrain.org/journal2/gardner.html> (accessed 12 September 2008).

GARRETT, GREG, *The Gospel According to Hollywood* (London: Westminster John Knox Press, 2007).

GEERTZ, CLIFFORD, *Interpretation of Cultures: Selected Essays* (London: Fontana, 1993).

GEYMONAT, ROGER, 'Introducción', in Roger Geymonat, ed., *Las religiones en el Uruguay: Algunas aproximaciones* (Montevideo, Uruguay: Ediciones La Gotera, 2004), pp. 5–8.

—— ed., *Las religiones en el Uruguay: Algunas aproximaciones* (Montevideo, Uruguay: Ediciones La Gotera, 2004).

—— AND ALEJANDRO SÁNCHEZ, 'Iglesia Católica, Estado y Sociedad en el Uruguay del Siglo XX', in Roger Geymonat, ed., *Las religiones en el Uruguay: Algunas aproximaciones* (Montevideo, Uruguay: Ediciones La Gotera, 2004), pp. 11–38.

GILSON, ÉTIENNE, *Painting and Reality* (Princeton: Princeton University Press, 1968).

GIRE, KEN, *Reflections on the Movies: Hearing God in the Unlikeliest of Places* (Colorado Springs, CO: Cook Communications Ministries, 2000).

GLASER, BARNEY, AND ANSELM STRAUSS, *Discovering Grounded Theory* (London: Weidenfeld and Nicolson, 1967).

GODAWA, BRIAN, *Hollywood Worldviews: Watching Films with Wisdom and Discernment* (Downers Grove, IL: Inter-Varsity Press, 2002).

GOODACRE, MARK, 'The Power of *The Passion*: Reacting and Over-reacting to Gibson's Artistic Vision', in Kathleen Corley and Robert Webb, eds, *Jesus and Mel Gibson's The Passion of the Christ: The Film, the Gospels and the Claims of History* (London: Continuum, 2004), pp. 28–44.

GORRINGE, TIMOTHY J., *Furthering Humanity: A Theology of Culture* (Aldershot: Ashgate, 2004).

GOULDING, CHRISTINA, *Grounded Theory: A Practical Guide for Management, Business, and Market Researchers* (London: Sage, 2002).

GRAHAM, DAVID JOHN, 'Uses of Film in Theology', in Clive Marsh and Gaye Ortiz, eds, *Explorations in Theology and Film: Movies and Meaning* (Oxford: Blackwell, 1997), pp. 35–43.

GRANT, PERCY STICKNEY, 'If Christ Went to the Movies', in Jolyon Mitchell and Brent S. Plate, eds, *The Religion and Film Reader* (London: Routledge, 2007), pp. 27–31.

GRENZ, STANLEY J., *Renewing the Center: Evangelical Theology in a Post-Theological Era* (Grand Rapids, MI: Baker Academic, 2000).

—— *Revisioning Evangelical Theology: A Fresh Agenda for the 21st Century* (Downers Grove, IL: Inter-Varsity Press, 1993).

GUBRIUM, JABER F., AND JAMES A. HOLSTEIN, eds, *Handbook of Interview Research* (London: Sage, 2001).

GUTTIEREZ, GUSTAVO, *The Truth Shall Make You Free: Confrontations*, tr. Matthew J. O'Connell (Maryknoll, NY: Orbis, 1990).

HALLBACK, GEERT, AND ANNIKA HVITHAMAR, eds, *Recent Releases: The Bible in Contemporary Cinema* (Sheffied: Sheffield Phoenix Press, 2008).

HAMMERSLEY, MARTYN, AND PAUL ATKINSON, *Ethnography: Principles in Practice*, 2nd edn (London: Routledge, 1995).

HARDY, ANN, *Film, Spirituality and Hierophany*, 2nd Series Occasional Paper 31 (Lampeter, University of Wales: Religious Experience Research Centre, 2002).

HART, STEPHEN M., *A Companion to Latin American Film* (Woodbridge, Suffolk: Tamesis, 2004).

HAY, DAVID, *Exploring Inner Space: Scientists and Religious Experience* (London: Penguin, 1982).

—— 'Religious Experience Amongst a Group of Post-Graduate Students: A Qualitative Study', *Journal for the Scientific Study of Religion*, 18.2 (1979), pp. 164–82.

—— AND A. MORISY, 'Reports of Ecstatic, Paranormal, or Religious Experience in Great Britain and the United States: A Comparison of Trends', in *Journal for the Scientific Study of Religion*, 17.3 (1978), pp. 255–68.

HEITINK, GERBEN, *Practical Theology: History, Theory, Action Domains*, tr. Reinder Bruinsma (Cambridge: Eerdmans, 1999).

HENNELLY, ALFRED, T., ed., *Liberation Theology: A Documentary History* (Maryknoll, NY: Orbis, 1990).

HENRY, CARL F. H., *God, Revelation and Authority—The God Who Speaks and Shows, 1: Preliminary Considerations* (Waco, TX: Word, 1976).

—— *God, Revelation and Authority—The God Who Speaks and Shows, 2: Fifteen Theses, Part One* (Waco, TX: Word, 1976).

—— *God, Revelation and Authority—The God Who Speaks and Shows, 3: Fifteen Theses, Part Two* (Waco, TX: Word, 1979).

—— *God, Revelation and Authority—The God Who Speaks and Shows, 4: Fifteen Theses, Part Three* (Waco, TX: Word, 1979).

HESKJAER, MIKKEL FUGL, 'Religion in New Danish Cinema', in Geert Hallback and Annika Hvithamar, eds, *Recent Releases: The Bible in Contemporary Cinema* (Sheffied: Sheffield Phoenix Press, 2008), pp. 30–49.

HIGGINS, GARETH, *How Movies Helped Save My Soul: Finding Spiritual Fingerprints in Culturally Significant Films* (Lake Mary, FL: Relevant Books, 2003).

HILL, ANNETTE, *Shocking Entertainment: Viewer Response to Violent Movies* (Luton: University of Luton Press, 1997).

HILL, JOHN, AND PAMELA CHURCH GIBSON, eds, *The Oxford Guide to Film Studies* (Oxford: Oxford University Press, 1998).

HUNT, KATE, 'Understanding the Spirituality of People Who Do Not Go to Church', in Grace Davie, Linda Woodhead, and Paul Heelas, eds, *Predicting Religion: Christian, Secular, and Alternative Futures* (Aldershot: Ashgate, 2003), pp. 159–69.

HURLEY, NEIL, P., *Theology through Film* (London: Harper & Row, 1970).

IÑÁRRITU, ALEJANDRO GONZALEZ, 'Interview', *Little White Lies: Truth and Movies*, Issue 9, December 2006 – January 2007, p. 19.

INSTITUTO DEL TERCER MUNDO, *The World Guide 2005/2006*, 10th edn (Oxford: New Internationalist Publications, 2005).

INTERNATIONAL MOVIE DATABASE, 'Paul Schrader', <http://www.imdb.com/name/nm0001707/> (accessed 12 December 2008).

JAGODZINKSI, JAN, *Youth Fantasies: The Perverse Landscape of the Media* (Basingstoke: Palgrave Macmillan, 2004).

JAMES, NICK, 'Hell in Jerusalem', *Sight and Sound*, April 2004, pp. 14–18.

JANCOVICH, MARK, AND LUCY FAIRE, WITH SARAH STUBBINGS, *The Place of the Audience: Cultural Geographies of Film Consumption* (London: British Film Institute, 2003).

JARMAN, BEATRIZ GALIMBERTI, AND ROY RUSSELL, eds, *The Oxford Spanish Dictionary* (Oxford: Oxford University Press, 1994).

JASPER, DAVID, 'On Systematizing the Unsystematic: A Response', in Clive Marsh and Gaye Ortiz, eds, *Explorations in Theology and Film: Movies and Meaning* (Oxford: Blackwell, 1997), pp. 235–44.

JEWETT, ROBERT, *Saint Paul at the Movies: The Apostle's Dialogue with American Culture* (Louisville, KY: Westminster John Knox, 1993).

—— *Saint Paul Returns to the Movies: Triumph Over Shame* (Cambridge: Eerdmans, 1999).

JOHNSON, RICHARD, DEBORAH CHAMBERS, PARVATI RAGHURAM, AND ESTELLA TINCKNELL, *The Practice of Cultural Studies* (London: Sage, 2004).

JOHNSTON, ROBERT K., *Reel Spirituality: Theology and Film in Dialogue* (Grand Rapids, MI: Baker Academic, 2000).

—— ed., *Reframing Theology and Film: New Focus for an Emerging Discipline* (Grand Rapids, MI: Baker Academic, 2007).

—— '*The Passion* as Dynamic Icon: A Theological Reflection', in S. Brent Plate, ed., *Mel Gibson's Film and Its Critics: Re-Viewing the Passion* (New York: Palgrave Macmillan, 2004), pp. 55–70.

—— 'Transformative Viewing: Penetrating the Story's Surface', in id., ed., *Reframing Theology and Film: New Focus for an Emerging Discipline* (Grand Rapids, MI: Baker Academic, 2007), pp. 304–21.

—— *Useless Beauty: Ecclesiastes through the Lens of Contemporary Film* (Grand Rapids, MI: Baker Academic, 2004).

JUMP, HERBERT, 'The Religious Possibilities of the Motion Picture', in Jolyon Mitchell and Brent S. Plate, eds, *The Religion and Film Reader* (London: Routledge, 2007), pp. 14–24.

KAES, ANTON, 'German Cultural History and the Study of Film: Ten Theses and a Postscript', in *New German Critique*, 65 (1995), pp. 47–58.

KEGLEY, C. W., and R. W. BRETALL, eds, *The Theology of Paul Tillich* (New York: Macmillan, 1961).

KELSEY, DAVID H., *The Fabric of Paul Tillich's Theology* (London: Yale University Press, 1967).

—— 'Paul Tillich', in David Ford, *The Modern Theologians: An Introduction to Christian Theology Since 1918*, 3rd edn (Oxford: Blackwell, 2005), pp. 62–75.

KERMODE, MARK, 'Review—*The Passion of the Christ*', in *Sight and Sound*, April 2004, pp. 62–3.

KING, JOHN, *Magical Reels: A History of Cinema in Latin America*, new edn (London: Verso, 2000).

KRACAUER, SIEGFRIED, *From Caligari to Hitler: A Psychological History of the German Film*, revised and expanded edn (Oxford: Princeton University Press, 2004).

—— *Theory of Film: The Redemption of Physical Reality* (Chichester: Princeton University Press, 1997).

KREITZER, LARRY J., *Gospel Images in Fiction and Film: On Reversing the Hermeneutical Flow* (Sheffield: Sheffield Academic Press, 2002).
—— *The New Testament in Fiction and Film: On Reversing the Hermeneutical Flow* (Sheffield: Sheffield Academic Press, 1993).
—— *The Old Testament in Fiction and Film: On Reversing the Hermeneutical Flow* (Sheffield: Sheffield Academic Press, 1994).
—— *Pauline Images in Fiction and Film: On Reversing the Hermeneutical Flow* (Sheffield: Sheffield Academic Press, 1999).
LAGO, GERMÁN, 'Pese a todo el testimonio', *La Democracia*, 8 February 1985.
LAMARQUE, RAÚL FORLÁN, 'Bodrio feroz', *El Día*, 19 September 1993, p. 27.
—— 'Historia Mínima', *La República*, 6 August 2004.
LAMN, JULIA A., '"Catholic Substance" Revisited: Reversal of Expectations in Tillich's Doctrine of God', in Raymond F. Bulman and Frederick J. Parrella, eds, *Paul Tillich: A New Catholic Assessment* (Collegeville, MN: The Liturgical Press, 1994), pp. 48–72.
LEWINS, ANN, AND CHRISTINA SILVER, *Using Software in Qualitative Research: A Step-by-Step Guide* (London: Sage, 2007).
LIEBOW, ELLIOT, *Tell Them Who I Am: The Lives of Homeless Women* (London: Penguin, 1995).
LITTLE, W., H. FOWLER, AND J. COULSON, eds, *The Shorter Oxford English Dictionary* (Oxford: Clarendon Press, 1973).
LOUGHLIN, GERARD, *Alien Sex: The Body and Desire in Cinema and Theology* (Oxford: Blackwell, 2004).
LYDEN, JOHN, *Film as Religion: Myths, Morals, and Rituals* (London: New York University Press, 2003).
—— 'To Commend or Critique? The Question of Religion and Film Studies', in *Journal of Religion and Film*, 1.2 (1997), <http://www.unomaha.edu/jrf/tocommend.htm> (accessed 28 August 2008).
—— ed., *The Routledge Companion to Religion and Film* (London: Routledge, 2009).
LYNCH GORDON, *Understanding Theology and Popular Culture* (Oxford: Blackwell, 2005).
—— 'Film and the Subjective Turn: How the Sociology of Religion Can Contribute to Theological Readings of Film', in Robert K. Johnston, ed., *Reframing Theology and Film: New Focus for an Emerging Discipline* (Grand Rapids, MI: Baker Academic, 2007), pp. 109–25.
—— AND EMILY BADGER, 'The Mainstream Post-Rave Club Scene as a Secondary Institution: A British Perspective', in *Culture and Religion*, 7.1 (2006), pp. 27–40.
MANNING, RUSSELL RE, ed., *The Cambridge Companion to Paul Tillich* (Cambridge: Cambridge University Press, 2009).
—— *Theology at the End of Culture: Paul Tillich's Theology of Culture and Art* (Leuven, Belgium: Peeters, 2005).
—— 'Tillich's Theology of Art', in Russell Re Manning, ed., *The Cambridge Companion to Paul Tillich* (Cambridge: Cambridge University Press, 2009), pp. 152–72.
MARCEL, GABRIEL, *The Mystery of Being I: Reflection and Mystery*, tr. G. S. Fraser (South Bend, IN: St Augustine's Press, 2001).
—— *The Mystery of Being II: Faith and Reality*, tr. G. S. Fraser (South Bend, IN: St Augustine's Press, 2001).

MARSH, CLIVE, *Cinema and Sentiment: Film's Challenge to Theology* (Milton Keynes: Paternoster, 2004).
—— AND GAYE ORTIZ, eds, *Explorations in Theology and Film: Movies and Meaning* (Oxford: Blackwell, 1997).
—— 'Film and Theologies of Culture', in Clive Marsh and Gaye Ortiz, eds, *Explorations in Theology and Film: Movies and Meaning* (Oxford: Blackwell, 1997), pp. 21-34.
—— 'Religion, Theology and Film in a Postmodern Age: A Response to John Lyden', in *Journal of Religion and Film*, 2.1 (1998), <http://www.unomaha.edu/jrf/marshrel.htm> (accessed 28 August 2008).
—— 'Audience reception', in John Lyden, ed., *Routledge Companion to Religion and Film* (Routledge: London, 2009), pp. 255-74.
MARTIN, JOEL W., AND CONRAD E. OSTWALT, eds, *Screening the Sacred: Religion, Myth and Ideology in Popular American Film* (Oxford: Westview Press, 1995).
MARTIN, MICHAEL T., ed., *New Latin American Cinema, Volume I: Theory, Practices and Transcontinental Articulations* (Detroit, MI: Wayne State University Press, 1997).
—— ed., *New Latin American Cinema, Volume II: Studies of National Cinemas* (Detroit, MI: Wayne State University Press, 1997).
MARTÍNEZ, VIRGINIA, *Tiempos de dictadura 1973-1985: Hechos, voces, documentos: La represión y la resistencia día a día*, 3rd edn (Montevideo, Uruguay: Ediciones de la Banda Oriental, 2005).
MASON, JENNIFER, *Qualitative Researching* (London: Sage, 1996).
MAY, JOHN R., AND MICHAEL BIRD, *Religion in Film* (Knoxville, TN: University of Tennessee Press, 1982).
MCGRATH, ALISTER E., ed., *The Blackwell Encyclopedia of Modern Christian Thought* (Oxford: Blackwell, 1993).
—— *The Making of Modern German Christology: From the Enlightenment to Pannenberg* (Oxford: Blackwell, 1986).
MCLEAN, GEORGE F., 'Symbol and Analogy: Tillich and Thomas', in T. A. O'Meara and C. D. Weisser, eds, *Paul Tillich in Catholic Thought* (London: Darton Longman and Todd, 1965), pp. 145-83.
MEDELLÍN CONFERENCE, 'Document on Justice', in Alfred T. Hennelly, ed., *Liberation Theology: A Documentary History* (Maryknoll, NY: Orbis, 1990), pp. 97-105.
MELZER, RONALD, 'Tango feroz', *Brecha*, 24 September 1993, p. 24.
MESSENGER, CHRIS, *The Godfather and American Culture: How the Corleones Became 'Our Gang'* (New York: New York State University Press, 2002).
MILES, MARGARET R., *Seeing and Believing: Religion and Values in the Movies* (Boston, MA: Beacon Press, 1996).
MILES, MATTHEW, AND MICHAEL HUBERMAN, *Qualitative Data Analysis: An Expanded Sourcebook*, 2nd edn (London: Sage, 1994).
MITCHELL, JOLYON, AND SOPHIA MARRIAGE, eds, *Mediating Religion: Conversations in Media, Religion and Culture* (London: T&T Clark, 2003).
—— AND S. BRENT PLATE, eds, *The Religion and Film Reader* (London: Routledge, 2007).
MITRY, JEAN, 'Cinema', in Lionel Richard, ed., *The Concise Encyclopedia of Expressionism* (Seacaucus, NJ: Chartwell, 1978), pp. 213-42.

MONTICELLI, SIMONA, 'Italian post-war cinema and Neo-Realism', in John Hill and Pamela Church Gibson, eds, *The Oxford Guide to Film Studies* (Oxford: Oxford University Press, 1998), pp. 455–60.

MORLEY, DAVID, AND CHARLOTTE BRUNSDON, *The Nationwide Television Studies* (London: Routledge, 1999).

MULHALL, STEPHEN, *On Film* (London: Routledge, 2002).

MULVEY, LAURA, 'Visual Pleasure and Narrative Cinema', in Leo Braudy and Marshall Cohen, eds, *Film Theory and Criticism: Introductory Readings*, 5th edn (Oxford: Oxford University Press, 1999), pp. 833–44.

MURPHY, ROBERT, ed., *The British Cinema Book*, 2nd edn (London: British Film Institute, 2001).

NIEBUHR, H. RICHARD, *Christ and Culture* (London: Faber & Faber, 1952).

——'Translator's Preface', in Paul Tillich, *The Religious Situation*, tr. H. Richard Niebuhr (London: Thames and Hudson, 1956), pp. 9–24.

NIEBUHR, REINHOLD, 'Biblical Thought and Ontological Speculation', in C. W. Kegley and R. W. Bretall, eds, *The Theology of Paul Tillich* (New York: Macmillan, 1961), pp. 216–27.

NOLAN, STEVE, 'The Books of the Films: Trends in Religious Film-Analysis', in *Literature and Theology*, 12.1 (1998), pp. 1–14.

——'Review: Screen Christologies by Christopher Deacy', in *Reviews in Religion and Theology*, 9.5 (2002), pp. 460–65.

——'Towards a New Religious Film Criticism: Using Film to Understand Religious Identity rather than Locate Cinematic Analogue', in Jolyon Mitchell and Sophia Marriage, eds, *Mediating Religion: Conversations in Media, Religion and Culture* (London: T&T Clark, 2003), pp. 169–78.

——'Understanding Films: Reading in the Gaps', in Anthony J. Clarke and Paul S. Fiddes, eds, *Flickering Images: Theology and Film in Dialogue*, Regent's Study Guides 12 (Oxford: Regent's Park College, 2005), pp. 25–48.

NUOVO, VICTOR, 'Translator's Introduction', in Paul Tillich, *The Construction of the History of Religion in Schelling's Positive Philosophy: Its Presuppositions and Principles*, tr. Victor Nuovo (London: Associated University Presses, 1974), pp. 11–32.

O'MEARA, THOMAS FRANKLIN, 'Paul Tillich in Catholic Thought: The Past and the Future', in Raymond F. Bulman and Frederick J. Parrella, eds, *Paul Tillich: A New Catholic Assessment* (Collegeville, MN: The Liturgical Press, 1994), pp. 9–32.

——AND C. D. WEISSER, eds, *Paul Tillich in Catholic Thought* (London: Darton, Longman and Todd, 1965).

OPPENHEIM, A. N., *Questionnaire Design, Interviewing and Attitude Measurement*, new edn (London: Continuum, 1992).

ORTIZ, GAYE WILLIAMS, 'World Cinema: Opportunities for Dialogue with Religion and Theology', in Robert K. Johnston, ed., *Reframing Theology and Film: New Focus for an Emerging Discipline* (Grand Rapids, MI: Baker Academic, 2007), pp. 73–87.

P., M., 'La más reciente revelación del cine argentino', *Busqueda*, 8 July 1993.

PALMER, MICHAEL, ed., *Paul Tillich: Writings in the Philosophy of Culture: Main Works II* (New York: De Gruyter—Evangelisches Verlagswerk GmbH, 1990).

PATTISON, GEORGE, *Anxious Angels: A Retrospective View of Religious Existentialism* (Basingstoke: Macmillan, 1999).

—— *Art, Modernity and Faith* (London: SCM Press, 1998).
—— *Kierkegaard, Religion and the Nineteenth-Century Crisis of Culture* (Cambridge: Cambridge University Press, 2002).
—— *A Short Course in Christian Doctrine* (London: SCM Press, 2005).
—— *Thinking About God in an Age of Technology* (Oxford: Oxford University Press, 2005).
PAUCK, WILHELM, AND MARION, *Paul Tillich: His Life and Thought, Volume I: Life* (London: Collins, 1977).
PAWLUCH, DOROTHY, WILLIAM SHAFFIR, AND CHARLENE MIALL, *Doing Ethnography: Studying Everyday Life* (Toronto: Canadian Scholars' Press, 2005).
PERCY, MARTYN, *Engaging with Contemporary Culture: Christianity, Theology and the Concrete Church* (Aldershot: Ashgate, 2005).
PHILLIPS, PATRICK, 'Spectator, Audience and Response', in Jill Nelmes, ed., *Introduction to Film Studies*, 4th edn (London: Routledge, 2007), pp. 143–71.
PICK, ZUZANA M., *The New Latin American Cinema: A Continental Project* (Austin, TX: University of Texas Press, 1993).
PLATE, S. BRENT, ed., *Representing Religion in World Cinema: Filmmaking, Mythmaking, Culture Making* (New York: Palgrave Macmillan, 2003).
—— ed., *Mel Gibson's Film and Its Critics: Re-Viewing the Passion* (New York: Palgrave Macmillan, 2004).
—— 'Religion/Literature/Film: Toward a Religious Visuality of Film', in *Literature and Theology*, 12.1 (1998), pp. 16–38.
—— AND DAVID JASPER, eds, *Imag(in)ing Otherness: Filmic Visions of Living Together* (Atlanta, GA: Scholars Press, 1999).
POLAND, BLAKE D., 'Transcription Quality', in Jaber F. Gubrium and James A. Holstein, eds, *Handbook of Interview Research* (London: Sage, 2001), pp. 629–50.
POPE PIUS XI, '*Vigilanti Cura*: On the Motion Pictures', <http://www.vatican.va/holy_father/pius_xi/encyclicals/documents/hf_p-xi_enc_29061936_vigilanti-cura_en.html> (accessed 28 August 2008).
POSTIGLIONI, ALBERTO, 'Drama Contemporáneo', *El Diario*, 2 November 1997, p. 11.
QUARESIMA, LEONARDO, 'Introduction to the 2004 Edition: Rereading Kracauer', tr. Michael F. Moore, in Siegfried Kracauer, *From Caligari to Hitler: A Psychological History of the German Film*, revised and expanded edn (Oxford: Princeton University Press, 2004), pp. xv–xlix.
RATSCHOW, CARL HEINZ, 'Preface', in Michael Palmer, ed., *Paul Tillich: Writings in the Philosophy of Culture: Main Works II* (New York: De Gruyter—Evangelisches Verlagswerk GmbH, 1990), pp. ix–xi.
REINHARTZ, ADELE, *Scripture on the Silver Screen* (London: Westminster John Knox, 2003).
RICHARDS, JEFFREY, 'British Film Censorship', in Robert Murphy, ed., *The British Cinema Book*, 2nd edn (London: British Film Institute, 2001), pp. 155–62.
RICOEUR, PAUL, 'Toward a Hermeneutic of the Idea of Revelation', in *Harvard Theological Review*, 70.1–2 (1977), pp. 1–37.
RIDDELL, MIKE, *Threshold of the Future: Reforming the Church in the Post-Christian West* (London: SPCK, 1998).
ROLDÁN, ALBERTO, 'El concepto de revelacion en la teologia de Paul Tillich', *Teología y cultura*, 2.3 (2005), <http://www.teologiaycultura.com.ar/arch_rev/a_roldan_revelacion_tillich.PDF> (accessed 31 August 2008).

ROMANOWSKI, WILLIAM D., *Eyes Wide Open: Looking for God in Popular Culture* (Grand Rapids, MI: Brazos Press, 2001).
ROWLAND, CHRISTOPHER, ed., *The Cambridge Companion to Liberation Theology*, 2nd edn (Cambridge: Cambridge University Press, 2007).
—— 'Epilogue: the future of liberation theology', in id., ed., *The Cambridge Companion to Liberation Theology*, 2nd edn (Cambridge: Cambridge University Press, 2007), pp. 304-7.
RUNIONS, ERIN, *How Hysterical: Identification and Resistance in the Bible and Film* (London: Palgrave Macmillan, 2003).
SARATSOLA, OSVALDO, *Función completa, por favor: Un siglo de cine en Montevideo* (Montevideo, Uruguay: Trilce, 2005).
SAUKKO, PAULA, *Doing Research in Cultural Studies: An Introduction to Classical and New Methodological Approaches* (London: Sage, 2003).
SCHAREN, CHRISTIAN BATALDEN, '"Judicious Narratives", or ethnography as ecclesiology', in *Scottish Journal of Theology*, 58:2 (2005), pp. 125-42.
SCHILLER, J. C. FRIEDRICH, *On the Aesthetic Education of Man: In a Series of Letters*, tr. R. Snell (Bristol: Thoemmes Press, 1994).
SCHRADER, PAUL, *Transcendental Style in Film: Ozu, Bresson, Dreyer* (London: University of California Press, 1972).
SCHUMAN, HOWARD, 'Artifacts are in the Mind of the Beholder', in Nigel Fielding, ed., *Interviewing, Volume 1* (London: Sage, 2003), pp. 180-90.
SCHWÖBEL, CHRISTOPH, 'Paul Tillich', in Alister McGrath, ed., *The Blackwell Encyclopedia of Modern Christian Thought* (Oxford: Blackwell, 1993), pp. 638-42.
SCOTT, BERNARD BRANDON, *Hollywood Dreams and Biblical Stories* (Minneapolis, MN: Fortress Press, 1994).
SEGUNDO, JUAN LUIS, *Liberation of Theology* (Maryknoll, NY: Orbis, 1976).
—— *The Liberation of Dogma: Faith, Revelation, and Dogmatic Teaching Authority* (Maryknoll, NY: Orbis, 1992).
SHAW, DEBORAH, *Contemporary Cinema of Latin America: 10 Key Films* (London: Continuum, 2003).
—— ed., *Contemporary Latin American Cinema: Breaking Into the Global Market* (Plymouth, UK: Rowman & Littlefield, 2007).
SKLAR, ROBERT, *Film: An International History of the Medium*, 2nd edn (New York: Prentice Hall, 2002).
SKRADE, CARL, 'Theology and Films', in John C. Cooper and Carl Skrade, eds, *Celluloid and Symbols* (Philadelphia, PA: Fortress Press, 1970), pp. 1-24.
SOBRINO, JON, AND IGNACIO ELLACURIA, *Systematic Theology: Perspectives from Liberation Theology* (London: SCM, 1996).
SOLANAS, FERNANDO, *La mirada: Reflexiones sobre cine y cultura* (Buenos Aires, Argentina: Puntosur Editores, 1989).
—— AND OCTAVIO GETTINO, 'Towards a Third Cinema: Notes and Experiences for the Development of a Cinema of Liberation in the Third World', in Michael T. Martin, ed., *New Latin American Cinema, Volume I: Theory, Practices and Transcontinental Articulations* (Detroit, MI: Wayne State University Press, 1997), pp. 33-58.
STAFFORD, ROY, *Audiences: An Introduction* (London: British Film Institute, 2003).
STAM, ROBERT, *Film Theory: An Introduction* (Oxford: Blackwell, 2000).

—— AND ISMAIL XAVIER, 'Transformation of National Allegory: Brazilian Cinema from Dictatorship to Redemocratization', in Michael T. Martin, ed., *New Latin American Cinema, Volume II: Studies of National Cinemas* (Detroit, MI: Wayne State University Press, 1997), pp. 295–322.

STIBBE, MARK, AND J. JOHN, *Passion for the Movies: Spiritual Insights from Contemporary Films* (Milton Keynes: Authentic Media, 2005).

STRAUSS, ANSELM, AND JULIET CORBIN, *Basics of Qualitative Research: Grounded Theory Procedures and Techniques* (London: Sage, 1990).

SUCHMAN, LUCY, AND BRIGITTE JORDAN, 'Interactional Troubles in Face-to-Face Survey Interviews', in Nigel Fielding, ed., *Interviewing, Volume 1* (London: Sage, 2003), pp. 191–216.

SUDMAN, SEYMOUR, AND NORMAN BRADBURN, *Asking Questions: A Practical Guide to Questionnaire Design* (London: Jossey-Bass, 1982).

SUTCLIFFE, THOMAS, 'Now Everyone Can See the Light', <http://www.independent.co.uk/opinion/columnists/thomas-sutcliffe/thomas-sutcliffe-now-everyone-can-see-the-light-819383.html> (accessed 12 September 2008).

SVENNIG, MICHAEL, IAN HALDANE, SHARON SPIERS, AND BARRIE GUNTER, *Godwatching: Viewers, Religion and Television*, Television Research Monograph of the Independent Broadcasting Authority (London: John Libbey, 1988).

SWINTON, JOHN, AND HARRIET MOWAT, *Practical Theology and Qualitative Research* (London: SCM Press, 2006).

TAYLOR, MARK KLINE, *Paul Tillich: Theologian of the Boundaries* (London: Collins Liturgical Publications, 1987).

TELFORD, WILLIAM R., 'Through a Lens Darkly: Critical Approaches to Theology and Film', in Eric S. Christianson, Peter Francis, and William R. Telford, eds, *Cinema Divinité: Religion, Theology and the Bible in Film* (London: SCM Press, 2005), pp. 15–43.

THATAMANIL, JOHN J., *The Immanent Divine: God, Creation, and the Human Predicament* (Minneapolis, MN: Fortress Press, 2006).

THOMAS, J. HEYWOOD, 'Foreword', in T. A. O'Meara, and C. D. Weisser, eds, *Paul Tillich in Catholic Thought* (London: Darton, Longman and Todd, 1965), pp. vii–x.

TILLICH, PAUL, 'Autobiographical Reflections', in C. W. Kegley and R. W. Bretall, eds, *The Theology of Paul Tillich* (New York: Macmillan, 1961), pp. 3–21.

—— *The Boundaries of Our Being* (London: Collins, 1973).

—— *The Construction of the History of Religion in Schelling's Positive Philosophy: Its Presuppositions and Principles*, tr. Victor Nuovo (London: Associated University Presses, 1974).

—— *The Courage to Be* (London: Yale University Press, 1952).

—— *On Art and Architecture*, ed. John Dillenberger and Jane Dillenberger (New York: Crossroad, 1987).

—— 'On the Idea of a Theology of Culture', in Mark Kline Taylor, ed., *Paul Tillich: Theologian of the Boundaries* (London: Collins Liturgical Publications, 1987), pp. 35–54.

—— *The Protestant Era*, tr. James Luther Adams (London: Nisbet, 1951).

—— *The Religious Situation*, tr. H. Richard Niebuhr (London: Thames and Hudson, 1956).

—— *The Shaking of the Foundations* (London: SCM Press, 1949).

TILLICH, PAUL, *The Socialist Decision*, tr. Franklin Sherman (London: Harper & Row, 1977).
—— *Systematic Theology, Volume 1* (London: Nisbet, 1953).
—— *Systematic Theology, Volume 2* (Chicago: University of Chicago, 1957).
—— *Systematic Theology, Volume 3* (Chicago: University of Chicago, 1963).
—— *Theology of Culture* (New York: Oxford University Press, 1959).
TOSCANO, HUASCAR, 'Cenizas del paraiso', *Sabado Show*, 1 November 1997.
TRACY, DAVID, *The Analogical Imagination: Christian Theology and the Culture of Pluralism* (London: SCM Press, 1981).
—— *Blessed Rage for Order: The New Pluralism in Theology* (New York: Seabury Press, 1975).
TRAVERSO, JORGE, 'Figuras en el paisaje', *El Observador*, 15 August 2004.
TREMBATH, K. R., *Divine Revelation: Our Moral Relation with God* (Oxford: Oxford University Press, 1991).
TUDOR, ANDREW, 'Sociology and Film', in John Hill and Pamela Church Gibson, eds, *The Oxford Guide to Film Studies* (Oxford: Oxford University Press, 1998), pp. 190–4.
VER STRATEN-MCSPARRAN, 'Polanyi's Personal Knowledge and Watching Movies', in Robert K. Johnston, ed., *Reframing Theology and Film: New Focus for an Emerging Discipline* (Grand Rapids, MI: Baker Academic, 2007), pp. 162–78.
WALL, JAMES M., 'Biblical Spectaculars and Secular Man', in John C. Cooper and Carl Skrade, eds, *Celluloid and Symbols* (Philadelphia, PA: Fortress Press, 1970), pp. 51–60.
WALSH, RICHARD, *Finding St. Paul in Film* (London: T&T Clark, 2005).
WARD, PETER, *Selling Worship: How What We Sing Has Changed the Church* (Bletchley, UK: Paternoster, 2005).
WARFIELD, BENJAMIN BRECKENRIDGE, *Calvin and Augustine* (Philadelphia, PA: The Presbyterian and Reformed Publishing Company, 1956).
—— *Revelation and Inspiration* (New York: Oxford University Press, 1927).
WEIGEL, GUSTAVE A., SJ, 'Contemporaneous Protestantism and Paul Tillich', in *Theological Studies*, 11.2 (1950), pp. 177–202.
—— 'The Theological Significance of Paul Tillich', in *Cross Currents* 6.2 (1956), pp. 141–55.
WHYTE, WILLIAM FOOTE, *Street Corner Society: The Social Structure of an Italian Slum* (London: University of Chicago Press, 1981).
WIEBE, PHILLIP, *God and Other Spirits: Intimations of Transcendence in Christian Experience* (Oxford: Oxford University Press, 2004).
WILLIAMS, ROWAN, 'Interview with Radio 4 on Redevelopment of St Martin in the Fields Church', <http://www.archbishopofcanterbury.org/1641> (accessed 12 September 2008).
—— 'Trinity and Revelation', in id., *On Christian Theology* (Oxford: Blackwell, 2000), pp. 131–47.
WOODS, ROBERT H., MICHAEL C. JINDRA, AND JASON D. BARKER, 'The Audience Responds to *The Passion of the Christ*', in S. Brent Plate, ed., *Mel Gibson's Film and Its Critics: Re-viewing the Passion* (London: Palgrave Macmillan, 2004), pp. 163–80.
WRIGHT, MELANIE J., *Religion and Film: An Introduction* (London: I. B. Tauris, 2007).
ZAPIOLA, GUILLERMO, 'Buen cine argentino', *Guía del Ocio*, 8 October 1993, p. 15.

Index

Acevedo, Hugo 222
Adams, Nicholas 128–30
Adorno, Theodor 94–5, 103, 119
Alea, Tomás Gutiérrez 109, 163, 189–90
Alien Trilogy 37
alienation 68, 96, 225
Alister Hardy Research Centre 144
Amarcord 184–7, 191
ambiguity
  contrasted with unambiguous life
    59 n. 158, 64–6, 72–5, 191, 198, 225
  in film 24, 25, 111, 184, 227
Amores perros 165, 167
analogia entis 71, 79–80
analogia imaginis 76
Anker, Roy 20, 35–7
anthropology 83–4, 122, 130–1
Antonioni, Michelangelo 96, 97, 113–15
anxiety 62, 64, 68, 71–2, 73, 105, 188, 199
Aparte 6, 167
Aquinas, Thomas 61, 80
Argentina 5, 11, 157, 164, 182, 183–4, 192, 215–7
  Buenos Aires 158, 183, 190–2, 215–17, 222
Argentinean cinema 161–7, 167–8, 183–5, 192, 215–7, 221–2
Arksey, Hilary 141, 142–5, 148–51
Arnold, Matthew 6 n. 8, 83
atheism 88, 145, 174, 176–7, 182–3, 185–8, 203–5, 206–7, 222
Atkinson, Paul 146
audience 2–3, 7–8, 15, 21, 25–30, 31–2, 35–8, 38–43, 45, 115, 165, 167, 174, 221
  history of study 118–22, 123–6
Auer, Gabriel 189
Augustine of Hippo 61, 93
auteur 17, 22, 32, 169–70

Babel 165
Bach, Alice 20
Bach, Johann Sebastian 195
Balazs, Bela 105
El Baño del Pápa 167
Barker, Martin 141
Barth, Karl 128, 129
Baugh, Lloyd S. J. 16
Bazin, André 97–8, 107–9, 109–12, 227
beatific vision 198
Beau Brummel 206

Beaumont, Harry 206
beauty 3, 6, 35, 52, 64, 66, 68, 83, 92, 101–2, 151, 207, 231
Begbie, Jeremy 79–80, 227 n. 10
being
  ground and abyss of being 61–4, 67, 68, 71, 73, 75, 81, 134, 143, 157, 187, 188, 191, 197, 199, 202, 233
  being itself 58, 63–5, 70–1, 79, 188, 191
  New Being 63–4, 65, 76, 78, 81, 97, 99, 188, 199, 226, 230
  non-being 58, 62, 67, 97, 188
Benjamin, Walter 82 n. 1
Bergeson, Albert J. 20
Bergman, Ingmar 10 n. 26, 17
Bernal, Gael García 177
Bielinsky, Fabián 215
Billotto, Dardo 222
Bird, Michael 50, 97–9, 100–1
Birri, Fernando 163
Blow Up 97, 113–5
Boff, Leonardo 233 n. 34
Bordaberry, Juan María 180
Bordwell, David 24, 30–1, 34
Borges, Jorge Luis 160
Botticelli, Alessandro *see Madonna with Singing Angels*
Bradburn, Norman 142–5
Brazil 1–3, 157, 212
  Rio de Janeiro 160
Brazilian cinema 1–3, 161–2, 166, 212
breakthrough (also rupture) 53, 55, 56, 58, 60, 68, 96–7, 99, 102–5, 108, 109–12, 165, 191, 197–8, 200, 211, 213, 227–30, 231
Bresson, Robert 17, 32–4, 97–9
British Board of Film Censors (BBFC) 17
Brown, Stephen 99
Browning, Don 85–7, 90
Buckingham, David 122, 125–6, 134
Buenos Aires *see* Argentina

Caballos salvajes 192
Cabinet of Dr Caligari 33, 102–5, 108
Cabra marcado para morrer (Guy Marked for Death) 1–3, 190, 212
Calvin (Calvinism) 7 n. 17, 52, 93
Carril, Manuel Martínez 167, 169
Casillo, Robert 42
catharsis 38, 201

Cenizas del paraiso 192
Central Station 166
Centre for Experimental Cinematography (Rome) 109, 163
Chalcedon 128
Chatman, Seymour 115
Chicago School 138
childhood film-experiences 3, 118–9, 171, 184, 207, 209–11, 221, 234
Chile 162–3 *see also* film festival, Viña del Mar
Christianson, Eric 36
church 16–19, 28–9, 75, 76, 87, 91, 96, 127–8, 130–1, 174–9, 226, 228, 231
Cinemateca Club 148, 167–71, 172–3, 205–6, 208, 210, 219, 223–4, 226
Cinématographe 15
City of God 166
Clarke, Adele 138
A Clockwork Orange 37
Cobb, Kelton 91–5
coding 153, 196, 199, 211
commercial cinema *see* Hollywood
concrete experience *see* phenomenological approach
congregational studies 130–1
conservative theology 53, 87 *see also* evangelicalism
constellations of revelation 68, 70, 145, 157, 179, 187, 190, 195, 223, 224, 226–7, 230
Cool Hand Luke 97
Cooper, John 18
Copa America 174–5
Coppola, Francis Ford 35–9
correlation 59–60, 77–8, 80–1, 84–91, 100
of revelation 72–3, 76
da Costa, Néstor 175–6, 178
coup d'état see dictatorship
Coutinho, Eduardo 1–3
Cox, Harvey 18
creativity 55, 64–8, 76, 93, 165, 169–70, 190, 211, 222; *see also* theoria
Creed, Barbara 121
Creswell, John 141, 146
El crimen del Padre Amaro 177
Cuba 2, 109, 162–4, 189–90, 212
Cuban cinema 109, 162–4, 199, 212
cultural linguistic theology 131–2
culture, definition of 83–4
CUREC (Combined University Research Ethics Committee, Oxford University) 155

Darín, Ricardo 215
data
 generation 124, 125–6, 140–2, 142–5, 148–51, 182, 211
 analysis 137–9, 151–3, 152–3, 168, 182, 190, 205–13, 223, 225
 validity 153–4, 172–3
Deacy, Christopher 19, 39–43, 84
DeMille, Cecil B. 17
demonic in Tillich's thought 57, 72, 75, 232
Denzin, Norman 122–3
depth of culture or artwork 55–8, 59, 66–8, 88–91, 94, 96–101, 101–12, 134, 191, 198, 224, 231–2
Diary of a Country Priest 17, 97–9
dictatorship 1–3, 164, 169, 179–81, 189–90, 198, 208, 212–13, 226
directing films *see* filmmaking
La Dolce Vita 17
Dreisbach, Donald 78, 234
Dreyer, Carl Theodor 30–5

Eagleton, Terry 83
ecstasy and miracle of revelation 67–8, 143, 144, 157, 173, 195, 202, 204, 209
Edison, Thomas 15
effect of revelation 72–4, 81, 96–7, 145, 198–202, 209, 230–5
Eisner, Lotte 105
Elena, Alberto 160, 163
Elgenius, Gabriella 145
Eliade, Mircea 38, 97–9
Ellacuria, Ignacio 132–3
Elliot, Charles 128–30
Emmet, Dorothy 80–1
empirical research *see also* qualitative research *and* quantitative research
 potential problems 115
 history of empirical research 118–22
 importance of 29–30, 31, 38–9, 43, 45, 77
encounter
 with an artwork / film 10, 60, 221–3, 225, 230
 with God / transcendence 3, 7, 8 n. 18, 33–4, 49–50, 58, 71–2, 98, 111, 133, 186
 ineffable 32, 184, 188, 191, 197, 202, 204
Espinosa, Julio García 163–4
essence and existence (essential and existential) 62–4, 65, 73, 75, 199, 202, 225
estrangement 61, 63–4, 73, 188, 199, 202
ethics 55, 67, 75, 93, 129, 177
 in empirical research 129, 155,
ethnography (ethnology) 121–22, 124–6, 128–9, 130, 135, 141
evangelical (evangelicalism) 6–7, 26–9, 53, 77

event of revelation 58, 67–8, 69–72, 81, 108, 144, 171, 172, 179, 190, 192, 194, 195–8, 227–30
exampling 146–7
existence / existential *see* essence and existence
existentialism 58–60, 86–7, 88, 188
expressionism 33, 55–6, 76–7, 101–6, 107–8, 110–11, 187, 202, 227, 231

Fackre, Gabriel J. 7 n. 17
Faire, Lucy 122, 123–5, 125–6
Fall, doctrine of 62–3
Fellini, Federico 17, 184–6
Fielding, Nigel 148–9
Figueras, Marcelo 222
film festivals
 Cannes (France) 201
 City of Angels (USA) 2
 Mar del Plata (Argentina) 167–8, 172
 Montevideo (Uruguay) 169–70, 172, 206
 Viña del Mar (Chile) 163, 178
film school 169, 183–4, 208
film theory, general discussion of 21–4, 44
film-watching experience 34, 50, 221–3, 230
 communal dimension 2–3, 124, 196–7, 209–11
 effect, impact, function 1, 7, 19, 21, 29, 38–9, 98, 118–22, 149, 151, 187, 194, 196, 199–200, 205–6, 211–2, 219, 233–4
 particularity of each film-viewer relation 2, 38–9, 124–5, 145, 190
 researching the experience 140–5, 148–51
filmmaking 1–3, 19, 32–4, 35–6, 40, 47, 104, 106–9, 111–12, 114, 162–7, 186, 201, 206
filter question 140, 143, 156–7, 204–5
Flesher, Paul V. M. 25–6, 29
form and substance 53, 53–8, 81, 88, 90–1, 92–3, 101–2, 108, 191, 197–8, 224, 232
formalism 30–1, 98, 106–7, 191
Forrester, Duncan 132–3
Foucault, Michel 129
Frankfurt School 93–5, 119
freedom 62–63, 89–90, 226, 234
Fresa y chocolate 189–90, 199, 212

Gambetta, Diego 139
Gardner, Colin 114
Geertz, Clifford 38, 83–4
general revelation 6, 73, 77
Gettino, Octavio 163–5
Geymonat, Roger 176, 178
Gibson, Mel 25–30
Glaser, Barney 137–9, 141, 146, 152, 223
The Godfather Trilogy 35–9, 40
Gomez, Cecilia 3

Goodacre, Mark 28–9
Goulding, Christina 136–7
The Gospel According to St Matthew 18
Graham, David John 99
Greeley, Andrew M. 20
Grenz, Stanley 7 n. 17
Griffiths, D. W. 161
grounded account 8, 136–9, 217
grounded theory 136–9, 223
Gutiérrez, Gustavo 132, 233 n. 34

Hamill, Heather 139
Hamilton, Kenneth 77
Hamilton, William 18
Hammersley, Martyn 146
Hansen, Miriam Bratu 110–11
Hart, Stephen 160, 163–7
Hay, David 143, 144
Hays Production Code 17, 36, 38
Hegel 53–4, 160
Heitink, Gerben 133–4
Henry, Carl F. H. 7 n. 17
hermeneutical circle *see* pastoral cycle
Hill, Annette 124–5, 139, 159, 196
history in Tillich's thought 55, 57–8, 70, 72–3, 78, 81, 89–90, 198, 226,
Hollywood 108, 161–2, 165–7, 184
 as pejorative 21–2, 170, 205–6
The Horitz Passion Play 16
Huberman, Michael 141, 147, 153
Hunt, Kate 141–2
Hurley, Neil 18, 22–3

idolatry in Tillich's thought *see* demonic in Tillich's thought
imperfect cinema 163–4
Iñárritu, Alejandro Gonzalez 165–6
intellectual puzzle 5–6, 60, 147
intercept technique 140, 145–6, 209
interdisciplinarity 9, 19, 21, 22–3
interviews 29, 123–5, 130, 140–2, 146, 148–51, 172–3, 182
 guarding against interviewer effects 126, 142, 143, 150, 200–1, 211
Italy 162–3, 186

Jancovich, Mark 122, 123–5, 125–6
Jagodinski, Jan 125–6
Jasper, David 21, 23–4
Jesus Christ 30, 40, 41, 56–7, 63, 69, 74–7, 78, 87, 89–90, 97, 128, 145, 179, 188, 202, 222, 232
 Jesus films 16, 25–9, 42
Jewett, Robert 19–20
Johnston, Robert K. 17, 19, 20, 27–9, 49–50, 232

kairos 55, 57–58, 162, 213
Kammerspiel 33
Kant, Emmanuel 54
Kelsey, David 73, 77–80
Kermode, Mark 28–29
King, David 160-2
King of Kings 17
kitsch 94, 223
Knight, Peter 141, 142–5, 148–51
Kracauer, Siegfried 97–8, 102–12
Kreitzer, Larry 19–20, 22

Lacan 23, 120, 125
El lado oscuro del corazón 190, 200, 204
Lago, Germán 213
The Last Temptation of Christ 32, 42
Latin American Cinema 5, 159–67, 177–8
Legion of Decency 17
liberation theology 132–4, 177–8, 228 n. 12, 233 n. 34
Lincoln, Yvonne 122–3
Lindbeck, George 131–2
López, Marína Diaz 160, 163
Loughlin, Gerard 37
Lumière brothers 15–16, 106, 160
Luther (Lutheranism) 52, 93
Lyden, John 19, 35, 37–9, 40, 43
Lynch, Gordon 84–7, 90

Madonna with Singing Angels by Alessandro Botticelli 50, 51, 52, 60, 68, 93, 150–1, 185, 188, 203, 205, 207, 213, 230–2
magic realism 190
Mangold, James 47–8
Manning, Russell Re 87–8, 91
Marsh, Clive 39, 41, 50, 99–101
Martínez, Virginia 180–1
Mason, Jennifer 147, 152–3, 154
mass culture *see* popular culture
MAXQDA (qualitative research software) 152
May, John 18, 22–3, 36
McClean, George F. 80
McGrath, Alister 78
Mean Streets 39–43
Medellín Conference (Columbia) 178
Méliès, Georges 106
Melzer, Ronald 222
Memento 37
Messenger, Chris 37
methodological priority without privilege 8, 12, 125–35
Mexican cinema 160, 161–2, 177
Milbank, John 127

Miles, Margaret 20
Miles, Matthew 141, 147, 153
military 1–2, 158, 164, 179–81, 198, 208, 212, 225
miracle *see* ecstasy and miracle
Mitry, Jean 105–6, 110
Mothers' Union 17
Mowat, Harriet 127–35
Mulhall, Stephen 37 n. 108,
Mulvey, Laura 120–1
music 183–4, 194–5
mystery 67–8, 68–9, 197, 216
mysticism in Tillich's thought 52, 61–2, 90
myth 37–9, 92, 107, 222

National Board of Censorship 17
neo-realism (Italian) 108, 109, 111, 163, 191
Niebuhr, H. Richard 54
Niebuhr, Reinhold 77
Nolan, Steve 22–4, 41–3
Nueve reinas 215-7
numinous 68, 80, 112, 178
Nuovo, Victor 54, 88–9

O'Meara, Thomas Franklin 61
Ortiz, Gaye Williams 19, 84, 99
Oxford University
    CUREC 155
    Department of Sociology 11, 145
Ozu, Yasujiro 32–4

painting *see also* expressionism 55–6, 69, 76, 94–5, 98–9, 101–2, 108, 109–11, 227, 231
Paisa 111
Palmer, Michael 78–9
participant observation 140
Pasolini, Pier Paolo 18
La Passion de Jeanne D'Arc 30–5
The Passion of the Christ 25–30
pastoral cycle 130, 132–5
Pattison, George 60–1
Payne Fund 118–9
pentecostalism 177
Percy, Martyn 130–2, 35
phenomenological method 59, 60, 64, 70, 74, 86, 141, 146, 234
pilot study 140, 143
Piñeyro, Marcel 183, 192
Pius XI, Pope 17
Pizza, birra, faso 190, 191, 207
Plate, Brent S. 21, 22–4
plot (narrative), importance in experiences 192, 193, 195, 221, 230, 234
poetics 30, 229

Poland, Blake 152
political / social context 1-3, 27, 31, 33, 37-8, 53, 54-8, 93-5, 101-6, 108-9, 111, 118-9, 123-5, 142, 149, 151, 157-9, 168, 175-6, 179-81, 189, 209, 212, 224, 225
popular culture 6-7, 82-95, 119, 163-4, 165, 178
portfolio (of interpretation) 125, 159, 196
poverty 132-3, 177
practical theology 127-35
prison 97, 164, 180, 189, 206, 208, 212
Protestant Principle 57, 165
psychology 61, 64, 74, 103, 105, 108, 120

qualitative interview *see* interview
qualitative research, an introduction 122-5, 215
quantitative research 122-3, 146
quest for revelation 63-4, 65, 68, 71, 179, 187, 188-90, 223, 226-7
questionnaire research 142-5, 146, 151, 172-3, 182-3, 195-6, 200, 206

realism 98, 101-12, 160, 162-3, 191, 227
  belief-ful 56, 98-9, 111-12
reason in Tillich's thought 61, 63-4, 65, 67, 71, 80, 90, 191, 228-9
Rebella, Juan Pablo 201, 233
reception theory 25-6, 30-1, 124, 144, 154, 212, 221
Red Cross 212
Red Desert 96
reflexivity 138, 154
religion in Tillich's thought 59, 66, 71-2, 84-91, 92-3, 188, 197, 224, 225, 233
religion and film 19
  biblical studies approach 19
  bi-polar approach 7, 21, 118
  cultural / religious studies approach 20, 24, 30-2, 48, 92, 121-2, 126
  film theory approach 23, 28, 30, 44
  ideological approach 21-2, 24, 39
  influential scholars (definition) 25 n. 54
  literary studies approach 18, 25-6, 29, 44
  theological approach 20, 27-9, 35-7, 39-43, 44, 92, 126
religious film, defining 24, 30-5, 41 n. 134, 44, 97
  Bible-based 16-17, 25
  educational potential 16
  missional potential 16, 26
  transcendence 18, 32-4, 97
Renoir, Jean 107
revelation
  individual or communal 58, 60-1, 207-9, 209-11

  knowledge 58, 68-72, 79-81, 90-1, 188, 195, 204, 231-5, 234
  momentary or gradual 58, 207-9, 212-3, 223-4
  salvation 58, 72-4, 80, 90-1, 143, 145, 188, 208, 225-7, 233
Ricoeur, Paul 227-30, 231-2
ritual 36, 37-9
Roldán, Alberto 145
Roman Catholicism 26, 27, 28, 42, 61, 175-8, 189, 203, 212
romanticism 51-2, 56, 83, 95, 184-6
Rossellini, Roberto 111, 227

Salles, Walter 166
salvation 72-4, 80, 90-1, 143, 145, 184, 188, 198, 202, 208, 225-7
sampling strategy 140, 145-8, 173
  critical case 147, 157, 173, 182-3, 188
  maximum variation 147, 183, 194, 200-1, 206
Sanguinetti, Julio María 181
Saratsola, Osvaldo 168-9
Saukko, Paula 126-7, 131-2
Schelling, F. J. W. 61, 78, 86-90
Schiller, Friedrich 83
Schleiermacher, Friedrich 54, 93
Schrader, Paul 30, 32-5, 195
Schuman, Howard 153
Schwöbel, Christoph 234
Scorsese, Martin 39-43
Scripture 17, 19-20, 25-6, 28, 48, 53, 61, 76-7, 127-8, 133-4, 202, 227-30, 230-2, 235
Segundo, Juan Luis 133
semi-structured interview *see* interview
The Seventh Seal 17
Shaw, Deborah 165-7
da Silveira, Pablo 175
Skrade, Carl 18, 50, 96-7, 100
Sobrino, Jon 132-3
socialism 56-7, 58
Solanas, Fernando 163-5, 211
spectator theory 23-4, 34, 120-2
spirit (Spirit, *geist*) 64-7, 68, 73, 89, 173, 191, 224-7, 235
spiritual community 213, 223-7
Stam, Robert 23, 112
Stoll, Pablo 201
Strauss, Anselm 137-9, 141, 146, 152, 223
The Student of Prague 103
style in Tillich's thought
  interpreting art 50, 56, 76, 101-2, 108, 111-12, 191
  interpreting a culture 58, 86, 165, 213, 226-7
Subiela, Eliseo 190

substance *see* form and substance
Sudman, Seymour 142–5
syncretism 203
Swinton, John 127–32
symbol 69–71, 75, 78–80, 97, 98–9, 187, 189, 193, 197, 202

Tango feroz 183–6, 190, 192, 199, 212, 221–2
Taxi Driver 32, 43
Telford, William 126–7
temporality and eternity 55, 57, 198 *see also* form and substance; history
The Ten Commandments (1923) 17
Tertullian 27, 93
Thatamanil, John 61
theatre 33, 109, 174
theonomy 56–7, 93, 213, 226–7
theoria 8, 66, 134–5, 191, 224 *see also* creativity
third cinema 164–5
Thomas, Hilary 148–9
Tillich, Paul
 biography 48, 51–3, 93–4, 213
 direct references to film 10,
 philosophical system 58–9, 77, 89–90
 The Courage to Be 64, 74, 188
 On the Idea of a Theology of Culture 53–4, 93, 102
 The Protestant Era 57, 58, 98, 102
 The Religious Situation 54–6, 98
 The Socialist Decision 56–7, 8
 The Systematic Theology 58–77, 143, 188, 202, 224–7, 232–5
 Theology of Culture 49, 69, 86–8, 90–1, 187, 232–3
Torry, Robert 25–6, 29
Toscano, Huascar 192
Tracy, David 85–6
transparent to the depths 197, 202, 230, 232, 234
transcendence 178–9, 195, 212
transcription 151–2

translation 145, 152, 173, 184–5
triangulation 154, 172–3
25 Watts 6 n. 6, 167
21 Grams 165

ultimate concern 70–1, 80, 87
Uruguay 5–6, 133, 150, 157–9, 167, 173, 174–7, 206, 210, 221–2
 dictatorship 179–81, 189, 190, 208, 212, 223–4, 225–7
 Montevideo 148, 156–7, 157–9, 167–9, 183, 201, 210, 226
 secularism (anti-clericalism) 174–7, 226–7
Uruguayan cinema 6, 167–70, 189, 190, 192, 201, 210, 212–3, 233

Vatican II 27, 178
Vigilanti Cura: On the Motion Pictures 17
Villa, General Pancho 160
violence in film 25–30, 35–9, 42, 124–5, 139

Walk the Line 47–8
Wall, James 18, 22–3
Walsh, Richard 25, 26–9, 36
war 51–2, 58, 93, 102–4, 108, 111, 119, 161, 234
Warfield, Benjamin Breckenridge 7 n. 17
Warm, Hermann 33, 104
Wegener, Paul 103
Welles, Orson 107
Weigel, Gustave 76, 78, 80
Whisky 167, 190, 201, 233
Wiene, Robert 104
Williams, Rowan 227–30, 231–2
world cinema 5 n. 2, 15, 159, 165, 169
world created by film 196, 209, 227–30, 231–2
 entering and inhabiting the film-world 196, 227–30, 231–2
Wright, Melanie 20, 22–4, 30–2, 40, 43

Les Yeux des Oiseaux 189, 199, 212
Y tu mamá también 166

BX 4827 .T53 B736 2012
Brant, Jonathan, 1970-
Paul Tillich and the
 possibility of revelation

MAY 2 4 2012